CONTAMINATED COMMUNITIES

Coping with Residential Toxic Exposure

SECOND EDITION

Michael R. Edelstein

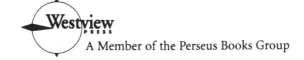

Westview PRESS

A Member of the Perseus Books Group

Copyright © 2004 by Westview Press, A Member of the Perseus Books Group

Westview Press books are available at special discounts for bulk purchases in the United States by corporations, institutions, and other organizations. For more information, please contact the Special
Markets Department at the Perseus Books Group, 11 Cambridge Center, Cambridge MA 02142, or
call (617) 252-5298 or (800) 255-1514 or email special.markets@perseusbooks.com.

Published in the United States of America by Westview Press, 5500 Central Avenue, Boulder, Colorado
80301–2877 and in the United Kingdom by Westview Press, 12 Hid's Copse Road, Cumnor Hill,
Oxford OX2 9JJ.

Find us on the World Wide Web at www.westviewpress.com

A Cataloging-in-Publication data record for this book is available from the Library of Congress.
ISBN-10 0-8133-4148-5 (hc)   ISBN-10 0-8133-3647-3 (pbk)
ISBN-13 978-0-8133-4148-4 (hc) ISBN-13 978-0-8133-3647-3 (pbk)

To my poet sister, Arlyn:
Forced to watch so much of life from the sidelines
you have captured the richness of human experience
better than most in the fast lane.
The most acute observer,
and best friend,
you prove that in reality
there are no sidelines.

CONTENTS

Foreword to the First Edition by Adeline Gordon Levine   ix

Preface to 2004 Edition   xi

Acknowledgments   xiii

1 Toxic Exposure: The Plague of Our Time   1

The Plague as a Metaphor for Toxic Exposure   2

Contaminated Communities   6

Contamination as a Widespread Event   7

Defining a Contaminated Community   9

The Stages of Toxic Disaster   19

Collateral Damage in the Risk Society   22

The Theory of Environmental Turbulence   24

Summary and Outline of the Book   32

2 Legler: The Story of a Contaminated Community   35

A Methodological Note   35

Groundwater Contamination in Legler   37

Period of Incubation   38

Discovery and Announcement   50

Disruption of Lifestyle: Water Delivery   55

The Hookup of City Water   59

Lingering Concerns   59

Afterword About the Landfill's Afterlife   62

**3 Lifescape Change: Cognitive Adjustment
to Toxic Exposure**   65

Defending Our Prior Assumptions   65

Perceiving a Changed Status   66

Perceptions of Health   71
Inherent Uncertainty   73
Confirmed Exposures   78
Environment   81
Loss of Personal Control   89
The Inversion of Home   93
Loss of Social Trust   104
Conclusion: The Lifescape Impacts of Toxic Exposure   118

4 **Individual and Family Impacts**   **119**
Coping with Exposure: Individuals   119
Outcomes: Positive and Negative   122
Coping with Exposure: Couples   136
Coping with Exposure: Children   141
Case Studies of Family Dynamics   147
Stigmatized Relationships: Outsiders
          Just Don't Understand   152
Neighbors: Proximate Support   158
Summary: Individual and Family Impacts   159

5 **Disabling Citizens: The Governmental Response
   to Toxic Exposure**   **161**
A Dialectic of Double Binds   162
Communicational Distortion in the Institutional Context   172
Distortion and the Communication of Bad News   176
Differing Paradigms of Risk Between
          Citizens and Regulators   178
Institutional Contexts   189
Conclusion and Summary   191

6 **The Enabling Response: Community Development
   and Toxic Exposure**   **193**
Enablement Through Community Development   193
Keys to Enablement: Leadership and Activism   195
Key Benefits of Community Development   197
The Consensus/Dissensus Continuum   201
Consensus and Dissensus in Legler   205
Consensus and Dissensus Elsewhere   209
Toxic Victims: A New Social Movement?   213

Sustainability as a Metaenvironmental Justice Issue   242
Conclusion: A Radical Environmental Populism   244

7 **The Societal Meaning of Pollution**   **245**
Denial and the Culture of Contamination   245
Rejecting a Contaminating Culture: Local Environmental
     Resistance   253
Changing the Culture of Contamination   274
Cultural Immunity: Last Defense
     of the Contaminating Culture   279
Sustainability as the Third Stage of Modernity   282

Notes   293
Bibliography   311
Index   339

FOREWORD TO THE FIRST EDITION

In the late 1970s, the Love Canal sounded a warning. Those who listened understood that a new type of disaster was emerging in our world in the form of an unanticipated price for the benefits derived from the post-World War II burgeoning of the chemical industry. Since that time, we have learned that the price goes well beyond money, for it also encompasses physical, psychological, and social distress. While the burden falls most heavily on individuals and families exposed to hazardous pollution, that price is being extracted as well from groups, neighborhoods, communities, and societies. It will continue to be paid long into the future, unless we collectively recognize that the human, social problems created by our technologies cannot be addressed simply in technocratic terms. Michael Edelstein is one of the people who heeded the warning of Love Canal. As he makes clear in this book, the problems must be addressed with an emphasis on the concerns, needs, interests, and rights of the people whom technology is supposed to benefit, in such fashion that our social fabric becomes stronger, or at least is not weakened.

In the late 1970s, when Edelstein, as a young professor, began to expand his academic studies of the environment to include the psychological and social effects of toxic pollution, he also expanded his own role to become an environmental activist. This book shows the results of his decade of work, which started at a time when the human problem of toxic pollution was scarcely recognized as an area of study for social scientists. In the ensuing years, the events at Seveso, Love Canal, Times Beach, and numerous other sites have drawn the attention of researchers who have produced a number of published pieces and papers read at conferences devoted to the issues. Meanwhile, a broad social movement has begun, which draws its members from communities threatened by toxic wastes and its inspiration from the example of the citizens' movement at Love Canal. Edelstein has drawn together literature from all these sources, and has coupled it with his own research and observations, to produce a coherent, soundly based picture of the broad, deep, and long-lasting effects of exposure to hazardous wastes, on every element of society.

Contaminated Communities is a solid addition to the literature of a new, growing field of study. The book is absorbing and enlightening because the author provides richly detailed pictures of affected people trying to cope with problems they had never anticipated having, problems that are so new that no one truly knows their dimensions, let alone what the solutions might be. It should be read by policy makers who will not only gain insight into the thinking of the affected people they are mandated to serve when toxic pollution strikes a community, but will also be able to reflect on the constraints and problems of their own roles in these cases. This book may help them avoid some of the pitfalls that have ensnared so many in the past decade, and have created alienation between some government officials and the people whose lives are massively disrupted by toxic pollution.

But *Contaminated Communities* should be read by a wide range of people. Edelstein makes us realize that in the broadest sense we are all policy makers, for we must all ask and try to answer the hard questions, we must all take responsibility to improve our society. It is books like this that will help us think about our choices, about the sort of physical and social world we want to maintain and create for ourselves, and leave as our legacy for generations to come.

ADELINE GORDON LEVINE
State University of New York at Buffalo

PREFACE TO 2004 EDITION

The World Trade Center Disaster as a Contaminating Event

Works are continually redefined by events that occur while they are in progress. I was busy putting final touches on this manuscript when the new ambient divide of September 11, 2001, occurred. On that day, I gave live commentary to my sustainable communities class as the horrors unfolded on the TV screen in the classroom. Obsessed with this new reality, as many are, I have read everything I could find, listened to radio, and watched TV. I have talked to survivors. I have watched a parade of funerals and mourners pass through the church across the street from my house. And I have made the sad pilgrimage to Ground Zero. Through it all, I am struck by the unfortunate relevance to much of what I have written here as a broader framework for understanding these new disasters.

The World Trade Center disaster, in my view, is a contaminating event. It exposed untold thousands to the smoke and dust and debris of a burning and collapsing modern architectural icon. Other than release of asbestos acknowledged publicly in the early days, there has been only scant information about exposures to dioxins and furans from burning plastics, heavy metals, burning petroleum products, particulates, and perhaps an array of additional poisons. It will never be clear how many died from acute exposures to smoke and toxins rather than fire and collapse. I predicted from the first moments that when the acute vestiges of this tragedy wear off, we will face the prospect of chronic WTC syndromes, physical and psychological. Already there are indications that my fears are correct.

The WTC disaster was contaminating in secondary ways as well. It made a different kind of threat palpable in our lives, one based on the prospect of harmful acts by others. Biological, chemical, and radioactive agents might join explosive events as an arsenal of new weapons in a war of contamination. The contemporaneous and continuing anthrax scare has given palpable proof of this potential and of the resulting psychosocial impacts. Problems of boundaries are evident, as future threats suggest that lower Manhattan and the Pentagon, and doomed flights, are not the only loci for victimization. There is no immunity from the fear and perhaps from the agents of terrorism.

These disasters caused vicarious victimization on a massive scale. In part, being able to watch the tragedy unfold made media watchers part of the events in such a way that there was little separation. This wasn't just happening to others but to us as well; the events shattered the divide between abstract and ambient environment. This horror was not limited to innocent victims and brave helpers, direct onlookers and survivors. The dissemination of the event by the media and the universal symbolism attached to the Twin Towers and Pentagon and to the safety of the skies combined to give this event a universal poignancy. The fact that victims came from across the map added to this immediacy. For the dead and missing, their pictures adorn sidewalk displays and the media remembers them with words so touching that their loss is made tangible to strangers. Many know victims and their relatives, or have other direct associations with the disaster. Even greater numbers of people have some connection with the places destroyed and sense the fatal vulnerability of the hijacked. The effect is a vicarious victimization on a massive scale. This event was so powerful that there is no room for denial and scant gap between insiders and outsiders to the events.

This tragic turbulence has shattered life assumptions on a massive scale, and our lives are unlikely ever to be the same. Our health is threatened in new, invisible, and unpreventable ways. We are helpless to protect our families and dependent on others for safety. Our fear of the environment extends to the mail delivery, offices and apartments in tall buildings, airplanes, and any place that we may become exposed and vulnerable. We distrust and stigmatize others out of fear and blame to the point of sacrificing our liberties and waging war. While the events differ, these outcomes parallel key findings of this study.

In short, many of the concepts that I have advanced to help understand the impact of contamination may have utility in our efforts to understand this other human-caused acute disaster and its sequelae.

Our normal and naive world has been spoiled. Life will never be the same.

MICHAEL R. EDELSTEIN, PH.D.
Goshen, New York

ACKNOWLEDGMENTS

I wish to thank my colleagues at Ramapo College of New Jersey, as well as the institution and its staff, for generous support and encouragement; my colleagues at Orange Environment, Inc., for courage, conviction, and talent; my students for their interest and motivation; my peers across the globe who share work on the predicament of contamination for their generous feedback, sharing, and synergy; the scores of young researchers drawn to this work for their new ideas and confirmation of old ones; the attorneys who have afforded me the opportunity to conduct research and present testimony; and the more than one thousand contamination victims I have interviewed for their openness, sharing, and inspiration; and to the future generations whose legacy is in our hands.

I also thank my wife, Ludmila, for her loving support and my sons, Joel and Boris, for their graphic assistance. And for patience, I thank my editors at Westview Press.

M.R.E.

"Why Must I Become Sicker and Sicker?" Painted by seventh-grader Olga Karzoba from Bryakunovskya School near Pestova, Russia.

1

Toxic Exposure: The Plague of Our Time

In *A Journal of the Plague Year*, Daniel Defoe chronicled the transformation of everyday life caused by the Great Plague of London of 1665, which killed some 100,000 people. As early news of the plague abroad reached them, Londoners nervously began to watch the "bills of mortality," the weekly reports of number and cause of deaths in each parish, which served as indicators of the plague's approach. Many fled the plague, leaving the city comparatively empty. The wealthiest were most likely to be able to leave. Others, employed in the trades or lacking resources, were generally forced to remain, only to face unemployment resulting from the disruption of London's economy. Many who left the city perished on the road from hunger and want of lodging.

A plague culture emerged within London. Fear of strangers became the norm. Books foretold the ruin of the city, and people appeared on the streets prophesying destruction. Others set up practices to treat the sick, some offering "charms, philtres, exorcisms, amulets."[1] In their alarm, some people confessed crimes long concealed. Many believed that heaven had sent the "distemper." At first people mourned the dead, but then the expectation that their own death would shortly follow hardened them. "A kind of sadness and horror sat upon the countenances even of the common people. Death was before their eyes, and everybody began to think of their graves, not of mirth and diversions."[2]

Parents, not knowing they were diseased, inadvertently infected their children. The Lord Mayor began shutting up sick people in their houses on July 1, 1665. Watchmen were set at their doors. Because entire families were quarantined with the sick persons, all were doomed to perish.

No one knew how the infection spread, so various superstitions emerged. People came to define any suspicious occurrence or symptom in light of the plague. Medical experts were of little help in clarifying the situation, arguing over whether open fires might help control the spread of the plague and, if so, what type of trees might best be burned. Not only was the daily life of Londoners dramatically affected by the plague, but their entire way of seeing and comprehending the world was altered. The psychological and social dynamics of combining uncertain, invisible, and unpredictable environmental causes and dreaded consequences was well demonstrated by these events.

The Plague as a Metaphor for Toxic Exposure

Beginning in the Middle Ages, the foundation for our modern paradigm of public health was laid with the emerging understanding of the relationship between plague, sanitation, and pollution control.[3] For example, in the 1890s, at about the same time that scientists traced the cause of typhoid fever to waterways polluted with human wastes, technologies for sewage and water filtration became available. Environmental hygiene provided sanitation, control of vectors (carriers of disease), and protection against bacteriological disease. At least in privileged societies, the known conditions that invited plague could be controlled.[4]

Slow Recognition of a New Toxic Plague

Despite the advances in public health that it brought, industrialization bequeathed a less beneficial legacy, a new form of widespread environmental pollution. Nearly 200 years after Defoe's plague year, in 1856, the first synthetic chemical, aniline dye, was invented by W. H. Perkin in London.[5] Over the next decades factories producing the chemical were constructed across Britain, inspiring Dickens to write in *Hard Times* of rivers "that ran purple with ill-smelling dye." Instructively, although bladder cancers had been linked to aniline dyes as early as 1895, the social recognition of such pollution would take much longer.[6]

Contemporaneously, in the United States, shortly after the Civil War, it was reported that industrial wastes supplanted sewage as the main cause of "foul and health-threatening conditions." However, due to an incipient "sanitary movement,"

> the priority placed by health officers and sanitary engineers on the dangers posed by sewage pollution reduced the amount of attention devoted to industrial wastes. The rationale for this prioritization was that, "from a purely pathogenic standpoint," industrial wastes were viewed as having a "remote" relation to sanitation. Bacterial research had shown that sewage pollution could lead to epidemics of diseases with acute health effects, but the health effects of industrial wastes were generally not explored and poorly understood.[7]

Thus, at a minimum, the paradigm of public health focused attention away from the new type of threat: exposure to toxic substances found in air, water, and food. Moreover, the very effort to control pests and pathogens often invited the new calamity. The synthetic transformation brought about an intense social dependency upon chemicals, exemplified by the wholesale institution of chlorination and use of chlorinated compounds for killing everything from germs, termites, and enemy soldiers.

After World War II public attention was captured by such dramatic events as the smog disasters in Donora, Pennsylvania, in 1948, London in 1952, and New York City in 1953, 1963, and 1966 that left thousands of people dead or injured.[8] The environmental era responded to oil spills, visibly polluted rivers, and Rachel Carson's pioneering work on the effects of pesticides. Intensive concern, evident by the 1970s, that exposure to toxic chemicals causes human cancers was supplanted two decades later by evidence of their broader consequences for hormonal disruption.[9] World War II also laid the foundation for recognizing the toxic consequences of radioactive exposures from both military and civilian activities.

With new illnesses such as SARS, and with AIDS, Ebola, and dengue fever emerging from the biodiverse organismic sink of the rain forest and mad cow disease demonstrating the danger of prions, it is premature to dismiss the pathogenic conception of plague.[10] While these threats mix both natural and anthropogenic causes, there is nothing remotely natural about the new technological plague that uniquely characterizes our time. Toxic exposure has demanded yet another revolution in the conception of environmental health.

In this book, I address some of the significant health consequences of toxic exposure that have received comparatively less recognition than such dreaded diseases as cancer. These impacts are the social and psychological effects caused by both residential toxic exposure and the social response it engenders. Such consequences are central to mental health and well-being, people's ability to enjoy their homes and property, family and community cohesiveness, the integrity of place, and other ingredients considered collectively as the quality of life.

The Extent of Contamination

The dimensions of toxic exposure are staggering, reflecting our dependence on an increasingly synthetic world.[11] There are some 70,000 chemicals in regular use just in the United States. Add to this seventy new chemicals invented every hour and another 500–1,000 added to American commerce every year. One billion pounds of pesticides, herbicides, and fungicides are utilized in the United States every day. Beyond toxic exposure due to the manufacture, transportation, storage, and use of these materials, by 1991, the National Academy of Sciences estimated that U.S. businesses were generating annually some 4.5 billion tons of hazardous wastes, 100 pounds per day for every individual American. Indeed, the amounts of waste produced have continued to rise.

The results of this societal chemical dependence are shocking, if not surprising. Again focusing on the United States, the former Office of Technology Assessment estimated that there were some 600,000 contaminated sites. Of these, 1,266 sites have been designated or proposed by the Environmental Protection Agency for priority cleanup under the Superfund program established through the 1980 Comprehensive Environmental Response, Compensation, and Liability Act (CERCLA), with another 41,000 sites under review. In addition, there are another 400,000 municipal landfills, more than 100,000 liquid waste impoundments, millions of septic tanks, hundreds of thousands of deep-well injection sites, and some 300,000 leaking underground gasoline storage tanks threatening groundwater. Hundreds of municipal and hazardous waste incinerators are generating new concerns about air pollution and toxic ash residues. It is estimated that one in six (i.e., some 40 million) Americans live within four miles of a chemical dump or suspected other hazardous waste site.[12]

Across the land, in streams, lakes, and rivers contaminated with persistent pollutants, pollution spreads in tides and flood waters, collects in river sediments that, when dredged, must be handled as a hazardous waste, volatilizes into the air, and biomagnifies up the food chain, contaminating fish, wildlife, and humans.

This list merely scratches the surface of potential causes for residential toxic exposure. A complete chronicle would also include countless sites of illegal or inadvertent waste dumping; contaminated industrial sites regulated under RCRA (the Resource, Conservation and Recovery Act); the use, production, and storage of hazardous materials by industries now partially tracked under the Emergency Planning and Community Right-to-Know Act (passed as part of the 1986 Superfund Amendments and Reauthorization Act, Title III); the existence of naturally occurring toxins such as radon gas; exposure to radioactive wastes; toxic substances in building materials, home heating sources, foods, and household items; and the widespread use of pesticides in agriculture, forestry, lawn care, termite control, utility right-of-way maintenance, and routine home applications.

Over the past decade, indoor air pollution has become an issue rivaling outdoor air pollution for attention; thousands of buildings, including the EPA headquarters in Washington, have been blamed for causing "sick-building syndrome." Along with outdoor pollution, sick buildings are blamed for a rash of incidents of asthma and diseases of the immune system, including "multiple chemical sensitivity" and other "environmental illnesses."[13] In one of the most fascinating issues of contamination, the use of mercury in Latin and Caribbean religions, such as Santeria and voodoo, has resulted in the exposure of countless thousands of individuals and the contamination of perhaps thousands of buildings.[14] Yet another symptom of growing mistrust regarding the purity of our environment is the multi-billion-dollar bottled-water business that has emerged in this interval. This blind trust of water commodified and packaged in plastic epitomizes our synthetic transformation.

By focusing on chemical pollution, I do not mean to minimize the importance of radioactive contamination resulting from mining, refining, and processing of nuclear fuel and the development, testing, use, storage, and disposal of weapons. The resulting pollution has led to a separate Superfund for radioactive sites administered by the U.S. Army Corps of Engineers called FUSRAP (Formerly Utilized Sites Remedial Action Program). FUSRAP was created in 1974 by the Department of Energy (DOE) to locate, control, and clean up radioactive contamination remaining from the early years of the U.S. atomic energy program. More than forty-five sites in fourteen states are currently listed for remediation under this program.[15]

Additionally, the civilian nuclear energy program and the use of radioactive materials in health care and environmental monitoring pose an array of exposure issues. Radioactive mill tailings in the United States have proven to be hazards around mining sites and manufacturing sites, as well as where they were used as fill beneath houses. Dangers resulting from the use of radioactive materials in health care were dramatized in the late 1980s by a tragic disaster in Goiania, Brazil. Scrap dealers scavenged a discarded nuclear medicine machine, breaking open a platinum container and dispensing a blue luminescent carnival glitter (in actuality a radioactive cesium compound) to family and friends. Of the 129 individuals exposed, fifty were hospitalized and seven died. In terms of direct deaths, Goiania was the worst nuclear accident after Chernobyl.[16]

The list of contamination events extends far beyond the ones just mentioned. However, what is perplexing about so numbing a list is that it took so long to recognize a phenomenon of such magnitude. Excellent journalistic accounts of toxic incidents during the 1970s produced global awareness of such disparate tragedies as mercury poisoning in Minimata, Japan; the dioxin release in Seveso, Italy; the contamination of food by mercury in Iraq and by PCBs in Japan and Korea; and Agent Orange poisoning in Southeast Asia. Americans' awareness was particularly aroused by numerous domestic toxic incidents, the most dramatic being the discovery of a major toxic waste dump beneath a residential community in the Love Canal section of Niagara Falls, New York. Love Canal bore witness to this new plague of toxic exposure. No previous environmental event had posed such a direct threat to the American Dream.

Contaminated Communities

Love Canal as a Signal Event

"Signal events" inform us of some novel circumstances demanding our attention.[17] The heavily publicized Love Canal event signaled the realization that toxic exposure can destroy a neighborhood.[18] An uncompleted canal, dug late in the last century to create hydroelectricity for industry, Love Canal was used by Hooker Chemical and others as a dump site for chemical wastes beginning in the 1940s. In the 1950s, a residential neighborhood and school were developed along the canal. The implications of residents' exposure to the dumped chemicals began to unfold after widespread chemical contamination was discovered in 1978 by federal officials studying pesticide pollution of the Great Lakes. Concerned over existing and future health problems, residents organized to represent their interests and to advocate government action. Using public demonstrations and political pressure, as well as their own scientific studies, they were eventually able to win government-sponsored relocation. By 1987, the Love Canal neighborhood was substantially abandoned. A subsequent "redevelopment program" achieved modest success in attracting new buyers for those homes now deemed to be "habitable" by the state health department finding that risk in the neighborhood was no worse than risks elsewhere in the heavily contaminated city.[19]

Of course there were other signal events of the toxic plague, likely to be familiar to many readers:

- The "accident" at Three Mile Island caused thousands of residents from areas near Harrisburg, Pennsylvania, to evacuate in the wake of a governor's advisory for pregnant women. The subsequent effort to block restart of the twin reactor reflected a new poignant symbolism—if the closed damaged reactor represented the disaster that was, the restarted reactor symbolized a new accident waiting to happen.[20]
- In Woburn, Massachusetts, a high incidence of childhood leukemia was explained by the discovery that industrial solvents had contaminated local groundwater. This incident was given notoriety by the best-selling book *A Civil Action*, made into a popular movie about the lawsuit filed on residents' behalf.[21]
- Throughout the 1970s, a waste hauler named Russell Bliss used dioxin-contaminated oil to treat roads and horse arenas throughout Missouri. The resulting statewide dioxin crisis caused human illness, killed horses, and resulted in the federal buyout of the town of Times Beach.[22]
- A long-simmering conflict raged in the Pennsylvania community of Centralia over the significance of a 1962 fire that started in a garbage dump and spread through a warren of subterranean mine shafts beneath the town. A combination

of carbon monoxide gas escaping from the fires, unpredictable subsidence, and a lack of means to put out the fire resulted in a congressional resolution to relocate residents in 1983.[23]

- A 1981 fire in the new State Office Building in Binghamton, New York, released 180 gallons of PCB coolant. As the PCBs vaporized in the fire, mixing with soot created from burning wires, huge emergency vents opened, drawing contaminants into every nook and cranny of the building, including the space between floors and walls. The result was an unrepairable building, lots of exposed workers, and a fascinating test of government response.[24]
- Thousands were killed and injured in the worst acute toxic incident to date globally, the 1984 release of methyl isocyanate from the Union Carbide plant over a sleeping Bhopal, India.[25]
- In 1985, the globe-trotting radioactive cloud released from the near meltdown of the Chernobyl nuclear reactor north of Kiev, in what is now Ukraine, erased any remaining reassurances about the safety of nuclear power.[26]
- In 1986 the spill of the *Exxon Valdez* in Prince William Sound in Alaska caused an acute and chronic crisis for regional ecosystems, with reverberating effects through the native and non-native populations.[27]

Contamination as a Widespread Event

Even as the events at Love Canal and other infamous locations captured media attention, residents in thousands of communities across the United States confronted similar circumstances. Here are examples from my own experience.

- Residents of the Relocated Bayway section of Elizabeth, New Jersey, had suffered extreme toxic exposures in April 1980 when between 50,000 and 60,000 barrels of chemical wastes exploded and burned at the Chemical Control facility. There were so many local chemical hazards that it was later impossible to prove responsibility for the toxic fumes that wafted through the neighborhood and made residents ill.
- The discovery in the early 1980s that radioactive mill tailings had been used for housing fill in a number of Essex County, New Jersey, communities revealed a threat to residents from elevated levels of radon gas and gamma radiation. A pilot effort at soil removal kept residents from their homes for years while disposal of the contaminated soil itself became a major source of controversy. Meanwhile the boundaries of the areas thought to have been affected have steadily grown.
- In the summer of 1983, extremely high amounts of the potent compound dioxin were discovered in the ethnically diverse Ironbound section of Newark, New

Jersey, the result of the production of Agent Orange by the Diamond Shamrock Company.[28]

• The discovery of the pesticide DDT in the Triana River and Indian Creek in the 1980s led to a ban on the consumption of fish, a staple in the subsistence diets of many residents of the rural black community of Triana, Alabama.

• In a 1988 industrial accident frighteningly similar to the one at Bhopal, a hazardous cloud of hydrofluoric acid was unleashed over the poorer neighborhoods of Texas City, Texas. Some residents were forced to flee the cloud on foot. Many breathed fumes and developed subsequent respiratory problems.

• In 1980, bicyclists riding along a rural road in Warwick, New York, just north of the New Jersey border, discovered twenty-two seeping barrels of organic chemicals illegally dumped on an alfalfa field near homes relying on well water.

• Residents in the strikingly beautiful Skagit River valley in northern Washington State, beset by a downturn in the forest industry, had their groundwater contaminated by the pesticide EDB, sprayed on local strawberry crops.

• A leaking landfill near a General Electric plant in upstate New York exposed neighbors to hazardous chemicals and released PCBs to the Hudson River, causing collapse of a major fishing industry, designation of a sixty-mile stretch as a Superfund site, and a controversial plan to dredge the river.

• In Cañon City, Colorado, a closed uranium processing plant held the secrets of how molybdenum had been spread throughout the community, leaving residents with telltale symptoms—huge bumps all over their bodies.

• In 1978, after a decade of concern, California neighbors of the Stringfellow acid pits organized when officials, fearing a break in the dam holding back 32 million gallons of toxic chemicals, pumped 1 million gallons into the community.

• South of Houston, residents of a new suburban community discovered that the Brio Superfund site was a close neighbor, unleashing decades of concern and litigation.

• Residents of Rushton, Washington, discovered in the 1980s that their entire community was included within the boundaries of a Superfund site because of arsenic and lead contamination resulting from the historic operations of the Asarco smelter.

• Thirty miles of the wild and scenic Middle Fork of Little Beaver Creek was designated a Superfund site in the early 1980s due to contamination by the locally manufactured pesticide mirex. Fish, game, soil, cow's milk and meat, garden crops, and soil contact along the creek and floodplain were placed off-limits.

• One of the nation's newest Superfund sites is the Claremont development and the Rustic Mall in Manville, New Jersey, built atop thirty-five acres of a former industrial site, Federal Creosote, which for more than forty years had soaked railroad ties in coal tar. Homes are to be removed from two sections of the neighborhood overlying large lagoons used by the factory to store waste products. Soil will be replaced in other areas.[29]

My point is that environmental hazards (1) are ubiquitous and (2) are often invisible in the landscape unless we are truly looking for them. One of the defining characteristics of average people is that such threats are normally the furthest thing from our minds. This assumption of "normal nature" is an important backdrop to the experience of contamination.

Defining a Contaminated Community

The ubiquitous presence of environmental hazards in itself does not define a contaminated community. Rather, as the events at Love Canal and other locations demonstrate, an explicit linkage between some released pollutant and an inhabited area must first be established. Accordingly, *I will use the term "contaminated community" to refer to any residential area located within or proximate to the identified boundaries for a known exposure to pollution.* Whether or not residents share a similar political, geographic, or social environment, the discovery of a toxic threat provides a basis for a new and shared identity that effectively defines a community of interest among those residing within this toxic territory. Graphically, a "risk perception shadow" is cast over the bounded area,[30] as well as over its margins, where exposure is less certain but perhaps suspected.

Contamination is bounded temporally as well as spatially. Thus, for example, when a Superfund site is designated (i.e., the site is placed on the national priorities list, or NPL), the host community is drawn into a predetermined sequence of events. The milestones along the tortuous path from site evaluation to the institution of some degree of cleanup are signified by acrimonious acronyms such as RI/FS (remedial investigation and feasibility study) and ROD (record of decision). The journey from listing to cleanup has taken on average nearly twenty years.[31] A subsequent period of monitoring extends the temporal definition of contamination on the order of another thirty years.

The focus on bounded contamination in this definition of a contaminated community is not meant to describe every circumstance of pollution. In reality, no community is free of multiple exposures to global, regional, and local contaminants that may never be bounded. We do not have the same ability to cognitively frame these unbounded events, to subject them to regulatory processes and schedules, and to address issues of responsibility and remediation.

It must be recognized that the psychosocial impacts of toxic disaster involve both issues of toxic exposure per se and the ways in which society addresses the exposure over time.

Toxic Exposure as Psychosocial Disaster

Scholarly attention to the psychosocial impacts of toxic exposure in contaminated communities dates from Adeline Levine's efforts to document the Love Canal disaster.[32] Since the first edition of *Contaminated Communities* was published in 1988, there has been an explosion of attention in the social sciences to this issue, both new documented case studies and theoretical work intended to develop a conceptual understanding of the meaning of toxic exposure to its victims.

The convergent message of this literature confirms the basic psychosocial facts of contamination events. With community contamination, there is a deterioration in the relationship between humans and their ecological surround. Tellingly, this lost intimacy is both to the natural and the built or human ecology. This change may occur in a sudden and acute fashion, as at Three Mile Island, Bhopal, and Chernobyl, or as a chronic and gradual development, as seen at such sites as Love Canal and Woburn or as some combination of both. As with naturally occurring disasters, such as floods and hurricanes, victims of toxic exposure experience stress because their way of life is disrupted and society cannot readily restore what was lost. Trauma associated with disaster affects the family and community as well as the individual. Threats to health and safety, social relationships, and the prevailing worldview are likely to enhance the perceived extent of the disaster.[33]

If we more closely examine these events, we can readily see why exposure to contaminants is inherently stressful. The exposure is generally not voluntary. The definition of the situation as exposure to a contaminant implies bodily contact with some harmful agent. And most aspects of the situation are likely to be unclear, uncertain, or unavailable for consideration. Thus intrinsic sources of stress come from a combination of the given uncertainties of the situation as well as from the "certainties," namely, what is known or believed to be true about the exposure. We will explore these uncertainties and certainties before examining the stages of toxic disaster.

Unknowns: The Role of Uncertainty and Invisibility

The fear invoked by disaster varies with the certainty and familiarity of the event and its causality.[34] Yet, for a given disaster, this vital information may be transparent, translucent, or opaque.[35] While floods and tornadoes are *transparent* (i.e., both event and cause are familiar and observable), earthquakes and airplane crashes are *translucent* (i.e., the events are familiar and observable, but their causes are unknown and/or their onset is unpredictable). In contrast, toxic events are *opaque*. Whether chronic contamination, an acute accident, or a global cumulative effect such as global climate change, they are neither familiar nor observable, and their cause and course are equally obscure. Let's explore the opacity of chronic contamination.

Because chronic toxic events are most often invisible in nature (otherwise they presumably would have been detected earlier and not become chronic), their cloaked quality contributes to their inherent uncertainty. Questions over the cause, extent, and history of the exposure are likely to be impossible to answer: How long has the release been occurring? What areas and what people are affected? What is its duration over time? Why has contamination occurred? Why was it not discovered previously? At what levels has it been manifest? Through what pathways might exposures have occurred?

But why are these questions important? Take the issue of who is thought to have been exposed. The way that the exposure is "bounded" spatially and temporally is key to the definition of victim. In many cases, victims are defined by government agencies. For example, New Jersey residents from areas filled with radium-contaminated soil who were notified by letter that their properties were within an expanding hot zone were instantly victimized with the very act of notification. Residents on the margins of defined contaminated areas may not draw solace from being outside the assumed boundaries. In this New Jersey case, boundaries have periodically expanded over time. To hold much faith in the permanence or validity of the boundaries at any given point would be a leap of faith. And, as was illustrated by the efforts of outer ring residents at Love Canal to be included in the boundaries of contamination, the significance of the territory defined for government assistance is highly germane. Experience suggests it may be better to be part of the area defined as impacted than to be at the margins, stigmatized with exposure, perhaps even exposed, but unable to get help.

Other uncertainties belong to the consequences of the exposure: What is the potential health effect of contaminants in this mix, form, duration, and amount? Are existing symptoms attributable to the release? What will the future consequences be? At what latency and temporal stretch? Will there be cross-generational effects? Are the impacts preventable or treatable? Will they be recognized as due to this release?[36]

And there are uncertainties associated with efforts to control the contamination, as well. Is there any real way to remedy pollution once it has occurred? Will dredging the river cause more hazards than leaving a persistent contaminant to degrade over time? Will contaminants reach a drinking water source sometime in the future, when no one is looking? Is the least expensive remediation strategy for a Superfund site, involving delayed action and monitoring, sufficient when long-lived contaminants may escape detection? Is a water treatment plant designed to "strip" the chemicals from the water causing new hazards by transferring the con-

taminants from the water to the air? Or will the effort to concentrate the most hazardous radioactive materials on earth at the planned repository at Yucca Mountain,
Nevada, succeed in creating a safe way to handle wastes toxic for tens to hundreds
of thousands of years?[37]

Complicating uncertainty is the fact that not all invisible consequences are
immediately human. For example, it is not unreasonable to ask, "Are sediments
loaded with contamination?" "How persistent are contaminants?" "Will this ecosystem recover?" And because primary ecosystemic impacts have secondary human
effects, other questions arise. "Are fish or other organisms safe to consume?" "Is the
water safe to drink?" "Is it safe to breathe the air coming off a given site?"

The drama of an acute toxic release raises immediate uncertainties, such as the
safety of responders and whether evacuation is needed and for what distance and
duration. Other than discovery during its occurrence, however, so that the time
and circumstances of release are known, all other attributes of the acute disaster
may be as opaque as those of chronic events.

*The net effect of these inherent uncertainties found with contamination events is
that, to a much greater extent than with most natural disasters, the "facts" of toxic disaster are often unclear, making the "perception" of the disaster central to its subsequent
effects.* In this sense, Steve Kroll-Smith and Steve Couch term contaminated communities as "ecological-symbolic disasters." Beyond damaged environments, per se,
one must consider how the damages are interpreted.[38] *Although spiced by uncertainty, this perception is likely to be driven by what is known and understood about
the nature of the toxic calamity.*

What Is Known: The Risk Personality

Uncertainty serves to magnify the significance of the available "facts" about a contamination event. By necessity, the appraisal of the situation rests more on what is
known about the exposure than what is not known. Therefore, it is useful to closely examine the known aspects of an exposure context for the defining characteristics that give it meaning. These presumed facts of the exposure are derived from
government statements, the media, expert sources, networking to informed organizations, and word of mouth, as well as from citizen research in libraries and
increasingly on the Internet. The important thing about these "facts" is not that
they are known generally or to some group of experts but rather that they are
known to the exposure victims. Cumulatively, the known "facts" about a contamination event make up the "risk personality" of the contaminant(s) in question.[39]
"Risk" is not generally a naive construct in the sense that people do not normally
weigh the risk of various conditions in the cost/benefit mode of economists, insur-

ance actuaries, and risk assessors.[40] Instead, people either perceive "threat" or have peace of mind.[41] Risk personality amplifies or attenuates risk according to its volume, drama, controversy, and demand for attention.[42]

The "3 Cs of risk"—its cause, consequence, and controllability—is a useful shorthand for the key ingredients of a personal risk evaluation.[43] First to be weighed are causal attributes of the hazard, such as its origins, its boundaries, and its nature. Second is the appraisal of the potential consequences of the threat, balancing the expected severity of the outcomes (the "dread" factor) and the estimated likelihood of its occurrence. Outcomes are most threatening when the observer feels vulnerable or susceptible and therefore sees the danger as personal—"it may (or will) happen to me"—rather than abstract—"it might happen to someone else, but it won't (or can't) happen to me." Third, there is less threat for hazards that can be prevented and controlled, and whose consequences can be mitigated, but only if there is trust and belief that controls will actually be exercised. Each contaminant and contamination event invites a risk personality based on its known traits. Furthermore, each trait potentially exerts a dual or ambivalent influence—simultaneously contributing to and discouraging an active response to the hazard.

This duality can be seen in comparing ratings of the 3 Cs for two environmental hazards having very different risk personalities: the persistent organic pesticide mirex, which is known to have contaminated parts of the Great Lakes, southeastern Ohio, and central Pennsylvania, and naturally occurring radon gas, found across much of the planet.[44]

Case 1: Mirex Contamination.   As part of the post–World War II rush to employ recent petrochemical weapons technologies in a profitable civilian war against pests, in 1961 the Hooker Chemical Company was granted a registration for a new pesticide generically called mirex and sold under the brand name Dechlorane. Mirex was employed during the 1960s as the principal pesticide used against the imported fire ant in the southern United States. It served as the active ingredient in pesticide manufacture by Hooker Chemical's Niagara Falls facility, later linked to mirex contamination of the Great Lakes and, as a result, to the discovery of the Love Canal. Mirex was primarily manufactured by Nease Chemical, which operated plants in State College, Pennsylvania, and Salem, Ohio. Bodies of water near both plants were contaminated with mirex and its daughter products, which include the compound kepone. In Ohio, mirex released from the plant contaminated a thirty-mile stretch of the adjacent Middle Fork of Little Beaver Creek from Salem, Ohio, as far south as Lisbon. This entire area was subsequently designated as a Superfund site. Contamination from mirex was found in sediments and floodplain soils, as well as in fish, wildlife, and in the blood of some residents of the creek

CAUSAL TRAITS	CONSEQUENCES	CONTROLLABILITY
Invisible	Not identifiable easily	Testing required
Human-caused	Anger	Superfund process
Toxic Chemical	Carcinogenic and other health problems	Medical monitoring
Released into natural system	Unbounded within the MFLBC	No resolution
Long latency diseases	Effects are delayed	Medical monitoring
Personal threat to People along MFLBC	Causes Environmental Stigma	None
Lipophilic	Mirex bioaccumulates in Fish, Game, etc.	Avoid consumption of local foods.
Hydrophilic	Mirex attaches to soils.	Avoid soils and floodplains
Contact and Consumption Advisory	Impacts enjoyment of the MFLBC Impacts enjoyment of home	Give up any contact with stream, game, fish, etc.
Long half-life	Persistent in environment and degrades to even more toxic substances	Avoid contact with MFLBC for generations

Table 1.1: The Mirex Risk Personality.
Note: MFLBC is the Middle Fork of Little Beaver Creek in Ohio.

corridor. Using the three risk characteristics—cause, consequence, and controllability—as a framework, Table 1.1 indicates the significance of the risk personality for mirex for those with confirmed or likely exposures.

As exhibited in Table 1.1, mirex's risk personality invites a sense of threat because mirex is an invisible, human-caused toxic chemical associated with health problems, including cancer and other long-latency diseases. Because mirex was released into a natural system, within which it is uncontained, its systemic characteristics are particularly salient. Mirex has a long half-life, it readily attaches to soils, and it magnifies or accumulates up the food chain. These personality attributes make mirex a past, present, and future threat to the physical and biological systems of the affected area. Not only do residents face danger from contact with the river system, but they and their property are stigmatized. In short, the immediacy and danger of mirex are accentuated by its risk personality.

Case 2: Naturally Occurring Radon Gas. The 1984 discovery of high levels of radioactivity in the home of a Pennsylvania nuclear engineer focused attention on

	Mobilizing	Qualifying
CAUSAL FACTORS		
Radon Is Invisible	X	X
Radon Is Natural and, Therefore, Blameless		X
Radon Is an Unbounded and Ambient Geologic Hazard		X
Radon is Radioactive	X	
CONSEQUENCES		
Radon Invades the Home		X
Radon Is Carcinogenic	X	
Radon Is Stigmatizing		X
Radon's Impacts Are Delayed—Another Day of Exposure Is Unlikely to Matter		X
CONTROLLABILITY		
Radon Is Identifiable	X	X
Radon Exposure is Preventable	X	X
Radon is Remediable	X	X

Table 1.2: Radon's Risk Personality

a naturally occurring radioactive substance, radon gas. A daughter product resulting from the radioactive decay of uranium and radium, radon rapidly breaks down into a chain of its own short-lived daughter products. Breathing air "contaminated" with radon exposes the lungs to alpha radiation. Given the uncommonly solid epidemiological record derived from the health records of uranium miners, radon was named the second leading cause of lung cancer, behind smoking, and campaigns developed to encourage testing and remediation.[45]

As a naturally occurring hazard, radon has a risk personality that presents an interesting contrast to mirex. Table 1.2 further distinguishes between the mobilizing (threat-enhancing, magnifying, amplifying) and qualifying (threat-reducing, diminishing) attributes of radon's risk personality.

Here we see that radon is blameless, avoiding the burden of anger found with human-caused hazards such as mirex. It is also easily remediable, producing an ambivalence to the risk. Thus, despite the serious risk associated with radon exposure, the risk personality is nonthreatening. We next expand this analysis by contrasting the two threats according to the 3 Cs.

The Cause of Exposure

The causal origin of the contamination, particularly whether it is natural or humanly caused, has long been recognized as an axial variable in understanding the significant psychological difference between contamination disasters and natural disasters. As a general rule, three key characteristics of the origin of an exposure have been viewed as influencing its perception.

Technological Failure. First, toxic disaster is technological in origin, implying that the technological control over nature that enables us to enjoy a high standard of living has failed. The resulting "loss of control" contrasts with our "lack of control" over natural disasters.[46] This reaction to technological disaster is evident in the increasing public concern over technological dependence, evident at the millennium in the extraordinary fears of a Y2K apocalypse due to limits in computer programming. Technological disaster carries the same hollow sense of fear felt in the tense moments that the space shuttles *Challenger* and *Columbia* hurtled to earth, or the tragic helplessness felt during the unfolding TMI or Chernobyl events.

It may be even more useful to speak here of a failure of technocracy than technology. Inevitably the release of toxins reflects a lapse in operations, oversight, compliance, and enforcement of environmental regulations, the critical lapse in judgment in issuing permits for risky activities, or a failure of corporate self-guidance. Thus Charles Perrow has observed that, when we consider the social and organizational context of technological disaster, we find that these events are "normal" and expected rather than exceptional. But the normalcy of such accidents pushes beyond the meaning intended by Perrow, for we now accept the likelihood of catastrophic accidents as "routine." It is as if we were inured to their occurrence, if not their consequences. We are just biding our time until the next disaster.[47] It is as if technological systems were no longer controlled by social values; but those values are now, in Brian Wynne's words, "*malleable* to the new experience and relationships which the technology creates." Potential technological changes are "*inevitably* unforeseeable," as well as often "unacceptably irreversible and inflexible."[48] The release of mirex was clearly a failure of an industrial technical system. In contrast, although radon exposure could legitimately be viewed as an indictment of the way we build buildings that suck in soil gases, in practice it is rarely viewed as a technological disaster.

Human Causality. Contrast perceptions of victims of the 1977 Johnstown, Pennsylvania, flood with those of residents of the Love Canal neighborhood, whom I interviewed two years later. The first disaster was seen as "an act of God," the latter as stemming from corporate greed and government corruption. Not all floods are "natural," however. The disastrous Buffalo Creek flood in West Virginia was caused by the collapse of a huge slag dam. Survivors did not blame God for bringing the rain; they blamed the coal company for damming the creek.[49] As these examples suggest, when victims realize that a disaster is humanly caused, they are likely to develop attributions of responsibility causing feelings of distrust and anger toward the perceived agents of harm.

Unlike mirex or other synthetic contaminants released into the environment by human activity, radon gas is natural and blameless, unbounded, and is considered easy to detect and remediate. In short, geologic radon, in itself, does not motivate concern or action. However, home buyers must increasingly be assured that their home is free of radon. Once someone else has been made responsible for making sure the house is safe of radon, its subsequent discovery is rendered as an insult. Finding a high radon level in spite of assurances to the contrary connotes that exposure is involuntary and someone is at fault—the seller for not disclosing the problem or hiding it, the tester for misdiagnosis, and so on. In this way, a blameless event is converted into a blamed one.[50]

Involuntariness. It follows from these causal characteristics that central to the impact of contamination is its involuntary nature. All three critical elements of voluntary risk are violated: victims lack awareness, volition, and the opportunity to evaluate their risk.[51] We do not expect to consent to participate in natural events, yet we hold dear the belief that, with events of a social origin, we have the right to choose to be involved. We are likely to blame those who have subjected us to undesired conditions and thus further deprived us of our volition.

There is little doubt about the involuntary nature of mirex exposure along the Middle Fork of Little Beaver Creek. No choice was offered. The creek and everything in and along it was polluted by industry. People, wildlife, fish, the river itself—all were victimized. Alternatively, blameless naturally occurring radon failed to inspire sufficient voluntary testing and remediation, with action occurring instead during the sale of homes, the most regulated and economically driven (i.e., the least voluntary) aspect of the private home ownership. Instructively, with radon exposures that are not natural, as in the case of mill tailings and industrial exposures, appraisal of the contaminant changes dramatically. In fact, appraisal of industrial radon exposures is more similar in its psychological characteristics to mirex than to naturally occurring radon.[52]

The comparison of natural radon and mirex demonstrates the significance of causality to the interpretation of hazards. Human-caused events are likely to produce a much greater sense of intrusion, involuntariness, and victimization, to cause anger, blame, and a desire for justice, and to make rationalization of the exposure difficult. Furthermore, blame readily extends beyond the parties who caused the release of hazards to begin with and includes those charged with protecting the public from exposure and helping address it once it has occurred. Government agents who failed to prevent the release, to quickly detect it, to make notification in a timely manner, or to offer needed assistance are all likely to be blamed. These later forms of blame may also attend naturally occurring hazards.

Consequences of the Exposure

The outcomes of exposure are a second important factor. Dreaded health consequences such as cancer and other severe outcomes will trigger concern, even if considered unlikely.[53] Although radon and mirex have widely divergent origins, they share dreaded health consequences—long-latency illness of a serious nature. Both hazards involve unseen contaminants of environment and home and place. As with most human-caused contaminants, the facts of exposure create a plausible scenario for believing that there is a tangible threat. Medical invisibility often makes it impossible to predict what outcomes will occur or to necessarily relate them causally to the exposure. Even if one knew what exposure occurred (amount and pollutants), one would not know the outcome. As a result, exposure is psychologically burdened with legitimate expectations of the worst outcomes. Adults worry about themselves and their children. Children may worry about themselves and their parents. All worry about the next generations. And adverse outcomes can readily be attributed to the exposure even if there is no way to prove the relationship. Such uncertainties serve to heighten this belief while limiting the extent to which the risk can be qualified and the victim reassured.

Controllability of the Exposure

Knowledge of a hazard without the reassurance of some recourse results in a phenomenon I have termed the *"mitigatory gap."*[54] In this regard, the comparative risk personalities of mirex and radon also reveal a difference with regard to controllability. Although radon is touted by the EPA as easily mitigated, mirex lacks any clear ecosystemic remedy. Thus, in the Ohio instance, controllability was particularly problematic because of the close overlap between the victims' lifestyle and the exposure pathways identified for mirex.[55] Hydrophobic, mirex attaches to soils, allowing for transport to residential areas through flooding surface water runoff and blowing. A lipophilic compound, mirex is added to the body's fat through consumption of milk, meat, fish, and wildlife. Completed exposure pathways, therefore, include eating, drinking, breathing, or coming in contact with contaminated dirt, air, water, or food. Individuals might receive potentially serious exposures from fishing or trapping, farming or gardening, raising cattle for milk or meat, swimming or boating, or even breathing along the shoreline or floodplain areas. The only way to truly avoid such exposures involves forgoing any of these activities. Given the close connection between life along the Middle Fork of Little Beaver Creek and the creek ecosystem, lifestyle, or the array of normal daily activities, had to be significantly altered in order to avoid exposure. Furthermore, because the half-life of mirex exceeds ten years, exposure pathways represented the potential for past, present, and future exposure. Although future mirex exposures can be limited by lifestyle modification, this strategy itself involves all of the secondary stressors associated with the willingness and ability to change. There is no simple "tech fix" as there is often thought to be with the use of well-established radon mitigation techniques.

In summary, the concept of risk personality is useful for evaluating how what is known about a hazard influences its perception. Despite similar types of consequences, the risk personalities of radon gas and mirex differ significantly in origin and controllability. As a result, although the risk personality of mirex helps invoke a sense of threat and concern, naturally occurring radon has an ambivalent risk personality.

The Stages of Toxic Disaster

Toxic disaster can be described in the generic stages used for natural disaster,[56] allowing for variations due to factors such as type of contaminant, mode of contamination, population characteristics, acuteness of the exposure, certainty about the consequences, and quality and quantity of assistance.

Predisaster Stages: Incubation

Because a toxic disaster may strike gradually and incrementally without people's knowledge, detection of the problem, warning of potential victims, and perception of threat may occur long after the disaster. During this "incubation" stage, the community is unaware that the disaster is developing and there are few if any preparations or premonitions. This failure to predict and recognize an incubating toxic disaster is understandable. Since it is a novel experience, the eventual victims have never learned to recognize signs of contamination; and because such disasters are not supposed to happen, it is assumed that they won't. Pollution is often barely detectable, both in occurrence and consequence. The threat may be invisible, and any resulting damage may be hard to relate to the pollution.[57] The subtlety of the clues makes them easy to discount. Community complaints are frequently ignored. Industry controls information that it has a vested interest not to share, or at least not to call attention to. Finally, it is generally assumed that government officials are watching out for us. Yet agencies we look to for protection are often not vigilant in monitoring environmental hazards, are woefully understaffed in light of the number of regulated facilities, or do not immediately share information they learn. No one may be reviewing self-reported violations, or the ability or will to enforce compliance may be absent. Cumulatively, these factors reflect the complexities and uncertainties of toxic disasters that make the risks hard to define.[58] This period of incubation has not been eliminated by anticipatory and predictive innovations in environmental regulation, such as community "right-to-know" and "cradle to grave" monitoring.

Disaster Stages: Discovery, Acceptance, Community Action

Alan Barton observed that while a gradually occurring disaster allows the existing social system to make adjustments, the sudden-onset disaster requires a new process for reducing chaos.[59] Ironically, because they are not anticipated, human-caused disasters are routinely experienced as sudden even when they actually develop gradually.[60] Accordingly, much of the initial psychosocial impact of a contamination event is due to the announcement of the disaster and the sharing of information about it. Beliefs formed at this point may persist even in the face of new evidence revealed at a later time.

Experts specially trained to measure and detect toxic substances are usually involved in the process of discovery and announcement. Victims quickly become dependent on such experts to help define the situation and forge solutions. The invisibility of the agent and its effects invites differing interpretations of the occurrence, as well as required responses regarding testing, protective measures, and remediation. Therefore, consensus about the cause, course, and possible outcomes of the crisis is less likely than with natural disaster. Each individual and family must make its own determination of the significance of contamination. The lack of shared beliefs about what has happened invites conflict within the family, the community, and between the community and potential helpers.[61]

Despite difficulties accurately identifying the affected area, government officials commonly hastily draw boundaries around the area they believe to be affected. Therefore, the boundaries of the disaster may become socially clear, even if the criteria for drawing them are scientifically fuzzy. The community defined by the pollution boundaries becomes isolated from its surroundings, not by the kind of destruction seen with natural disaster but by the subtle changes in perception signified by stigma. This collective isolation of victims sharing common concerns frequently contributes to internal cohesiveness and formation of emergent ad hoc community organizations that fight for recognition, assistance, relocation, and cleanup.

Postdisaster Stages: Mitigation and Lasting Impacts

Whereas natural disaster is often of brief duration, human-caused disasters such as toxic exposure may be chronic and indefinite.[62] A contaminated site may remain unsafe for generations given the persistence of toxic hazards; individual impacts may cross generations. A sense of finality is elusive for the toxic victim, in part because toxic disasters lack a "low point" from which things would be expected to improve.[63]

Because it is not clear what damage has occurred to property or finances, or what long-term health effects may develop, it is difficult to inventory losses. Basic needs such as water may be allocated on an emergency or even a permanent basis, but rarely is rescue quickly forthcoming. Helping professionals may not define the events as a disaster to which they must respond. Bureaucrats may lack vested interests or authority to help in a definitive way. Friends and relatives may not know how to help. As a result, the affected community is left to fend for itself.

Remedy may involve mere mitigation, as with the provision of a new water source or the building of a water treatment plant. Such remediations inevitably signify the severity of the original threat (i.e., there would be no treatment plant operating if the groundwater were not polluted) and, should the mitigation fail, the hazard will return.[64] A lawsuit may be brought to seek some form of compensation or medical monitoring, but not to restore the naive security that previously existed. Toxic disaster is hard to completely remedy because its impacts are impossible to measure. Because relocation is rare, people usually continue to live in the context of contamination. Much as with the prediction of pollutants moving underground, it is difficult to gauge what the genetic implications of toxic exposure will be—neither of these outcomes can be seen, and the effects may be slow to emerge. Various studies have suggested that human-caused disasters result in greater, longer-lasting, and different kinds of stresses than those associated with natural disaster.[65] Furthermore, the recovery to a "postdisaster equilibrium" possible after a natural disaster is here problematic.

It is notable that even the program intended to resolve this problem of continuing jeopardy, Superfund, has often acted to compound it. The initial challenge of getting a toxic site evaluated and listed on the coveted National Priorities List involves a perverse "lost beauty" contest. Sites are subjected to a hazards rating system to qualify. To date, some 41,000 sites have been evaluated under Superfund, with less than 5 percent reaching the national priorities list. The remainder are pushed back into limbo, left for states or other EPA programs to eventually address.[66]

Once on the NPL, the contaminated site must pass a gauntlet of milestones—assessment, study, choice of remedy, remedial design, and construction to achieve "site remediation." Identification of potentially responsible parties (PRPs) and other start-up issues may cause serious delays, as may missed schedules by consultants and the pervasive shortages of funds that leave many NPL sites dangling. The actual remedial investigation and feasibility study (RI/FS) process easily stretches past a decade in duration. The remedial action selected in the record of decision (ROD) frequently fails to achieve the level of cleanup sought by the affected community. Twenty years in the making, the remediation itself may come to be viewed as yet a new community threat, such as when permanent in-place disposal of hazardous wastes is allowed, a hazardous waste incinerator is constructed, or a water purifying plant discharges pollutants into the air. Thus, aside from the personal and even cross-generational health issues, the social process of addressing contamination easily preoccupies a significant portion of victims' lives, corresponding to a typical transition between life cycle stages or a generational turnover. Postclosure monitoring of at least thirty years extends this intrusion across additional generations.

Considerable progress has been made to expedite cleanup of federal Superfund sites. In 1991 only 60 (or 5 percent) of the 1,200 sites on the national priorities list had been cleaned up. As Table 1.3 shows, 12 percent had been cleaned up by 1993. And over a third have had remedial activity completed by 1997. Considerable progress made during the Clinton administration in completing Superfund sites was potentially reversed when George W. Bush became president. Although the number of sites completed in Clinton's second term averaged 87 per year, the first two years of the Bush administration produced almost half the completions (averaging 45). Still, Figure 1.3 reveals some 850 sites now remediated under Superfund, more than five times the completions a decade earlier. [68]

It is certainly premature to conclude that the Superfund process has been made so efficient that its adverse effects have been eliminated. The above figures still show a roughly twenty-five-year lag in addressing listed sites. Furthermore, thousands of toxic sites and their neighboring communities languish in the limbo created by positive evaluation of contamination but lower priority of cleanup. And Superfund fails to restore some semblance of order in victims' lives or to provide compensation for their losses. [69]

Collateral Damage in the Risk Society

Cumulatively, the toxic plague described in this volume represents to Erikson a "new species of trouble" characterized by its human cause, invisible toxic poisons, uncertainty over time, loss of personal control, anger and anxiety and distrust, negative changes to the environment, lost trust in technology, and a new way of seeing the world. These problems reflect the ecological and social destruction caused by a modern industrial era organized to exploit nature in order to ensure human sur-

	Pre-Remedial Assessment	Emergency Cleanup or Study-RIFS	Remedy Selected	Design Underway	Work Underway	Work Complete	Total Sites
January 1993	73 (06%)	367 (34%)	92 (7%)	213 (17%)	380 (30%)	155 (12%)	1280
End of FY 1997	55 (04%)	180 (17%)	63 (5%)	124 (9%)	477 (34%)	498 (35%)	1397
By Dec. 31, 2002	61 [72] (4%) [5%]	248 [256] (16%)			382 (24%)	846 (54%)	1560

Table 1.3. Figures showing progress in accelerating cleanup across stages of the Superfund process based upon www.epa.gov/superfund/. 1993 and 1997 data was taken on Dec. 14, 1999 and 2002 data on May 18, 2003. The 2003 data was not reported in a fully compatible manner with previous figures and the two left columns should be considered approximations.

vival and produce wealth. The result, as the German theorist Ulrich Beck observes, is a shift into a new "reflexive" phase of modernity, the "risk society," focused on the production and distribution of hazards and insecurities produced by modernity itself. Accordingly, "risk" has become the preeminent concern of postmodern people. Where early moderns enjoyed consumption and comfort as tangible indications of progress and growth, late moderns stare into the existential void created by the unknown and unintended, often invisible and abstract consequences of our own perhaps irreversible actions.[70]

I want to stress three attributes of the risk society. First, as William Freudenburg notes, the "risk crossover" between pre-modern and modern society involves a substantial drop in traditional risks of death while paradoxically making moderns increasingly vulnerable to risks associated with the interdependencies that make the system work. This vulnerability is less to dramatic events such as nuclear catastrophe than to the ordinary use of hazardous technologies. Such risks are socially divisive, occurring at the hands of those who purport to be our friends—the government officials, industry public relations people, and experts involved in selling and permitting the hazardous tradeoffs that enable modern society.[71]

Second are the implications of this transformation of risk. British social scientist Brian Wynne cites a description of the terror experienced by GIs in Vietnam who were never sure if they were receiving hostile or "friendly" fire.[72] By the Gulf War, we had come to rework "friendly fire" as "collateral damage," with the expectation that shooting at the enemy invariably includes taking out some of our own. This metaphor of collateral damage captures the dilemma of the risk society, as the rebounding consequences of our own actions make us cringe. The "friendly fire" we fear is illustrated by my colleague's description of panic as a low-flying plane strafed Sunday morning shoppers on a Brooklyn street in late summer 1999 with a mist of pesticides as part of New York City's effort to destroy mosquitoes carrying West Nile virus. The incident raises the issue of whether intensive pesticide exposure by the broad population offsets the risk of the disease. Maybe it is important to try to eradicate the mosquitoes that carry the disease, but what are the costs in terms of collateral damage? This is the dilemma of a risk society.

Finally, in the risk society, social thought atrophies as all are dependent on science to make unseen contaminants visible and on experts to address them. In the process, Beck acknowledges that the victims are subjected to "terrible psychological stresses."[73] In what follows, I detail the causes and consequences of these psychological stresses.

The Theory of Environmental Turbulence

This volume presents a "theory of environmental turbulence" that makes concrete the abstraction of the risk society, identifying the major social and psychological impacts stemming from residential toxic exposure and examining their significance against the baseline of victims' previous lives. The theory was inductively derived from field observations in scores of contamination sites and tested and refined across multiple observations.[74] Findings have been compared with other researchers using varied approaches. The resulting theoretical framework is based on four postulates:

- The social and psychological impacts of toxic exposure involve complex interactions across various levels of society in a particular ecohistorical context.
- These impacts not only affect how victims behave but how they perceive and comprehend their lives, in both the short and long term.
- Environmental turbulence is stressful, forcing victims to adopt some form of coping response.
- Contamination is inherently stigmatizing and arouses anticipatory fears.

Postulate 1: The Impacts of Toxic Exposure Occur at Interacting Levels of Social Process in an Ecohistorical Context

The essence of my approach is to understand how the inhabitants of polluted places make sense out of their daily lives, contrasting before and after contamination is discovered. I believe that there is an inherent structure of meaning in our life context that can be recognized and defined. After all, people live in places and communities, not a vacuum. I seek to understand people in these life contexts, examining their thoughts, behavior, and feelings. Rather than try to isolate the causal effect of one influential factor occurring in a simple situation, I search for the mutual causal influences of multiple factors occurring simultaneously in a

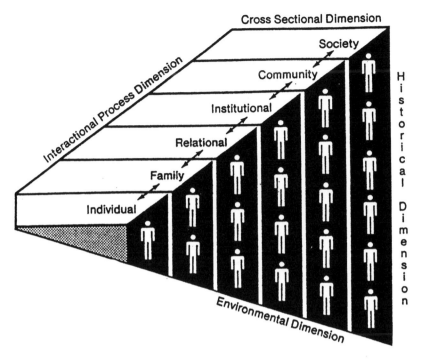

Figure 1.1   A Model of Social Process in Ecohistorical Context

complex situation. The approach is not purely deductive and narrow but rather explores complexity while developing and testing theory.

I conceived of such an approach in the face of an interesting challenge. In August 1985, I traveled to Richton, Mississippi, as part of an interdisciplinary social science team charged with preparing a social impact study of the preliminary proposal to site a high-level nuclear waste repository in the nearby Richton (salt) dome. Our client, the state of Mississippi, wanted to understand the full ramifications of this potential federal action. But how could one quickly learn enough about this community and place to cogently create a social impact study whose conclusions might be valid in predicting the consequences were the proposal to be carried out? In a thought piece to the team entitled "Modeling Mississippi," I proposed the *model of social process* depicted in Figure 1.1. The model assumes that for any contaminated community (or other study context), a given cross-section (or observation taken at a given point in time) must account for the mutual synergy of three very distinct parts of the puzzle: the social, the historical, and the ecological.[75]

- *The social dimension.* Trained in group and organizational psychology, I was aware that impacts of the siting process and potentially resulting facility might occur at varied mutually synergistic and interdependent levels of psychosocial process, namely, individuals in isolation and within their diverse social contexts—families, relational groups, institutions, community, and society. Assessment of psychosocial impacts challenges us to capture the essence of each level of process without losing the sense of the whole dynamic.
- *The ecological dimension.* Moreover, human interaction occurs within an ecological and geographic setting, often within a continuing relationship and identity associated with place. The health of this environmental surround is a baseline determinant for human health. Even undetected and unknown environmental forces may exert great influence over the course of our lives. The perceived contamination of the environment simultaneously overlays and undermines the quality of social interaction at each level of social process.
- *The historical dimension.* Finally, the historical dimension is used to place any cross-sectional observation into the chronology of locally important events or key milestones that shape the identity, coping capacity, concerns, and relationships for every level of social process. As Shkilnyk correctly notes, toxic impact combines in complex ways with prior insults to produce "cumulative injuries" for the community.[76]

Together, the latter two dimensions produce an *ecohistorical context* of social process. If the meaning of contamination involves the complex interactions of people and the environment, collectively as well as individually, it must be understood that such patterns do not occur miraculously. Rather, they take root and develop over time. Thus, in addition to cultural, social, and individual differences between people, there can be important idiosyncrasies in the ecohistorical context that influence how the discovery and announcement of contamination is understood. The challenge to any observer is to understand the event studied at that discrete point in time and to place that event in the evolving ecohistorical context for meaning in that setting.

Thus, for some residents in the Richton area, consideration of a high-level nuclear waste site by the federal government was a continuation of the insults from Washington that could be traced to the Confederate loss in the Civil War and the disabling conditions of the reconstruction period. Furthermore, if the facility were built, the Richton dome would hold a swath of the Gulf Coast region in jeopardy for millennia. And even if the Richton dome were not selected for the repository, it would still remain in *perpetual jeopardy* as a site identified as environmentally suitable for hazardous waste disposal.

The baseline for any pollution event involves identifying the prior status of the community on these three dimensions.[77]

Postulate 2: Toxic Exposure Affects Both Action (the Lifestyle) and Cognition (the Lifescape)

For each level of social process, we can identify a pattern of functioning that reflects a normal set of behaviors, the "lifestyle." "Lifestyle" refers to people's way of living, including their pattern of activities and the relationships, places, and props needed to sustain these activities. Lifestyle embodies the core assumptions of a society as reflected in the pursuit of personal goals. The achievement of these goals and related social expectations allows the attainment of "quality of life," encompassing such factors as economic security, secure family life, personal strengths, friendships, enjoyment of home and property, and an aesthetic physical environment.[78] Normal life before a contamination event provides a baseline against which we can compare later behavioral and cognitive changes.

Beyond lifestyle, the precontamination baseline also reflects our normal assumptions about life, what I term the "lifescape."[79] The lifescape reflects both unique individual interpretive frameworks and shared social paradigms used for understanding the world. Such core assumptions generally are hidden. However, in the face of their disconfirmation by contamination events, they are forced to the visible surface. A pillar of the lifescape becomes evident for each of five core life assumptions: health, self, home, the environmental surround, and trust for others (Figure 1.2).

In addition to disrupting personal paradigms, disconfirmation of the lifescape may challenge core assumptions held by families, communities, institutions, and even the overall society. Thus toxic exposure directly assails fundamental social beliefs that humans hold dominion over nature, people control their own destiny, technology and science are positive and progressive forces, environmental risks are acceptable, people get what they deserve, experts know best, the marketplace is self-regulating, one's home is one's castle, and government exists to help. It is not easy to discard such beliefs, unless they have previously been cast into doubt. Some may so strongly adhere to these assumptions that they deny, rationalize, or ignore issues of toxic exposure in order to maintain their existing lifescape.[80]

Postulate 3: Environmental Turbulence Is Inherently Stressful

For the individual, the physiological, psychological, emotional, and social costs exacted by everyday life are commonly referred to as stress.[81] Toxic exposure may

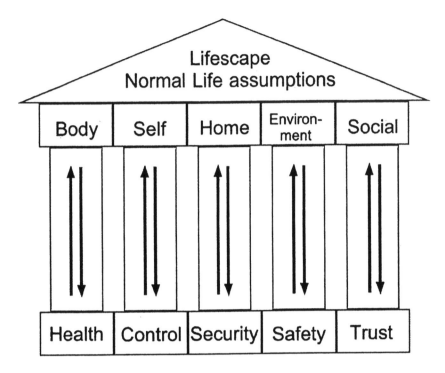

Figure 1.2   The Lifescape

cause new strains in victims' lives, intensify existing strains, or give new meaning to old problems. It may be blamed for such major life crises as the death of a loved one, marital discord, ill health of family members, and financial difficulties. None of the key spheres of life activity—home, family, work, friendships—is free from disruption due to exposure.

Stress is not solely the property of the individual, however. It occurs at every level of social process, affecting family, relational, institutional, community, and societal dynamics as well. For example, at the institutional level of analysis, an environmental agency may be affected by its involvement in a contamination issue. The case may affect individuals within the agency, the public image of the agency, its institutional standing as an arm of government, its success at meeting organizational goals, its use of available resources, and its ability to attract new resources. Given that stress exists at all levels of process, it may be meaningful to think of a "system's" response to stress, rather than merely an individual's response. Any level of social process—from individual to the society as a whole—is thus recognized as a system responding to stress.

The stress process itself is depicted in Figure 1.3. Although much psychological emphasis has been placed on the system's resources for coping with environmental challenge, our examination of the psychosocial impacts of contamination places the greatest emphasis on the nature of environmental stressors, understood within the overall ecohistorical context of the system. These stressors are threats or challenges from outside the system that by their very nature disrupt its balance. Stress occurs as the system responds to the stressor. The impact of the stressor may vary according to the state of the system, including such factors as its preparedness, its vulnerability, and its resources for coping. Environmental stressors take various forms—noxious physical stimulation, recognition of a threat that might cause or has already caused disruption, harm or loss, and confrontation by challenges that vary from simple problems to complex dilemmas. Toxic exposure often involves all three types of threat simultaneously—exposure to noxious physical conditions, fears over realized and future consequences, and the need to make decisions based on scant, novel, complex, and ambiguous information under great pressure.

Once a threat is recognized—for example, with the public announcement that a community's water is polluted—the cognitive component of the stress process kicks into play. Here the stressor is appraised by the system to ascertain the potential implications, their severity, the system's susceptibility, and whether anything can be done about it. Because appraisal is a subjective analysis, varied interpretations of a given event are likely, ranging from taking the threat seriously to engaging in defensive avoidance. Factors affecting appraisal include the beliefs of the appraisers, their knowledge of the threat, the threat's visibility (e.g., amount and kind of publicity), and the significance of the threat. The "risk personality" of a contaminant determines its appraisal as a stressor.

After a threat is appraised as legitimate, alternative responses are considered. In the absence of easy solutions or choices, the system may be forced to continue its existing practices. Thus, for example, most toxic victims remain in their homes despite concerns over risk of continued exposure. Some victims will cope with this imbalance or dissonance (e.g., "I'm at risk, but I'm staying") by engaging in a form of denial ("If it were truly dangerous, government would relocate me"). Other residents, however, regarding themselves as stranded in a hazardous situation, may panic or become hypervigilant. Still other victims will vigilantly survey and evaluate alternatives, searching for the most desirable outcomes.[82]

Resulting coping responses may also vary. Some responses are focused on controlling feelings of upset and disruption rather than on controlling the source of the threat. Systems may accommodate to the stress, as when people adjust their behavior or beliefs to fit changed circumstances (e.g., either stop drinking the contaminated groundwater or stop worrying about drinking it) or adapt their sensitivity to environmental stimuli (e.g., just get used to the altered taste of the water).[83]

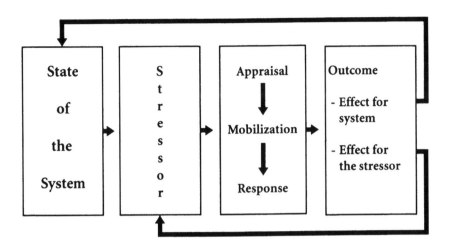

Figure 1.3 The Contextual Stress Process

Other examples of adjustment include the use of background sounds (music or air conditioners) to filter traffic noise and the personalization of pollution detection equipment in living rooms by giving the equipment names such as "Old Harry" and "Darlene."[84] Other examples of adaptation include the Love Canal resident who reacted to being told that the house smelled just like the nearby chemical plants by commenting, "We got so used to living in the house, so the odor could have been there all the time." Such individual accommodations to stress have parallels in relational groups, institutions, and communities as well. However, although they assist in coping with stress, accommodations do not necessarily reduce the perceived severity of environmental problems.[85]

Accommodations may themselves become new stressors. In the case of living with the threat, for example, one parent became a television addict to avoid dealing with pollution. Now he and his family faced the secondary impact of his listlessness and unwillingness to deal with problems. And, in the case of acting on the threat, consider parents who attend so many meetings in an effort to be vigilant about the contamination issue that their absence causes tension at home.

It is widely recognized that different life events cause different degrees of stress.[86] For example, the loss of a family member, serious illness, relocation of one's home, and the like are extreme stressors. In contrast, the stresses associated with such common occurrences as being stuck in traffic, being aggravated by a teenager, having a computer crash, or feeling burdened with too many chores are less serious "daily hassles." But how does one measure the level of stress associated with a complex set of events caused by contamination? Citing studies involving stress measurements collected at one point in time on a generic stress survey, some researchers conclude that stress due to contamination is only of modest daily hassle intensity.[87] This conclusion is suspect for two reasons. First, in a large enough sample, those most victimized (and thus most stressed) by contamination may statistically disappear or their scores become washed out; an average of modest stress does not mean that there is not a subpopulation experiencing much greater stress.

Second, contamination involves a complex array of stressors that arise, to varying degrees of severity, at different points spatially and temporally. Assume that the long-term chronic average stress due to contamination is in fact no worse than having additional continuing daily hassles added to one's life. This stress baseline, however, is likely to be punctuated by "acute" high stress events. For example, when there has been no new news about the pollution for a long interval, life in a contaminated community may appear to be quasi-normal and the chronic stress level modest. However, at crucial milestones—such as key meetings, the release of new information, or an important decision point—levels of acute stress may skyrocket precipitously.

A final distinction can be made between the internal, primary, and direct stress due to the actual exposure and the external, secondary, and indirect stresses caused by the response to the contamination event. The first category includes any resulting physiological changes and illness and also the fear of illness, adjustments due to the knowledge of exposure, and the need for medical monitoring and precaution. The second incorporates the social response to the contamination and its consequences, including stress due to the response of government, friends, and relatives, coworkers, others in the community, the media, and neighbors. Both forms of stress are inherent in the contamination situation, although either may dominate in certain situations. Regardless of whether or not they believe they have been contaminated, contamination events have primary victims who have been exposed or live proximate to the hazard and secondary victims, those injured only by the public response to the disaster.[88]

Generally, however, we can assume that at least half of the stress caused by contamination is external—it is due to the social response rather than the exposure itself.

Postulate 4: Exposure Is Inherently Stigmatizing and Arouses Anticipatory Fear

Contamination events (1) arouse environmental stigma and (2) cause anticipatory fears. Environmental stigma is a consequence of being "contaminated."[89] In the classic formulation by Erving Goffman, stigma always involves a victim identified by an observer as marked (deviant, flawed, limited, spoiled, or generally undesirable). When an observer notices the mark, it changes, in a negative and discrediting way, how the observer sees the victim, whose identity is now spoiled. And because we tend to assume that people deserve what happens to them, stigma readily invites a tendency to blame the victim. Environmental stigma routinely accompanies the announcement of contamination and the identification of its boundaries, affecting a variety of targets, including affected residents, buildings, objects, places, animals, and products.

Edward Jones and colleagues suggest a number of criteria that observers use in evaluating a stigma that are applicable to toxic exposure. Accordingly, one can evaluate how disruptive an exposure event is, whether its existence is concealable, whether it affects aesthetic qualities, whether the victim is in any way responsible for its occurrence, what its prognosis is, and the degree of peril it portends. Once contaminated, many exposure victims view themselves differently, in part because they fear dreaded health impacts, such as cancer, threats to unborn children, and cross-generational genetic effects. Victims also discover that others see them differently as well. And their homes and neighborhood are downgraded by observers who exhibit "anticipatory fears" about place.

Anticipatory fears are perceptions of threat associated with future outcomes that are causally connected to current events.[90] The initial lack of vigilance that results in toxic exposure reflects an absence of anticipatory fear. But once contamination or its potential is recognized, much greater vigilance can be expected. After people mentally rehearse an anticipated danger, they may take protective actions. Drawing on the experience of others, people may even learn to rehearse disasters that they have not personally experienced and, therefore, to anticipate threatening events not as yet set in motion. The "ticking time bomb effect" associated with toxic disaster, its protracted period of anticipatory concern, is a consequence not found with natural disasters.[91] Opposition to stigmatized facilities such as waste disposal sites is partially a consequence of anticipatory fears.

Summary and Outline of the Book

The turbulent impacts of toxic exposure need to be analyzed across the levels of social process in an ecohistorical context. They involve effects on both lifestyle and lifescape and can be explained in light of a stress process involving threats, appraisal, and coping efforts, which include accommodation as well as more assertive and successful actions. Toxic exposure also inherently invites stigma and anticipatory fears. These four postulates form the framework for analysis in what follows.

In Chapter 2, I use a detailed case study to describe the lifestyle impacts of toxic exposure. In Chapter 3, I discuss the five lifescape changes resulting from toxic exposure. In Chapter 4, I review the cumulative family impacts of contamination, highlighting individual and relational impacts as well as effects on children. Chapter 5 describes how toxic victims are disabled (or rendered powerless) by the institutional and expert context of an exposure incident. Chapter 6 explains how citizens regain power through grassroots organizations. Chapter 7 examines the rational basis for community resistance to stigmatized and hazardous facilities and the overall societal impacts of environmental turbulence.

2

Legler: The Story of a Contaminated Community

At the heart of my research on contaminated communities is the preparation of a detailed case study describing how victims in a community have been affected. I refined the approach in 1981 during my study of the impacts of groundwater contamination on the Legler section of Jackson Township, New Jersey. Before using the Legler case study to illustrate lifestyle impacts, I will further describe this research method.

A Methodological Note

The meaning of any disaster is most clearly indicated by what has been involuntarily lost or changed for the worst from the ordeal. Accordingly, my approach for field study of the psychosocial impacts of toxic exposure is grounded in a comparison of victims' lives before and after an exposure event, the first serving as a baseline for analyzing the second. It is by understanding how "normal life" may have been affected by contamination and related events that one can make tangible these consequences. I have sought to use approaches that maximize my ability to learn the meaning of such changes as understood by the victims. I review all available documents about the case, often thousands of pages of government and court documents, as well as media files. Using these materials, I construct a detailed chronology of events for the community—a profile of the ecohistory.

Next I visit the affected community, tour it in detail, and sometimes live there for a short time. I generally conduct a series of in-depth interviews with a sample of affected residents chosen to highlight key impact variables. The interviews reconstruct the precontamination baseline, subsequent changes due to contamination, and their meaning. In-home family group interviews lasting between two and six hours are used to provide depth, while shorter focused group interviews with unrelated individuals from the community offer breadth. Although the sessions utilize a basic set of questions, the specific shape of the interview is fluid, acting like a conversation that takes its own course as much as possible. The conversation continues until the topics contained in the interview format are "saturated" with information, even if not all questions have been asked.

Classified by colleagues as "ethnographic,"[1] this approach varies from the quantitative one frequently employed by psychologists.[2] Rather than compare samples from control and affected communities, I focus on victims from the contaminated community to gain insight into the dynamics and meaning of contamination over time. I am less interested in the question "Is this community significantly different?" than "How has it been impacted?" As an alternative to "statistical validity," this qualitative approach judges the "logical validity" of any new piece of information as it makes sense within the larger social and ecohistorical context.[3] This difference is vital because conventional studies using standardized measures to compare affected communities to an uncontaminated "control" may identify significant differences in stress or psychological dysfunction but may not be able to explain how the differences were caused by contamination, what they mean, and the associated dynamics. Comparison communities may be matched on superficial similarities. Lacking some historical baseline, these cross-sectional studies measure only one point in time, offering no basis for weighing the influences of the ecohistorical context. I am pleased that over the twenty-plus years I have worked on contamination, such qualitative approaches have become as mainstream as are quantitative studies.

Three final methodological notes are in order. A victim-focused approach is useful for trying to understand the most important effects of a contamination event, simply because it best represents those most impacted. In contrast, randomized sample studies may confound impacts by mixing those who believe in the contamination with those not viewing themselves as affected or harmed. Such data is useful for a blended assay of the overall community or to identify percentages of believers versus nonbelievers in the population, but may obscure victims and how they have been affected, minimizing the effects. The perceived victims may be a small percentage of the overall community and thus easily underrepresented in a randomized sample and their impacts washed out.

Second, my research often involves preparation for testimony in toxic torts. I have found litigation to be an unusual opportunity to do logically valid research. I routinely encounter motivated participants and gain unusually full access, or "entry," to affected communities. Despite plaintiffs' apparent vested interest to exaggerate their harm, I have not found them to be biased informants. Beyond their availability and willingness to spend much more time than the average person would give to a researcher, plaintiffs in litigation have relaxed their customary veil of privacy and generally offer uncommonly high levels of disclosure. At the levels of depth and detail attained during lengthy conversations, logical inconsistencies become apparent, providing a truth check on victims' self-reports. Litigation offers other unique safeguards. Plaintiffs are subject to discovery, answering of interrogatories, and examination at both deposition and trial. They are under close scrutiny by defense attorneys seeking to impugn their integrity and could be punished for perjury if they are caught lying under oath. These are uncommonly strong truth motivators.

Finally, the complementary strengths of qualitative and quantitative approaches invite efforts to collaborate on convergent research. On a number of occasions, I have had the pleasure of inviting collaborators to do a parallel study of the same community as I.[4] After reports are written, evidence of convergence (or divergence) can be examined. The Legler study was the proving ground for both my qualitative approach and the benefits of such collaboration.

Groundwater Contamination in Legler

This case study is drawn from a report that I prepared in 1981 for the law firm representing ninety-six Legler families in a legal action against Jackson Township and others. The study sought to identify the social and psychological impacts on families belonging to the Concerned Citizens Committee resulting from the pollution caused by the municipal landfill.[5]

A study sample of twenty-five families was carefully chosen to be representative of all ninety-six families. Adult members of each of the selected families participated in a lengthy, intensive interview which reconstructed life in Legler at the time respondents had moved there and reviewed other key junctures in the chronology of the Legler incident. Interviews were held in the home and children were often present.

All of the selected families were middle-class homeowners.[6] They differed on four key factors, three reflecting residents' possible feelings of vulnerability to toxic exposure. Age was the first factor. Predominant in Legler were married couples under forty years of age. Not only did most already have children at home, but they were young enough to produce more. Given their age, they were themselves susceptible to slowly developing diseases such as cancer. As a result, I expected that their concern over health effects, both for themselves and their children, would be quite different from that held by older residents. In picking the sample, therefore, I tried to assure a mix of ages. Similarly reflecting vulnerability were differences in length of residence and direction and distance of the home from the pollution source. Activism was the final factor; the sample included all members of the executive committee of the Legler Concerned Citizens Committee as well as people comparatively much less involved.

In asking questions and in analyzing the data, I sought to understand how residents interpreted events rather than to test hypotheses quantitatively. Each interview was carefully reconstructed from notes and typed in as close to verbatim form as possible. Each interview was subsequently read intact as a narrative from start to finish, keeping its own inherent longitudinal logic, flow, and integrity as a conversation. In addition, interviews were dissected cross-sectionally according to each question, in order to compare across respondents to ascertain the cumulative logic of the community on that topic. Although it was therefore possible to tally the responses, such totals miss a key point of this qualitative research, namely, that an observation found only once within scores of interviews may have incredible explanatory power for the entire population despite no one else having mentioned it. Thus the number of times a given response occurred was less important than its depth and contribution to elucidating the overall picture. Using this qualitative approach, I was able to reconstruct respondents' baseline residential expectations and identify the psychosocial impacts of the pollution incident.

Because the Legler case involved a new topic then little represented in the literature, it offered an opportunity to create a new body of theory that emerged directly from the interview findings. But the paucity of literature also limited heuristic influences. Fortunately, Jackson's proximity to Long Beach Island, where Dr. Adeline Levine and her husband, Dr. Murray Levine, were vacationing, allowed me to accept their kind invitation to visit. Addie had already been helpful in making key suggestions based on her study of the then ongoing Love Canal incident, stressing the importance, for example, of age and the presence of children as influential variables. As we sat on the beach, I carefully laid out my findings and we compared and contrasted my Legler findings with hers from Love Canal. Our conversation confirmed the validity of my emerging understanding and suggested that the theory developed out of one contamination event might be generalized to and be confirmed by others.

Period of Incubation

There were several phases of incubation for the Legler groundwater contamination event. Early residents formed their residential expectations when Legler was pristine. Later, they were forced to adjust to the development and operation of a mining site, subsequently the location of the municipal landfill that caused the pollution. Each phase was a baseline for what would follow.

Residential Expectations in Legler

Legler was distinctive in its basic similarity to many other residential areas lacking its notoriety. Located southwest of New York City, Legler was a suburb laid over an older rural landscape in a way that parallels thousands of other developments of the prior and subsequent decades. In every way, the area symbolized the search for the American Dream.

Achieving the American Dream.   Located at the edge of the sandy Pine Barrens in a remote section of Jackson Township, Legler is surrounded by open spaces. Atlantic Ocean beaches are nearby. The section reflected the intensive development that characterized Jackson and all of Ocean County during the fifteen years preceding the discovery of contamination. The spatial plan of Legler emphasized privacy and seclusion. The development was dominated by bi-level and ranch homes on large lots. During a visit in 1981, I saw swimming pools in many backyards. Stores and other amenities, where neighbors might meet one another, were absent from the area. People depended on cars for obtaining almost all their needs. A firehouse was the only visible evidence of community.

Legler was only sparsely populated prior to the late 1960s. Single-family houses lining the highway attest to an initial period of growth from 1968 through 1971. A similar growth spurt from 1973 through 1975 began to fill in a road running parallel to the highway. A final and major surge of development that pushed back from the major roads began in 1976 and peaked in 1978, virtually ceasing by 1979.

The new residents came primarily from dense urban areas of New Jersey or from New York City, where they tended to have had a surprisingly stable pattern of residence. Half the sample had previously owned a starter house. In contrast, all considered their Legler home to be permanent. The move to Legler often reflected more than just having outgrown the prior house. It also involved an escape from a hectic urban lifestyle in crowded neighborhoods. The dominant factor cited in the selection of Legler, mentioned in some form by nearly everyone in the sample, was its rural ambience. Legler was viewed as undeveloped and isolated—it had woods, fresh air, well water, open space, sparse population, little traffic, and abundant quiet. Work-related considerations (e.g., commuting distance, job transfers, or room to park one's truck) also influenced Legler's selection.

Typically, the search for a new home coincided with some milestone, such as marriage, starting a family, outgrowing the prior house, or achieving the savings necessary to afford moving beyond a starter house. Prospective home buyers learned of Legler from advertisements or when taken to a builder's model. For many, financial considerations led to Legler. It was a comparatively inexpensive place to acquire an acre of land and build a new custom home. The $40,000 to $50,000 price range was considered a bargain during the peak years of development in the region.

Residents used words such as "Shangri-la," "countrified," "beautiful and peaceful," and "clean and refreshing" to describe their recollection of Legler at the time they moved there. The country was seen as a place where children, free of the perils of crime, traffic, and "Cancer Alley," could have wonderful adventures that many of their parents had never experienced. In nearly all cases, it was seen as a generally healthy place compared with the new residents' prior homes.[7]

Privacy and Community in Legler. Not only the physical but also the social environment changed as the area was developed. The relatively few residents predating the period of intensive housing development knew Legler as sparsely populated and isolated. Residents depended upon each other for social stimulation and developed a tight self-help network as well, as one old-timer recalled,

> *Everybody was friends. They were the best, most beautiful people; there were no enemies. We had parties at Halloween, Thanksgiving, on every holiday. On Christmas we'd ride through the area on horse and buggy. If anyone was in trouble, everybody would help.*

Although people were close in this way, a strong sense of reserve and respect for each family's privacy was also evident.

> *It was a quiet, no-pressure place. We weren't coffee klatch people. We were here for our neighbors if needed, but we didn't want people visiting all the time.*

During the first major influx of development, old-timers extended help to their new neighbors, inviting them over for a drink or assisting them in the move. These newcomers shared their rural expectations for the area even if they lacked their communal spirit. Proximity was the newcomers' sole basis for association. They established a "hello basis" for neighboring and helped each other readily. However, they did not seek to establish close ties with their fellow residents.

> *We felt cut off from people and that's how we liked it.*

In selecting Legler, the new residents had deliberately avoided housing developments. Given the way they valued solitude and a rural way of life, it is not surprising that they wanted to shut the door to Legler. Accordingly, they resented the predominantly young families with children who came several years later during a much larger phase of development from 1976 to 1978. Earlier residents derided these latecomers for their suburban "coffee klatch" mentality. In fact, if reserve and solitude were the main components of privacy for the earlier residents, intimacy and neighboring characterized this later group—their expectations favored a suburban rather than rural way of life. Given the difference in residential values between these groups of residents, it is not surprising that they had little contact prior to the pollution incident.

For the latecomers, social relationships were initially affected by the pace of development when they moved in. While it might be lonely for the first family in a new subdivision, strong local ties quickly developed once neighbors arrived.

> We had nice neighbors in our age-group with children similar in ages to ours. We had met the people when we checked on the house before we moved in. The whole line of six houses is very close-knit. We picnic, share a garden, and let the kids play together. Our neighbors are either here or we're there. We share a pool and party together almost nightly. Given that we all have seasonal jobs, we even help each other out when we're having a slow period.

Elderly residents, adrift in the sea of young couples with children, came to play a role as honorary grandparents.

However, not every new section of Legler was so cohesive. In one area, settled largely by people from outside the region, problems with the builder led to continuing tensions among the families. Other residents who had moved from nearby areas retained their friends outside of Legler and thus felt less pressure to relate to their new neighbors. The overall social dynamics of the community reveal that the closest friendships were based on residential proximity—until the water crisis, when people from across Legler began to relate as a community.

In fact, Legler's status as a community was very nebulous before a pollution boundary was drawn. Arrivals during the period of development had only the vaguest conception of Legler. Many knew little about the area before moving there. Jackson was seen as a sprawling town lacking either a center or orienting landmarks. Earlier residents viewed Legler as the "boonies," the rural, undeveloped part of town. But given realtor's reports, later residents, with their suburban orientations, expected Legler to grow into a more urban center with shopping facilities. As a further indication of the limited sense of community, only one respondent reported having joined a community organization (the fire company) that gave him a basis of association with fellow township residents.

Disrupting the Dream

Respondents recalled no major drawbacks to Legler at the time they moved there, noting only concerns with commuting distance, distance from shopping, and problems with builders. Otherwise, Legler was the American Dream achieved. But then things began to change. The origins of these changes predated the arrival of most of the residents.

The Glidden Mine Site. In 1961, the Glidden Corporation began mining on a 135-acre site in Legler for a mineral, the titanium ore ilmenite, used in manufacturing paint. The strip mine redeposited mine wastes and tailings in pits created from excavating the ore. Although many local families were unaware of the operation, nearby families were heavily affected. A key local road was severed. One family's home, surrounded on three sides by the sandy soil left over from the operation, came to be called "the island." The mine site itself acquired the name "2001" because of its moonscape-like terrain. Area teenagers later frequented the site at night, swimming in the water-filled craters. Despite the aesthetic loss to their neighborhood from the mine, residents appreciated the jobs it brought. Moreover, they had been promised that the site would eventually be reclaimed as a park and the truncated road rebuilt. Picturing a rosy future, they tolerated the operation.

A Landfill for a Neighbor. However, in 1971, when Glidden faced the prospect of closing the site and undertaking an expensive reclamation job, Jackson was seeking a new site for its municipal landfill. In a true marriage of convenience, Glidden deeded the site (for one dollar) to the township. When Legler residents found out, they were alarmed. They had long awaited reclamation of the site. Moreover, they did not want garbage from the entire town dumped in their area, especially when they felt that beneficial services were already concentrated on the other side of Jackson. Finally, residents viewed the landfill as a threat to the peaceful ambience of their neighborhood.

> We didn't want it because Lakehurst was a country road; it was quiet. We didn't want to go from an isolated area to Grand Central Station.

But the greatest concern was about pollution. The sandy site was full of sixty-foot-deep holes filled with water. Nearby wells tended to be shallow—often less than fifty feet. Moreover, the dump across town was being closed because it had caused water pollution, it smelled, and it was a breeding ground for rats. Legler residents foresaw inheriting similar problems.

A group of Legler homeowners quickly organized to oppose the landfill. A petition with 365 signatures against the Legler site was presented to the township. Many residents attended meetings to voice their protest. In the view of my respondents, however, the decision had already been made in secret. It was too late.

The township went to great lengths to reassure residents that the new landfill would be run properly.

People believed the promises, for example, that there would be gate passes and dump tickets and other safeguards, that someone would carefully watch the dumping and that there would be security.

Residents were also told that after ten years the landfill would become a golf course, enhancing their properties. Despite the failure of Glidden to keep a similar promise, some residents accepted this commitment as well.

Their unsuccessful protest left many residents feeling bitter toward the township. They felt that the landfill siting decision had been manipulated. Furthermore, township promises quickly proved to be short-lived. Yet, seeing no other course of action, residents ceased organizing against the landfill and accepted it as a reality. As one resident explained, "We didn't like it, but we had no choice. You can't fight city hall."

This incident laid the foundation for later developments in Legler. People who had never before mobilized for a cause learned to be community activists. They also learned to distrust local officials. Although no general community organization emerged for some time, Legler activists successfully unseated the dominant local party in the 1972 township election.

The municipal landfill operated in Legler from late 1971 until late 1980 on twenty acres of a 135-acre parcel. The landfill officially accepted liquid and solid sewage and septage, as well as solid wastes. As many as 50,000 gallons per day of human waste were deposited in the landfill during its years in operation. Illegal disposal of construction wastes, as well as chemical and industrial wastes, also occurred. Waste was disposed of in unlined trenches created by the former mining pits.[8]

Despite the concerns of earlier residents, new arrivals during landfill operations were often unaware of its existence, even when the homes they purchased bordered the facility. When apprised of the facility, others were surprisingly unconcerned. This naïveté and lack of information reflected the fact that people did not explore their future neighborhood for possible hazards; instead they assumed it was safe. And when they learned about the landfill, most saw it as benign, some even viewing it as a convenience. Residents pictured the landfill as a sand pit or a local dump for residential garbage. They appreciated neither the scale of the landfill operation nor the range of wastes accepted. Many of the residents had moved from areas where it was common to build on landfilled ground, visualizing the common practice of filling in wetlands for development. Finally, residents were misled by real estate agents, lawyers, and township officials, as related here:

> We never walked to the back of our property because of the weeds. I did ask the real estate agent what was behind the property. He said that there was a closed landfill that had just been for local garbage and that the property was going to become a park. We didn't give it a second thought. We didn't even know what a landfill was. We figured it was a pit that you take sand out of. After the first week in the house, I took a look at the back of the property. They were dumping right at the end of our lot—tons of garbage.

Some new residents were mollified by town officials who told them that there was a greater chance of well pollution from their septic tanks than from the landfill. Others, living as close as one-quarter mile and as far away as three miles, believed that the landfill was too far away from their homes to affect them. Thus, even though they had been deceived, most newer residents rationalized the presence of the landfill. Unlike the begrudging acceptance of early residents, latecomers were unconcerned. For most residents—new or old—the Legler facility settled into the background of the neighborhood.

The Direct Impacts from the Landfill

Although a fixture of the Legler section, there were constant reminders of the landfill operation for residents exposed to such environmental stressors as odor, noise, traffic, visual impacts, litter and dust, and vectors. For strongly impacted families, the facility contributed substantial life stress long before it was labeled as a polluter, suggesting that nuisances and environmental conditions which detract from our peace of mind, enjoyment of home, property, and community surround are, in themselves, significant forms of contamination.[9] Figure 2.1 shows the approximate distribution of direct impacts within the Legler area, illustrating the situation faced by all proximate local residents during the period when the issue of water contamination was still in incubation (note there were no residences adjacent to the landfill to the east, where the abandoned quarry is located). Let's examine some of these key direct impacts.

Odor.   Odor was one of the worst impacts for those living near the landfill, as the following comments suggest:

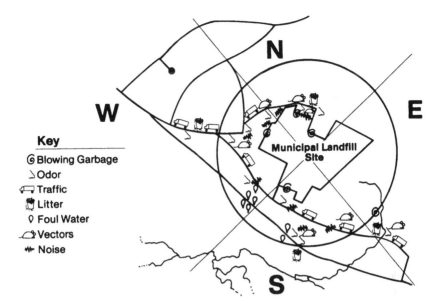

Figure 2.1   Map Showing Direct Impacts of the Jackson Municipal Landfill on Residents of Legler

> *Depending on which way the wind blew, we would get the odor. We had built a patio prior to the landfill's opening so that we could use our backyard. By the following summer, we couldn't stay there. We put in air conditioning in the house because we couldn't open the windows in the summer.*

> *We couldn't hang out our clothes on the line; the smell would get to them.*

> *The smell came right through the house. Sometimes you'd wake up in the middle of the night and think you were in a sewer. If you'd start a barbecue, the smell would come and spoil it. Our children couldn't have company or sleep out at night.*

As these statements suggest, foul odor is uniquely intrusive, spoiling the enjoyment of home and use of property. Although odors may or may not indicate exposure to hazard, there is the sense that being able to smell the facility means breathing contaminated air. Thus odors make visible the otherwise unseen movement of pollutants. We see this effect at other locations too.

Studies at three California hazardous waste sites found close relationships between detecting odors and both environmental worry and such physical symptoms as nausea, eye and throat irritation, and especially headaches. The researchers concluded "odors serve as a sensory cue for the manifestation of stress-related illnesses among individuals concerned about the quality of their neighborhood environment."[10]

Residents of Florence, New Jersey, moved there for the beautiful views of the Delaware River, never anticipating that the Tullytown landfill would be built directly across from them on the Pennsylvania side. Odor was the most cited problem of the many impacts reported to the Pennsylvania DER. One resident tersely complained that "wind is blowing from the dump across the river to my house. Also last night it rained. Odor permeated the entire house (windows are open on such a beautiful day)." Under the section on the complaint form where physical effects and conditions were to be listed, the resident added, "Nasty temperament! God knows what else!" Such complaints rarely led to enforcement actions, however, because by the time DER employees would reach the scene, the odor had usually dissipated.[11]

At the administrative hearings for an expansion permit at Al Turi landfill in Goshen, New York, a nearby resident testified that odor problems had continued for years. Yet what drove her to finally put her home on the market was one particular experience. While jogging one morning, she was overpowered by sickening odors. Now she was determined to move her family at any financial cost.

Noise.   Facility noise comes from both traffic and equipment. Heavy equipment, used at landfills to cover garbage with soil, operates at high-decibel levels that destroy peace and quiet and can even harm hearing. But even if a nearby resident got used to the rhythm of this noise, they could not accommodate to irruptive or unpatterned noises such as the "beep-beep-beep" emitted when equipment is shifted into reverse. Unpredictable and demanding of attention, these noises are particularly stressful. Waste trucks add the constant roar of engines, and sounds of shifting and braking, beeping of horns, and banging of metal bodies on rough roads. A thorough literature documents the adverse impacts of noise as a general stressor, as disruptive of thought, and as emotionally debilitating.[12] The meaning of noise is related to the ecohistorical context. In Legler, landfill noises punctuated the rural quiet. In contrast, my discussion of stress with a neighbor of Midway landfill, south of Seattle, was drowned out every sixty seconds or so as a jet airplane roared at rooftop level over her house to land at SeaTac Airport. She was so fully adapted to the airport noise that she seemed not to notice. It was the landfill that was on her mind.

Traffic.   Typical concerns with traffic in residential areas include safety, intrusion on local roads by cut-through traffic, noise, congestion, litter, and air pollution.[13] It is common for the character of surrounding areas to be affected by trucks traveling to and from waste sites. These traffic impacts extend all along the routes used to reach the facility. Landfills also bring congestion, particularly in the early morning, when waste trucks are likely to be lined up before the gate, and at times when the public has access. Traffic safety concerns are often focused upon children, as this Legler resident indicated:

> We worried about the kids on the road. We had to curtail their activity. We wouldn't allow them to ride their bikes until after the landfill closed for the night.

Additionally, neighbors of landfills report that idling trucks fill the air with fumes.

Litter and Dust.   Blowing refuse and dust are frequent problems at landfills. Litter results when truck beds are inadequately covered or when deliberate dumping occurs along roadways. In Legler, properties near the landfill were covered by trash, as this person recalled:

> First people would dump in front of my house and then litter would blow onto the back of my property. I was surrounded by garbage. The garbage in the back was even floating in my stream. The township agreed to clean it up but they didn't. Later the health department ordered me to do it. I took three truckloads out.

Such impacts are common. An ominous indicator of exposure from the Tullytown landfill was the constant problem of dust particles that coated houses within days of cleaning. Not only was the dust an unsightly nuisance, but it caused trouble with breathing. Residents feared what effects ingesting the particles might have on themselves and their children.[14]

Other Impacts.   Additional direct impacts include those from loss of aesthetics and from fire, explosion, and corrosion. In Legler, as elsewhere, vectors were associated with landfilling.

> We had mosquitoes—we never had them before the landfill nor since it closed. Also we had rats in the yard. The township poisoned them. We feared smallpox from the sludge lagoon transmitted to the children by animals.

Waste sites may cause serious visual impacts, particularly when landfills rise hundreds of feet above the surrounding area. Not only were the visual impacts of the Tullytown landfill unsightly and depressing, but lights from trucks would shine into people's houses after dark. At the Tacoma landfill, the site was surrounded by apartment buildings. From the windows of these apartments, residents looked down directly into the center of the landfill. Aside from the odors, noise, and other issues, the facility so dramatically changed the aesthetics of living in the area that occupancies dropped. Perhaps most memorable were the tens of thousands of seagulls and crows that attended religiously at the open face of the landfill. Bird droppings are frequently an additional direct impact to the area.

Finally, additional disturbance may occur from the meaning associated with the constant intrusions from the facility. In addition to odors, noise, and litter, residents are reminded of the unwanted changes forced on a community that otherwise they had seen as ideal. Thus, even before there was evidence of contamination, the Jackson municipal landfill had dramatically changed the character of the Legler area in stressful, stigmatizing, and dissonant ways. The result was a loss of serenity, pleasure, and enjoyment of one's home.

Portents of Disaster

Despite the stress, Legler residents generally learned to live with the inconveniences. There was little that could be done to stop direct impacts once the facility was permitted to operate. Active opposition to the landfill would demand some major event, such as a particularly frightening incident or notification of contamination. Ironically, the period of incubation is often accompanied by numerous clues that disaster is brewing, yet the concern generated by such clues is below the threshold for action. Residents occupy the unenviable position of the frog adjusted to gradually boiling water.

In Legler, before the pollution was known, seemingly random water quality problems appeared. As with health problems affecting some area families, these were treated as private problems, with neighbors unaware of each other's concerns.

> One month after we moved in, we thought that the water was funny. We spent $1,300 on a water purifier. Soon it was bad again. We talked to another person with this problem. They didn't feel good either. We had itchy, dry skin.

> Every time we'd drink coffee, we'd immediately have to go. The water had the worst smell. You had to open the windows. You couldn't run the water in the kitchen.

In some cases, one member of a family perceived a change in water quality unnoticed by others. Such instances lacked social confirmation of the individual's suspicions. As a result, there was usually no sustained response, even if concern continued.

There were also indications that landfill security was inadequate. Legler residents reported,

We took pictures of them trying to cover 300,000 tons a day of garbage with sand. It didn't work.

I saw them dump forty-three barrels of chemicals. I tried to move one of the fifty-five-gallon drums, and I couldn't. Then I noticed that something had eaten a hole right through my pants.

I saw green- and purple-colored sludge in pits thirty feet deep. I didn't recognize this as a problem at this time.

I've dropped garbage off and seen pools of water with garbage down to the water table. I didn't realize that our well was so shallow. It's easy to connect the two—I saw it with my own eyes.

I had a friend who was offered money to keep quiet about a truck that was not licensed to dump there.

That residents could view these clues and yet not recognize the pattern suggests a frightening aspect of lifestyle and lifescape accommodation—the rejection of anomalies that undermine basic assumptions about life. Although Legler residents found the health, water, and security problems disturbing, they failed to comprehend the significance of these events as signposts of contamination.

The Legler disaster came to light in November 1978, only a few months after Love Canal hit the press. And yet nearly half of the Legler residents interviewed either claimed never to have heard of toxic pollution previously or ignored it. Others recall hearing of incidents and thinking that it could never happen to them. The awareness of the landfill, whether among old-timers who had accepted it or among newcomers who barely knew of its existence, was not at first associated with the dangers of toxic pollution. As two Legler residents reported:

We had heard of Love Canal, but it wasn't really relevant to here. We were two miles from the landfill; nothing could happen to us.

We heard of Love Canal on the news. I felt sorry for those people, but I didn't lose any sleep over it. We didn't think it could happen to us.

Caught up in their families, work, home, and the other concerns of the American lifestyle, Legler residents did not expect what was coming despite clues that would serve as the basis for explanations after the fact. What was about to happen to them was, at that time, virtually inconceivable. Thus, after the initial period of incubation during which they accommodated in various ways to sources of stress associated with landfill operations, Legler residents entered the next phase of toxic exposure—the period of discovery and announcement.

Discovery and Announcement

Unknown to most residents, the New Jersey Department of Environmental Protection had responded in the summer of 1978 to a request from the Jackson Township board of health to test Legler's groundwater, part of the vast Cohansey aquifer. Although no pollution was found, residents' complaints about water quality continued. In the fall, the DEP did further testing for contamination by organic chemicals. In October, the first indication of significant pollution was found. As testing continued over the next eight months, some thirty-four chemical pollutants were found in private wells.[15]

In response to the October discovery of organic chemicals, on November 8, 1978, the Jackson board of health issued a notification to residents south of the landfill that their water was polluted. Referring to the board meeting held to review the test results, the notice read in part: "It was recommended that because there was enough evidence for concern, area residents are advised *not* to use water for human consumption, but limit use for sanitary purposes only." Later versions of the message additionally recommended that residents ought "not to soak for extended periods of time" when bathing. With this notification, Legler families began experiencing a period of disruption that was to have continuing ramifications.

Notification was originally given for only a portion of Legler. Others outside the original boundary were reassured that their water was drinkable. But over several weeks, official identification of the area affected by pollution was changed, so that by early 1979 all of Legler's approximately 150 families had received the warning. It was coincidental that the identified boundaries of contamination so closely mirrored Legler's own boundaries. And it was ironic that, not having previously heard the label "Legler," most residents only became aware of their neighborhood's identity with the advent of the disaster.

Reactions to Notification

In Legler, as is often the case, government played the role of announcing the contamination problem. A representative of Jackson Township was sent in person to notify residents. Sometimes the messenger's demeanor intensified the warning in the letter. Thus, one respondent recalled, "I knew from the look on his face that it must be serious." Other people, however, returned home merely to find a form letter left for them.

Initial Coping. How did people react to notification? In moving their young families to the suburbs, most Legler residents had just invested their hopes and their savings in new homes. A number had just been issued a certificate of occupancy (CO) certifying that their new home could be legally occupied. With the announcement of contamination, nearly all were caught by surprise.

> *Four days after our certificate of occupancy was issued, we were eating dinner with our neighbors. A man came to the door and announced that we might get cancer if we drank the water. Our neighbor refused to finish her spaghetti because it had been cooked in our water. She was quite sick. We couldn't believe it—four days after our CO! What were we supposed to do now?*

Initially, people were confused by the notification. Women called their husbands at work to relay the news. People frequently called neighbors to see if they too had been notified and to find out what they were doing. Many residents also called the township for clarification. This latter step did not necessarily prove helpful, as illustrated by one resident who was told, "It's too technical for you to understand."

Reactions to the notification varied. There were some indications of initial panic. One resident spoke of "going berserk." Others viewed notification as an attack and called the police. Some residents remained calm in the face of notification, believing, at least initially, that this was a "problem" that could simply be fixed.

> *My husband was calm. "It's no big problem, they'll fix it. It's like fixing a water main that breaks." Then we went to a township committee meeting and we learned fast. We had expected this to be fixed in a couple of weeks.*

Alternatively, other residents minimized the risk associated with the chemical exposure.

> *Nothing bothers me. I hate to sound blase, but I see in the paper something that causes cancer almost every single day.*

One resident, her family already reeling from a series of disasters, commented:

> *This was just another blow in a long line of blows—we were dumbfounded.*

Trying to Define the Uncertainty.   As they began to assess their predicament, residents turned to their elected officials for guidance, only to be frustrated with the township's inability to clarify their situation.

> *When I asked at a meeting how long before we would get clean water, the health department official didn't know. There was no light at the end of the tunnel.*

Residents began to realize that their elected officials didn't know how to remedy the situation. The officials responded to the uncertainty with extreme caution, causing concerned citizens to feel abandoned in a state of extreme uncertainty.

> *This was like someone shooting you and then not having the decency to finish you off.*

To Drink or Not to Drink.   As they sought to understand their new situation, Legler residents had to decide whether or not to use their well water. Most of them ceased using it immediately upon notification. Some made transitional steps toward stopping use. The transition was hard, with people falling back on longstanding habits.

> *I would go to the faucet and fill up a pot and then remember and have to spill it out.*

Most residents continued to shower in the water, and some used it to bathe. Generally, parents were more careful with their children than themselves. Most discontinued use of the water in cooking, although some apparently believed that the water was safe if boiled. Some residents continued using the water for an interim period until they became convinced that it was polluted. A few others continued to use the well water until forced to join the local water district several years later.

Rising Frustrations.   As they were left in uncertainty, residents increasingly directed their anger at the township. From the beginning, residents were enraged to have been put in this situation. Earlier residents were angry that the township had forced the landfill on them and then not operated it carefully. Recent newcomers had a different historical perspective. They wondered how the township had approved certificates of occupancy (COs) for their houses, making the new owner rather than the developer responsible for addressing the water problem. Now these residents feared the loss of their COs due to the contamination.

> *My mother had read about the pollution in Legler. The builder said there was no problem. Two weeks after we moved in, I called the board of health to make sure our water was okay. They said there was no problem. Later that same day, the notice was delivered that we couldn't drink the water. I was angry at the builder and the township over the CO. The builder had lied that he lost the water tests to give him time to finagle with the town to let us move in.*

The degree of anger resulting from this situation was indicated by another respondent.

> *I went to three meetings to ask the mayor how I got my certificate of occupancy after they knew about the pollution. Each time I got so mad that I couldn't speak; I just walked right out.*

Whether people actively believed that the water was polluted or not, they were quick to appreciate the implications of losing COs, being unable to sell their homes and having to finance a new water source. Young families had invested every penny in their homes; older residents had limited financial resources.

> *At first we thought we'd abandon the house, but everything we owned was sunk into it. We were in debt. We were trapped. There was no place to go. No one wants to buy Love Canal.*

> *We were all set to sell our house. We were supposed to sign the next day. We lost our CO; we lost our sale. Our concern wasn't health—we didn't know about this yet. Our investment was destroyed.*

A major by-product from the lack of an easy escape was that residents were forced to face the problem head-on.

Developing a Social Consensus. Beyond the lifestyle impacts of forgoing tap water, however, there were actions necessary to clarify an uncertain situation and bring about its resolution. When local government failed to provide a timely and adequate remedy, people were forced to adopt increasingly sophisticated means of involvement. As Legler residents met at township meetings, they began to communicate with one another. From their shared frustration, revealed during the confrontations with the township council, came the potential for local cooperation. Under the leadership of community residents who had initially fought the landfill, an organization called the Concerned Citizens Committee of Legler was created.

The meetings of this organization played the vital role of creating a tangible bond, a way for this community in distress to come together to confront the issues.

Nearly all residents interviewed saw the pollution notification as pulling people together. Initially, the old-timers had organized while newcomers, who lacked local acquaintances, were left to fend for themselves. But as the organization began to develop strategies requiring broad participation, it recruited the new residents. People met others whom they might never have known otherwise. As one observed,

> This pulled a lot of people together at meetings. We met a lot of people. We had concern for each other. Sympathy. We felt bad for people who lived here a long time when we saw what they'd gone through.

As people became more involved, they encountered a growing social consensus regarding the severity of their situation. Thus, even if they initially doubted the notification, their new milieu made it hard to continue denial. New information about the landfill and well pollution reinforced their concerns.

Substantiating the Threat.   A number of developments contributed to the growing consensus in Legler about the nature of the problem. The informational meetings held by the Concerned Citizens Committee provided the first firm information. At an early meeting, a geologist from the Department of Environmental Protection (DEP) spoke frankly about the dangers associated with the chemicals that had been found. This straightforward information challenged residents' remaining skepticism. As one resident recalled,

> I didn't view this as a serious problem until the DEP meeting with Concerned Citizens. Then I knew we were in big trouble. When I heard about the chemicals in the water, I felt sick.

In addition, results from a state groundwater study ended residents' misconceptions about the water's purity.

> When we found things like benzene in the water, I was shocked, worried, and frustrated. I thought the test would show that we were clear.

Residents having technical expertise were particularly quick to grasp the severity of the situation.

Also contributing to the emerging consensus was media coverage that took the situation very seriously, reinforcing the fears of some residents and adding additional information about the implications of toxic exposure. As one couple recalled,

> We heard about the cancer-causing chemicals on the news. We worried about the kids. They were scared too. They asked us questions about cancer.

After notification, people noticed new symptoms, such as rashes and skin irritations associated with showering. As people compared symptoms, the view was reinforced that their problems derived from a common source, the water. People then began to rethink previous health problems and to link them to the consumption of the water. In this way, continuing health problems took on a new meaning in light of the contamination.

> We mothers began to compare notes and decided that the ear infections and other problems with our children were no coincidence. I saw our family as being in jeopardy.

> You hear so much about the water. I heard that benzene can be absorbed through the skin, yet the town told us we could still shower. I heard about cancer clusters and the kidney problems. I was scared.

On the day after notification, Jackson Township began to supply water to Legler residents. Later, planning began for a central water system to replace residential wells. Such actions convinced reluctant believers that the crisis was real.

Disruption of Lifestyle: Water Delivery

Shortly after the first notification, water tankers were placed at both ends of a local main road. After Liquid-Plumr® was dumped in the outdoor tanks, the township began delivery of large metal civil defense containers to each of the affected households. After protests, the clumsy and unsanitary metal containers were replaced by large plastic containers, each outfitted with a spigot. Residents signaled the need for more water by placing a flag in front of the house. For some two years, until their homes were connected to a central water main, most families received all their drinking water through deliveries. At the time of the interviews, in the summer of 1981, several families were still drinking delivered water.

As many Legler residents pointed out, Americans take for granted having a ready supply of usable water at their fingertips.

Water is a life source. We lived in the city. You just had to turn the tap on. We didn't think of these things. We never thought about it.

The way in which we organize our homes, our schedules, and our activities depends on a ready supply of water. When this supply is disrupted, the ramifications are felt as a disruption of lifestyle itself. Daily activities now had to be reorganized around this new reality.

Impacts of Water Delivery

Various impacts were associated with residents' inability to use their tap water. Although most respondents spoke of the period of water delivery as one of inconvenience rather than difficulty, it is evident that this was a stressful time. It was easy for people to quarrel. Daily life became a chore. A general sense of well-being was hard to maintain.

Water Containers.   The logistics of getting water into the home disrupted lifestyle during this time. The containers were heavy and difficult to bring inside, contributing to secondary health impacts and family friction.

My wife would carry the seventeen-gallon jugs. She did nerve damage and got disc problems in her back. Now she has to take it easy.

I was not able to carry the water because of my health problems. This hurt my ego. And my wife was mad because she had to do it. We'd argue about this.

Water-Quality Issues.   The quality of the delivered water was a further concern. Some residents refused to drink the delivered water because it tasted worse to them than the polluted well water. Additionally, delivered water might be muddy or overchlorinated. It might contain cigarette butts, aluminum, sand, or, after the township repainted the containers, paint chips. One woman pulled a big jar of water out of her cupboard to show me. At the time of delivery, the water had been slimy. More than a year later, the solids had separated out to reveal a quarter inch of black particles at the bottom. And an argument with the delivery workers might bring water tainted with urine.

Water Availability.   Families had to manage water use carefully to ensure an adequate supply. Water deliveries were sometimes unreliable, as when trucks broke down. Also, to arrange delivery, people had to remember to put their flags outside the night before.

Having trucked water adds responsibility. It's something you have to keep in mind all the time. If we run low, there's no way to get any on the weekends. We have to ration on Saturday and Sunday.

People always had to judge how much water they had and how much they needed. Too much water might stagnate. Too little water had obvious shortcomings. And if no delivery was made, residents had to call town officials who might blame them for failing to put out the flag, even if that had been done. Winter brought another problem. The cans of water froze if left outside, creating huge ice cubes capable of splitting the container and, upon thawing indoors, flooding the floor.

The Pioneer Life.   Even when people mastered the logistics of using delivered water, they still had to contend with the difficulties of not having tap water in the home for housework and for personal and recreational use. A number of residents characterized their ordeal as "the pioneer life." Although some people had access to alternate washing facilities (e.g., at the home of friends or at work), most residents learned to live with minimal bathing. Most utilized the tap water for showers. One family whose shower water tended to burn their eyes learned never to face the shower stream. Later, after their home was hooked into the central water system, they still maintained their aversion to facing the water. Some adults who had severe skin reactions from the water bathed with the delivered water. Although several of them heated the water in pots on the stove, one woman reported washing in a barrel of cold water each morning. Despite these problems, few residents accepted invitations to shower at a local school: winter was seen as an unhealthy time to shower prior to being outside and open shower rooms were not viewed as private enough.

People had to remember to carry a cup of water from the storage can to brush their teeth. This was one task about which people reported "cheating" and using the tap water.

Homes often were not kept as clean as they previously were. People varied between using the tap water, the delivered water, or no water in cleaning. Housework took much longer.

I'd be home alone. I'd try to bathe the baby, cook, and clean with the delivered water. I'd live out of a jug. It was a real strain. I have a bad back; it was impossible for me to carry the water to the tub. It would take longer to do anything using the water. It was inconvenient.

Many young parents bathed their children in the delivered water. This entailed carrying water from the garage, heating it on the stove, and then carrying it to the tub. Most people continued washing clothing and dishes in the well water. A few even used it in cooking. With delivered water, cooking became a major chore. Vegetables had to be soaked to clean them.

If you were making spaghetti, you couldn't rinse it. You'd have to pour water over it. It was aggravating, especially because this wasn't your fault. Who needs this?

Families with animals had to hand-carry their water as well.

Recreational use of the property was also affected. It was more difficult to use backyard pools. Some residents delayed plans to build pools until after the central water system was installed. Although some gardeners had been told that aerating the tap water made it safe to use for watering vegetables, others chose to rely only on rainfall or gave up the hobby altogether.

It also became harder to have guests during this time.

What happens if you have thirty people coming for dinner and you have no water?

We put big signs on the faucets—"Don't drink the water." It was embarrassing.

People would bring water with them when they came to visit instead of bringing cake.

As these examples illustrate, the period without tap water was one of constant personal frustration. Even the small steps of daily life reminded residents about the fundamental crisis in which they had been trapped.

A Dominating Concern.   Beyond these complications and disruptions of routine, for many victims, the exposure incident became a central life focus, dominating free time activity, conversations with neighbors, friends, and relatives, and family life itself. Daily decisions had to be made under conditions of great uncertainty. Some were large in scope, such as whether to stay in the home or move. Others were small yet significant, for example, what degree of exposure to the tap water was allowable (e.g., should the children play underneath a sprinkler?). Meanwhile, residents' understanding of the situation was limited by the paucity of information, the complexity of issues about which they had little prior experience, and distortion by the media or by agencies anxious to minimize the problem.

Secondary effects compounded these impacts. For example, as a resident began to devote greater attention to the pollution incident, the person's family life, friendships, work, and recreation were adversely affected. Friends and relatives grew tired of the victim's obsession with the incident. Spouses became resentful of an activist mate's absences.

The Hookup of City Water

Connections to a new central water line provided by the township began in July 1980. This water district used the deep well beneath the Glidden mine site as its source. Given the lifestyle disruptions that characterized the period of water delivery, it is not surprising that having homes hooked up to the central water system was a major event. For most Legler families, water had been transformed from a resource assumed and taken for granted into a prized and valued possession.

> *The water was like gold. We let it run; we drank it. We all cheered; we were elated.*

> *We had a party in the neighborhood when the water came in. We ran five hoses [one from each neighbor's house] to fill our pool. We filled it in four hours. The whole neighborhood jumped into the water that night. We didn't drink beer for once, we drank water.*

However, some residents had difficulty forgetting the bitter legacy associated with their water supply.

> *I broke the well pipe when we put in the city water. I just felt like locking the front door and leaving, like in* The Amityville Horror.

By the summer of 1981, twenty-one of twenty-five families interviewed had hooked into the new system. The others were unable or unwilling to pay for the connection but were later forced by the township to join.

Lingering Concerns

It might seem reasonable to assume that having a new water source would end the disaster. But only one respondent indicated that having central water ended their concern with toxic exposure. It is an important lesson of toxic disaster that its scars are not easily mitigated; replacing what was lost in Legler involved more than obtaining a different source of water. Some losses seem beyond mitigation.

Legler residents had several lingering concerns. Sensitized to the pollution of the aquifer beneath them, they feared the contamination of the well at the Glidden mine site by chemicals migrating from the adjacent landfill, as this quote suggests.

> *I just hope and pray that this water is safe. You never know. A worker came and told me recently that he was taking a test for chemicals. I got upset and asked why. When I called the township, they said it was just a bacteria test. But why should they take this from the tap?*

The same resident also remembered one of the township's arguments against the digging of new private wells.

> *When the town talked to us about deep wells, they explained that you need double casing to prevent chemicals from getting into the water. Well, does Glidden have double casing?*

Furthermore, the polluting landfill had created a history of distrust toward the township, now operating the new water system.

> *We suspect the new well. We don't trust the town. They're the same people who pulled this stunt to begin with.*

An additional concern was the quality of the water, perceived to be excessively chlorinated. One resident noted that his family was still buying bottled water. Another said of the new tap water,

> *It tastes yucky and disgusting. It's like drinking Clorox out of the bottle. We boil it and refrigerate it.*

Others indicated that their concern for chlorine was more than a matter of taste. They were concerned that chlorine is itself toxic. Further adding to water quality concerns was the use of asbestos pipes, viewed as a potential health threat, in connecting the water system.

> *How will we know when the pipe eats away?*

> *We get killed either way—if not from the water, then from the pipe.*

Residents' fears were later substantiated when tests revealed detectable amounts of asbestos in their new water source. All of these fears merely illustrate the extent to which Legler residents had become critical, suspicious, and distrustful of their homes, their environment, and their government.

Moreover, the water system was now seen as being out of residents' control. The supply was viewed as unreliable. One resident recalled being stuck lathered in the shower during a service disruption. The township's approach during the hookup phase fueled this frustration because "they didn't listen to people." Residents reported that the township was heavy-handed in forcing recalcitrant residents to hook into the system, threatening to condemn their houses if they did not. The practice particularly angered old-timers on fixed incomes who minimized the threat of drinking the well water and therefore saw no great advantage to hooking into the new water system. As one noted,

> *The town says that I have to connect to the water! Why? What law did I break? We own a well. They have not proven to us that the water is contaminated. There is no solid evidence of a problem.*

Additionally, the hookup represented a major financial burden for some residents. Once the township provided the central water main, it was up to each household to pay a hookup fee and to connect into it. If the house was far from the main, the costs of trenching and burying the pipe were high. A few families could not initially afford the connection. One family sold its horse to pay for it. Others borrowed money. A number of residents dug their own trenches for the hookup. In some sections, there was a cooperative effort among neighbors. These residents told of various roadblocks to their work, including trenches that collapsed and inspectors who demanded deeper ditches.

Once hooked up, residents then had to pay for the water they used. This additional financial burden irritated residents, who perceived themselves as double-taxed because they had already paid for wells and now had to pay for the water system. Compounding the anger was their view that rates in the Legler water district were high compared with those in other parts of the township. The costs proved a barrier for some.

> *We paid the hookup fee, but we haven't plumbed in the water. We're on social security—fixed income. We can't afford to pay thirty dollars a month for water. This would be an awful burden on our income.*

Beyond contamination of the new water source, residents also feared exposure through soil, leaky basements, and surface water, and even toxic residues in their plumbing.

>   *I figure it's in the ground. I wonder if they dumped it near our wild blue-berries.*

>   *I still have a well; I'm still in the affected area; the chemicals are in the air and ground—they could still ooze out! I think about it in the summer when I'm gardening. Will the ground contaminate the plants?*

In addition to problems that persisted in the environment, residents had concerns about damage already done to themselves and their children. Thus whether the new water was good or not failed to obviate the concerns raised by the fact that the old water was bad. As one resident remarked, "Cancer does not show up right away." Another referred to this persistent health theme:

>   *We still worry about our children. It will always be on our minds for a while yet, until they grow up.*

As these ongoing concerns demonstrate, a new water supply represented only one step toward reestablishing some sense of normalcy in Legler. Although lifestyle disruptions generally ceased as a result of the hookup, return to normal lifestyle did not end the disaster. Many residents experienced profound changes, which are deeper and more permanent than those accompanying disrupted lifestyles. These persistent changes involve the way that residents view their world. It is to these lifescape impacts of toxic exposure that I turn momentarily.

Afterword About the Landfill's Afterlife

In 1993, the New Jersey Department of Health filed a public health assessment on the Jackson Township landfill under the terms of its agreement with ATSDR (Agency for Toxic Substances and Disease Registry). Along with the EPA Superfund report, this document is useful for summarizing subsequent developments and research in Legler regarding the municipal landfill site.[16]

A protracted process of evaluation occurred in Jackson, stretching sixteen years from the point of discovery in 1979. The New Jersey DOH had concluded, on the basis of its 1980 health surveys of a substantial number of residents, that reported skin and eye irritation was in fact related to exposure to residential well water. By December 1982, the Jackson Township landfill had been added to the National

Priorities List for remediation under Superfund. However, it was not until August 1988 that Jackson Township entered into an order on consent with New Jersey requiring the township to produce a Remedial Investigation and Feasibility Study. This RI/FS, completed in late 1990, found contamination of the landfill soils, continuing pollution of the groundwater, some indications of ambient and indoor air contamination, and contamination of stream sediments.

A subsequent Public Health Assessment looked for environmental pathways that might transport contaminants, exposing the local population. Although unable to evaluate exposures due to errors in data collection, the report confirmed "indeterminate" and past risks. Residents had ingested, inhaled, and experienced skin contact with volatile organic compounds (VOCs) through their tap water and may also have breathed VOCs in outdoor and indoor air. Given a new water source and fencing of the landfill site, continuing risk was not anticipated. EPA concluded in the Record of Decision that no further action was needed at the landfill as long as there was continuing maintenance and monitoring. The site was deleted from the National Priorities List in September 1995. It remains under a long-term monitoring program. Along with the issues of incubation, discovery, and mobilization to address the threat, the Legler case also illustrates how sites move into a regulatory and regulated existence under Superfund until, deemed sufficiently remediated, they are let out to pasture as monitored sites, perhaps, if lucky, to someday become the site for Brownfield Redevelopment.

3

Lifescape Change:
Cognitive Adjustment to Toxic Exposure

If daily life is behaviorally structured around lifestyle, it is cognitively organized by "lifescape." The framework of understanding that governs our perception of "normal" life, the lifescape is central to our psychological well-being. Like all social paradigms, the lifescape remains invisible until challenged. Lifescape and lifestyle interact. Lifescape represents the underlying premises around which daily life is organized. Any forced change to our routine activities, in turn, upsets these core assumptions. Thus exposure to toxic materials not only changes what people do but also profoundly affects how they think about themselves, their families, and their world. As we previously saw (Figure 1.2), there are five fundamental pillars of the lifescape: health, control, home, environment, and trust. All are transformed as a result of toxic exposure (see Figure 3.1).

Defending Our Prior Assumptions

There is a natural inclination to preserve the assumptions of normalcy and to insulate oneself from the disruption of a toxic incident. The old reality can be only tenuously preserved through such rationalizations as used by this Legler resident:

> *Today you can't pick up the paper without finding something else that's killing you; we might as well dry up and die. If the water is bad, the hell with it; everything else is bad!*

The uncertainty of the situation gives great latitude for interpretation. One doubter at Love Canal viewed declarations of emergency by Governor Carey and

Core Lifescape Assumptions	
Previous to Contamination	*After Contamination*
Health Optimism	Health Pessimism
Personal Control	Loss of Control, Disabled
Home is Secure and Valued	Inversion of Home and Place
Environment is Benign	Environment is Malevolent
Social Trust	Social Distrust and Stigma

Figure 3.1   Fundamental Lifescape Shifts

President Carter as entirely political.[1] This "safe" social explanation denied the more threatening alternative of a severe health danger.

As a prerequisite for most lifescape effects of toxic exposure, victims must move from denial to belief that they have been affected. Perception, not reality, is the key.

Perceiving a Changed Status

As risk perception links the external hazard to victims' appraisal of danger, they reach a new, deeply held, and persistent understanding, a nonempirical or symbolic construction that Steve Kroll-Smith and Steve Couch call a "threat belief system."[2] We can see from the Legler and Love Canal incidents how some victims come to believe the reality of contamination.

Acceptance of Legler's Groundwater Contamination

How did Legler residents respond to notification of water pollution? For most, the news was a serious blow. For many, it was literally unbelievable. And for a few residents, it was even a relief! Several factors influenced whether residents were shocked by notification and their subsequent perceptions of vulnerability to exposure.

Hints of Problems.   In the prior chapter, I noted that the announcement of Legler's contamination was foreshadowed by a number of clues which enhanced residents' readiness to believe the warning once it arrived. Not all residents witnessed such clues, however. Their absence made it initially easier to deny the threat.

When we were notified in December, we didn't want to believe it at first. Our water wasn't foul. It tasted good. But when they tested it, it contained acetone and benzene.

Some clues were more abstract and others personal. While knowledge of the lack of landfill security made plausible later threats from pollution due to illegal waste dumping, such information was not as influential as anomalies closer to home. Thus for families previously reporting detectable deterioration in water quality, the notification confirmed their concerns.

I had suspected this for a long time. I wasn't that surprised. It confirmed how I felt. I was angry. I had been complaining for a long time, and the township told me I was crying wolf.

In such instances, the notification was a sign of hope that finally the township would act; what had been viewed as a private problem was now seen as a community-wide issue.

The report of pollution also provided an explanation for what had previously seemed inexplicable health problems.

I made a connection between the water and health problems. In Staten Island we didn't have diarrhea and the water didn't smell.

For those living outside the first area designated as polluted, the period during which the contamination boundaries were gradually extended outward provided an opportunity to prepare for the bad news. However, it more often created false hopes for residents that their homes were safe. Government officials directly encouraged this denial by reassuring those outside the current pollution boundary that they had no problem. When these hopes were dashed, trust in government was strained.

We had received no notification, but I read about the pollution in the Asbury Park Press. *I called the township and they said that if I didn't get a letter, there was no problem. A person moving onto the street called to ask if the water was polluted, and we said no. I had been reading in the paper about [Route] 571 and Lakehurst. It got closer and closer. I kept thinking about those poor people.*

Perceived Vulnerability.   Location was also an indicator of vulnerability, with residents who perceived themselves to be far from the landfill feeling most secure. However, the most important correlates of perceived vulnerability to pollution impacts were less locational than temporal, reflecting the life cycle issues of the residents' age, particularly the presence of children in the home.³ Even more than belief in pollution, this factor influenced residents to heed the health advisory and cease using their groundwater. People were not willing to take a chance with their children, even when they doubted the veracity of the notification.

It took two weeks for us to gradually accept that our water was polluted. We would forget and drink the water during this time. We were more careful with our daughter than we were with ourselves.

In ceasing use of their tap water, these young parents were motivated by concern about the health effects of toxic exposure.

When I heard that the chemicals were carcinogenic, I didn't know what that meant. When it was explained—cancer! My stomach fell. I worried what I had brought my son into.

This childless adult held a contrasting view.

We'd be a lot more concerned if we had kids.

Younger adults also recognized that they might themselves suffer health effects from exposure, as this resident noted,

I still don't know what will happen in ten years. My husband knows all about Love Canal. I'm very worried about cancer—period! We both have been losing our eyesight: Is this related? We don't know what will show up with the chemicals. We were swimming in it!

In contrast, the few elderly couples in Legler were relatively free of personal health concerns about exposure.

What do we have to lose? Cancer takes twenty years to develop.

However, some still worried about the effects on children.

We had brought up three grandchildren who spent much time here. Is it possible that this will affect their lives? How can you tell?

Length of residence also affected perceived vulnerability, although parents tended to be deeply concerned over their children's health whether long- or short-term residents. Perhaps reflecting their family role, women were particularly vigilant.

Acceptance in Love Canal

A similar pattern of acceptance occurred at Love Canal, although the specific dynamics varied given differences in the incidents and communities. Love Canal was considerably larger and more urban, with a stronger blue-collar presence. Development had occurred in the 1950s after dumping stopped. A substantial proportion of the population was older and had lived in the community for a greater length of time. Whereas Legler residents had sought a rural, suburban life, residents of Love Canal accepted trade-offs by living in an urban industrial environment and, in many cases, by working for the area chemical companies, a factor that contributed a slight tendency to minimize the problem. The presence of minority residents who rented their units in Love Canal was a further difference.[4]

At Love Canal the key conflict concerned the delineation of safe from unsafe areas. While Legler's water problem was "fixed" so that relocation was unnecessary, Love Canal residents faced the closing of a local school and either forced or voluntary residential relocation.

Anomalous contamination clues also preceded the Love Canal incident. A child was injured by exploding rocks, soil suddenly subsided, chemical drums popped from the earth, and on some plots plants would not grow while elsewhere they underwent accelerated growth. Those believing the contamination to be severe tended to have suffered from "a strong pattern of unpredictably recurring, debilitating and diagnostically elusive illnesses."[5]

The degree of concern did not vary with location at Love Canal. However, age was an influential factor, with older residents, highly dependent on neighborhood stability as they neared retirement, likely to minimize the problem. Age was positively correlated with length of residence; the median length of residence for families who refused to relocate was twenty-four years. As in Legler, younger families were likely to be concerned about their children, consequently recognizing the potential risk, and thus were more likely to relocate. These families had lived in their homes between eight and a half and ten years; half saw themselves as permanently settled in the community.[6]

Overall, relocation decisions reflected residents' belief that the contamination was a real threat. These beliefs, in turn, were related in part to educational levels and particularly to the residents' social values, as suggested by sociologists Marcia Fowlkes and Patricia Miller:

"Nonbelievers" espouse a highly individualistic and meritocratic set of values. They are defenders of the status quo, and subscribe to the view that life in present-day American industrial society is inherently and pervasively risky. Accordingly, they hold that the major burden of responsibility legitimately resides with each family to secure the information and resources necessary to safeguard its own welfare. The "believers" live in less privatized and more sociable worlds. They articulate an inextricable linkage between individual and collective welfare and an expectation that the polity properly stands for the interests of the individual where these would be compromised or jeopardized by the interests of the industrial order.[7]

Believers and nonbelievers also differed in their approach to defining the disaster. Believers were more likely to have had uncommon health problems and other direct experiences that they related to chemical exposure. They actively searched for clarification of the situation, attending meetings, questioning officials, and seeking tests. In contrast, nonbelievers had fewer direct impacts from chemicals and relied on their own limited experience and that of close acquaintances. Compared with believers, they were far removed from events and information sources, conditions that reinforced their denial.

This perceptual gulf between believers and nonbelievers is common to contamination issues.[8] In fact, it is an inherent feature of an often invisible and intangible phenomenon that invites divergent perceptions rather than consensus and conformity. We will later discuss the consequences of this divergence for community cohesion, social support, and environmental stigma.

Summary of Factors Affecting Acceptance

In summary, prior anomalies help prepare some residents for the possibility of contamination. Additionally, a family's vulnerability creates a predisposition or readiness to believe in the threat and a willingness to employ protective measures. Factors affecting acceptance of threat include location, education, and length of residence. Age, gender, employment, and especially presence of children in the home are even stronger factors. Acceptance requires a belief in the threat and is further affected by core ecosocial values.[9]

Belief in exposure is victimizing. It contradicts previously held views of life. The resulting disconfirmation of meaning is perhaps the most commonly noted effect of toxic disaster.[10] Five fundamental lifescape changes are involved.

- A reassessment of the assumption of good health.
- A shift to pessimistic expectations about the future, resulting from victims' perceived loss of control over forces which affect them.
- A changed perspective on environment; it is now uncertain and potentially harmful.

- An inversion of the sense of home involving a betrayal of place. What was formerly the bastion of family security now exposes all to danger. Having chosen to live there, the person is now deprived of the choice of leaving.
- A loss of the naive sense of trust and goodwill accorded to others in general; specifically, a lost belief that government acts to protect those in danger.

In the remainder of this chapter, each of these long-term lifescape impacts is explored in detail.

Perceptions of Health

Given the plethora of diseases and illnesses that people typically confront in the course of life, it is a fascinating testimony to the power of denial as a coping response that people routinely are health optimists rather than pessimists.[11] In effect, we are healthy until proven otherwise and, for most of us, we plan our lives with a certitude that our good health will continue. Illness therefore comes as a shock to us because it disconfirms this basic lifestyle assumption. While the probabilities of illness are denied, its prospects are often dreaded. Thus the health consequences of contamination are central to the anticipatory fears that accompany it.

Such fears are particularly evident with regard to cancer. Ablon notes that "cancer carries the mystique of death. In Sontag's words, it is 'The disease that doesn't knock before it enters . . . a ruthless, secret invasion.'"[12] Half of a national sample in an American Cancer Society study cited by Stephen Berman and Abraham Wandersman reported fear even of the word "cancer," and a third felt that cancer was the worst thing that could ever happen to them. These authors conclude that exposure to toxic hazards particularly inspires a fear of cancer for at least three reasons. First, synthetic chemicals are reputed to be carcinogenic and potentially fatal to humans. Second, given the invisibility of pollutants, toxicity is inferred simply as the result of knowledge of a proximate hazard. And, third, cancer is inherently frightening due to "its mere association as a fatal, loathsome disease which can cause prolonged suffering, pain, disability, disfigurement, dependence, social stigma, isolation, and disruption of lifestyle."[13]

Beyond their carcinogenicity, chemicals may be mutagenic (affect the genetic structure), teratogenic (affect the fetus), somatogenic (affect the organs or body), and neurotoxic (affect the brain and nervous system). Furthermore, certain chemicals are endocrine disrupters, with disastrous results.[14] Beverly Paigen, the cancer researcher who advised the Love Canal Home Owners Association, established the principle that the fetus is the point of earliest reliable detection for exposures, our analog of the canary in the coal mine.[15]

Illness comes with inherent lifestyle and lifescape impacts. A classic study of lifestyle notes that

poor health appears to have a peculiarly insistent ability to reduce one's sense of well-being, an ability which most people find impossible to resist. Not very many people say they are dissatisfied with their health, about one person in ten, but those who do show an impressive pattern of ill-being—not very happy, dissatisfied with life, and high feelings of strain.[16]

Thus Frank, a sociologist, reflected on the loss and mourning his experience of cancer entailed for him and his wife.[17]

Together Cathie and I lost an innocence about the normal expectations of life. At one time it seemed normal to expect to work and accomplish certain things, to have children and watch them grow, to share experiences with others, to grow old together. Now we realize that these events may or may not happen. Life is contingent. We are no longer sure what it is normal to expect. . . . Those losses of future and past, of place and innocence . . . must be mourned. The ill person's losses vary according to one's life and illness. We should never question what a person chooses to mourn. One person's losses may seem eccentric to another, but the loss is real enough, and the reality deserves to be honored.

Illness focuses the attention of family members inward as resources are marshaled to deal with health problems now a cause of worry, financial hardship, missed work, and lost loved ones. Inattention to extraneous issues was evident as a 1979 informant explained she had only learned of Love Canal the prior spring.

I had no idea whatsoever. I was so tied up with my child being sick, with our own illnesses. And then we went away for vacation, and we came back, and my best friend said, "Hey, the state's going to move me out of here!" And she was totally confused. Her husband died from cancer. Her son died from cancer. She had a hysterectomy! I lost a child here.

The numbing list went on and on. Every time I tried to change the subject, my Love Canal informants resumed their litany of maladies: their own, their family's, friends', and neighbors'. Given all of their other issues, I was perplexed by this obsession with health problems. Obviously, unexplained illness now dominated their experience. Now linked to contamination, ill health had become an interpretive overlay for life itself.

As toxic victims become preoccupied with health concerns, past and current symptoms are attributed to exposure. Given the delayed onset of environmental health problems, expectations about the future are captured by what victims believe will happen as the result of exposure. A frequent outcome is that anxiety about future illness, a shortened life span, and genetic damage cast a shadow over the future. This perceived health threat does not require tangible health symptoms, as an observer at Times Beach noted, "We kept hearing phrases like 'possible carcinogen' or 'suspected mutagen.' These phrases strike a person like the rattling of a chain—with a sense of dread."[18]

It is hardly surprising that a comparison of different toxic disasters by Duane Gill and Steven Picou identified a significant relationship between perceived health threat and elevated levels of chronic community stress.[19] As my Love Canal informant illustrated, this new health reality represents an insurmountable emotional burden.

> *I have a friend who lives two doors down from me. And she just got out of Memorial Hospital for the fourth time in the last six months. She's suicidal. She's classified as schizophrenic. She lost three babies here. She used to hold a secretarial job with a prominent firm. Now she can't function. We're in the process of getting her into a home. Her family can't handle anything anymore. I have another friend who committed suicide. Why? We don't know. The nervous system just can't tolerate it. I myself have been under extreme depression—no reason. It just comes on you and you don't know how to handle it.*

Inherent Uncertainty

The stress is further magnified by the mystery surrounding the health effects of toxic and radioactive exposure. In considering this "medical invisibility," Henry Vyner has delineated uncertainties over past, present, and future medical conditions, the dose of exposure and its effect, the latency before the effect manifests itself, what actually causes the effects, how one detects the symptoms and ties them to causal factors, the prognosis, the cost of treatment, and the potential consequences for future generations.[20] Such uncertainties have at least two implications.

First, uncertainties affect medical diagnosis and response. During a period of health concern, the family must depend on physicians often reluctant to accept environmental explanations for symptoms, relying instead on conventional explanation and treatment. If a "normal" diagnosis can be made, the illness becomes demystified; there may be no reasons to search for environmental causes. Even "unconventional" diseases rarely prod physicians to look for environmental sources.[21]

Uncertainty persists even for labeled environmental illnesses. For example, Steve Kroll-Smith and Hugh Floyd note the absence of medical consensus about "chemical hypersensitivity disorder," which lacks a commonly accepted terminology and uniform description. The cause, patient prognosis, prevalence of the disorder, and its incidence in the population are not known.[22] It is no wonder that many victims have the jaded view of the medical establishment held by my Love Canal respondent.

> *Last summer, I scrubbed my basement. Soon after, I felt real sick. And my hands felt like they were being crushed, and my feet and my spine. And I went to the doctors, and I had steroid treatments. And nothing helped. And I went to specialists. I still have it, [it's] affecting my hip now. They don't know what's wrong with me. I don't even want to take my son to the doctor anymore. It's bullshit. They're afraid to open their mouths for fear of losing their license.*

In short, what people experience as symptoms are medically invisible to the very professionals on whom they depend. Doctors' failure to "legitimize" toxic exposure as the cause of health problems renders victims' claims as irrational.[23]

Second, uncertainty complicates social diagnosis and response. Plainly put, it is hard to link health symptoms to an environmental cause.[24] Health studies, mandated under Superfund, routinely fail to find such relationships. For example, residents of Goshen, New York, blamed Al Turi Landfill, Inc., for the seemingly large number of cancers in their neighborhood. The Agency for Toxic Substances and Disease Registry (ATSDR) of the Centers for Disease Control and the New York State Department of Health failed to find corroboration. They reasoned the neighborhood too small for valid assessment, the cancers too diverse to have shared one environmental cause, and overall cancer so prevalent in the region that the numbers, albeit high, were not unexpected. No matter how justified, these conclusions merely added to the negative psychological toll of contamination. In a situation where the burden of proof carries so much weight, we have the presence of effect but the absence of conclusive evidence. Despite perceived excess cancers and potential environmental pathways, risk studies readily find cause and effect to be unrelated. Yet people know that something caused their tragedies. Such "orphaned events"—exposures with no proven consequences or illness clusters without a clear cause—leave victims in limbo because government lacks enough proof to act.

Ironically, at Love Canal, a precedent was set for action without acknowledging health damages. Adeline Levine describes how government carefully neutralized compelling health data, justifying this first instance of government-funded relocation on other grounds (the first phase to allow capping of the dumpsite and the second for mental health reasons).[25]

Given the medical system's inability to recognize, describe, and treat their symptoms and government's failure to justify protective action, victims commonly resort to "popular epidemiology." In contrast to grassroots organizing concerned with such goals as environmental cleanup, provision of clean water, and property relief, popular epidemiology reflects a perceived disease cluster, a naive hypothesis linking environment to illness, or the desire to identify possible consequences of known pollution. As they undertake their own health research, lay epidemiologists move from viewing illness as a private problem to the search for patterns of illness in the community. They use an approach for gathering information that circumvents the shroud of privacy surrounding health information, be it informal communication among neighbors or conducting a health survey. Serendipity may play a role, as when the leukemia cluster in Woburn, Massachusetts, was recognized because victims traveled to the same specialized health clinic in Boston.[26]

Health Preoccupation and the Changed Perception of Health

There is ample evidence of the importance of health concerns in contaminated communities.[27] A significant relationship was found between proximity to a South Carolina hazardous waste dump and higher levels of perceived health and cancer risk.[28] Twenty months after a train derailment caused a toxic spill, health concern and fear of cancer among residents of Livingston, Louisiana, was greatest for those most proximate to the accident, whose family members were evacuated longest and who were separated during the accident from family members.[29] And, using the MMPI, Margaret Gibbs documented a clinically significant preoccupation with illness for toxic victims.[30] Such preoccupation reflects a changed perception of health across all time frames: past, present, and future.

Reinterpreting Past Health Problems.   Discovery of toxic contamination provides a perceptual framework for explaining previous health problems, particularly those originally inexplicable.[31] For example, the tragic loss of a Legler child to a rare form of kidney cancer was explained definitively (in the view of the family and others in the community) by the later discovery of toxic chemicals in the groundwater. Other examples of the reinterpretation of health problems were suggested by my Love Canal informants.

My son quit growing. He lives in the lower level of a raised ranch. He developed ulcers; he has sugar; three out of five of my kids have ulcers. And it's not because my wife is a bad cook.

My son had to come home for lunch. And I had to go pick him up and take him back because by the time he'd get to school he'd have an asthma attack. And I used to think it was pollen! He'd get it in the dead of winter!

In response to the health concerns in Legler, the Concerned Citizens Committee conducted a health survey of residents using a form developed by Love Canal activists. When a subsequent report by the state health department concluded that the survey showed no health problems beyond possible skin and eye irritation, it only served to heighten public awareness of the health issue. The state's argument that no conclusive test of health effects could be done with such a small and uncontrolled sample suggested to Legler residents that other health effects could not be ruled out. And the statement that long-term illness such as cancer was "the only plausible health consequence of consuming this water" was hardly reassuring.[32] In sum, the state report failed to dissuade residents' belief in a link between chemicals known to cause symptoms and the occurrence of those symptoms.

When the state described the problems from the chemicals, my husband's kidney problems seemed to fit. Within a thousand feet of here, we have eight people with kidney problems. Do people with a predisposition to kidney problems choose to live near a landfill?

I had blamed my physical problems on getting older. Now I started to think that maybe they were due to the water. I had skin problems, stomach aches, and menstrual disorders. I lived on Maalox. Now whatever goes wrong, I think that it's the water, and it's going to kill me. I'm a hypochondriac.

Although some suggest that unconventional diseases are most likely to be questioned in this manner, my own data shows that even conventional health problems are reinterpreted in light of known toxic exposure. Thus a Love Canal informant indicated:

We have several women right around where I live who had hysterectomies. Five men have had open-heart surgery. Almost every child from twelve years on down has allergies, asthma, hyperactivity, above-normal intelligence, or below-normal intelligence; there are very few normal children. On my street alone, one woman moved in next door to me. She'd had two small children when she came, so she could conceive. She's lost five sons. She's twenty-six years old and had her tubes tied. The woman across the street moved in with one child and lost three. The woman next door to her was two weeks away from having her baby when she moved in. The week before she was due, the doctor said everything was okay, "you're beautiful." Well, the child was born dead.

Reinterpreting Current Symptoms. Reinterpretation of present health status is also found, as this Legler resident explained.

It seems silly sometimes when you fear something. For example, I had a tumor in my ankle during the water situation. I thought it was cancer from drinking the chemicals. I expected to find cancer. I was really upset. Even when the doctor said it was benign, I was still worried.

Similarly, at Love Canal, an informant displayed a picture of a girl with chloracne, a skin condition found with exposure to dioxins and other chlorinated compounds.

When they started digging, my daughter did not have one blemish—nothing—on her face. And she broke out in the "Hooker bumps," which several other children did in this area.

Beyond reassessing their health, people may question what behaviors are "healthy." In the Michigan PBB contamination case, many mothers grew to fear the consequences for their infants of breast-feeding, creating a dilemma because they otherwise viewed this as a superior means of providing sustenance.[33]

Future Health Concerns. Long-term health expectations also change after toxic exposure. The potential for long-latency health problems such as cancer clouds the future. Other threats extend to future generations—mutagenic (changes affecting the genetic material) and teratogenic (fetus-threatening) effects. A Legler woman recalled her concerns as she anticipated the birth of a child:

The doctor said that the baby would be aborted if there was a chemical problem. It was in the back of my mind until it was born that it would be deformed. It wasn't until after it was born that I could learn to cope with the water problem.

Such effects involve more than a sense of violation and intrusion; the seeds of future misery have been planted, and it is only a matter of time before they germinate. As a result, as this comment by a Love Canal resident indicates, formerly happy anticipations may be shifted dramatically:

*When a child is born in this area, no one says, "was it male or female?" They
say, "was it normal?" That's the big thing, "was it normal?"*

Children are not spared such concerns. While her son stood at her side, a Love
Canal mother explained:

*I'm thinking about my son. What kind of kids is he going to have if he lives—
he has to have a blood test twice a year for leukemia—are they going to be mental retards?*

A Legler teenager reflected similar concerns.

*What worries me is my genes. This stays with you. It may not show up for
twenty years. It may hit the next generation. Having a deformed child can be an
emotional crisis. I think of the mentally retarded class at school. I don't know
how to handle this situation.*

Ironically, government programs aimed at ongoing health screening for toxic victims may serve as a continuing reminder of the potential for future disaster, reinforcing this lifescape shift. Testing may also serve to dehumanize victims, as this
Love Canal resident intimated.

*We're human beings, we're not guinea pigs. We've had blood. We've had all
kinds of tests. They treat us like we're a better strain of white mice.*

Confirmed Exposures

What happens when toxins are detected in these human guinea pigs? In most
instances of contamination, people may know that they have been exposed, but
they do not have confirmation that exposure resulted in detectable levels of poison
in their bodies. Blood tests identified serum mirex in some residents along the
Middle Fork of Little Beaver Creek in Ohio. Residents I interviewed there who
received positive test results now had proof of their exposure but little idea what it
meant.[34]

*The results had been given to the family "straight." There were no limitations
on it [to judge the results of the blood tests]. We did not know if it was good or
bad. There was no scale to go by.*

> *Nobody knew what it meant. What could I do about it? What would it do to me? Nobody would tell you. I asked the doctor and he did not know what it meant either. Anybody you would ask would say they did not know. I still do not know what it means. They said it was a carcinogen. A cancer-causing agent. But they could not tell what might happen. What we should look for, other than glowing in the dark.*

Thus uncertainty does not end with testing. Rather, the assumption of bad health found generally with toxic exposure is merely experienced with even more confidence, as expressed by this Ohio resident. "If anything comes along, we wonder if it is caused by this. Or if we have got over it now." This comment illustrates that knowing of confirmed mirex exposure at one point does not suggest when it will have passed through the system or at what levels it will have what effects. And when health problems occur, there is no certainty as to whether the mirex is the cause. Confirmed presence of mirex does not prove mirex consequences, as this comment suggests. "My brother has had three premature children. One was two and a half pounds. Was that caused by this? It is a question." And do people treat health conditions differently now that they know? "It is in me. I have a lump on the back of my head. I am not going to lance it. Just leave it alone. Is it malignant? Does it have mirex in it?"

Some now knew, and knowledge of confirmed exposure itself became an impact. I interviewed three generations of a family in which seven of eight members tested had shown confirmed blood mirex levels. A mother of the second generation worried about the implications of her son's confirmed exposure.

> *My son is marrying a girl in May. . . . She asked him if their kids are going to be affected. Will they be able to reproduce? She sees people and asks questions about this.*

After her son returned, he confirmed her concerns.

> *Next year, I hope to marry. My fiancée is a big worrier. What will happen when we have kids? . . . Now that I have come to the age where these things could start happening, she is asking these questions. How do you answer? Will my life be shorter? What can you say?*

Some residents refused the tests because exposure along the Middle Fork of Little Beaver Creek was a foregone conclusion.

> *I don't want to know. I spent a lot of time in the creek. I was continuously in it from the time [I was young]. I trapped, went digging, and so on. I chewed my*

fingernails. I know I got it. I figure if it is a problem, if I live past fifty-eight years, I will be so happy. I live my life accordingly. I do as much as I can with my children. I figure my life will be fifteen to twenty years shorter. If not, then the rest is a bonus. If I make fifty-eight or sixty, I will have achieved what I want to.

Knowing was not always seen as empowering, as a resident, who had declined testing for the family, suggested.

What would we do about it if we tested? I am concerned that if it was positive, what could I do? We do not know what to do about it. So we passed up the opportunity to test.

Here we see the palpable confrontation with contamination. Worst fears are confirmed, but the confirmation brings little clarity. Or confirmation is not sought because it is not necessary. Difficult questions do not have clear answers. Toxic victims who accept the full "worst scenario" of health outcomes are haunted by the possibilities, suggesting the palliative virtues of denying such impacts.

Of course, MFLBC residents had feasible steps they could take to minimize future exposures, including avoidance of the creek and flood plain, and local milk, meat, and vegetables. Action-focused coping was also practiced in the lead-contaminated Australian town of Broken Hill, described by Tara McGee's work.[35] Although concern over lead and health effects stretched back a century, it was not until 1991 that lead was documented in the dust of Broken Hill homes and subsequently found at levels of concern in the blood of 30 percent of the community's children. A successful two-year-long effort to reduce lead exposures through parental education was undertaken. Children were discouraged from eating soil, playing in the dirt, and sleeping or eating on the floor or outside and encouraged to stay clean, to wash their hands before meals, and to eat a low-fat, nutritious diet including lots of fruit. Carpets were vacuumed no more than once a week, and floors were wet-mopped two hours after vacuuming. Cracks in ceilings and walls were repaired. Residents were also advised to seek consultation prior to renovating, painting, or altering their gardens. Although limiting to normal childhood activities, costly, and difficult to follow, the guidelines allowed parents to regain a sense of partial control over their children's continuing exposures.

Conclusion: Health Lifescape Change

Perceived loss of health in the face of toxic exposure causes a reinterpretation of life suggesting ill-being. This threat to health is rooted in the environment where we live. Our second lifescape shift involves our view of this surround.

Environment

After many years, desperate to escape, a family had sold their beloved home to the mobsters who ran the adjacent landfill. The house was demolished, the land was cleared, and a waste transfer station was built directly atop the site. Only one reminder of their former homestead remained. Somehow, in the midst of this devastated landscape, growing tall and defiant, there survived the gnarled tree their grandmother had called "the hanging tree." As children they had feared and avoided it. Now, its brilliant flowering heralds the triumph of evil over good. All that was loved about this place is gone. Only a twisted tree thrives in the twisted landscape, symbolizing precisely the transformation of the environment that occurs with contamination.

Perhaps most perplexing, this transformation was overseen by environmental engineers and scientists and approved by the state's Department of Environmental Conservation. How could the fields and pond and hills that were home, setting, and surround for this family be so defiled in the name of the environment?

The answer was suggested long ago in the work of the German biologist and gestalt psychologist Jakob Von Uexküll, who distinguished between two frames of understanding. One, signified by the term "environment," connotes an abstract realm, effectively separate from people, that is described by scientists and manipulated by engineers. The second, the "ambient," refers to our immediate and intimate surround. Although we can be objective and distanced in considering the environment, what happens to the ambient happens to us.[36]

Environment as Abstraction

Indeed, for most Americans, environment is an abstract concept. It is a sphere of reality that is somehow separated from us and our lives. We know there are terrible problems with the environment, and we want them to be addressed, but we do not necessarily associate these problems with ourselves and our homes. We know that people are victimized environmentally, but we are confident that it could not happen to us. Furthermore, we frequently think of these problems as belonging to others or society to address and not as our own responsibility.

In a more immediate vein, we think of the environment as a benign backdrop to our lives, the background for what really counts, namely, our selves, families, and friends, our social worlds, our workplaces and our homes. It is, to use the old gestalt conception, the "ground" to our "figure." And reflecting its distance from us, we often think about environment as "the view." Spoiling the view detracts from the focal point of the scene. Instructively, this perceptual framework for the environment is dominated by the use of vision as a distance receptor. Unless there are foul odors, disruptive noises, a bad taste to the water, or other intrusions into the more immediate sensory realm of our other modalities for understanding the world, we readily place the environment at a visual distance. We are distressed by the aesthetic degradation of our surround, but the effects are still far off.

In focusing our attention on objects, not what surrounds those objects, we confuse object perception with environmental perception. Environmental psychologist Bill Ittelson long ago noted that, although object perception involves the separation of the perceiver from the perceived, environmental perception requires participation and involvement. You can't stand back and look at the environment; you are part of it.[37]

Awakening to the Ambient Realm

This emergence of the environment as a major force in our lives is a significant shift, exposing an inherent flaw in our worldview. With the transition to an industrial society, environment came to be perceived as an object rather than as a surround. By extension, we can easily view the environment as a resource to exploit while overlooking the partnership with nature that we belong to as living organisms.[38] Insensitive to our interconnectedness, we act as if we were wearing blinders. Or, as Von Uexküll put it, we act toward the abstract environment nonchalantly, "as though we have another one in the boot."

Thus our distancing from the environment can be seen as a cultural distortion. In reality, we live *in* the environment. It is our surround. We swim in it like a fish in water. The environment begins at the boundaries of ourselves, forming what Von Uexküll termed our "second skin." And as living organisms, we have a total interdependence with this surround. Try not breathing while you read this page and you quickly realize this intimacy. We continually borrow air from "the environment" to meet our need for oxygen, returning the spent air to the surround. To not do so is to die quickly. And whatever was in that air is clearly now inside our bodies, some to remain as part of us—whether good or bad, desired or not. Exhaling, in turn, we taint the surrounding air. In similar fashion, we take in water, food, light, and stimulation. We cannot exist outside this nurturing and forgiving surround, and anything that impedes the ability of the environment to nurture us or to accept our released pollutants is a direct threat to our existence. In contrast to our abstract environment, any changes to our ambient environment cause us to reflexively respond as we would to some direct attack on our bodies.

The challenge poised by Von Uexküll's work, then, is how to remove the cultural separation of person and environment, awakening an awareness of the ambient that will transform our behavior. It is as if we need a wake-up call. For toxic victims, that shock has already occurred, paralleling the old parable, cited by the gestalt psychologist Kurt Koffka:

> On a winter evening amidst a driving snowstorm a man on horseback arrived at an inn, happy to have reached a shelter after hours of riding over the winter-swept plain on which the blanket of snow had covered all paths and landmarks. The landlord who came to the door viewed the stranger with surprise and asked him whence he came. The man pointed in the direction straight away from the inn, whereupon the landlord, in a tone of awe and wonder, said: "Do you know that you have ridden across the Lake of Constance?" At which the rider dropped stone dead at his feet.[39]

Contamination victims also learn of unknown danger beneath their feet or in their water or food or air. Like the traveler, they trusted a seemingly safe environment only to discover that it was treacherous. Gone is the sense of protection formerly assumed to be present in the environment.[40] Shocked to attention, victims are forced to recognize the vulnerability of natural systems and their intimate interconnectedness and interrelatedness with their surround. Environment is now central to their understanding of life.

Confronted with the realities of contamination, victims find themselves suddenly and acutely aware of the ambient surround, almost as a revelation. Suddenly they see patterns of drainage on the land and the resulting movement of water. Now they comprehend the implications of drawing water from a well that taps a shared underground body of water exposed to influences far beyond their control perhaps long ago. Air patterns and their implications for movements of pollution become obvious when previously they meant little. Airsheds and watersheds are now as visible as viewsheds. Bioaccumulation and magnification of pollutants up through the food chain is now comprehended. The potential threat to environmental health can be understood as they begin to see themselves as biological organisms whose viability depends on the quality of the ambient surround. We cannot be healthy organisms living in an unhealthy place. Thus the effect of contamination is to suddenly shift into focus an entire heretofore hidden realm of ecological reality, like an amoeba appearing on the microscope's glass with just a turn of the knob.

It is a parallel awakening to that described by David Abram for the aftermath of a great storm that, having frightened us with its fury, now forces us to live without electricity, attending to what we otherwise would ignore.

The breakdown of our technologies had forced a return to our senses and hence to the natural landscape in which those senses are so profoundly embedded. We suddenly found ourselves inhabiting a sensuous world that had been waiting, for years, at the very fringe of our awareness, an intimate terrain infused by bird-song, salt spray, and the light of stars.[41]

The analogy has its limits, however, for the breakdown involved in contamination doesn't quite parallel the deep quiet that follows the storm. Here it is not the natural landscape that emerges, but rather the denaturalized environment. Realization of the sensuousness of nature and our interconnection places us at risk; for our terrain is hardly intimate but estranged and suspect, infused not by bird-song but by silent springs, and not by starry skies but by unblocked ultraviolet sunlight. Our awareness fails us, and we know it. We cannot see, smell, taste, or feel the pollution, yet it is palpable to us.

It is in this context that toxic victims experience what I call a "de facto environmental education." In the antithesis of distance learning, they become ecologically literate studying independently in their own backyards: naively grasping the laws of ecology and thermodynamics, the inevitability for complex, unpredicted outcomes, the interconnectedness of all and the wisdom of nature's way. The cascade of insights offers a primer in the interdisciplinary and comprehensive field of environmental studies. Now it is expected that environmental problems become ambient problems. Abstract and the personal merge into one.

The Environment as Malevolent Force

Perceptions of the environment have shifted dramatically throughout history. A little more than a century ago, hatred of the wilderness characterized Western culture. Conquering the wilderness and civilizing it were the goals of American settlers moving west. With the wilderness since vanquished and reduced to scattered controlled parklands, the human-dominated landscape now became the place of danger. As Joel Kameron noted, "Ironically, the wilderness experience is now seen as being enriching and enlightening, while the city, which was formerly associated with virtue, is now often seen as the bestial jungle."[42]

In a further cultural modification, the merger of the abstract and ambient environments after toxic exposure forces a reassessment of the idea that the environment is a benign backdrop. Instead, as it comes to be recognized as the carrier of the contamination, the environment becomes a much more significant, and ominous, component of one's world. Such requisites as air, water, and soil, normally assumed to be freely available in desired purity, are no longer trusted to be safe.

Children learn to ask of hosts, "Is the water safe to drink?" I have noted the same phenomenon at every toxic site that I have visited—urban, suburban, and rural.

Threatening Urban Livability. In the neighborhood around the Asarco Superfund site, which encompassed the entire town of Rushton, Washington, and parts of Tacoma, residents had to contend with the issues of arsenic and lead contamination in the local soil. Recalling a warning by EPA officials to take precautions with gardening, to wear gloves outdoors, and to prevent small children from eating dirt, one resident remembered, "I started to realize how this was going to affect small day-to-day decisions."

The experience of a single father raising two young girls illustrates the resulting transformation of parenthood.[43] EPA instructed him to keep his kids out of the dirt, dress them in long pants and shirts all year round, put blankets on the floor to keep them off the carpet, and do the laundry daily. However, "They were one and a half and three and a half at the time. It was not possible to follow this advice. The kids would move around, and it was impossible to keep them on the blanket."

Now, a year and a half later, he humorously reported a comedy of errors. Watching them caused him constant stress from the time the kids awoke until bedtime. To keep them out of the dirt and off the grass, he stopped gardening, put in a swing set, and bought bikes. But even when he yells at them, they still play in the dirt. "You can't just suspend the kids from the ceiling, you know." He tries to talk to the kids about it, but they have a short attention span. One daughter keeps taking her shoes off. She then sits on the floor to put them back on, violating a second taboo. And when he tells her the floor is dirty (i.e., contaminated), she looks at the freshly shampooed rug and says, "It doesn't look dirty." Even when they are sleeping, he wonders if their sheets and pillows are clean. "I wash them constantly. But I don't know that they don't have lead on them just because they look clean. All I can do is wash them." This worry is on his mind all the time. The kids get their blankets on the floor, and then he has to wash them before bedtime. "I can't keep up with it. I have one washer, one dryer, and a life." Sometimes it gets to be too much for him. "When you start to yell at your kids, you are being stressed. It compounds the normal stress factor."

Another Rushton parent captured the dilemma posed by this pressure to avoid contact with the surround. "These are questions that our generation never faced. It is not an easy thing to hand down to the next generation. We were never raised with our parents having to explain this to their children."

Ruining the Suburban Myth. The move to the suburbs and quasi-rural areas, undertaken by many of the toxic victims discussed in this volume, was part of an escape from the city to a rural idyll. Likewise, settlers in the 1700s and 1800s saw America as a new Garden of Eden that could cleanse and purify the blight of industrial pollution that had enveloped Europe. As a result, Americans failed to anticipate the conflict inherent in the image of America as a bucolic paradise and the unchecked industrialism that soon followed the pioneers.[44]

This conflict was evident in the new suburbs of Legler. It was also seen in Love Canal at the edge of Niagara Falls, New York. On the way to the canal, one drives toward the falls along a "scenic drive" that juxtaposes massive chemical plants and the roaring Niagara River. When I visited the canal in 1979, huge earth movers were in the process of making a clay cap atop the site. During the workers' lunch break, my informant and her son led me out onto the canal behind a boarded-up brick house, formerly the home to their closest friends. When the mother said of the barren landscape, "This used to be a yard," her son interjected, "The most beautifulest yard that you could ever think of." She continued:

> Tony, who died, spent many years filling in topsoil in this yard. And it kept sinking, and they didn't know where it was going. Right here there was a cherry tree and a pear tree, and we canned. And she had a garden right here. And she had huge tomatoes, and we used to say, "Why are the tomatoes and zucchini so big?" And we found out that some of this stuff [the chemicals] accelerates growth and some of this stuff kills. There were spots where the grass wouldn't grow.

The contamination of the garden represents a shift full circle. Now there is no escape, not even to the most remote settings. We have brought an end to nature and the natural.[45]

Contaminating the Bucolic Retreat.   For generations, the small communities along the Tennessee River in northern Alabama had lived in close harmony with the water.[46] Around the small town of Triana, the largely black population had evolved a local culture centered around the river and its tributaries. The major sources of protein were catfish and other aquatic creatures. Fishing was more than a source of subsistence and income—it was a way of life. Fish fries were important family and community events. Swimming and fishing outings occupied vacations and weekends. People spent a major portion of their time with friends and relatives at their favorite fishing spots. They returned again and again to these locations, learning the habits of the fish in each locale.

With the growing recognition of the dangers of the pesticide DDT in the 1960s, attention had gradually turned to the possible impacts of discharges from a major DDT manufacturing site located upriver from Triana. Although domestic use of DDT was banned in 1971, the compound continues to be present throughout the region. As with other complex synthetic substances, DDT does not break down in water. Instead, it persists in the environment, bioaccumulating in the fatty tissues of animals up through the food chain. DDT was found to have significantly contaminated much of the wildlife around Triana, including the fish.

It was not until the late 1970s that the implications of this contamination dawned on people. A study by the Centers for Disease Control (CDC) found evidence of DDT in the blood of local residents. Warning signs were posted along the river. A series of lawsuits sought damages from the manufacturer and others. As residents heard about the contamination on their televisions or at local gatherings, they were faced with a choice analogous to that confronting other toxic victims. They could continue eating local fish or they could stop. The choice had major financial and social implications. But it altered the lifescape in still another way by changing the perception and role of place in the lives of residents, as one described to me.

> *The river—you don't dare touch it with your hand. It's poison. I remember the pleasure and enjoyment. Now it's a dirty place and I wish it would go away. Now I don't go that way.*

Along the Middle Fork of Little Beaver Creek Superfund site, discussed previously, residents had been asked to make major changes to their lifestyles, avoiding exposure to the creek, its fish, and wildlife, as well as the soils of the floodplain. Gardens had to be abandoned and grazing cattle kept from the stream. Children and pets had to be watched carefully to keep them from harm. A small trailer park along the river had to close its pool and recreation complex. Several residents painfully decided to sell their beloved homes to keep their children and grandchildren from being exposed, but only after finding people to buy their homes who not only knew about the problem but also had no plans to have children there.

Perhaps the most infamous contamination of bucolic nature was the 1989 *Exxon Valdez* accident in the Prince William Sound area of Alaska. Both native and nonnative inhabitants of "natural resource communities" in the region exhibited an extreme vulnerability to ecological disaster because of their cultural and physical dependence on renewable natural resources.[47] Comparing longitudinal data from Cordova and Valdez with a control community unaffected by the spill, Picou and Gill found evidence in the oiled communities of significant and persistent impacts: social disruptions in work, personal, and community life, as well as higher levels of stress, generally, and occupational stress for fishermen.[48] Additionally, loss of tradition led to cultural chaos in native communities affected by the spill that had historically relied on natural cycles, social cooperation, and sharing.[49]

A second study, by Impact Assessment, Inc., was conducted for the "Oiled Mayors" on thirteen spill affected communities.[50] They identified as key impacts the importance of uncertainty over future resource availability, the boom associated with work on the cleanup, and the demand that communities deal with oil company representatives to address cleanup issues. The aftermath of the spill for the most exposed individuals was associated with greater depression and loss of traditional relations for both natives and nonnatives. Anxiety and Post Traumatic Stress Disorder were evident, particularly in natives, women, and younger adults. And increased drinking, drug use, diagnosed medical conditions, and domestic violence was also evident after the spill.

The third major research effort relevant to the spill involved a comprehensive government funded longitudinal study of native Alaskan communities by Jorgensen. Beginning three years before the spill and expanded afterward, the study documented how natives live a communitarian and traditional life based on an intimate knowledge of the land, harvesting of natural resources, and local networks of interdependency, visiting, and sharing. While the spill limited access to resources, native sharing afterwards increased even further. Jorgensen concluded that the spill caused "cultural deprivation" for natives.[51]

> They experienced a real, empirical loss of wild resources; real, empirical damage to the areas in which they gain their livelihood and which define their homeland; real empirical alterations in their customs of harvesting, preparing, sharing, and consuming products and by-products; and real empirical threats to the future generations of animals on which they rely.

None of these projects was intended for litigation, however the first two became embroiled in the momentous trial held to sort out the damages and responsibility for the *Exxon Valdez* spill.[52] The Jorgensen study failed to influence litigation on behalf of natives seeking compensation from Exxon for damage to native culture. Based instead on "bad and irresponsible social science," the two trials resulted in awards to nonnative commercial fishermen of $253,333 each while natives were to get only $4,570 apiece.[53]

Conclusion: Environment as Lifescape Change

As place becomes defiled by invisible contaminants, a realization of their interconnectedness with their surround dawns on victims. Any abstraction is replaced by an intimate violation of the closest and most intrusive kind. Perhaps in a manner more in line with the Grassy Narrows Ojibwa who were the subject of Anastasia Shkilnyk's powerful *A Poison Stronger Than Love*, environmental destruction is seen as a signal from the gods that the world has been unbalanced by our actions.[54] This is a difficult leap for Westerners taught that we hold dominion over the earth. Ironically, it is this core belief, false as it is, that is a key basis for the individual's sense of personal control. It is therefore not surprising that, beyond a reassessment of environment, with contamination there is also a parallel shift in the understanding of self and the future.

Loss of Personal Control

The social psychology of Western society has at its core the postulate that people need to understand, feel in control of, and be effective in producing changes in their physical and social environment.[55] Threatening events can shatter the victim's basic assumptions about the world, giving way to new perceptions marked by threat, danger, insecurity, and self-questioning. Central to the experience of disaster is the breakdown of the ability to believe in a predictable and controllable world.[56] In the wake of toxic exposure, victims not only lose their sense of control, but corollary challenges confront many other of their most cherished personal beliefs. The result is a loss of our cultural norm of optimism about the future and confidence in our ability to shape it.

The origin of this slide rests in the involuntary nature of contamination events, as this observation underscores. "Lung cancer to a heavy smoker [is] accepted [as] a person's choice to smoke. Miscarriage to a young mother is not so easily accepted, particularly when there are existing fears for the safety of one's drinking water."[57] Not only does contamination contradict plans and wishes, but caused by others' actions, it represents an intrusion into life. Much as with crime and rape, those affected are victimized. Their sense of justice is affronted, for how could they deserve what happened to them? And they are rendered helpless to protect themselves and their families from harm due to the contamination insult, originally, and then subsequently by all of the disabling issues that arise as key decisions about their lives are made by corporations, government agencies, politicians, and lawyers, judges, and juries. As if blinded by pollution's invisibility, they must even rely on others to tell them when the contamination is present and when it is not. Once contamination is announced, victims may feel as if they are pulled onto a continuous conveyor belt with no opportunity to stop, moving from one bad situation to the next, as if in a house of horrors.

There are other dimensions to the loss of control as well. Jerome Bruner notes that the sense of self consists of both an agentive and an evaluative component. Selfhood demands that we see ourselves as active agents, having the skills and knowledge to competently carry out key life activities. Our past record of efficacy is used to extrapolate future success, thus influencing the evaluative self (i.e., our self-esteem, a balance of beliefs about our capabilities and limitations).[58] As elaborated in Chapter 5, contamination robs its victims of their sense of agency and thus diminishes their sense of self-esteem.

There is ample empirical support for these conclusions. Longitudinal studies of area residents in the aftermath of the Three Mile Island accident showed a persistent association between feelings of helplessness and higher levels of stress.[59] In two studies of toxic exposure, lower levels of self-control were evident in victims than in comparison groups and psychopathology correlated with loss of control. In another case, for opponents of a hazardous facility, perceived control inversely correlated with the emotional response and evidence of psychological symptoms.[60] And compared to controls, those living near a hazardous waste site were both significantly more helplessness as well as uncertain about future effects of possible toxic exposure.[61]

In my study of Legler, the issue of lost control was a dominant theme for residents.[62] When I asked Legler respondents to contrast their sense of control before and after the water pollution, only about a fifth indicated feeling in control at both times. The largest group of residents reported going from a previous sense of control to a current loss of control, as suggested by this comment.

> *I tell myself that I'm in control, but I don't feel it. I feel like I'm in the Twilight Zone. Simple things are out of control. You get to a point where you don't know whether you're coming or going.*

Aside from activism, virtually every element of the Legler situation robbed residents of control. Their predicament was human-caused; others acted to disrupt their lives. It was an involuntary situation. Management of the threat was controlled by outside forces (see Chapter 5). Dependence on delivered water resulted in small hassles that reinforced victims' feelings of helplessness. Legler residents also lost control over their private wells; being forced into an expensive central water system represented a further limitation of their freedom.

> *I had always thought I was in control. I own my own home, but I have no say over it. I've been hit financially. Now I can't water the grass with the old well; I have to pay for the new water.*

Beyond the mundane, their loss of control also came home to people in contemplating significant life issues. Neither their physical nor social environment appeared to deserve continued trust. And, most disturbing of all, victims feared that their ability to secure a healthy future for their families was now compromised, as this Legler resident suggested:

> *I'm never going to go into another house with the naive enthusiasm that I had here. I'll be wary and distrusting. I hope the kids don't get sick. I don't believe it though; I think they will get sick.*

A key element in the loss of control was the inherent uncertainty of the situation.

> *There is no sense of certainty. People have plans and they're shot to hell. I thought I'd live here the rest of my life!*

Even Legler residents who claimed to maintain a sense of control felt it was usually diminished in some way.

> *I'd say yes [that I'm still in control], but I don't think that I'm as smart as I did because I wouldn't have got myself into this situation to begin with.*

Others saw the loss of control as temporary.

> *During the crisis we lost our control. We couldn't do anything about the problem. We talked. We fought over what to do. It didn't make any difference. We had control when we bought the house; afterwards we had no control. We'll return to feeling in control when this is solved or the lawsuit is over and we know where we stand.*

But in most cases, Legler residents no longer felt secure.

> *I'm always under tension. This has disrupted my peace. I have anxiety. I worry about the future. I'm down on this piece of property. I'm at the mercy of forces over which I have no control.*

> *I felt secure, but not now. I don't know what will happen. I live in fear. What will come next? I'm a confused person.*

Exposed to unanticipated events beyond their control, Legler residents had lost their illusion of invulnerability. No longer could they claim "it won't happen to me." Not only had they failed to protect their families before, but there was little to suggest that they could be protective in the future.[63] The sense of immunity characteristic of our culture helps to explain the otherwise seemingly careless behavior of homeowners who either failed to seek out or else ignored clues that might have suggested future danger. Yet after a disaster, the immunity is gone. This point is elaborated by Martha Wolfenstein:

> It would seem for a disaster victim that the world has been transformed from the secure one in which he believed such things could not happen to one where catastrophe becomes the regular order. In his drastically altered view a catastrophic universe has come into being. His underlying feeling may be that the powers that rule the world have turned against him, have declared their intentions to get him, and, if he has escaped this time, they will try again.[64]

Another related outcome of victimization is the loss of a meaningful world.[65] People are likely to question why they were struck by undeserved disaster. Furthermore, victimization contradicts the "belief in a just world," whereby we believe that people get what they deserve. Although victims may feel that they did not do anything to deserve this unfair fate, they also may think that they were somehow to blame. Others may similarly blame them. In any case, victims feel that they are no longer in control of events which confront them. For some victims, one consequence of this uncertainty, insecurity, and vulnerability is a loss of the ability to plan. Thus Legler residents commented:

> *I've switched between being in control and fate. I feel that I make a few decisions but that circumstances control.*

> *Before, I had great expectations. I looked for better things. Now I'm afraid to make a move because I don't know how things will result.*

The sense of future among Legler residents now revolved around whether they intended to remain in the community despite the problem or would choose to leave if they had the resources. Those planning to relocate tended to think of reformulating their lifestyles through the move. They spoke of creating a simpler and better life for their families and of escaping government interference. As one resident commented,

> *I never want to have to depend on the state for happiness. We need self-sufficiency. We don't want police, taxes, and a disinterested government. I'll decide what I want to do with my own life. That's what I thought I had here.*

Some residents revealed little concept of the future at all, speaking of living in the short run because of the uncertainty involved in thinking too far ahead. In fact, if there was one projection uniting residents who planned to stay with those who wanted to leave, it was a recognition that wherever one goes, there is no escape from the worry associated with the past exposure to toxic chemicals. All share a changed lifescape regarding health. As a result, their image of the future is clouded, as bluntly indicated by one of my Love Canal informants.

> *If you stay here, you're going to die. And then they say that they don't know what you died from. 'Cause cancer looks like cancer. If anybody's lived here eight or ten years, they will develop cancer.*

Health psychologists confirm that the questioning of people's health status causes them to feel more vulnerable. This vulnerability is, in turn, a cause for worry and a loss of native optimism.[66] Another point of vulnerability involves a new distrust for the security of home, our fourth lifescape shift.

The Inversion of Home

The meaning of home as haven from a complex society is inverted by toxic exposure. The psychological importance of this lifescape shift can best be understood in light of the significance of home in American society. "Home" refers to more than a structure. It connotes a private place separate from the public that helps center our lives. It is a place for relating to intimates. Home serves as a basis for two key psychological factors—security and identity. The home permits us to separate and defend ourselves and our possessions from external threat. We further assume that the home itself will not harm us. As a result, we feel secure.[67]

Beyond providing us with a defensible boundary, home serves as the basis for anchoring our sense of self. Houses encode a variety of messages that may be seen as reflective of the owners or occupants in various ways, affecting both how we are viewed by others and how we view ourselves. Much as the facade serves to impress others, the interior of the house may come to express the self-concept of the occupants. The house is thus simultaneously supportive of self and revealing of its nature.[68]

Cultural identity is also expressed by the home. Although millions live in apartments and condos or settle in urban areas by choice, the dominant American Dream centers on the nuclear family in the context of ownership of a home surrounded by trees on an acre of land. Single-family houses express the American values of independence and individuality, managing social contact by fences rather than norms.[69] And when the home is separated from the workplace, the suburban home comes to further symbolize both the ability to differentiate private life from work life and to achieve distance from others, including the extended family. Furthermore, in the United States, the ownership of a house signifies a family's achievement of a desired developmental status, as well as what might be called the economic "creditability" necessary to obtain a mortgage loan. The status results from being found worthy of indebtedness. The result: "Not being a 'nation of shopkeepers,' America is one of homeowners, busily investing in plant maintenance and expansion with both money and time, keeping the product attractive for both use and sale." This focus on possible resale makes the homeowner a producer, not just a consumer. It follows, from this perspective, that as "small-scale traders," homeowners are on guard against any threats to the value of their property.[70] This vulnerability from factors that may adversely affect their investments influences people in a deep, rather than superficial, manner. Reinforcing concern with the economic exchange value of the home is the American propensity for mobility.[71] Contamination becomes a major constraint to mobility because of its inherent environmental stigma.

Not all Americans are mobile, however.[72] Some resist moving even in the face of hazards, making an apparent trade-off between the advantages of their living place and the recognized hazards.[73] Take as an example the rural Appalachian community where, several years ago, I traveled to study the effects of a contamination event. A nearby industry had paid a local landowner to dispose of its hazardous wastes on his property, which he did in open fires and by pushing barrels of chemicals off the hill into the hollow. Interviewing mostly entire kinship groups, I learned of the unique ecohistorical context. For many generations, these very kinship groups had lived in the same hollows. Beyond relying on the local environment for game and fish, community members exhibited a close identification with the land. The belief that the hollow was now contaminated and no longer a safe place to live meant that these historic bonds had to be rethought. Relocation meant separation from land and kin, and the graves of one's ancestors. But staying on did not assure that the old relationship to place would be maintained. Either way it was gone. This community is devastated whether it stays or leaves.[74] Thus, although forced relocation causes a grief response over the loss of home,[75] the inability to leave in the face of threat represents a further challenge.

Although the inversion of home is primarily a phenomenon for homeowners, there are many instances of renters being trapped in unwanted homes or apartments, fearing and disliking their homes due to the contamination, or being forced into undesired and costly mobility, perhaps to a less desired place. Therefore, one cannot assume that renters avoid significant impacts because they are not property owners.

The Meaning of Home in Legler

Residents in Legler were primarily young families with young children. People owned homes that were not "starter" homes but represented the achievement of residential ideals. The home was the central locus of their activity. For many, home was synonymous with recreation. For a working person, a typical evening might include gardening, house chores, playing with children, some socializing with neighbors, or collapsing before the television. For housewives in the daytime, the focus was on chores, children, and some socializing. On weekends, a substantial proportion of residents divided their time between housework and either visiting or hosting relatives or friends. For a few residents, weekends included attending church activities, visiting social clubs or the nearby beach, going camping, or engaging in hobbies or small-scale farming. Overall, Legler was seen as an ideal place to center one's home life.

The psychological significance to residents was suggested by their answers when asked what home meant to them. The surprising range of answers reflects a varied image of home within the Legler sample.[76] Thus for some Legler residents, home was a place where they were in control; here no one could tell them what to do. It was a place for independence.

> *You can go about your business in your own private way—you can have a dog, hang a picture.*

Residents also saw home as a place of security and permanence where they were not at the mercy of landlords. Some saw the home as a refuge, a place to relax, be themselves, and escape from the pressures of life.

Some residents thought of home as the orienting point for their scattered lives; it was the place they came back to. It was a place where they could feel "at home," a place that they could get used to and arrange in a way that felt comfortable. It was a place for enjoyment and socializing.

> *Our family is built around our home. We stay here when we have time; we don't take vacations; this is it. We have a pool. We stay home and enjoy what we have. We party here in our and our neighbors' backyards. We avoid a babysitter this way because we can go in and check on the kids.*

For some Legler residents, home was a place for solitude, tranquility, and seclusion. It was a repository of memories—of what they put into it and of their lives as a whole.

> *Home is my life—hard work, tragedy, heartache, happiness, love, and [picking up a picture of a dead child] tragedy; my life is my home—both the good and the bad memories.*

Home was a place for observing changes over time and for attaining a sense of achievement.

> *I enjoy seeing the plants grow, to see changes. It's like taming the wilderness. We've accomplished so much in ten years. There was nothing here when we moved in. We are proud that we did the work ourselves.*

Home was, for many residents, a place to personalize, for connection and expression.

> *I built this home, and I'm going to die in it. That's how much I love this home! I built a home, not a house. I built this home from the bottom of my heart; I built everything here. My heart and soul are in it.*

Home was a place for raising children and gathering family.

> *Home is a place to have togetherness within the family circle, a place to enjoy holidays with friends and family.*

At the same time, home offered the possibility for avoiding crowding.

> *It's nice to have the space so that the kids can each have their own room; we like having privacy.*

Finally, home connoted ownership, responsibility, and investment.

Accentuating their significance was the fact that many Legler homes were custom built. They were thus more likely to express the individual taste and desire of the owner than does the average house. Because people helped create their homes, they were likely to be "invested" in them. The tremendous importance of home in the matrix of people's activities is striking. A new home and an acre of land—these were the lucky Americans who had achieved the American Dream in Legler.

The Inversion of Home in Legler

Inversion of home negates the hopes, dreams, and expectations that surround the cultural institution of home. In Legler, a "home-centered" repertoire of activities was converted from a primary source of pleasure to a cause for dread.

One indication of the inversion of home was the expressed inability of most residents to recapture their ideal life in Legler. Reasons cited included distrust of the new water, fears of the landfill reopening, and belief that soils were also contaminated. This inability to regain normalcy involves more than fears about continued exposure. It also reflects something as subtle as a changed feeling about the place.

> *Just the experience that we had in the beginning, the emotion—it will never be erased. It will always hinder us being able to settle here and raise a family the way we want to. I know that this is my home, but I don't feel as comfortable as if this never happened. I want to feel the way I feel about my parents' home, the way they feel about their home. I wanted these type of feelings; I can't have them here.*

Home is no longer the secure place that it previously was for Legler residents. They were effectively trapped in their homes even as they saw them as places of danger. Suggested by this change in the meaning of home is its virtual inversion as a naive concept. The process of inversion of home appears to have two related foundations—psychological and financial.

Home as a Psychological Refuge.   Rather than a place to escape to, with contamination, home had become a place from which residents could not escape. Parents particularly feared the consequences of continued residence for themselves and their children. Thus home was inverted; it now was accompanied by a strong sense of fear and insecurity. Instead of buffering the family from the dangers of the outside world, home embodied these dangers. Lingering fears about possible alternative routes of exposure other than through groundwater suggested to some residents that they could no longer regain a sense of security there.

Inversion is also revealed in the way the home was used as an expression of identity. Personalization and even routine maintenance halted as people became reluctant to invest more time or money in homes that they saw as valueless. With the costs of the new water system, others could ill afford home improvements. Many appeared to lose their motivation for their homes; they were disinclined to do work that just a short time before had been a major focus of their lifestyle. For many, this loss of motivation continued even after the central water system was provided.

> *We went to Florida. We hoped the house would burn down while we were away. We had a lot of plans for the house when we moved in. But after the water situation, we didn't paint, landscape, carpet—we didn't do anything. There is no joy in this house at all. I hate the floors, the walls. But I'm not going to fix it up. We won't get our money out of it.*

There was a time when I stopped cleaning the house. What difference did it make? I couldn't invite anyone over. No one would want to come. I was ashamed and embarrassed. I'm usually very organized. But not then.

Of course, there were exceptions to this inattentiveness to home. One woman reported that during the period of water delivery she made compensatory efforts to have her house neat and clean and free of chemical odors.

I'm a Dutch girl. I kept working on the house all along. I kept washing and scrubbing to get the smell out. I tried to be extra clean.

With the provision of another water source, the Legler incident entered a new phase. On the surface, residents now had the opportunity to recreate their previous lifestyles. But could they regain their lost sense of security in their homes? Some two and a half years after the pollution incident began, about half the families in the sample indicated a desire to leave, although few had actually tried to move.

With the completion of the central water system, some residents expressed rekindled satisfaction with their homes and neighborhood. These tended to be more recent arrivals who viewed the pollution as a technological problem that was now fixed. They felt that few other places could offer them the same quality home at the same price. They looked forward to continued development in the area. They tended to be more comfortable with a central water system under government management than with private wells. And they shared the belief that pollution problems, already confronted in Legler, might occur elsewhere. For these residents, a return to a privatized lifestyle in Legler was eagerly sought.

Why should we move somewhere else? All towns are alike. We hope they learned a lesson here. We would only move if we were forced to. We worked too hard to get this house in the first place.

Although some residents were remotivated to work on their homes, many showed signs of ambivalence.

We accomplished everything but the yard, and I still plan to do that. I figure, if we're stuck with the place, we might as well give it our best shot.

This was our first house. No matter what, we do not want to lose it. We'll rectify the problems. We'll stay here.

I hate it here, but I'm making the best of it. I keep the house up so we'll be able to leave.

Some residents sought to stay less out of enthusiasm for Legler than out of a dread of encountering new horrors elsewhere.

We didn't consider moving. If we were looking for a place, we would not know where to go. The problem is everywhere. If it's not smog, then it's the water. No matter where you move, how do you know you're not moving into the same nightmare elsewhere?

Even the view that the water problem was fixed did not erase concerns.

If we moved, it would not eliminate the problem that we had. It would still not erase our worry about the kids. The water problem here is fixed. It's like the house had breast cancer; it was cut off, and now it's okay.

In contrast, residents frustrated in their desire to leave Legler tended to doubt that it would ever regain normalcy.

I would hope to get everyone out of here; make it into an industrial park. No one should live here.

Home as an Investment.   It was difficult for Legler residents to separate the pride they felt in their homes from issues of economic value. The concern reflected both the cultural significance of home and the feeling that residents had been misled when they invested in Legler. The landfill and the barren "2001" were a far cry from the promised parks and golf courses. Additionally, residents had been confronted with unexpected costs, including water hookup fees, water bills, and other expenses during the period of water delivery. They feared loss of their certificates of occupancy. The direct threat to the value of home as an investment was magnified by the situation of most of the residents, who had just made twin investments in homes and in beginning their families.

Although a few homes were sold during the incident, residents uniformly perceived a loss of property value and potential for sale. Several reported lost opportunities to sell their homes or recalled real estate agents advising them not even to try. One resident recollected, "If you tried to list, they'd laugh at you." Even as they faced difficulty selling their own homes, it became harder for Legler residents to relocate. Home costs elsewhere were soaring, mortgages difficult, and interest rates were substantially higher than those paid on Legler property. Virtually all the residents felt a sense of financial entrapment. Having invested everything they had in their homes, they had lost the option to capitalize on their investment but also the option to leave.

> *We want to move, but we haven't tried. The only place we could go is to an apartment, and my husband won't do that. We can't sell; we can't rent another house. So we have to stay here until everything is rectified.*

> *I turned down the job in LA partially because the realtor said I'd never get what my house was worth because of mortgage rates, and because the* Asbury Park Press *was running ads for real estate in Jackson that had "not Legler" across the top. This may be our last house; am I going to lose my butt on it?*

Beyond such stigmatizing advertisements, real estate agents often aggravated already high tension by reminding residents that it was community-generated publicity that had given Legler its bad name. This was truly a dilemma; without publicity, residents had no means of pressuring government for assistance.

Real estate stigma appears to have affected the entire township, as evidenced by demographic data for Jackson Township as a whole.[77] Jackson Township shared the generally fast growth rate experienced by Ocean County during the decade between 1970 and 1980, going from 4,804 households in 1970 to 6,514 in 1978. From 1977 to 1979, Jackson led Ocean County in its growth rate, but then the Jackson rate tapered off sharply. Similarly, records suggest a rapid growth in the number of Jackson subdivisions between 1975 and 1978, before a dramatic decline beginning in 1979. Although other factors may also have influenced this trend, Ocean County as a whole continued to grow at a time when Jackson Township, widely identified with a pollution problem, abruptly ceased its growth. It would appear that this discrepancy reflected environmental stigma.

The lawsuit filed by the Concerned Citizens Committee was seen by residents as a means of achieving a sense of finality to the period of disruption; affording an opportunity to move, even if houses did not bring full value. As with many toxic tort actions, legal claims over loss of enjoyment of one's home and of quality of life were largely based on the inversion of home.

The Legler case study shows how the inversion of home undermines normal feelings of residential security. Home is no longer a place of either psychological or financial refuge. The interaction of these two types of security represents a further dilemma. Although many Legler residents saw staying as being harmful to their family's health, to leave was to commit financial suicide. They were damned with either choice.

Generalizing to Other Settings.   The basic process of inversion of home appears to be a consistent outcome of toxic contamination,[78] but with some variations across communities.

At both Love Canal and Times Beach,[79] the first instances of government-sponsored relocation in the United States, some residents chose to remain behind. Presumably, they were able to retain or regain their sense of home. Some may have been too attached to the home to give it up. Others may have seen few other options for themselves and felt that they could make the best of it by staying in their homes. At Love Canal, families who remained tended to be nonbelievers in the scope and severity of the problem. Their privatized lifestyle allowed them to overlook the loss of community and the abandonment about them.

Relocation is also stressful. For example, the federal/state buyout at Times Beach involved complex bureaucratic procedures and delays that seemed inequitable and unfair. And the required property assessment was painfully judgmental, as this family's experience revealed: "They knew they would be talking about money, but what they felt was that ten years of work and effort would now be evaluated. To the company, the buyout offer was a measure of currency; to Art and Karen it was a measure of worth."[80]

Absent government or industry assistance, it has been most common to find victims trapped in their contaminated homes in the manner described to me by one of my Love Canal informants.

> *We can't afford to move out. We have everything invested in these homes. We are so swamped with medical bills! My son's allergist said last fall to get the kid out of the house. I'd like to, but I have no place to take him. If I get another house or rent an apartment, how am I going to keep that up and the house too?*

However, some families have swallowed their losses and abandoned their contaminated home. Some fifteen years ago I was given a child's drawing. In it, he gazed out his back window at bulldozers moving piles of waste around a landfill just a stone's throw from his house. When I saw his mother a few years later, she reported that the family had taken a total loss on their home in order to move their son away from danger. The only other time I encountered voluntary abandonment of property was in the neighborhoods nearby the Brio hazardous waste site south of Houston. However, there was an extenuating ecohistorical context here. In the mid-1980s, after the local oil-based economy went bust in Texas and Colorado, it was not uncommon for homeowners saddled with expensive and heavily financed homes to "walk" their mortgages. The Brio neighbors emulated this phenomenon.

Inversion of Community as an Extension of Home

Of course, the term "home" may well encompass more than the individual dwelling.[81] Home may also be synonymous with community, where the individual residence shares weight with the collective definition of place, built environment, collective identity, organization of amenities, social contacts, and physical support for a wide array of available activities.

Community inversion frequently accompanies contamination events. Following a two-week evacuation and a year-long cleanup studied by Steve Picou and Duane Gill, residents affected by the Louisiana train derailment and toxic release felt stress, fear, dissatisfaction with their quality of life, and vulnerability to future accidents. Now aware of the danger of living near railroad tracks, many sought to leave. Similarly, as described by Steve Kroll-Smith and Stephen Couch, the underground mine fire that ripped apart the formerly cohesive community of Centralia, Pennsylvania, proved not merely a threat to home but to the collective fabric of the community, as well. And Anastasia Shkylnik describes how both forced relocation and mercury contamination not only shattered a sense of community for the Grassy Narrows Ojibwa but severed their attachment to place.[82]

Of the classic contaminated communities, Times Beach appears to have been most cohesive. Facing evacuation, a resident observed, "We are a community without a community. We are lost in so many ways."[83] In order to deal with their loss, a group of residents planned a memorial service for Times Beach. Several hundred gathered on a bridge before the town. Reflecting the importance of religion in the community's cohesion, they threw flowers into the river and recited the following prayer:[84]

We Remember:
Building Our Houses
Raising Our Children
Running Our Businesses
Talking With Our Neighbors
Having Happy Birthdays
Going To School
Playing With Our Pets
Fishing In The River
Coming Home Over This Bridge

We Remember:
This Community

We Believe:
That Life Follows Death
That God's Son Was Born Among Us And Lives With Us Today
That As Jesus Was Raised From Death, Rise Daily To New Life In Him

We Hope:
To Remember Our Community
To Begin A New Life
To Remember Our Community
To Begin A New Life
To Walk With God

Inversion of Home as Livelihood. Home and livelihood impacts can also merge.[85] When a neighboring landfill contaminated groundwater beneath a nursery owned by an elderly couple, they were less concerned about their adjacent home than about their beloved plants. They had taken great pride in raising prized ornamentals, particularly azaleas and rhododendrons, without the use of pesticides. The plants not only represented their present and future means of support but were the focus of their daily activities, their relationship, and their friendships with others. While a new central water source served their home after the incident, unable to afford to water their plants from this metered source, they were forced to use polluted water. The resulting predicament was described by the husband:

> *Dilemma! If dry weather—water, will contaminate—will die. If not water, also will die. What to do? Very lousy feeling. When I see them wither away, I say "give them a shot." Then they die. It's a useless fight!*

The couple's own disappointment and disenchantment with the land in turn discouraged their customers. Stigma was reinforced by media coverage. As a result of these disclosures, their business declined; their social relationships were also affected. An inversion of livelihood, as well as home, had occurred.

An important rule of thumb for estimating the effects of contamination is that residential toxic exposure is likely to have the greatest impact where the various spheres of life (family, work, relationships, recreation) coincide with the home. *The greater the dependency on home*—for those working at home, housewives and househusbands, the retired, children, the homebound, and members of clustered extended families—*the greater the degree of stress due to a toxic incident*. These groups lack the opportunities for escape and ventilation available to others whose life spheres are more spatially diversified.

Inversion of Home: Conclusion.   Beyond the psychological and financial losses, the inversion of home signifies other lifescape changes. Home is the locus of health danger, exposure to a harmful environment, and loss of protective control. Confronted by a confusing and frightening challenge to the safety of their homes, it is not surprising that victims seek help from their friends and that citizens expect assistance from their government officials.

Loss of Social Trust

We have seen the global erosion in trust represented by contamination. No longer is one's health assumed. The ability to make decisions for one's self and family is thrown into doubt. Both home and environment are now feared. As these areas of personal and contextual trust collapse, victims' dependency on their social networks is magnified. Yet this final lifescape shift involves an additional betrayal of normalcy: a general loss of trust in others and in the polluter and in government specifically. There is a breakdown of any presumption that others, the polluter, the community, and particularly government officials, will restore justice and aid innocent toxic victims to make their lives once again whole.[86] In effect, in Steve Kroll-Smith's words, there is a loss of "civility" itself.[87]

The scope of these losses in trust is disconcerting. It is hardly surprising to see distrust of the polluter, but the failure of victims' social support networks is a fundamental disappointment. And the loss of the naive trust in government as helper is perhaps most notable of all, far exceeding what one would expect even given a trend toward government distrust in national polls.[88] Furthermore, this loss of trust shows a revealing gap between the experience of natural and toxic disasters. While the response of government frequently falls short of the expectations held by natural disaster victims,[89] with toxic exposure, official actions particularly exacerbate the victims' distress. *As a result, toxic victims are likely to be as adversely impacted by the social response to contamination as they are by the knowledge of the exposure itself.*

In this section I explore the concept of trust as it relates to environmentally stigmatizing situations, arguing that loss of trust is an inherent outcome of contamination. I then focus on some of the specific targets for distrust—local officials, politicians, and state and federal officials—drawing principally on examples from the Legler case study. I explore the situational roots of distrust inherent in toxic contamination episodes, indicating why victims are likely to be disappointed by the response of government officials. Finally, I review the differing expectations of the principal actors in a toxic incident.

Some Thoughts on Distrust

Distrust involves feelings of unacceptable vulnerability within a relationship. One becomes vulnerable in several ways—by disclosing information about oneself, by placing one's safety in the hands of another, and by allowing physical proximity to another. Such vulnerability is important to the development of a trusting relationship; with distrust, however, one seeks to limit vulnerability through reserve, keeping one's distance, and not placing one's safety in the other's hands. With distrust, openness is replaced by vigilance.

Trust is a dynamic situational attribute of the interpersonal social relationships between people (or people and institutions). As efforts to cope with contamination are made over time, the victims' trust in their social and institutional support systems is tested again and again. The person beset with a toxic threat "reads" the social environment and assigns various expectations to different actors. As trust and distrust grow and sometimes invert over the course of a relationship, situational attributes can become reified as dispositions. Disappointment becomes permanent distrust. And when one formerly relied upon this fallen relationship, such distrust is particularly bitter.

Distrust is an inherent consequence of contamination events.[90] As a human-caused phenomenon, contamination from hazardous materials forces victims to seek an explanation for what has occurred. As they ponder why the disaster was made to or allowed to happen, they question whether government, industry, or others had the ability either to cause or to prevent the exposure and whether they attempted or intended to do so. These questions make issues of trust and distrust central to the experience of a contamination event. Thus after the Times Beach disaster, 92 percent of the dioxin victims blamed both those responsible for improper disposal of the hazardous wastes and government agencies for their failure to regulate the waste disposal.[91]

Even as the occurrence of proven contamination alters relationships, the siting of potentially hazardous facilities also raises inherent questions of trust. Often there is outrage over one's community's selection to host a feared and undesireable facility. After all, it is hard to accept someone's rationale for deciding that your life can legally be disrupted and threatened. Siting is thus in itself a form of stigmatization involving a class bias or categorical distrust of people and place. That the community was chosen indicates it was viewed with a stigma and its selection, in turn, devalues and marks the community further. Environmental stigma can thus be seen as both a direct cause and consequence of social distrust. A stigmatized environment is a distrusted environment.

Invariably, contamination is understood by those who share the experience and ill understood by others. As a result, this process of trusting and distrusting can be viewed as forming a mutually unsupportive dialectical relationship between "insiders" and "outsiders." Their lack of understanding makes it easy for those outside the situation to violate trust simply because they don't know how to respond to contamination victims, and they tend to disconfirm and reject victims' perceptions and experience. Outsiders' normal mind-set is so different from the new "contaminated mind-set" held by victims that relationships are easily disrupted. There is a significant difference in perspectives. Outsiders don't understand why the victims have changed from their prior normal perspective and are now needy in a new and baffling way.

Even intimate outsiders misjudge the situation and stigmatize victims, blaming them, viewing them as devalued or tainted by their exposure. These outsiders may also discount, rationalize, or deny outright the exposure itself or the ramifications of the exposure and the exposure event. These separate realities invite a gulf of distrust between victims and their former social support systems. Victims become cynical, in part, as the stigma causes them to become disassociated from the assumptions of the larger community, feeding their tendency to be more critical and, as a result, less trusting. We can see how these dynamics of distrust played out in Legler.

Distrust in Legler

Legler residents lost trust in others generally and developed a specific disenchantment with government.

The General Loss of Trust.   General social distrust was evident in my Legler interviews.

> *I view others differently now. I'm suspicious of their motivation. I expect them just to seek personal gain. Before, I used to worry about what others think. I don't consider it anymore because nobody does anything for you unless there's something in return.*

> *I was very naive; I trusted everybody when we bought our house. Now I can't trust anybody—which is terrible, but I've become very cautious and cynical.*

Trust and Stigma.   As with any incident that has negative ramifications for an entire community, Legler residents faced a hostile and unsympathetic reaction from some of their fellow residents of Jackson Township. The issues of responsibility and cost were subjects of controversy, conflict, and blame. As they became isolated and were seen as contaminated and troublemaking "others" rather than neighbors in a bad predicament who needed help, environmental stigma became a major factor in their evolving feelings of distrust.

> *We were the scapegoat for all their money problems because of the cost of delivering water. They gave no support; they looked at us as lepers who caused stigma and publicity. The township committee put us down as publicity hungry.*

> *When they closed the landfill, people dumped their garbage on our front lawn. A lady chased me down the street with a broom.*

> *At the award ceremony at the high school, the principal spoke about the need for a positive public image for the town. This was directed at Legler. I wonder what they say at Jaycee meetings? It's as though we are blamed for the situation and don't deserve a remedy!*

> *When a park on the other side of town used fill from the landfill, parents wouldn't let their kids play there. And yet they boo Legler people when we complain at meetings. They give us hell. There have been cops there to stop fistfights. We can drink it, but they can't play in it!*

Jackson Township even appointed a committee to undo the stigma that had arrested the town's growth, as described in a local newspaper editorial.[92]

> This new group may not be able to completely wipe out the media's negative depiction of our town, but maybe they'll be able to finally put to rest the north Jersey impression that every damned one of our 6,500 households in our 100 square miles has a water problem.

Stigmatized, disillusioned, and distrustful, many Legler residents adopted a vigilant mode of decisionmaking based on caution and deliberation.

> *We do more investigation. We don't believe what we hear; we don't trust too many people. When we go to buy something, we think twice.*

Loss of Trust in Government.   The general level of distrust found in Legler was overshadowed by victims' loss of trust in government. Jackson Township was viewed both as the polluter and the expected agency of remediation. It was first in line for blame.

If my children get sick, I'm going to hold each individual on the township board responsible for it. I have this fermenting, boiling emotion.

The lawsuit against Jackson expressed this blaming. Residents felt that they had been wronged. Their lawsuit was a means of rectifying this moral injustice.

I want justice—revenge! This was criminal negligence. Watergate has nothing on Jackson.

Furthermore, Jackson Township officials were seen as decidedly unhelpful during the Legler water crisis. The fact that the township was the polluter as well as the source of government assistance had political, legal, and financial ramifications. Their difficulty in accepting responsibility for the situation appears to have affected how officials responded to residents.

They didn't believe that the water was polluted even when their own staff said it. They believed that the state had gone wild. They couldn't believe they caused the pollution.

Although newer residents were particularly angry that the township issued certificates of occupancy permitting the builders to sell them houses, all residents were angered by the township's unsympathetic response.

The township board totally humiliated us. For example, one time when I had waited a long time to speak, a board member remarked to me as I took the floor, "Isn't it past your bedtime, little girl?"

When we appealed for help, they badgered us and made us into the bad guys. It was like dropping a bomb on us and then making us feel responsible. They even swore at me.

Local government was generally viewed as complicating the victims' attempts to cope with their disturbing situation. As a source of information during the crisis, government officials were seen as evasive, saying only what was expedient, and distorting information that they grudgingly shared. Moreover, the township was viewed as having violated its own promises in the way it responded to the situation. Although local officials may have been sincere in their early estimation of their ability to deal with the problem, the fact that they were wrong in these estimates led to questioning of their sincerity as well.

We trusted the town to be adult and to take care of the problem. The mayor promised that it would be fixed in six weeks: "By the time you empty the first barrel of water, the problem will be taken care of."

Residents were also angry at the way the township responded to their attempts to organize and work on their problems. Some residents charged that the township used threats to try to quiet residents. One active Legler resident was allegedly fired from a township job. Officials were accused of deliberately trying to cause tension within the ranks of the community group.

Much as did residents of Love Canal and Times Beach,[93] Legler residents spoke about how astonished they were that their status as taxpayers meant so little. Many felt that the township sought to avoid the problem or even deliberately covered it up. Board members were suspected of playing down the problems before election time. Legler residents voiced a virtually unanimous belief that local government cannot be trusted. Some reported that they would no longer vote. Some of the most bitter disappointment was voiced by young people.

It makes you wonder when grown people in authority do this; it makes you wonder where it's all going to.

Immigrants who had adopted this country were also upset.

My husband was a superpatriot. Now he refuses to vote.

State agencies were seen as comparatively more sympathetic than were local officials.[94] However, Legler residents were also disappointed by their response.

At an early meeting we saw different agencies bickering over who was responsible. It was scary. There was rhetoric, but no action. It was frustrating. The people believed that the water was bad, they were hypochondriacs. And there was no one to ease their minds. The government was waiting for a dead body which could be proven to have been caused by the chemicals. One agency after another said we had to prove this. Tests were done, but no one ever came back to warn us about the findings. No one had a sense of responsibility.

Meanwhile, Legler residents found state politicians to be exploitative, to the extent that they paid any attention at all. Governor Byrne was probably the most disliked for making an appearance to cut a ribbon at Great Adventure amusement park, a few miles away, while ignoring Legler's plight.

This resident's comment sums up the perception of government in Legler after the contamination incident:

> *I've lost my belief in government. I always thought that in order to say things in public, they had to be true. Now I realize that government exists to pacify people.*

Although details differ, similar disillusionment and loss of trust for government are a universal characteristic of contaminated communities. How do we explain this loss of trust?

The Situation Invites a Loss of Trust

Distrust is in large part the result of a negative dialectic between citizen and government officials (see Chapter 5). Based on his experience working for the Missouri Department of Health at various dioxin sites, Robert Miller identified three key situational characteristics that contribute to this dialectic: the role of government in discovering the problem, the inherent uncertainties, and the pervasiveness of exposure.[95]

Discovery as the Starting Point.   Because of their part in the discovery of localized environmental disasters, health and environmental officials play a special role in defining that a threat exists. As a result, residents are drawn into encounters with government agencies at every turn in their attempts to deal with the crisis. For officials, Miller observed, "It means actions which are usually viewed as exclusively technical matters are transformed into public issues which come to be an object of observation, criticism, and intervention."[96]

Under public scrutiny, government decisions are no longer cut-and-dried. For example, at Love Canal, understanding of official response was hampered by residents' unfamiliarity with regulatory procedures and guidelines. While for citizens the distinction between a health "emergency" and a "disaster" had little meaning, for officials it defined their role by determining the allowed response.[97] Also, an agency's role in discovering the exposure places it center stage in the process of clarifying the threat. It is no wonder that officials sometimes are afraid to release news of their discovery due to a "fear of alarming people."

Uncertainty and Localized Environmental Disaster.   Local environmental disasters are inherently fraught with uncertainty. The pollution is not easily identified nor are its characteristics easily described. There is likely to be no reliable basis for estimating the consequences of exposure over the long run. Miller cited an EPA statement that embodied this uncertainty: "Dioxin in Missouri may present one of the greatest environmental problems in the history of the United States. Conversely, it may not."[98]

Miller further notes that uncertain conditions, such as unexplained illness, serve as a "risk enhancement" for the public; reasonable conclusions of danger are drawn from misleading data. When officials term this reaction panic and hysteria, residents dismiss them for deliberately playing down the severity of the problem. Russell Stone and Adeline Levine similarly observe that officials' tendency to allay fear rather than share uncertainty, given the lack of public participation in decisions, creates a pattern likely to engender distrust.[99]

Miller suggests that the problem for officials is not so much the uncertainty per se, but rather the need to make an assessment that can serve as a basis for a response. For example, defining who in Missouri was highly exposed to dioxin resulted in a range of psychological and financial consequences that exacerbated the stress otherwise inherent in the situation. Similarly, Barr, a physician, described the pressures on medical experts to clarify fears aroused by numerous incidents involving exposure to polyhalogenated biphenyls (such as PCB and PBB), even though little was then known about their health implications.

> In the face of all this ignorance, we are nonetheless asked by mothers whether or not they should breast-feed their babies. There is no simple answer to this question. It is an area in which passions may prevail over admittedly weak science. Over and above questions of toxicity, consideration must be given to the adverse effects of anxiety about breast milk contamination on the mother-infant pair. Denying that a problem may exist can, in many cases, lead to increased anxiety. Reassurance should help reduce anxiety, but how can one say "I don't know" and sound reassuring?[100]

David Harris, a county health commissioner in New York State, was considerably less sympathetic in his explanation for why the public has no tolerance for ambiguity.

> Used to neatly packaged television dramas like *Quincy*, where all loose ends are tied and all answers are in before the final commercial, the public finds it hard to accept incomplete knowledge and ambiguity. Far easier to believe some newspaper columnist or community leader who offers certainty than a cautious health official who tries to explain precisely what is or is not known. To a frightened and impatient public, health officials' punctilious concern about the thinness of scientific evidence and their disinclination to draw conclusions from

insufficient data are easily mistaken for lack of resolve or abdication of the responsibility to act.[101]

The inherent uncertainty of toxic exposure situations thus has implications for both the government official and the toxic victim. In some cases, the official's role is rather like that of solving a very intricate puzzle. This was seen, for example, in the complex detective work necessary to trace the Michigan PCBs back through the food chain to the industrial accident that released them.[102] Although the official may wish to tackle the puzzle sequentially, victims press for early clarity and action. The regulatory response is often described as careful science, but, as Reich notes, there is another interpretation of it. "The definition of a problem tends to become frozen in the position of a bureaucratic agency, and thereby to resist change." The routines established by agencies to deal with uncertainty divert them from anticipating problems. As a result, they must continually react to situations that demand their response.[103] A further complication is that numerous agencies may become involved, each with its own experience and expectations.[104]

As a result, having discovered and disclosed the threat, government is unable to provide much further clarification. This affects all residents of a contaminated community, even those engaging in denial. Thus at Love Canal, Fowlkes and Miller found that "ironically, whether residents were disposed to remain or anxious to leave, they received no confirmation or reassurance about the hazard or safety of the situation."[105]

Miller writes that to avoid distrust, officials must learn to communicate about complex and uncertain issues in an understandable and timely fashion, share their constraints, and seek to understand residents' needs. Residents in turn must learn to comprehend and interpret such information in a way that allows them to make decisions, to effectively organize, and to learn what government can and cannot do for them.[106]

The Pervasiveness of Localized Environmental Disaster. Catastrophic technological or natural disasters tend to follow an observable pattern, appearing via a single route and then disappearing. With localized environmental disasters, in contrast, the contaminant appears in an "occult fashion." By the time of discovery, residents are threatened through multiple routes of exposure. Soil, air, drinking water, dust, and moisture seeping through basement walls may all carry the pollutant. In the Missouri dioxin cases, residents were hard-pressed to avoid exposure because of pervasive contamination. Officials faced a hopeless task in separating people from contamination because the pollution was literally everywhere. Even after relocation, some Times Beach residents feared that their furniture had absorbed dioxin and thus posed a continued hazard of exposure for their families.[107] Such fears were corroborated when I walked out on the bleak landscape of Love Canal during the workers' lunch break during the laying of the clay cap in 1979. My guides took me to one of the abandoned houses that lined the canal, describing how tests of the wood from the owner's piano had showed uptake of toxic chemicals. Even the music had been contaminated.

Toxic disaster is a challenge for both regulator and victim. At Love Canal, there was a recognition by many residents that official response was hampered by the newness of this type of disaster and the corresponding lack of organizational experience in dealing with it. And although toxic incidents have their honeymoon period, it ends when officials fail to produce clear solutions (as they seem inevitably to do) and a collision course is set. The elements of distrust are inherent in the situation; the dynamics of localized environmental disaster result in controversy that is invariably polarizing.

Responsibility for Toxic Exposure

Another key source of distrust in toxic incidents involves confusion over the assignment of responsibility. Such attributions allow the victim to understand why exposure has occurred and who is at fault. Even more important for their attempts to gain control over the situation is the identification of responsibility for remedying the situation.[108] Government officials are routinely blamed on both accounts. First, they are blamed for failing to prevent the contamination and toxic exposure to begin with and therefore for failing to protect the affected public. They are further blamed for delays in discovering the contamination and for the way it is announced. And they are blamed for subsequently failing to rectify the pollution adequately, for secondary problems, and for failing to restore the victims' lives, homes, and place to a level of quality and security previously enjoyed and expected.

It's the Victim's Responsibility. Citizens' anger and distrust is particularly aroused because they "get stuck" with the problem. A "dumping" of responsibility results from several factors. First, government action often is statutorily limited, as when pollution is termed the problem of the owner because a well is private property. Residents confront a contradiction involved in the failure to protect aquifers—underground water sources—as a common resource when reservoirs—aboveground water sources—receive government protection.

Government may also lack the interest, expertise, and resources to act. As a result, citizens may have to bear the burden of proof that instances of poor health are caused by an environmental source, a difficult burden to meet under the best of circumstances. And "citizens attorney general" acting under the "citizens suit" provisions of such laws as the Clean Water Act have an enormous burden. My own experience intervening in administrative hearings and bringing citizen suits through the nonprofit environmental organization I lead removes any illusions to the contrary. The human, financial, and organizational costs, and need for technical expertise, place these avenues for meeting the burden of proof outside the reach of any but the most resourceful and dedicated actors.[109]

Another situation that shifts the burden to the citizen is the reality of "cumulative sources." For example, in the early 1980s, when I visited with the few remaining residents in the Relocated Bayway section of Elizabeth, New Jersey, there were so many potential air polluters nearby that it was impossible to prove that any one party was responsible for the unbreathable air and equally difficult to think about solutions. As a result, no one can be forced to remedy the situation.

Victims are also left with the burden of watch-dogging government and consultants to ensure that their work is accurate and thorough. Although Superfund was intended to allow government to act independently on contaminated sites, in fact, the paucity of funding and the complexity of governmental involvement has meant massive delay and the reliance on potentially responsible parties (PRPs) to conduct studies and develop remedies. This pattern raises what should be obvious issues of vested interests where consultants paid by the PRPs do the key work with minimal independent oversight, quality control, and corroborative information. The process commonly fails to provide affected residents with a trusted measure of exposure, any consequences, and the best protective actions.

My own experience illustrates the problem. Because Orange Environment, Inc., had spent more than $100,000 on hydrogeological research in a citizens suit over the Orange County landfill, we were in the position to discover a systematic pattern of serious error in the work of the consultant preparing the remedial investigation for the county. It appeared that the consultant had colluded with the county to overlook crucial information. When we presented state officials with a complete reanalysis of the county consultant's work, they admitted that we were right but excused the errors as an artifact of how Superfund contracts are bid. Thus, they argued, the consultants had underbid the job in order to win the contract. Having won it, however, they lacked adequate resources to do the remedial investigation studies properly. And, having fewer resources yet, the Department of Environmental Conservation had relied on the consultant's data. In explaining that the consultants were not in collusion with the county, however, the DEC staff admitted to a different kind of collusion—between themselves and the consultant—a collusion that guaranteed poor practice. These errors would never have come to light had not Orange Environment's experts been better prepared to understand the movement of contaminants beneath the site than were the consultants developing the remedial action plan.[110] Because such informed independent expertise is rarely available to citizens, the adequacy of data and interpretation in Superfund practice is not generally so scrutinized.

Finally, citizens may even bear the burden of defining the scope of both a problem and the response. Toxic incidents often begin as a private problem to later be more broadly generalized. For example, the Michigan PBB herd poisoning was initially found in a single farmer's cattle. For an entire year, he sought an explanation for his herd's illness only to be told by government agencies that they could not study a problem experienced only by one isolated farmer. The farmer's persistence eventually helped identify a pattern of contamination that had affected hundreds of farmers and thousands of consumers. Yet Michigan officials still left to farmers the responsibility for dealing with the PBB problem, as described by Michael Reich.[111]

> But state officials decided not to condemn any animals and not to order disposal, because they did not want to open the possibility for farmers to file suit against the state or for the state to be held financially responsible. The state thus quarantined farms and monitored the disposal operation, while the farmers and the companies decided on their own whether to destroy the animals. Farmers, in turn, felt enormous pressure to dispose of their animals.

Farmers could depend on neither the polluter nor government to help them. They were left either to privately absorb the costs or to organize to force solutions. Protests resulting from the Michigan PBB case culminated in a march by farmers to the steps of their state capitol, where the carcasses of contaminated cows were dumped.[112] Although organizing enabled farmers to force a remedy, being forced to solve problems that they did not create was a bitter experience.

It's the Polluter's Responsibility.   An "ideal" solution to existing toxic contamination would hold the polluter responsible for cleanup and compensation. Most federal and state approaches are based on compliance and enforcement models for achieving precisely this outcome.

However, in practice, the model of polluter responsibility has been fraught with problems. Where a polluter is identified, available laws may not provide an adequate basis for prosecution. Polluters may seek protection in bankruptcy or in legal delays. Evidence linking the polluter to the incident may be inadequate.[113] Government efforts may be dominated by "making a case" against the perpetrator to the detraction of cleaning up the pollution. Government agencies often negotiate "orders on consent" with the polluter, settling the case without full remedy from the victims' perspective. Time delays are frequent. And the Superfund model, although attempting to place solutions ahead of blame, has failed to expedite timely remedies to contamination.

Regardless of whether polluters escape prosecution, it is ironic that the polluter often receives less than its share of victims' blame. Anger may be mollified where the polluter is a major source of local employment. At Love Canal, for example, Hooker Chemical was able to keep a remarkably low profile during the disaster in part because local residents were adapted to and dependent on the chemical industry.[114] Hooker's efforts to minimize public health concern were not vilified even though similar efforts by the state health department to allay panic met with public anger. Beverly Paigen offered this explanation.

> The community made some allowance for Hooker because the chemicals were
> buried many years before the chronic toxicity of chemicals was understood and
> before regulations concerning disposal of toxic waste existed. Hooker Chemical
> claimed that it had used state-of-the-art technology in burying the waste and
> that furthermore they had warned the Board of Education not to build a school
> on the site. The community also understood that the goal of industry is profit
> and that Hooker was acting accordingly by using the cheapest method of dis
> posal.[115]

In short, the state was responsible for acting for the community's welfare; Hooker was not. The state was supposed to have expert knowledge about the risks from Hooker's chemicals that Hooker was not expected to have. The state should have foreseen problems from the Love Canal disposal that Hooker was excused for causing. The state should have regulated Hooker when the company failed to regulate itself. In the absence of regulation, Hooker was not at fault. Although the school board was irresponsible in allowing development of the area, Hooker comparatively escaped such judgments by the residents.

The case of Dow Chemical Company in Midland, Michigan, sheds further light on how corporations get away with such acts of "elite deviance."[116] Dow was the principal employer in the town. Keeping a high profile, it further established a reputation as a good citizen so that its deviance was overlooked.[117] When widespread dioxin contamination was discovered, Dow actively managed public perception of its responsibility. The corporation stressed the minuteness of the quantity of dioxin found, presented its viewpoint in a brochure called *The Truth About Dioxin*, involved its executives in a public relations campaign, and generally maintained that "Midland is a better, healthier place to live because of the corporation." Citing state studies that found no proof of health problems, the city and many residents firmly backed the corporation, overlooking evidence suggesting that Dow had lied previously about dioxin and had secretly edited a key Environmental Protection Agency report.

Rushton, Washington, grew up around the American Smelting and Refining Company (Asarco) copper smelter, and the identity of the community was symbolized by the tall smelter stack. Many local residents had worked for the plant, and it was integral to their pride of place. Others had long sought to curb stack and fugitive emissions from the plant and even close it down. There was a true schism in Rushton. After the entire community was included inside the Asarco Superfund site, people evaluated the risk according to their historic connection to the plant. Nevertheless, nearly all blamed government for the problems associated with the protracted cleanup activities. Not only did Asarco receive comparatively less criticism, but they successfully involved the community in a forum on the future of the community and waterfront through redevelopment of the remediated smelter site into a new residential and commercial neighborhood. While residents had mixed reviews of the permanent storage of hazardous materials and the upscale development proposal, all mourned the subsequent demolition of the Asarco stack.[118]

It's the Government's Responsibility.   Does government deserve to receive more blame than corporate polluters? We have already seen, given uncertainty, how easily government fails to exhibit the first requisite of trust, the technical competence and expertise to make correct decisions. Government frequently fails a second basis for confidence, as well, committing what William Freudenburg terms "recreancy." Recreancy involves violations of public trust, as when public servants fail their fiduciary responsibility or moral obligation to act on the public's behalf.[119] As we have seen, even when government is not blamed for causing the contamination or sponsoring a hazardous project, it is frequently blamed for inadequate prevention, oversight, and response.[120] The belief that government will not fulfill its duties is a principal basis for opposition to proposed facilities. Recreancy not only adds to distrust but explains how distrust is itself a cause of stigma.[121]

A third principal source of distrust might best be termed *dynamic distrust.* When the contaminated community's residents realize that they can not depend on government to solve their problems, they are spurred to collective action aimed at forcing a solution (see Chapters 5–6). When they confront angry citizens, government officials who expect that citizens will be passive and respectful quickly find otherwise. As a result, distrust emerges from the varied attributions made and expectations held by different parties at different points in a toxic disaster. Miscommunication and mistrust ensue because the parties have increasingly divergent views.

Loss of Trust: Some Final Thoughts

Central to the loss of trust with contamination are the myriad ways it causes promises to be broken and expectations to be violated.[122] Industry operates on an implicit—and sometimes explicit—promise that its activities will not harm the public. Government is charged with enforcing environmental laws and regulations and protecting broad civil rights. It is expected that, when in need, government will come to the rescue. Such promises are often formalized in permits that set forth the conditions for operating a facility. The public is asked to trust the operator/regulator relationship to establish a level of safe operation for the facility. When such promises are broken, it is difficult to reestablish faith. Promises associated with the safety of the site over time (e.g., "it will be safe," "it won't leak," "it will be carefully monitored," etc.) require believability that has as its requisite trust of those making the promises. Such promises may be rejected if they are seen as implausible or unrealistic, if they are contradicted by beliefs or information, or if the character of those making the promises has been impugned. Once a facility is sited, its performance represents an ongoing test of such promises.

Conclusion: The Lifescape Impacts of Toxic Exposure

The loss of trust, the inversion of home, a changed perception of one's control over the present and future, a different assessment of the environment, and a decided tendency to hold pessimistic health expectations are all indications of a fundamentally altered lifescape. Such changes do not just occur out of the blue. They result from a process of coping whereby the individual, family, institutions, and community attempt to deal with the newly accepted realities of toxic exposure. Next we will examine the dynamics of coping with contamination.

4

Individual and Family Impacts

Because toxic contamination represents a revolutionary change in lifestyle and lifescape, it is inherently stressful. The challenge for its victims, therefore, is to find a way to cope with unexpected and novel turbulent conditions. This chapter examines individuals, their families, and the social relations and networks that normally support people during life crises. For individuals, the focus will be the elements of personal growth and psychological damage associated with exposure, and for families, the pressures that pull some families together while forcing others apart. Effects on children will also be explored. Finally, the isolation of toxic victims from their customary support relationships and the development of new sources of support in the affected neighborhood will be analyzed.

Coping with Exposure: Individuals

Contamination events are highly disruptive for almost everyone involved. Although those believing in the occurrence of toxic exposures face the most stressors, even doubters confront numerous challenges from the social response to the incident. What are the common psychological consequences for these victims?

In Legler, Margaret Gibbs carried out a companion study to mine, using quantitative clinical measures in order to independently confirm my qualitative data.[1] In her sample of the Legler community, 96 percent of the respondents reported emotional reactions due to the incident. Beyond health worries, they reported (in declining order of mention) feelings of disturbance, anger, depression, family quarrels, mistrust of others, financial worries, feelings of being trapped or helpless, divorce or separation due to the crisis, nervous breakdown, and interpersonal aggression (such as a child assaulted at school) linked with the crisis. Roughly parallel findings are reported for Love Canal and other sites.[2] All together, these findings suggest that beyond coping with primary stressful life events, toxic victims also must deal with the secondary effects of their stress.

Robert Gatchel and Benjamin Newberry compared residents living along the mirex-contaminated Middle Fork of Little Beaver Creek (MFLBC) with two control areas more than five miles from any known toxic waste site. MFLBC residents evidenced significantly greater stress, worry about pollution and health effects, diminished proofreading ability, higher resting diastolic blood pressure, and high scores on a symptom checklist (the SCL-90R) for somatization and hostility. Results confirm the inherent stresses found in this situation.[4] Unless they relocate, victims are forced to cope with the uncertainty and fear associated with living next to a toxic site. As a result, they suffer from chronic stress. Additionally, human-caused disaster has proven to be more stressful than natural disaster and its effects are much more persistent.[3]

Coping with Exposure

How do toxic victims attempt to gain some measure of control over their stress? As in the case of any stressful event, some people are likely to cope by confronting the problem in an attempt to master it. Others will engage in denial, changing the way they think about the problem; feelings of stress are reduced, but the problem is unaffected.[5]

For example, more than half of some 100 new mothers tested in the 1970s for the chemical PPB in their breast milk had conflicting feelings about whether to breast-feed, and half felt guilt over endangering their children. Only about one-third of the group attempted to master the situation by changing their behaviors in order to reduce their infants' exposure to the PPB. Their responses included actively searching for alternatives, altering diet, changing grocery stores, reducing the frequency of nursing, switching to bottle-feeding, moving away, and consulting experts about what to do. The remainder engaged in denial, as indicated by a lack of protective actions, forgetfulness about their levels of exposure, and inability to articulate their feelings. Mothers with the highest levels were found to engage in the most extensive denial.[6]

Toxic victims confront a situation characterized by extreme ambiguity and capable of being construed in varied and contradictory ways. Possibly the most perceptive analysis of the effects of this uncertainty on whether a toxic victim adopts mastery or denial was this comment by a Legler activist:

> This was a crisis situation with no specified reaction. There was no grief ritual. You don't know what to do. There are divergent emotions and reactions

needed to cope. People prefer that this didn't happen. They can't see water pollution; they don't feel bad. They believe it, yet they can't cope, so they rationalize it. Even I have a point where I say "enough, I can't believe any more." When the [neighbor's] child died, I reached my breaking point. I couldn't believe that he died from the water because I couldn't live here with the kids if I believed this. Other people shut off at the beginning. One person got an ulcer, and the next didn't believe that there was anything wrong. My one neighbor was happy with her coffee klatch water club because it gave her something to do. We didn't know what we were supposed to be doing! Are we paranoid, hypocritical crazies? Other times, I didn't take it seriously enough. Then I called Michael Brown [author of Laying Waste*] and talked to him. He made me into a "basket case."*

Given their participation in the community group, my Legler respondents were not ideally suited for studying denial. Some engaged in palliative behaviors, as with the "burned-out" activist who so excessively watched television as an escape that he became dysfunctional. Overall, Legler residents participating in the lawsuit tended to employ strategies for active coping.

Communication Strategies.   Legler residents learned to use subtle communication strategies for managing stress. They would adeptly change the subject to deliver themselves from endless conversations about the groundwater pollution. They would avert being kidded about their problems by initiating a joke about the situation. Thus one couple told their friends,

> *You can go to Mexico or you can come to our house—but whichever, don't drink the water.*

Social Escapes.   Social activities served as an escape from problems and a means of relaxation. Although much normal social activity was interrupted by the crisis, residents of one neighborhood continued to party on a nightly basis. Other residents realized that they needed to escape periodically from Legler. One couple joined two clubs and went dancing every weekend. Another would call up a babysitter and take off. Another couple joined a camper club to get away.

> *We met sympathetic people who didn't know us well enough to kid us—this gave us a lift. There is something about camping. You can be only twenty miles away and be in a different world. We could run the water in the camper.*

Some people learned to escape at home.

I'd take a day to rest. If bills were due, I'd put them off. I'd watch TV, read, go for a ride, visit my mother—I'd stop thinking about it, relax, and try to work things out.

The Helper Role.   Still another active coping technique involved escaping into the situation. Some people took on the role of helper, coming to grips with their own situation by assisting others in dealing with the crisis. Although activism increased the helpers' own burdens in many respects, it allowed them to step outside the role of victim for a while. It was also a means of learning and discovering things that were useful. Helpers rationalized that by using their experience to teach other communities how to avoid similar problems, their suffering was not in vain. In this way, a negative experience was reconstructed in a more positive light, inspiring the fortitude expressed to me by a woman at Love Canal:

We did not ask for Love Canal. It came into our homes, our yards, our vegetables, and it's a principle now because we want to fight for everybody in this country.

Keeping a Positive Attitude.   As the last technique illustrates, cognitive adjustments were also made in the interest of coping. Some people sought consciously to put problems into their proper perspective and to attend to their immediate lives. As one person commented,

I'll keep on planning what I want to do. If a problem comes, I'll deal with it when I can. I'm not going to sit around and worry about day-to-day life. It's always in the back of my mind, but I don't think about the water problem when I have to change a diaper.

A related cognitive adjustment was the acceptance that circumstances were beyond the person's control.

My sister asked what we'd do if one of our kids got a kidney problem. I pray there is no problem, but I can't do anything else. Sitting and worrying won't help.

Outcomes: Positive and Negative

The stress resulting from toxic exposure is a powerful but double-edged force for personal change. On one hand, new experiences encourage new competencies. On the other hand, even in the face of positive growth, coping with the stress from exposure may cause serious and long-term psychological damage.

Exposure as a Growth Experience

Positive growth can result from the effective and assertive coping engaged in by activists.[7] Mastery of the exposure situation requires innovation outside the normal repertoire of behavior and the normal boundaries of thought. Unlike the tried-and-true ways for maintaining the status quo, the toxic activist adopts an assertive approach to coping that involves making new relationships and finding innovative solutions.[8] Their "de facto environmental education" challenges toxic victims with opportunities for learning and growth, albeit often it is "learning the hard way." Improved competence and confidence are simultaneously the prerequisites and benefits of such coping.

Despite their generally negative experience, many Legler residents revealed impressive personal growth. A good percentage learned to assertively fight for their interests. The leaders of the Concerned Citizens Committee were particularly effective in guiding the community's coping response. For the leaders and involved members, activism may not have been part of their prior normal lives, but now it was essential for effective coping.

> *It was an education. I never knew you could get active in anything. I became outspoken; I was a fighter!*

> *You have to keep fighting and trying. I can never again let someone else do the work for me.*

Along with a shift to mastery came opportunities to gain personal confidence. As people investigated their predicament, they frequently found themselves in novel situations. Responding to the township committee at a public meeting, for example, they might find that despite a prior fear of public speaking, they now could articulately explain their views. Television cameras presented another testing ground. Many residents who faced them came away from such opportunities with a strong sense of self-confidence. Furthermore, finding themselves in a situation of being forced to express themselves, residents learned that it was legitimate for them to show their anger. Expressing their feelings was now an acceptable alternative to hiding them.

A toxic exposure incident provides a course in the dynamics of modern politics and bureaucracy. In Legler, as people observed the response of the government that they had always trusted, they experienced a loss of naïveté and a dose of cynicism. The result was a less gullible community capable of critically examining future situations. Residents reasoned that, if they could pull through the toxic disaster, they could survive almost any crisis.

> *It was hard for me to think under pressure. I felt the responsibility of having my first home, my first child, a new situation, and a new area. I had all of this dumped on me at one time. Now when things come up, it's nothing!*

The most prominent role model for personal growth in the face of toxic adversity is Lois Marie Gibbs, president of the Center for Health, Environment, and Justice. Her transition from housewife to the savvy leader of the Love Canal Homeowners Association has been chronicled in a television movie and in her autobiography.[9] As the national symbol of toxic victim turned dragon slayer, Gibbs is not in a class by herself. Rather, many thousands of Americans and others abroad have developed on the same toxic training ground, adopting a vigilant response instead of accepting the conditions presented to them.

Psychological Costs of Exposure

The emotional costs of coping with exposure must also be considered. We have noted the impacts to lifestyle and lifescape due to exposure. Paralleling other forms of victimization, toxic victims have shattered their prior assumptions about life.[10]

Personal Changes. In contrast to the growth experiences discussed above, numerous negative changes were evident in Legler.[11]

First, bad habits indicated behavioral manifestations of stress. An increase in smoking was reported for at least one member of nearly half of the sampled families. Other stress-related behaviors included nervous eating and insomnia.

One can question the extent to which smoking, eating, or insomnia were due to toxic exposure as opposed to other possible contributing causes. In fact, an interaction of contributing causes was likely. For example, one insomniac had fallen into a "midlife crisis" about the time that the pollution became known. In thinking about new professional directions, he had begun to question his current job. The pollution incident further drained him of energy, making his job even less successful and satisfying. Not surprisingly, pressure at work began to mount, interacting with the intense pressure from the exposure incident and from his strained relationships at home. He reported being aggravated at work, an outcome that may also have been related to his inability to sleep.[12] In sum, his insomnia may have been due to any or all of these factors, or none of them.

Second, dreams of pollution tormented some residents.

I had bad dreams a lot. It was the same dream. The kids were in the pond. I'd always say, "Don't drink the water," but when they'd dive in they'd always drink some. In the nightmare, I'd see the kids floating in the water dead.

I shout out in my sleep all night long, especially after meetings. I fight with officials in my dreams. It started in 1978 and has gotten worse over time.

I'd have an occasional nightmare. I'd go into the shower and come out with open sores. There would be straight benzene coming out of the shower.

Third, changes in temperament were also reported, reflecting increased irritability and even a shift toward general hostility.

I'm antagonistic. Everything sets me off. I feel guilty about exposing my child. I fly off the handle more easily. I'm more intense than if this thing weren't hanging over my head.

Hostility was particularly heightened by the community meetings held to discuss the water crisis.

I'm only now getting my control back. Then I didn't have it. The only way to get it then was violence. My brain tells me that this isn't right, but I would have blown up city hall with the council in it.

Fourth, defensiveness in social relationships was a factor. Some residents reported an inability to relax with others and a paranoid suspicion of their motives.

I'm not as nice a person as I used to be. I was trusting and patient. I was willing to listen to the other side. Now I listen, but I'm quick to be judgmental.

Fifth, depression was another outcome.

My daughter would get depressed and start drinking the polluted water. She'd say, "I don't care if I get cancer!"

I tried not to let it bug me. Some days I could ignore the problem; some days I got too depressed—I almost had a nervous breakdown.

In some cases, depression led to a loss of motivation and lethargy, as if one might cope by ignoring much of the world.

Ever since the water problem, he's been unhappy with everything—his job, this place. He is melancholy and pessimistic. He thinks that things won't work. If something minor goes wrong, it's as if he says, "Let's all lay down, we're going to die anyway." His energy comes in spurts. Last summer, there were two weeks in which he didn't want to do a damn thing.

I used to grab my wife when I heard a rhumba on the radio. Now I'm too tired.

We don't go out like we used to. I don't dance anymore.

Sixth, guilt and self-blame were additional symptoms of stress. About half the respondents blamed themselves both for getting into the situation and then staying there.

We feel guilty that we just didn't leave, particularly when friends say we should have. Am I so terrible that I made my kids stay here under these circumstances? But to leave is to give up.

I felt guilty because I talked my husband into buying this place. We brought the kids here and poisoned them. Can you imagine how it must feel to stick your kid in poison? Incredible. What did I do to them?

Other stress symptoms also appeared, including somatic problems, such as migraine headaches and skin rashes.

Evidence of Psychopathology After Contamination

Margaret Gibbs's convergent study in Legler provided clinical evidence for many of these changes identified in my qualitative interviews. She found comparatively high scores on indicators of health concern, above normal hostility toward authority, and clinical levels of paranoia and depression. Given her findings, she concluded:

It seems to the author an inescapable conclusion that although many individuals in the litigation group may be well-adjusted, nevertheless the proportion of individuals with psychological problems, and especially the proportion of individuals with serious psychological problems, is much higher than one would expect in a comparable group which had not undergone the same stress. It is particularly impressive that these consequences remain two or three years after the period when most of the stresses occurred. The presence of serious pathology today, especially in areas other than health worry, attests to the power, pervasiveness and long-term nature of the stress experienced.

In her Legler work, Gibbs further posited that depression and other psychopathologies result from a loss of control caused by environmental stress. Although a subset were uncommonly likely to take control over events affecting them, the majority of Legler residents in her sample scored lower on measures of control than did comparison populations. Further support for these findings can be drawn from Gibbs's later studies of toxic victims from two other New Jersey sites, one a landfill and the other the scene of a gasoline spill.[13]

There is now considerable confirmation of Gibbs's findings.

- Demoralization was evident in New Jersey for victims of both the Chemical Control fire in Elizabeth, and a malathion pesticide release at an American Cyanamid plant in Linden.[14]
- Residents in a small poor, rural, and cohesive community whose water was polluted by a nearby hazardous waste landfill suffered significantly impaired personal functioning in such areas as daily living, work, parenting, and overall social adjustment. Psychiatric symptoms, somatic complaints, obsession, depression, and anxiety were also significantly greater than in a control community. Symptom levels in the contaminated community were similar to those found for depressed and anxious individuals receiving treatment in an outpatient clinic.[15]
- Baum and colleagues found higher levels of chronic stress for residents living within a mile of a hazardous waste landfill than those living near Three Mile Island. Compared to suitable control communities, both representations of environmental disaster evidenced significantly more self-reported emotional, somatic, and cognitive distress, as well as cognitive dysfunction (measured on proofreading tasks). When these results were triangulated with physiological measures, significantly higher levels of norepinephrine and cortisol, as well as blood pressure and heart rate, were found.[16] Furthermore, significant correlations were found between measures of chronic stress and feelings of helpless-

ness and between depression and feelings of future uncertainty (and uncertainty about future illness).[17]

• After the "cotton poison," methyl parathion (MP), was illegally used indoors by exterminators over a ten-year period to combat cockroach infestations in Jackson County, Mississippi, some 1,800 homes in primarily poor and minority areas were found to have been contaminated. More than half the victims tested as significantly depressed, particularly the poorest victims, predominantly African Americans and women. Length rather than level of exposure was predictive of depression.[18]

• Posttraumatic stress disorder (PTSD) reflects persistent effects of traumatic events. The Baum group found significantly higher levels of intrusive thought and avoidance thinking for both their TMI and landfill samples. PTSD correlated significantly with other chronic stress measures.[19] After the release of an organic chemical in California, Rosemary Bowler and colleagues found evidence of PTSD in more than half of their interviewees. Not only were PTSD symptoms elevated, but so were scales of depression, anxiety, and anger. More than two-thirds of their respondents suffered also from memory and cognitive functioning impairments, and almost all from dysphoric mood.[20]

Preexisting Psychological Problems.   Do these symptoms merely reflect that part of the population that has previously suffered psychopathology and therefore lacks the coping resources to address this new threat? While Bowler's PTSD results could not be accounted for by previous problems before the chemical release, a history of prior psychological symptoms was significantly associated with subsequent psychopathology in the above study of the Elizabeth and Linden, New Jersey, toxic accidents.[21] And a history of depression was the best predictor of the significant levels of depression, somatization, phobia, and generalized anxiety found in the Missouri dioxin disaster victims.[22] These findings suggest that, in the face of low to moderate stress due to toxic exposure, those least able to address such challenges are most likely to suffer personal consequences. However, if the stress is extreme enough, such differences will disappear, and all victims will be equally at risk of psychological damage.[23]

Coping Style.   Vulnerability to psychopathology also appears to be affected by the victims' coping style—whether they try to actively change their external circumstances or merely palliate their feelings.[24] Here the evidence is mixed. After the Buffalo Creek flood, men who became actively involved in the cleanup fared better than men who did not.[25] Activists responding to a proposed hazardous waste site in Arizona had more intense emotion but were less emotionally upset than less involved individuals.[26] At Love Canal, activists were less likely to report being negatively affected and held higher self-regard and personal efficacy.[27]

In contrast, at TMI, Andrew Baum and his colleagues found that a coping style aimed at reappraising the threat was most successful in reducing stress and that emotion-focused approaches were more useful than problem-solving approaches.[28] Similarly, Gibbs and Bedford found a positive correlation between activism and psychological symptoms among residents of a neighborhood where the state of New Jersey planned to dump radium-contaminated soil. Such findings have been interpreted to indicate that activism is psychologically costly. However, Gibbs correctly reasons that "active coping styles may allow the individual more opportunity to change the situation, but may not lead to less symptomatology." Both active and palliative coping styles may prove to be functional, depending upon the point in the disaster and potential for change that the victim can actually accomplish.[29]

Physical Versus Psychological Causality. Following chemical exposure, changes in a victim's psychological functioning may have multiple causes, physical and psychological. For example, physical causes for poor cognitive functioning might include actual damage to the brain, hormonal or chemical changes of a permanent or temporary nature, and impairment from drugs or toxins. Conversely, cognitive deficits may reflect the person's psychological state in a long-term or permanent manner (their dispositional self) or reflect their ability to cope with an overwhelming press of demands in the situation. Likewise, personality changes involving mood swings, aggression, and other emotional symptoms might reflect physical exposure (e.g., to mercury), the victim's dispositional tendencies, or their anger due to a frustrating or frightening situation. It may be difficult or impossible to identify root sources. More than one causal factor may be occurring, factors may interact, or symptoms may themselves be secondary or tertiary impacts of other factors. Thus it may be most useful to think of toxic impacts to psychological functioning as reflecting a complex synergy that takes into account physical exposures, changed personal characteristics, and situational attributes. Writing specifically about Post Traumatic Stress Disorder, Bowler concludes on this point that "similar neuropsychological deficits in concentration, memory, disordered information processing, and mood can be attributed to neurotoxic exposures and to PTSD."[30]

Physical symptoms may also be caused or influenced by psychological stressors. Around a California hazardous waste landfill, reports of health symptoms and worry were particularly associated with zones where odors could be detected. Such symptoms as headaches persisted even after the odors ceased following site remediation. The continued symptoms were attributed to the worry caused by proximity to the landfills rather than toxicological effect.[31]

Stress from Natural Versus Humanly Caused Disaster.   We previously noted that toxic disaster is both human-caused and technologically rooted. With minor exception,[32] evidence suggests that such disasters cause greater levels of stress than do natural disasters. Thus Davidson and colleagues conclude, "Whereas the negative effects of natural disaster appear to be rather short-lived, typically not extending further than the immediate period of impact and recovery, the consequences of technological disasters seem to be more long-lasting and hence more likely to lead to chronic stress." Much as the Gatchel and Newberry study cited earlier, these researchers found stress that was subclinical, within the normal range encountered with daily hassles, and not indications of psychopathology.[33]

Smith and colleagues found even more serious consequences. Their fortuitous studies of Missouri flood victims began before it was learned that some had additionally suffered from massive dioxin contamination, making it possible to compare victims of flooding, relocation due to dioxin exposure, and both disasters.[34] Against 3.6 symptoms for persons not exposed to either disaster, the mean number of psychiatric symptoms was 4.5 for flood victims, 5.3 for dioxin victims, and 5.9 for victims of both disasters. Significantly elevated among direct disaster victims were symptoms of depression, phobia, somatization, generalized anxiety, and post-traumatic stress disorder, as well as alcohol abuse. Almost a third of Times Beach victims (who suffered both disasters) evidenced symptoms of PTSD, 6 percent at a diagnostic level. Disaster exposure, especially flooding, also contributed to extended duration of symptoms, although it appeared that symptoms had recurred rather than persisted. Regarding the comparison of natural and caused disasters, the authors call a draw. Both can cause symptoms of psychopathology.

Duration of Stress.   Various studies suggest that psychological impacts from human-caused and toxic events are highly persistent over time.

- Longitudinal sampling after the TMI accident revealed greater psychophysical symptoms among TMI residents than in a control population at a year, at a seventeen-month interval, and again at five years. In particular, a marker of urine catecholamines, an indication of stress, was prevalent in the TMI sample, along with reports of physical and mental symptoms and decreased task performance.[35]
- Even fourteen years after the Buffalo Creek flood, significant psychopathology remained for a quarter of the survivors and some new symptoms had arisen, including global impairment, anxiety, and depression. These symptoms were strong but not sufficient to suggest a need for outpatient treatment. Although 25–30 percent of the Buffalo Creek sample evidenced clinically significant levels of impairment, only 10 percent had impairment in the moderate to severe range.[36]

- Seven years after closure and interim remediation, close neighbors and those previously able to smell odors from California's McColl hazardous waste site continued to report significantly more adverse health symptoms than controls.[37]
- Duane Gill and Steve Picou studied effects persisting a year and a half after the acute disaster in Livingston, Louisiana, caused by the derailment of a train carrying toxic chemicals. Even though the physical effects of the spill were quickly dissipated, except at the actual site, residents suffered lasting social and psychological consequences. Some key characteristics of an acute toxic event were particularly deterministic of later fears for health and desire for relocation, namely, proximity to the spill, lengthy evacuation, and separation from loved ones during the chaotic aftermath of the event.[38] These stress impacts were particularly strong for women, the elderly, adolescents, and younger children.[39]

This persistent stress effect, however, raises the issue of the levels at which the stress is maintained. Is containing stress significantly severe?

Acute and Chronic Stress

All credible evidence points to a significant level of continuing psychological impact from contamination. But what conclusions can we draw about the level of this stress? We earlier cited two studies which found only subclinical levels of stress similar to that encountered with the daily hassles of life. How do we reconcile this evidence with that suggesting that toxic exposure results in significant levels of psychopathology?

The findings of subclinical persistent stress reflect random population studies that, by their very nature, water down the effect by mixing those heavily impacted with those less so. The assumption that those living within five miles of a landfill are likely to see themselves at high risk does not fit with evidence about perceptions of risk. It is indeed notable, then, that such random populations evidence a persistent detectable stress effect.[40] In contrast, the work by Gibbs and by Edelstein reflects instances of litigation in which, presumably, there is a potential self-selection toward those believing themselves to be most impacted. Such populations reach levels of psychopathology well beyond that caused by daily hassles.

Clearly chronic and acute stresses both deserve consideration. As visualized in Figure 4.1, the reality of contamination can only be understood in a longitudinal frame, since contamination events frequently stretch across decades of the victims' lives. In the theory of random sampling, one would assume that peaks and valleys would average out over the sample. Indeed they may. However, any cross-section, or single point of assessment, may fail to be temporally representative. The sampling point may reflect extreme periods of crisis involving new discoveries, chal-

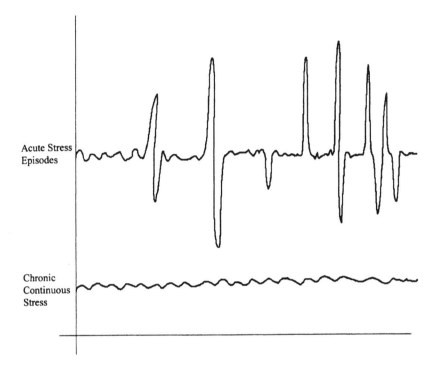

Figure 4.1   Chronic and Acute Stress

lenges, announcements, conflicts, and decisions, likely to amplify stress. In contrast, data collected during a relative period of calm may reflect the ongoing daily challenges of contamination but not the adrenaline pumping points that occur around important milestones.

The point is that the stress history of a contaminated community is a composite of chronic and acute events, threats, and responses. Thus measurements of chronic stress at the Three Mile Island reactor are not representative of stress levels during such acute events as when radioactive gasses were being vented. Chronic stress may reflect cumulatively a "bundle of acute events." Acute events may become chronic, as with PTSD, where trauma is relived for extended periods. Or secondary life changes due to contamination may expose victims to a repetitive pattern of diverse acute stressors experienced as one cumulative stress.[41]

Finally, stress levels may reflect the adequacy of coping resources. Successful coping may entail only moderate stress while difficult or failed coping is more stressful. In sum, all toxic victims are periodically thrown into crisis by the events of contamination. The mix of chronic and acute stress events over time assures a blend of modest with major stressors. That stress persists is hardly surprising. Toxic problems are stubborn, continuing and evolving for decades as new information emerges and they move through the regulatory and legal processes.[42]

Recovery

The persistence of contamination effects speaks to the resistance of such effects to recovery. It is hard to rebuild life when one is stuck in a feared home, expects some dread disease to be manifested, feels captured by distrusted agencies or industries, or believes themselves to have been unfairly victimized. Thus barriers to recovery range from the hurt of exposure to the life complications it causes. Lifton and Olson note of the Buffalo Creek survivors that "a sense of moral inversion—of wrongdoing going unpunished and responsibility unacknowledged while innocent victims undergo pain and suffering—further prevents psychological resolution and leaves people embittered and confused."[43] Mississippi parathion victims were subjected to extreme continuing stress regardless of whether they remained trapped in their home or were relocated.[44]

Survivors of the 1986 Chernobyl nuclear accident also have recovered slowly. A study done by the International Atomic Energy Agency several years after the accident found that levels of anxiety and stress greatly exceeded radioactive exposures. Most residents of the contaminated villages believed that they had an illness related to radiation, reported chronic fatigue, and desired relocation. Many still distrusted the safety of milk and believed that radioactive levels were not diminishing. Of course, relocation was also disruptive, with neighbors often being separated permanently.[45] These responses show recovery being hampered by distrust of the environment; belief in prior exposures, continuing health effects, and potential for new exposure; depression; and perhaps by relocation. Interestingly, the control population also showed surprisingly high levels of stress impact, as if they believed that they were also exposed to past and continuing radiation from the accident even though they came from villages designated as non-contaminated.

As these cases show, contamination is a raw scab, the wound easily reopened. Mixing chronic low level stresses with major stress events, toxic victimization places multiple barriers in the way of recovery and a return to some semblance of normalcy.

Treating Toxic Trauma

Given the psychological turmoil caused by contamination, how do we help the victims? Four issues arise here. First, is there a need for assistance? I find Margaret

Gibbs's Legler findings to be a compelling answer to this question. Half of her respondents indicated problems that normally justify psychological counseling. A quarter were in serious need of such help.[46]

Second, do toxic victims use counseling services? There are ample reasons to believe that the conventional mental health service model has not worked to support toxic victims. I have encountered only a handful who sought counseling after their exposure. The literature supports this gap. For example, although half of the Mississippi parathion victims were found to be clinically depressed, few were using mental health services.[47]

None of the Legler residents reported seeking help from professional counselors. While reflecting a general cultural bias against therapy, there were specific reasons why psychological help was avoided. Legler residents feared that anything divulged during therapy might be exposed because of the lawsuit. Residents also distrusted the community mental health agency because it received funding from local governments. At Love Canal, an official admitted to me the limited success of outreach to the affected residents by the community mental health center.

Of course, much counseling occurs by other means, such as through houses of worship. In southern African American communities, I witnessed clergy and congregations offering organized support for toxic victims. In contrast, in Legler, clergy did not appear to play a major role in counseling residents. Religious residents drew strength from prayer, not from pastoral support.

> *I never told the clergy, but I prayed. I believe deeply that help through the period was from up above—He is the mightiest!*

In Legler and elsewhere, I have witnessed the power of personal religious belief as a palliative tool and means for rationalizing toxic exposure. When people focus on otherworldly concerns, the trials of this world became substantially less important. Residents of a minority community contaminated by a New Jersey landfill told Margaret Gibbs that "they could not have dealt with this problem without God."[48]

Third, are conventional counseling and therapeutic services capable of following the contortions of contamination? Psychology suffers from almost a universal gap in theory and practice in recognizing environment as a factor in stress and coping issues requiring intervention. A fledgling effort has emerged within social work aimed at preparing community mental health workers to address environmental issues such as toxic contamination. And, under the guidance of psychiatrist Pamela Tucker, the Agency for Toxic Substances and Disease Registry has begun offering training for disaster responders and agency personnel.[49] Additionally, disaster relief organizations, such as the Church World Service, have long included contamination events within the scope of their disaster response training programs. Many clergy have become more informed about contamination and how to help their affected parishioners. These developments point toward a time, as yet unrealized, when there may be better community resources available to aid coping with contamination events.

Finally, what is the proper target for intervention? Both Gibbs and I have questioned the applicability of conventional person-centered psychological counseling to a situation in which causes are so clearly environmental.[50] Given the circumstances, true abnormality might involve the failure rather than propensity for victims to show symptoms of stress. In fact, there is a personalistic bias to the assumption that the person and not the situation is aberrant that is not only unfair and inaccurate but also insulting to the victims. This bias fits with what is called in psychology the "fundamental attribution error," the basic tendency to assume that behavior is controlled by people rather than situational factors. In an environmental context, this error is a common characteristic of press coverage of contamination events.[51]

A particularly blatant instance of the personalistic assumption occurred during the expansion hearings for the CECOS hazardous waste complex in the mid-1980s. Through its expert witnesses, CECOS countered my testimony on psychological impact by proposing to treat and cure community stress with mass therapy aimed at helping the community accept the facility. In this way, the community's "irrational" fear of the waste site could be "cured."[52]

By treating the person, under this model, one avoids having to address the underlying condition of pollution. Furthermore, to treat the person is to take a palliative approach—an absurd formula for "how to feel good about (or despite) contamination." An alternative assertive model of treatment would focus on the causes, the risks, the cleanup and restoration, and the prevention of further harm. In this vein, Steven Becker's comprehensive overview of response to the psychosocial impacts of contamination makes clear the need for interventions to complement rather than supplant citizen activism.[53]

Conclusion: Individual Stress

Toxic exposure is associated with persistent levels of significant stress, ranging from the nagging hassles of daily life to the trauma of a major life crisis. This stress is never experienced by individuals in isolation. Rather, following the model on social process, we have seen that residents of communities such as Legler and Love Canal were part of a relational web including their families, friends, and coworkers. These relations influenced the extent of the victims' stress as well as their coping strategy. The nuclear family is at the core of this relational web, organized around the couple.

Coping with Exposure: Couples

Given the relative isolation and mutual dependence of the couple in a privatized relationship, successful coping often depends on the supportiveness of one's mate. For most relationships, coping with toxic exposure involves a mix of destabilizing and stabilizing characteristics, as seen in Legler.

Destabilizing Characteristics

The toxic incident in Legler was immensely trying for the predominantly young parents who lived there. In combination with other stresses confronting these couples, the added tension contributed to the dissolution of some relationships and caused problems in others. As many as eleven divorces and twelve near divorces were attributed to the Legler pollution crisis. It may be useful to examine some of the contributing dynamics.

Blaming.   Spouses sometimes held their mates responsible for getting them into the situation or for their coping strategy.[54]

> *This didn't draw us together at all. We would have fights in which we'd blame each other for getting into Jackson. He had broken his promise that we would never have to move again. It was his fault.*

> *We would have awful fights. He would blame me for liking this house. He felt trapped. When he overreacts and wants to send our daughter to my sister's [to get her out of Legler], I miss her and he accuses me of overreacting.*

Such blaming was not always overt, and it sometimes smoldered below the surface for a long period of time. One Legler woman surprised her husband during the interview by admitting,

> *There were times I blamed him for the problems. I never told him about it. I'd think about it while I was hauling water around. I didn't want to live here, and he did. I'd particularly blame him if the cat got into the water, or I bumped into it.*

As this quote suggests, much of the resentment surfaced over lifestyle impacts, such as those entailed in water delivery.

Many housewives also resented their husbands' ability to escape to work during the day and thus avoid water-related problems. Their separation at times allowed husbands to be unappreciative of these problems. For example, in one home where well water stained clothing and dishes, the husband commented,

> *I didn't want to hear about the problems; I couldn't do anything about them. I was tired of hearing her complain about the clothes being ruined. We couldn't afford to buy new ones. It was frustrating. I looked like a slob. My mother said, "Doesn't your wife use bleach?" We'd argue about the dishes [which were stained from the water] or whether to buy a new dishwasher—they would just stain too!*

In part the blaming and anger stemmed from the inherent tension in the situation.

> *There was a lot of push and pull on us. We were so mad and aggravated that we'd yell. I'd yell when I was discouraged; we'd blame each other. The water was on my mind. The kid would be up all night itching from a rash. I just wanted to yell at someone.*

Participation Costs.   Beyond the blaming, the stress of the incident was itself distracting. In some cases, one spouse lost interest in joint activities formerly important to the relationship.

> *He stopped wanting to go dancing; we never go to clubs anymore. We fought like cats and dogs. I almost got a divorce.*

Not surprisingly, sex lives also suffered.

Pressures to be active in the community organization also stressed couples. Involvement of at least one mate allowed the family to be represented and informed. However, this new role invited various tensions, as this wife reported of her husband.

> *We usually argued after he returned from a meeting. He'd come home and tell me about it. I'd lash out. I expected him to know all the answers.*

In other cases, one mate resented the other's inactivism.

> *I'd yell and try to get answers at a meeting, and he wouldn't say a word. Why didn't he do his share of screaming? I started screaming at other people too—like the bank about our mortgage. Why didn't he do his share? It might have been good if they'd heard a man's voice.*

All but one of the families of Concerned Citizens Committee board members suffered marital strife caused by the continual absence of the activist mate, constant intrusions as the home became a key link in the community's communications network, and the pressure and tension brought home by the leaders.[55]

> We'd fight. He wanted me to quit Concerned Citizens because I was always bothered and upset.

> I blamed him for being too involved in Concerned Citizens, for never taking a day off. He is chained to that committee.

> Our home became a battleground. People would come in for help; they'd blame the executive committee for things. He'd be gone, and I'd be home all alone. He brought what should have been said to the township committee home to me. For a period, we just stopped discussing our problems.

Multiple Pressures.   Also contributing to the destabilizing impacts of exposure were other existing pressures within the family. Multiple and simultaneous sources of stress might overwhelm a couple's resources for coping.[56] For example, in one family that experienced a divorce the water crisis was felt to have "aggravated the situation." Thus contamination strains interact with other pressures on relationships.

Stabilizing Characteristics

Not all Legler couples experienced relationship problems during this time. Several factors contributed to stability.

Life Cycle Factors.   The most stable couples tended to be elderly. The experience of long marriages helped buffer problems. They lacked reasons to blame each other, nor were they as stressed by health concerns. Elders had generally lived in the community longer, avoiding the adjustments of moving, owning a first home, having young children, encountering problems with builders, and handling all of the other pressures confronting younger newly arrived couples.

For younger couples with children, the responsibility added to the stress. However, children provided a reason to persevere.

> Each time I had a problem with the kids and I couldn't cope anymore, I'd think I was going to have a nervous breakdown. But at night I'd feel that if I didn't have the kids it would be senseless to go on.

We would fight and blame each other. Our son was a help because he was a joy. At least we had him.

Coping Style.   The likelihood of tension was influenced by the couple's coping style. "Laid-back" couples avoided relationship problems.

We're calm, slow to get bothered. We have no choice. Why get upset over something that we have no way of doing anything about?

Couples might argue over the pollution incident but keep the conflict productive, releasing tension verbally without causing hurt feelings. Others had complementary styles of handling stress, differing in degree of optimism or excitability.

Sometimes it was hard to accept, like when the container leaked and the floor came up. I punched the walls, I was so pissed. I felt stuck; it was beyond my control. My wife calmed me down and convinced me that it would all work itself out.

Gained Confidence.   Despite its tensions, the water crisis sometimes brought couples a closeness that comes only from working through difficulties. For a family to survive, there was a need for disclosure and sharing, for the development of trust, and the willingness to learn new things about each other. Successful couples developed resiliency and a stronger relationship.

Nothing can bother us now. In some ways this brought us together. We feel precious to each other.

Long-Term Issues

Once the new water system was installed and there was a return to relative normalcy, stress from the pollution incident continued to surface for some couples. One reason was finances.

When we had the water system put in, we had to go into arrears on our mortgage. We can't catch up. It's harassing us.

Additionally, couples might even revive the tension.

For a while we had argued every day; then it was only after meetings. Now we only argue when someone reminds us about the water. Even with good water, the feelings are still there. We still occasionally have the same old argument, "If you would have listened to me!"

A continuing source of concern for caring parents were unsettling genetic and teratogenic threats to their children's health. Expectant parents were also affected. Kleese provides insight into the psyche of the expectant mother acting as a mediator of her child's level of environmental hazard.[57]

> One of the true enlightenments of pregnancy is the realization that the mother does not merely bear a child—as she might bear a load of books or wood. Instead, the mother represents the environment of the child; this situation is perhaps most analogous to an individual's relationship to the ecosphere. The mother is not merely a setting within which the child reposes, but she is a sphere of life wherein all of the interactions of natural systems necessary to sustain the child occur.

These fears colored how Legler couples viewed childbirth.

> *We argued over having another kid. I refused unless we first had genetic counseling. If it weren't for the water, we would have conceived another child.*

> *We are afraid to have children because of the possibility of chromosome damage. The baby we just had wasn't planned. We worried during the pregnancy. The doctor did tests. When the doctor came out to announce the birth, my husband asked if it had all its fingers and toes.*

Whether the stress of a worrisome pregnancy affects the fetus is uncertain. What is clear is that the decision about whether to have children is one of the most agonizing legacies of toxic exposure (see also Chapter 3).[58]

Once born, the child is subject to continuing parental concern about the next generation.

> *I'm deeply worried about my sons genetically. They still have their lives ahead of them. They drank the water since 1971 and they swam in our pond. I told my sons to use genetic counseling. I don't want them to have the heartache of a deformed child.*

> *I'm concerned for my children's children. They have a cousin who is mentally retarded. This may happen to their kid someday; the children know this. I'm scared to someday be a grandfather—what will be born? Do you ask your kids not to have kids?*

Parental concern for children is the strongest factor motivating response to the announcement of contamination (see Chapter 3). Ironically, in communities such as Legler parents commonly had moved to the suburbs in search of an ideal place in which to raise their families.

Coping with Exposure: Children

Children suffer similar lifestyle and lifescape impacts of pollution as do adults. Although it is difficult to conclude that they are affected in the same way, it is clear that they are stressed by the experience. Parental worry is passed along to them, as are tensions due to parental stress. Children also experience direct impacts from waste sites, peer pressures, and the consequences of being taught to fear. The result is the sensitization of the child to the issues of toxic exposure.

Parental Sources of Child Stress

As members of a family dominated by the concerns of adults, children experience much of the stress of exposure incidents vicariously from their parents. They must adjust to their parents' attempts to cope with the situation. In fact, there may be no more important indicator of the child's emotional response than the success of the parents' efforts to cope.[59]

The Effects of Parental Stress. In locales such as Legler, the high level of community stress resulted in a corresponding level of intrafamily tension. Beyond the strain on marriages, there were instances in which children took the brunt of the parents' frustration.

> *Before, I was very calm and in control. But during this time, it didn't take much to set me off. My nerves were shattered. If the kids dropped a drink, I'd fly off the handle.*

> *When I was depressed, I'd take it out on her. I'd pick on her. We'd have screaming contests. At least I can say that I'm sorry.*

Children of community leaders paid the costs of activism much as did their parents. Their homes bustled with activity. The entire family was under stress. As one Legler leader recalled,

There was nothing normal. The phone rang, there were meetings we had to attend, there were reporters. They [the children] were scared. They saw the tension and the emotion. It was far from peaceful and tranquil.

Activist parents may neglect the normal attentions that a child expects. For example, returning hungry from Washington, D.C., late in the night of her son's birthday, Lois Gibbs not only forgot the birthday but ate much of the cake baked by the child's aunt. The next morning, her son was in tears. Buying a new cake and presents, she squeezed an impromptu party into her busy schedule.[60]

By now it was 7:00 P.M. and we had to be at the meeting by 7:30. So we lit the candles on the cake and quickly sang happy birthday. It may have been the only birthday party for a six-year-old that had four attorneys and two doctors as guests. Michael opened his presents and cut the cake; then the adults left for the meeting. I hope Michael will understand and that he will forgive me someday.

The young son of another community leader accustomed to accompanying her as she engaged in her activist work would inquire each morning, "What's our schedule today?"

The Effects of Parental Worry. Parental fears for children's safety put a damper on the joy of family life. In one case in Legler, a mother feared retaliation against her child because of the father's activism.

We worry that she might be harmed when she leaves the house. They might try to get even. Our fear has given her fear. Now she worries about the "bad man"! She is explosive like her father. She has trouble sleeping. She's not as secure as she used to be. She doesn't like being alone or being away from her parents.

At times, total panic swept Legler. When a child died, some children were sent to stay with relatives. Moreover, Legler children were exposed to clear communications that all was not well. As couples argued and agonized over leaving their homes, they expressed explicit and understandable messages of fear.

Parental self-blame also affected parent–child relationships. This was particularly evident in the behavior of a young mother during a lengthy interview in which she continually reinforced her son for clinging to her. The mother admitted,

I became possessive because of my guilt over having exposed him to this. I'm overprotective. I don't let him experience what three-year-olds usually do. I like to keep him near me.

The Child's Experience

Children experience many of the direct impacts of a facility, and suffer some of the secondary impacts. They hear conversations and watch television. They interact with peers, teachers, and others with reactions to the pollution. And they confront explicit communications from their parents about their safety. Thus even younger children, incapable of understanding the full dimensions of toxic exposure, are quite aware of the disruption to a normal and secure home life.

Direct Impacts.   In Legler, children's activities (e.g., playing outside, having company, and camping in the backyard) were limited by landfill traffic, putrid odors, and parental fear of vectors. Similar impacts affected nine siblings growing up near Al Turi Landfill, Inc., in New York State. One sister recalled doing her homework after school to the rhythm of the equipment noise. Her brother suffered landfill-related nightmares. At the sound of garbage trucks arriving early in the morning, he would jump out of bed still asleep and awaken standing bolt upright. The children became increasingly sensitive to changes in the environment, observing the pollution of their favorite ponds and streams by leachate and litter. On their way to the school bus, the children had to walk a gauntlet of giant eighteen-wheel trucks, trying to ignore the threatening taunts of the drivers. And to top it off, the owner of the landfill ran over their dog.

In such situations, the cumulative sense of intrusion exceeds the incremental effects of each nuisance. Normal life comes to be dominated by the facility. For children, whose entire world revolves around home even more narrowly than it does for their parents, the psychological threat is all the more powerful.

The transformation of a benign environment into a feared one represents a disconcerting constriction of freedom for a child. Two young adults from Legler recalled the rural environment that preexisted the mining site and the landfill some fifteen years earlier. It was a place where children made their own adventures, spending time exploring the local woods and following old stagecoach paths. Subsequent changes in Legler, the girl bemoaned, made "my whole childhood disappear." The boy recalled that he stopped drinking the water shortly after the landfill opened. His father ridiculed him over this for eight years until the announcement of pollution. Both remembered having to pick up trash scattered along roads leading to the landfill.

Teaching Children to Fear.   As part of their adjustment to exposure, parents have to change their children's behavior. In Legler, parents literally taught children to fear the tap water. This lesson was not particularly difficult for older children. But younger children, who were able to use the faucet but not to comprehend complex reasons for refraining from its use, posed more of a problem. Parents resorted to blunt messages that would be understood.

We told them that the water was poison, like cleaners. None of the kids went near the water.

We told the kids that there was poison in the water, that they couldn't even brush their teeth with it. One time our son forgot and drank some. He came out screaming, "I drank the bad water, I'm going to die now."

Children, in turn, acted as agents to inform others.

They'd often tell people that our water is bad. If we had company, they'd say, "You can't drink that; it's poison." Then a guest drank some water one time; they expected to see him drop dead.

Once they learned that tap water was poison, children next had to define the generality of this phenomenon.

If visiting my relatives, they'd ask if the water is poison.

Younger children were additionally confronted by a confusing set of new rules inconsistently applied within Legler.

I can hear the kids talking outside. Some of the kids were allowed to use an aerated sprinkler. We let our daughter use it, but other kids were not allowed. This caused confusion. The kids would talk about how each parent says different things. The neighbors' children were so afraid to touch the water. Our daughter wasn't—she bathed in it.

For a while, nobody played with our daughter. They would be allowed to go under the sprinkler and our kids weren't. They would taunt our kids with "ha, ha, we're having fun."

After the central water system was installed, children had to learn to trust this source of water. As parents recalled,

Later it was hard to get them to use the faucet again.

For us the faucet is like a new luxury, but for the kids it's like a new invention.

There were other opportunities for children to learn about the situation. During interviews, Legler parents often spoke freely of their concerns with their children present. This was presumably not the first time that they had heard these concerns expressed. These were children who knew that all was not well, regardless of their ability to fully comprehend just what was wrong. At Love Canal, a boy of ten stood mutely by, shuffling his feet and averting his eyes from my video camera, while his mother listed his various physical and psychological problems.

> *My son has respiratory problems; he has asthma; he has been sick all of his life here. He has been hyperactive. He has been on sedatives from the time he was seven months old to eighteen months old. And now he's having psychological problems associated with this because he had to change schools. My son refuses to go. We changed schools again, but then he had another bad attack of asthma.*

Peer Stigma.   Children also learned of events from peers who were not necessarily supportive. In fact, their peers engaged in the same patterns of victimization as adults, as one Legler teen recalled,

> *At school, one kid told me he saw me on TV and that I was really stupid for moving into this area. Another said that he felt sorry for me. I hate both of them. I don't want pity. I was so mad I hit him.*

And peer group dynamics played out in mirror image the conflicts that divided Jackson Township's adults. Thus one Legler leader reported of her daughter,

> *She took abuse from other kids because of my involvement. She got punched on the bus; they called her names and told her that her mother is a trouble-maker. "My dad said that your mom is going to make our taxes go up."*

Similar dynamics at other sites suggest that children face social isolation as the result of toxic exposure incidents.

Media Coverage.   Children were exposed to media coverage. It was particularly frightening for children of activists to see what their parents said publicly. Lois Gibbs described her son's experience: "For example, picture yourself five years old watching the 6 o'clock news report. Your mother is being interviewed saying, 'There is dioxin in there. Dioxin kills. I don't want my babies to die.' What is the child supposed to think?"[61]

Sensitized Children

Some children became highly sensitized to the possible dangers of water. During the Legler study (after a new water source had been provided), I observed a young girl refuse to join her playmates under a sprinkler despite her parents' permission. Her mother explained that her daughter could not get past the belief that the sprinkler was dangerous. A few doors away, a teenager's parents reported that she continued to face away from the shower even though her home was hooked up to the new water supply. Parents gave other examples of children's sensitivity:

> *What hurts us is to see our six-year-old be paranoid—"Can I drink the water?" "Can I swim here?" "Can I bathe?"*

> *When we go camping, the kids don't want to swim in a pond if "it looks polluted." If we see a fifty-five-gallon drum, they say "look at the toxics." If there is a rainbow in a puddle, they say "looks like chemicals."*

Toxic concerns may become a factor in a child's ability to sleep. For example, Freedman describes very young children at Love Canal who had "chronic nightmares of toxins oozing from their bodies, while others have regressed to bedwetting, baby-talk, and clinging to their mothers."[62] Such worry might carry over into behavior at school, as this Legler parent recalled:

> *Our son was bothered by the situation. He wondered if someone made his little sister die. He was moody in the second grade. The teacher talked to him and found out that he was afraid of dying. He wouldn't study water pollution in class; he avoided the topic. The teacher said that he can pick out Legler kids.*

Both Freedman and Lois Gibbs note that younger children at Love Canal feared premature death. Older children were more able to appreciate the abstract horrors that so affected their parents. They too adopted a view of future as promising evil. Gibbs observed the effects of this on Love Canal teenagers.[63]

> The young people already had normal teenage problems and strains, and the Canal made growing up just that much harder. Young women suddenly had to face the fact that they might have chromosome damage or that their eggs might already be damaged by the chemicals in their environment. They feared that they might not be able to carry babies or give birth to normal children. These facts were devastating to the young women with their whole lives in front of them, and

especially in our community where most people marry within a short time after graduating from school and immediately begin their families.

In a similar vein, Freedman writes of one of three child suicides at Love Canal in the summer of 1980.[64]

The fourteen-year-old who killed herself with sleeping pills reportedly feared that she would develop cancer, as members of eight out of twelve families living on her block already had. She feared that it might be breast cancer or a cancer that would leave her unable to bear children. She worried that she would be unable to have a normal marriage. So, at fourteen, barely into puberty, she took her life.

Legler teens expressed fears over what toxic exposure might mean for their futures.

What will happen to me twenty to thirty years from now? I get scared about it.

Conclusion: Children and Coping

In summary, children underwent many of the same lifestyle and lifescape shifts that adults faced. In some cases, they may have been buffered by a child's view of reality. In other cases, they may have had enlarged fears. In either case, they were robbed of a normal childhood.

Case Studies of Family Dynamics

Family stress due to toxic exposure continues throughout the time that the family remains exposed, with certain stressors extending even longer. At the onset of the Love Canal crisis, two-thirds of Levine's respondents reported a high level of family strain. The next year, when nearest residents had moved to new homes, nearly half of these families showed improved relationships.[65] Therefore, removal from the situation can be seen as a key element in stress reduction. In the vast majority of toxic exposure cases, however, no such removal occurs.

As victims cope with life in their contaminated homes, family dynamics vary. Contamination intensifies problems in some relationships; coping with contamination draws other couples together. A family consensus about the exposure is required if the family is to stay unified through the experience. The contrast between united and divided families can perhaps best be seen by looking at two case studies of toxic victims from different sites in the eastern United States. I studied both cases in 1983 at the request of the lawyer representing the families in separate lawsuits. As with other instances drawn from my own interviews, the names of the families have been changed.

Case 1: Family Disintegration from Exposure

Louis, a retired man in his sixties with one college-age child, had been blind since his late teens. Some twenty-five years prior to our interview, he and his wife purchased a rural home with an adjacent rental property. The financial independence this property afforded allowed them to spend much of their time at home. Despite his blindness, Louis was independent to an extent amazing to a new acquaintance. He moved about freely outside his home. His ability to describe the natural features of the area surpassed that of many sighted people. He actively participated in maintaining his property, doing such chores as splitting wood for the stove. Particularly since his retirement, his life had been centered almost entirely around the home and property.

After a chemical factory moved in next door in the early 1970s, Louis and his wife suffered various direct impacts from its operation. Increasingly preoccupied with the factory, they came to spend the bulk of their free time seeking help from the government. Even when it meant neglecting their child, Louis would spend hours dictating letters to be sent to various officials who might help them. His wife typed the letters and mailed them. When groundwater contamination was later identified in their well, they felt certain that the factory was the source. As a result, they increased their efforts to get assistance.

Unsuccessful in eliciting help, Louis's preoccupation with the pollution intensified. He believed that he and his family were exposed to dangerous chemicals that affected their health and threatened genetic damage. He saw himself as fighting a wrong brought against not only his family but also the entire community. For Louis, the key issue was his family's exposure to chemicals and the inevitable consequences.

In contrast, over time, his wife began to rethink their obsession with the factory. She felt guilty that her child had been raised during protracted turmoil that prevented a normal home life and caused the boy mental strain evident in his teenage years. But to Louis, his son's mental strain resulted

> from the physical problems from the water. His nerves are affected from ingesting the water by drinking, eating, and bathing.

Over time, Louis's wife developed new interests. She was "reborn" through religion and also began a career. As his wife and son became increasingly mobile and centered elsewhere, the pollution issue became correspondingly less important for them, even as it became increasingly central to Louis. Continual misunderstanding resulted from this different emphasis. During their 1983 interview, Louis's wife and son maintained that the incident was over and that it was time to get past it and go on with life. But to Louis, "you can't walk away from something that is now within your body." Rejecting their attitude as a "Band-Aid," Louis became increasingly bitter at his wife's disinterest in pursuing the case. Of himself, he proclaimed,

> *I don't give up. If you're going to beat me, you're going to have to kill me.*

As a blind man, Louis was particularly dependent on his wife to maintain his high level of activity. She acted as his secretary, collaborator, and chauffeur. But as she refocused her energies, Louis was increasingly hampered in his ability to fight for restitution and achieve the resulting catharsis. Sitting alone much of the day, he was unable to distract himself through reading or traveling. Instead, he was left to stew in anger.

Increasingly, he perseverated on the need to complete actions that he felt were necessary. For example, at the time of the interview, a form sent by their lawyer had sat uncompleted for a week. Louis was obsessed with getting the form finished. He was outraged that his wife had not helped him fill it out immediately. He alienated her with continuous reminders. It became obvious that as the pressures had mounted in the family, Louis had lost not only his secretarial support but also his emotional support.

> *It's hell for me. I'm here all the time. I cannot leave. She refuses to read and write for me. She's out all day. When she comes home, I'm in bed. I eat sandwiches. I'm like a prisoner. I have no nourishing meals. It's not a normal relationship. She eats standing up in a rush all the time.*

As his wife avoided the issue, she needed also to avoid him. As he sat pondering what needed to be done and composing letters that he was unable to send, he felt caught in a true dilemma. To maintain the ongoing battle to protect his family and community, he needed his wife's help. When a response was required, he reminded her. Seeing her but infrequently, the topic dominated his conversations, motivating her to avoid responding. This dynamic is seen in the following exchange from their interview.

WIFE: Louis always mentions pollution. I went along with that for a long, long time.

LOUIS: My only regret is that I don't have more time to devote to this. It's a necessity.

WIFE: He talks about it all the time. Every time he sees me he says, "We have the letter that has to be sent."

LOUIS: The percentage of time devoted to this is about two minutes a day on the average.

WIFE: Do you deny that every time we get company, two-thirds of the conversation is about the factory?

LOUIS: That's an exaggeration—it's a lie!

WIFE: I'm tired. We've been sending letters since 1974.

LOUIS: I'm stronger than you are. I'm a human being too. I regret that I don't have more time to spend on it. It's wrong to let him [the factory owner] get away with it. I only devote two minutes a day, on the average.

Louis was being prevented from dealing with the issue that consumed him, but to mention it was to make it even less likely that the issue would be dealt with. From his wife's perspective, creating a normal home life required that the topic of pollution be expunged from their interaction. Yet the more she fought to eradicate it from the limited family communication, the more obsessed Louis became. He even began to lose the powers of concentration that had allowed him to organize his thoughts despite his blindness. Once proud of his competence, he became increasingly embarrassed by its loss. He periodically suffered from choking episodes during periods of extreme frustration.

Although Louis sought justice, revenge, and relocation, which would further provide confirmation of his perceptions, his wife and son just wanted the crisis to be over. They accomplished this cognitively—it was over because they decided it was over. Their view was that even if the pollution issue never got resolved, it was more important to bring something positive into their lives. This exchange captures their conflict:

LOUIS: It's a scientifically proven fact that there is chromosome damage.

SON: I realize it. But there is nothing there now!

WIFE: You can't only worry about physical effects, but mental effects also. We could go crazy fighting all the time.

SON: Physically I was young, so it didn't do much to me.

WIFE: You can't expect a child to go through this.

LOUIS: It's not a manufactured thing. You have to try to do something.

SON: The situation is gone.

LOUIS: You can't put a paper bag over your face and say it is not there.
WIFE: You put holes in the paper bag and keep on going.
LOUIS: That's silly.
SON: That's not silly.

Their coping strategies were totally divergent, although neither Louis's fixation nor his wife and son's defensive avoidance was particularly adaptive. The wife and son sought to make up for the years lost due to the incident; Louis couldn't get past it. The wife, feeling guilty for subjecting her son to so distorted a home life, was just as fixated on eradicating the issue from their lives, no matter its merit, as Louis was on keeping it as the central issue. This difference formed a barrier between them. Louis claimed that he no longer trusted his wife and wanted her to leave. She wanted to stay until their son was older. Both blamed the pollution incident for destroying their relationship.

Were there causes for the schism in this family besides the contamination? Louis's wife might have developed new interests and sought increased independence from her husband in any case. At the very least, the pollution issue contributed strongly to family conflict, driving Louis's wife to other interests as much to avoid the pollution situation as to find new interests and independence. Her changed role was more than a liberation from being a homemaker or a rebellion against the dependency of another; it had the added significance of ending the years of shared collaborative activity against the polluter that had become their dominant context for relating. It is neither surprising that she evaded her husband nor that Louis interpreted her evasion as a break in trust.

This case illustrates how a family can be split by the stress of a pollution incident. For Louis to persist in seeking answers to the fundamental questions of health and justice was quite reasonable. And yet, because our society is so ill-prepared to tackle these questions, he was stalemated in pursuing them. His task was Sisyphian. What appeared at first to be a competent and direct approach to the family's needs thus became an unproductive and dysfunctional element of the family's life. In contrast, his wife and son chose to reorient their lives to more constructive purposes, a healthy decision for their mental health although it avoids dealing with persistent issues of their experience. In a sense, therefore, neither choice is ideal. In fact, people in this family's situation lack an optimal option.

Case 2: Mutual Support During Toxic Disaster

Sonia and her husband had enjoyed their simple rural life together close to the soil. They coped well with the constant infringement from the neighboring industrial waste site even after their well was contaminated. They sought not to bother others or to be excessively disturbed. Their coping strategy drew heavily from their faith, as well as from a conscious effort to appreciate each day and to maximize the positive. Sonia noted,

> You know, we're studying the Bible. And there were certain phrases we picked up. If you think good thoughts, they will multiply. If you think bad thoughts, they will multiply. You talk about these bad things, and it spoils your whole day. I won't be able to fall asleep tonight because all these bad thoughts are on my mind. So we try to dwell on good thoughts constantly.

Accordingly, they refused to hate their neighbor, the polluter, despite what he had done to them. Sonia noted,

> All my life, the kind of policy I work with—if a person has one percent of goodness in him, appreciate that one percent and forget about the rest. And this is the way I lived all my life. And I believe Erik is the same way. I don't hate [the polluter]. He's doing this for a living. If this is what he went into, it's his business—I can't be critical of that.

Equally forgiving, Erik spoke of the landfill operator,

> He's a genius. He only should be pushed in the proper direction. Like a bank robber who can cut metal—he would make a great EPA guy.

Both share a profound sadness at the change that has overtaken them. Sonia is severely depressed; her husband is equally despondent. Yet their shared understanding allows them to be mutually supportive. They actively help each other cope with the situation. In contrast to Louis's family, coping with toxic adversity has brought them even closer together.

Stigmatized Relationships: Outsiders Just Don't Understand

Social support is well recognized as a key factor in the ability of victims to cope with disaster.[66] An enigma of contamination is that, outside the immediate family, victims frequently find a souring of their relationships with friends, relatives, coworkers, and others not in their circumstances.

Friends and Relatives

Beyond the nuclear family, our relational web encompasses a range of friendships and associations with kin. Under normal circumstances, and in the face of most major life crises, this network provides the individual and family with various kinds of help, aiding in efforts to cope with the crisis and offering socioemotional support.[67] The Legler case shows limits in how well this support network functions during toxic disaster.[68]

As a sprouting development within the New York metropolitan area, Legler was readily within reach of the major urban centers from which most Legler residents had moved. Many maintained close ties with friends and family, exchanging frequent visits on weekends. In most areas of Legler, where intra-neighborhood privacy norms were strong, the prior network of relationships continued to be primary while neighbors were kept at an "acquaintance level" of association.

Friends and relatives assisted victims in a variety of ways: they brought them water and offered the use of showers; some offered financial assistance; several offered to take children until the crisis was over. Yet most residents felt that such help was not commensurate with their needs.

What might account for this perception? First, it was as unclear to residents as it was to their friends what concrete actions might be beneficial. Sympathy was usually offered and at times it was very helpful, as when parents reassured their adult children that they should not blame themselves for buying a home in Legler. But often mixed with sympathy was the contradictory message, "How can you keep living there?" Residents already had conflicting feelings about choosing to stay in Legler; such "support" made them either defensive or doubtful. Sometimes blatant criticism was offered, arousing parents' guilt for staying in Legler or at least not removing their children.

Instead of being intensified as a support network, friendships often were weakened by the situation.[69] People who had frequently visited Legler before the water crisis just stopped coming, as these recollections illustrate:

> *Only my mother will come here. It's like we have the plague the way they [the rest of the family] avoid Legler. They feel that they don't want to expose themselves to our house. My wife's parents don't even want to know about it.*

> *Before the water, we entertained every weekend. Now only immediate family come. The others are afraid. We're afraid to invite them. People even called to ask us whether they were exposed to pollution from our water during their visits. This drains; it doesn't help!*

As these quotes indicate, friends and relatives at times showed self-concern as much as support.

Toxic victims sometimes helped close relatives pretend the problem didn't exist. The wife's parents sat watching television upstairs during one interview because the couple didn't want them to know how bad things had been.

Parents who knew of the situation might not be supportive. A young Legler father clenched his fists and assumed an angry look and tone as he spoke of the pressure he received from his family.

People act like we're diseased. They say, "If I was you, I'd get out of there." But where are you going to go? Everybody is a doctor or a lawyer! They're not in our situation. I'd get upset with them and say that the problem is being looked into. People say, "If I were you, I'd sell my house." The water is fixed; we went through the tough part already. My relations are not supportive; they always criticize— "sell the house; get out." They don't know the situation! We couldn't afford an apartment and a mortgage. But they won't accept this explanation. Our water stained all our clothes. My mother would ask, "Do the kids have any unstained clothes?" Then she'd buy the children "nice outfits."

Parents might use the pollution incident to bolster prior prejudices about how their children lived.

Our parents hate our lifestyle. They think that this place is a step down from our former bi-level. The water just emphasizes our mistake in moving. It reinforces their belief that this was a bad idea; they won't accept our lifestyle.

After a media interview, residents were sometimes objectified by friends and relatives as "celebrities."[70]

With the newspaper picture, no one ever wanted to let me alone. Friends would ask about it; they'd make me lose my concentration at bowling. They'd get nervous when I'd talk about it. They didn't really understand what I went through.

As already noted, the theme of "outsiders don't understand" is echoed in virtually every toxic exposure incident I have investigated. It is as though the victims share a private experience that can only be known to those who have undergone it themselves.

Distancing also occurred when friends grew tired of victims' preoccupation with their problems.

Our friends say that they don't want to be with us anymore because we are so caught up in the water problem.

Ironically, the only Legler family not reporting a change in relationships was an elderly couple undeterred by the pollution from continuing to use their well water. They reported,

Everyone who comes here even now wants to drink the water. We have friends here all the time. They're not concerned about the water.

A mirroring effect is suggested. Residents believing their water to be dangerous may have convinced their social network of this. The reverse appears also to be true. Ironically, for those disbelieving the severity of the incident, social support among friends and relatives may have been greater than it was among those for whom this was a true and complete disaster.[71]

Coworkers

For the men and few working women of Legler, the job provided a major life context outside the community. At times, this helped victims' ability to cope by giving them a space separated from the crisis and an opportunity to have an outside perspective on the situation at home. But this separation was often undermined by encounters during the course of the workday. Although generally intended to be supportive, inquiries and comments tended to break down the separation and deprive residents of their escape from the pressures of the crisis.

My coworkers and people I deliver to would ask about it; it was nice, but it dwelled on my mind that way.

In some cases, coworkers ridiculed the victim.

The other workers would laugh at me for overreacting. You're standing there and being hurt by it.

A few made jokes like "If you need a light, take a bucket of my water; it glows."

As it did with friends and relatives, the inherently private experience of the problem made it genuinely hard for outsiders to appreciate the severity of the situation.[72]

Most people were sorry that it happened, but they didn't appreciate the problem.

Other Outsiders: Stigma and Community Corrosion

Alan Barton notes conditions under which disaster victims are likely to be blamed: when the impacts of the disaster are specific to one group, the impact occurs gradually, others have vested interests in the source of the victims' deprivation, media content suggests blame, victims are isolated, the blaming dynamic is widespread, and altruistic values are absent.[73] Such conditions create stigma and related intra-community conflict.

Stigma. Refugees from the Chernobyl disaster were shunned openly in parts of Russia, as Marples's tale of a woman from Prypyat, at the epicenter of the accident, clearly indicates.[74]

> For pregnant women, their reception at health centers often resembled that of Biblical lepers. In May 1986, for example, some pregnant evacuees were driven to Belaya Tserkov health clinic and the staff came out to meet them wearing gas masks and protective clothing, and checked the women for radiation levels on the street before they even entered the clinic. The same applied to those who were hospitalized after the disaster. Aneliya Perkovska . . . was warned at the hospital not to say she was from Prypyat. . . . Perkovska ignored the advice because she felt it was beneath her dignity to lie about her background. However, in the hospital during a meal period, two women . . . joined Perkovska at a table. Upon hearing that she was from Prypyat, "they immediately ran away." Instead, Perkovska was seated next to "comrades in misfortune."

An unpublished study by Bebeshko and Korol nine years after Chernobyl reports adolescent victims who hid their identities for fear of discrimination in work, marriage, and education.[75]

Stigma requires a "mark," a discrediting feature observable to others.[76] Mere identification with the contaminated community marked Legler residents for stigma.

> *If someone sees I'm from Jackson, they ask, "Are you from that water area?" It's terrible.*

Neighbors of other landfill sites reported to me that their homes also acquired a stigmatized identity due to proximity to the facility.

Conflict. Researchers, following the work of Kai Erikson, speak of "corrosive communities" in the wake of contamination.[77] Stigma and blaming the victim are key elements of community conflict, as reported in Legler.

> *Every place I go on the other side of town, they mock us: "There's nothing wrong with your water; you're only out for the money."*

> *The local papers say you can't let two square miles affect the township. This hurts. We didn't create this situation.*

They don't give two hoots. People at the town meetings tell us to shut up, that they're sick and tired of hearing us and that we take too much time up at meetings.

I saw people on the other side of town who said that their well isn't polluted so why should they have to pay for mine. They blame us for all the news coverage convincing people not to move here.

Ironically, as township officials focused on overcoming the stigma directed at the entire town because of the Legler contamination, residents of the Legler section were further blamed and stigmatized.

Similar dynamics have occurred elsewhere. At Love Canal, for example, Martha Fowlkes and Patricia Miller describe stigma directed at those believing in the contamination by those who did not. The latter group viewed themselves as having "normal identities," while the believers were seen as abnormal and thus illegitimate.[78] In this way, the believers' perception that the canal was hazardous, so threatening to the disbelievers, was also characterized as illegitimate.

Steve Kroll-Smith and Stephen Couch report that Centralians were also stigmatized by outsiders. For example, overheard in a bank was the comment, "Here comes a Centralian; the money is hot!" The believer/disbeliever dichotomy also characterized Centralia. Residents from the hot side of town, who experienced imminent danger from explosion and subsidence, understandably were more eager to relocate than those from the relatively safe side of town. That lines of contamination represented lines in a serious community conflict is reflected in the authors' title for their book on the subject, *The Real Danger Is Above Ground.*[79]

Beverly Cuthbertson describes the interaction of the community of Globe, Arizona, during a period of protracted asbestos cleanup as "conflictive adaptation."[80] In the resulting "adversary disaster culture," government did not act definitively, the media debated the risks, and residents of the affected subdivision were increasingly labeled as "opportunists." While the community sought to downplay stigma, hazard-endangered residents believed that they were being victimized. As they argued for relocation, they clashed with residents who wanted to repair the community. When, on September 17, 1985, bulldozers crushed and flattened the Mountain View Mobile Home Estates, emotions were juxtaposed. Residents who had mourned the contamination of their homes were now free to leave; it was the disbelievers who now mourned the loss of their community.[81]

Conclusion. A few years back when I sought to describe the axial variable in the experience of contamination victims for a presentation at Oxford University, I observed of the experiential and practical gap that separates insiders and outsiders:

In sum, when toxic victims inevitably complain that outsiders don't understand their plight, what do they mean? Such victims have come to accept that they, and perhaps family, home, and community, as well, have been exposed to health threatening environmental contamination. The step into this non-normative reality now separates their experience from that of friends, kin, co-workers, and even from the government officials with whom they must now deal, all of whom are still living in the previous reality of the "non-contaminated" person. The result is an insider/outsider divide. Except for those neighbors or others who also perceive themselves to be toxic victims, other people are not privy to the meaning of contamination. They are ill-prepared to be supportive, informative or helpful because their reality is drastically different.[82]

McGee adopts the concept of "social undermining" to reflect this absence of support from family and others in the victims' social network. One of the interesting dynamics of contamination is that this relational net, perhaps not formerly based on proximity, is often supplanted for victims by a spatial net.[83]

Neighbors: Proximate Support

Although they previously knew each other, it was not until Legler's isolation in the throes of the water pollution crisis that neighbors began to develop close relationships. These relationships were particularly helpful in coping with the disaster because of the distancing of friends and relatives formerly central to residents' social networks.

Thus, if outsiders could not understand, then neighbors who shared the same situation could now offer one another significant social support. Much of this support came simply through conversation. Because they were in the same predicament, neighbors frequently were willing to listen to each other. They could test their ideas, discuss their fears, and seek empathy. This sharing gave them the opportunity for both emotional release and supportive feedback. They were also able to gain a basis of comparison with others in a similar situation.

> *Neighbors were very helpful. They were supportive in every way. I'd go to talk to them over a cup of coffee; then I'd feel better.*

> *I could let my aggravation out. I wasn't alone. And when I'd see others' problems, mine didn't seem so bad.*

Neighbors traveling together to meetings of the Concerned Citizens Committee had the opportunity to discuss options and impressions. They were not alone in the complex and frightening situation facing them.

Despite the overall climate of social support within Legler, tensions occurred. Some residents did not believe that the pollution was important. Others did not approve of the lawsuit against the township. And, over time, the internal obsession with the crisis became counterproductive for some residents. Some noted that all they ever talked about with their neighbors was the water, "even when we're tired of talking about it." One woman became so nervous when the issue came up that her husband would not allow her to speak with neighbors.

Considerable variation existed within sections of Legler as to the development of close neighborhood ties. Thus in some areas neighbors' help came readily; in others it had to be requested. Note the difference between the following comments:

You could borrow water from your neighbors, but you had to ask; they wouldn't just offer.

People borrowed water if they forgot to put the flag out. We exchanged spring water. We were lucky to have good neighbors. This helped bring us close together. We would not be as close now if it were not for our water problem. We wouldn't know many people in the community. We're like a family.

Overall, the interdependence among neighbors added a dimension of community spirit to Legler, demonstrated when the new water lines were ready. In several sections of Legler, neighbors worked together to dig the ditches for hooking up the city water. Strong feelings of cohesiveness were expressed:

All of the people were in the same boat. I love our neighbors. I fight more for them than for us. We felt like an "us."

This neighborhood dynamic helps explain Russell Stone and Adeline Levine's comment based on their Love Canal analysis that only one-third of their residents reported losing friends while half reported making new friends.[84]

Summary: Individual and Family Impacts

Toxic exposure places the adults in the family under particularly severe stress. Successful coping depends in large part on the ability of the couple to avoid being destabilized by these pressures. Moreover, the family is likely to be isolated from friends, relatives, and coworkers from outside the affected area, who do not share the perspective of the victim. Those outside the victims' relational web are even less likely to be supportive, particularly if their vested interests are countered by the pollution event or the demands and actions of the victims in coping with it. These "strangers" may form a hostile group of outsiders viewing activist victims as using the situation for their own ends.[85] Meanwhile, expectations that government will step in to solve the problem are likely to be disappointed. In the face of the resulting isolation, the support that neighbors give one another becomes increasingly important. As proximate relationships serve as the basis for a sense of community, people combine forces to overcome their disabling relationships with government, discussed in the next chapters.

5

Disabling Citizens: The Governmental Response to Toxic Exposure

With the discovery and announcement of contamination, toxic victims suddenly find themselves in a complex institutional context made up of the various local, state, and federal agencies having jurisdiction over their contamination incident. This is an unfamiliar life context for most people, one for which they lack experience. Their lives are essentially captured by agencies on which they become dependent for clarification and assistance. Technical experts and lawyers, from government and industry, now dictate the terms defining such core issues as safety and risk and whether they will be helped to find safe water or to relocate. The essence of this relationship is depicted by Adeline Levine in her description of how Love Canal residents perceived their treatment by the New York State Department of Health.

> Because DOH officials did not pay serious attention to the task of providing information to them and working through the implications of the information, the residents felt that they were being treated not as rational, respected adults but rather as though they had somehow lost their mature good sense when they became victims of a disaster they had no way of preventing.[1]

Effectively, toxic victims become "disabled," to use Ivan Illich's term, as suddenly they are dependent on professionals to expertly handle various areas of life formerly governed by their own naive wisdom.[2] What is lost is their ability to participate directly in understanding and determining courses of action important to their lives. Thus disablement is a key cause of the lifescape shift toward a sense of lost control.

The implications of disablement for the stress and coping issues discussed in the previous chapter should not be underestimated. To a substantial degree, psychological recovery from contamination is pegged to ecological recovery. It is not possible to restore mental health and well-being if one knowingly continues to live in a polluted environment. The dilemma is that there is rarely a quick fix for contamination; often there is no real fix at all, at least on the time scale of the human life span. Inasmuch as solutions to problems as defined by industry and government routinely do not correspond to restoring the health of affected ecosystems, what I term the "mitigatory gap" becomes a vital factor. It is much easier to identify and label contamination than to remove it. The gap between identification and recognized solution is key to contamination's consequences. Thus discovery of contamination pushes the victims onto one of two tracks. If they are "lucky," their place (and life) is captured by the remedial process, with all the related trade-offs, delays, expert-defined processes, and likely dissatisfaction with the eventual level of cleanup. Alternatively, their site is not considered to be a priority and is excluded from a process of cleanup, creating a different type of protracted limbo for the victims, one in which the condition has been initially diagnosed but all further treatment has been denied.

A substantial part of the psychosocial cost of contamination results from this social process of action or inaction. In effect, these costs are iatrogenic—caused by the treatment employed.[3] Like the staph infection picked up during a hospital stay or the dangerous interaction of prescribed drugs, they are a side effect of the way society addresses issues of contamination rather than of the physical effects of the toxins themselves.

Overall, the process of disabling reflects how in postmodern society the regulation of environmental risks embodies the *pseudotechnocratic* character of society. The criteria by which decisions are made do not reflect social values expressed through the political process, but rather political decisions hidden behind the rationale of technical standards set by experts.[4] In risk assessment, for example, acceptable risk is defined by professionals whose actions may less reflect public values than economic and political forces vested in permitting facilities and limiting the costs of environmental standards. The result is that victims are dependent on government officials whose will and competency to master the situation they come increasingly to doubt.

A Dialectic of Double Binds

The result of this change in circumstances for most victims is their virtual entrapment in a double bind. They learn that they are neither sufficiently at risk to warrant definitive action by government nor sufficiently free of risk to return to life as usual. For their part, government officials working with them are in an equally conflicting situation. They must respond to the public's concerns but without agreeing to take steps that extend beyond their regulatory authority, budgets, professional norms, or political realities.

For both parties, the "double bind" that results is one that is particularly evident in the context of communication between them. The term "double bind" originated from Gregory Bateson's efforts to explain schizophrenia by looking at family communication. Schizophrenia, in his view, results from contradictions between communications and meta-communications (communications about communications) that simultaneously send a message and negate that message. The result is endless interpretation that leads to "an experience of being punished precisely for being right in one's own view of the context." Repeated experiences lead the parties to behave habitually as if they expected such punishment. A mutual double bind develops, and "neither person can afford to receive or emit meta-communicative messages without distortion."[5]

The prolonged dialectic that evolves from the inherently contradictory yet mutually bound relationship of regulator and contamination victim represents a form of social schizophrenia. Victims are stressed by their initial dependency on government officials who simultaneously communicate such double messages as "You are at risk/You are safe" and "I will help/There is nothing I can or will do." In turn, citizens demand help from regulatory officials but reveal increasing degrees of frustration, anger, distrust, and hostility as they realize that officials are not clarifying and solving problems, at least not quickly. When regulators receive such mixed messages as "Do for me as much as you can/What you are doing is not good enough" and "I am relying on your help/I not only don't trust you but I blame you," they become embattled. This dysfunctional pattern of communication was illustrated during a meeting in the Washington Heights section of Wallkill, New York, in the mid-1980s.

It was a tense public meeting. Residents from the neighborhood crowded into the fire hall to learn more about their recently discovered contamination problem. The solvent tetrachloroethylene (PCE), a suspected carcinogen, had been found in wells at one end of the section. The concentration in one of the homes was among the highest ever recorded for a residential water source; a glass of tap water was said to be one-fourth PCE. Testing showed the PCE levels declining as samples were taken at greater distances from the worst wells. Beyond a cluster of some ten homes, no other wells exceeded the 50 parts per billion (ppb) standard used by New York State to define the acceptable level of contamination; many wells showed no pollution at all.

Midway through the meeting, the county health commissioner arose to address the question of whether people should drink their water. Earlier, he had been quoted to the effect that water below the 50 ppb standard was safe to drink. He now sought to distance himself from this advice, noting that the aquifer beneath the neighborhood might never again be free of PCE. Residents would themselves have to weigh the risks of continued use of their wells. As he followed this new line of reasoning, however, the commissioner was caught in a bind. Although water lower than the standard was legally safe, it is hardly the same as pure, uncontaminated water. And if PCE was in the aquifer, it might later be found at levels exceeding the standard. It follows from this line of reasoning that the water could never again be trusted and, accordingly, should not be used.

As he followed this chain of logic, the commissioner suddenly realized the danger of overstressing the hazard. Thus if the water could not be used, residents required assistance. However, since most of the tested water fell within allowable limits of contamination, his hands were tied in offering this assistance. Illustrating the mitigatory gap, the commissioner recognized that if people were made to fear their water source, there might be nothing he could do to help them. He grasped at the chance to balance his message, concluding with reassurances that most wells did not exceed standards and were "legally" safe. He thus garbled the message, with residents being simultaneously advised that their water was safe and unsafe.

Taking him aside, I explained just how confused his message had become. But his subsequent efforts to restate it also became garbled. Only after most people had filed out the door did he find the words to shout a clear warning about the potential risks of drinking water with detectable contaminants. Many residents, having been told that their water supply was "safe" by government standards, believed the threat was over and subsequently resumed use of their wells. Others, hearing of a potential ongoing threat, continued to believe that they were at risk. But these believers were not supported in their belief by most government communications or many of their neighbors. Denial of the threat was clearly an easier route than acceptance, in part because of the regulatory response. The dialectic of double binds had created a disabling situation. Two truths introduced into local belief had contradictory implications for personal, family, and community response. The prudent citizen might well suspend action until a better definition of the situation was given.[6] But, as it was left, in effect, the standard would be followed but without confidence that safety was achieved.

As this example shows, such double bind situations are often true dilemmas, in which response is limited by a combination of the realities and uncertainties of the situation. There may be no clear right answer, but there are many decidedly wrong ones.

The Citizens' Bind

Victims of contamination quickly find themselves in a double bind. Given the ambiguity of their situation, they can either wallow in uncertainty or push for a clearer definition of the situation. The double bind occurs with the twin risks of clarity: the risk may simultaneously be considered too low to justify assistance yet great enough that environmental stigma results.

Marginalization and Citizens' Bind. Most Washington Heights residents were thrown into limbo by the manner in which triage is practiced with all but the most extreme contamination events. While their wells were not polluted quite enough to trigger the state's "action level" (the threshold at which contamination demands action), their "fortunate" neighbors with higher levels of pollution were quickly provided with a new water system. Ironically, these highly contaminated residences escaped stigma because they were fully mitigated. In contrast, marginally affected residents could accept continued uncertainty or publicly argue that their levels showed enough danger to warrant assistance, with stigma as the only certain outcome.

Similarly, at Love Canal, residents who lived just outside the arbitrary boundaries delineating "safe" from "unsafe" areas were deprived of tax benefits, offers of relocation, testing, and other government aid. In toxic events, the epicenter may be physically dangerous, but the margins are a social catastrophe.

In 1975, in the aftermath of the tainted feed incident, citizens' bind similarly affected Michigan farmers with cattle classified as having "low-level" rather than "high-level" PBB contamination. Low-level farmers received no compensation even when their herds showed severe symptoms of PBB poisoning, resulting in economic losses. Ironically, some high-level herds were comparatively healthy yet qualified for assistance.[7]

Arbitrary Decisions and Citizens' Bind. Health officials routinely attempt to play down victims' overriding concern for health risk by citing legalistically defined rational criteria for categorizing different pollution cases.[8] Their response is triggered by exceeded action levels or by clear "exposure pathways" linking contamination to health risks for a proximate population, all pending their having the available staff, resources, and technology to test.[9]

But what happens when the rationality of decisions is questioned? For example, Washington Heights residents discovered from PCE victims in Vermont that a lower level for state action had been adopted there. Had New York used the same level, assistance would have been triggered for many additional residents.[10] Similarly, around the Asarco smelter in Washington State, residents with insufficient soil arsenic levels to trigger mitigation of their yards complained to me that other states had more stringent action levels. One can almost envision states' soliciting new residents with the slogan "We clean up to higher standards," much as industry is attracted by the inverse.

The existence of multiple different definitions of safety calls into question the seeming certainty with which government officials surround their decisions. Despite ambiguity, having made a decision, agencies are likely to use a scientific rationale to legitimize the position and to defend it stubbornly. Thus what may begin as an open inquiry under the scientific method is transformed into a politically distorted approach.

Also indicative of administrative rationality are efforts to avoid setting precedents by disguising the reasons for protective actions. To diffuse and bound the crisis there, officials defined the Michigan PBB contamination as an agricultural rather than a health problem.[11] At Love Canal, the political decision to eventually relocate marginal "outer ring" residents was justified on mental health rather than physical or environmental health grounds and under the guise of urban redevelopment.[12]

Decisions about the cleanup of contaminated sites often impugn regulatory credibility, as when the least expensive and involved remedial approach is chosen over a full restoration of both damaged ecosystems and residents' confidence in the security of their homes.[13] Further demonstrating the "damned if you do" nature of contamination's double bind, the remedial effort may replace the original contamination as the primary source of concern. For example, in a community I studied in the southern Appalachians, a visible and intrusive treatment plant built to strip chemicals from the polluted groundwater became a new symbol of fear and stigma, compounding concerns over invisible water pollutants with new worries about air pollution.[14] And, the cleanup process in the arsenic-contaminated Tacoma/ Rushton area negatively affected everybody. Ironically, disbelievers often faced removal and replacement of all the topsoil on their property; believers, desiring remediation, as often owned property with arsenic levels too low for action.[15] These examples suggest the restatement of our double bind as the entropic principle of contamination: *victims are likely to lose no matter what happens.*

Dismissing Disease. Citizens' bind also occurs when residents believe that a cancer or other disease cluster is affecting their community. Lay efforts at cluster identification are a good indicator of the lifescape shift in health expectations. Sometimes perceived high disease rates precede and trigger the discovery of contaminants. In other instances, disease incidence gains attention only after the community is "bounded" within or near a known contamination site. Either way, a normally private health crisis is now advertised, stigmatizing person and place simultaneously.

To address community risk of illness related to Superfund sites, the U.S. Congress established the Agency for Toxic Substances and Disease Registry, now a part of the Centers for Disease Control. ATSDR/CDC conducts health risk assessments and, in conjunction with state health departments, attempts to confirm or disconfirm disease clusters associated with waste sites. ATSDR and CDC have long been the subject of criticism. A scathing review in the early 1990s charged the agencies with using inappropriate testing techniques, relying on statistical methods inappropriate for small and transient populations living near waste sites, overlooking the sickest populations within a community, using consultant researchers known to be biased against finding cause and effect relationships, ignoring nonlethal exposure effects such as respiratory or reproductive problems, and failing to take precautionary measures in affected communities. Despite spending more than $30 million per year, the critics concluded, the agencies failed to find an association between disease and exposure and results have been used to quell public fears and justify cutting back on remedial measures.[16]

ATSDR has attempted to address some of these criticisms and to improve the sensitivity of its field staff to community concerns.[17] However, given the inherent disharmony between regulatory and scientific demands, the limits of community-based epidemiology, and its significance to toxic victims, it is hard to avoid health research having a disabling effect. Since Love Canal, where a protracted disagreement over health effects became a war of paradigms,[18] health research has often served to deny relationships seen by community members as patently obvious.

After politicians brought in ATSDR and the New York State Health Department to assess a potential cancer cluster near Al Turi Landfill, Inc., the agencies concluded that the cancers were too diverse and the likelihood of a single source too remote to warrant a full epidemiological study. Residents were told that the incidence of cancers is so high generally that their alarming levels might not exceed the norm. Furthermore, environmental investigations, focused on groundwater, failed to identify a pathway between the facility and the neighborhood despite the presence of groundwater contamination. Air as a possible exposure pathway was ignored, despite the candidate cancer cluster's location directly downwind from the facility and more than a decade of noxious odors plaguing nearby residents. While residents felt that the matter had not been thoroughly investigated, with the agencies bowing out, there was little they could do to prove that exposures caused their sickness. The most vocal resident died of cancer. Illness again became a matter of private suffering, not a rallying point for community action.

Winning a health study, however, is no panacea, considering methodological limits and choices and the barrier of vested interests. I learned this firsthand when my nonprofit organization won a state-ordered health study around Orange County landfill, encompassing the adjacent Al Turi site. Although I had feared that the approach based upon comparison to a control community was unlikely to prove much, the long-delayed study in fact identified significantly high levels of somatic symptoms when compared to either the control group or national norms.[19] Research problems made these findings even more compelling. In a reversal of expectations, I ended up defending the study while the county self-servingly dismissed the results as invalid and refused to conduct further investigations.

Conclusions About Citizens' Bind.   We have seen that uncertainty is maximal for marginally contaminated toxic victims. However, given the inherent uncertainties of exposure, nearly all toxic victims are marginalized. Most suffer from citizens' bind. In seeking publicity, they invite stigma. In actively seeking answers, they enhance their level of stress. In depending on government for assistance, they face likely disappointment. And facing a "mitigatory gap" between the discovery of the exposure and the determination and execution of corrective steps, they are trapped in a situation where they are damned no matter what they do.

The Regulators' Bind

Regulators' bind, in contrast, involves the frustrations of local, state, and federal environmental and health officials. Forced to make decisions under uncertainty and limited in their allowed response, they face a public extremely sensitive to what they say and do.

Regulators operate within a delimited role. Acting as public servants seeking to solve a complex problem, they find themselves bound by regulations, political realities, limited resources, and their own perspective toward their task. Moreover, they are caught between two conflicting visions of a public official's role, a traditional desire to mediate between differing interests to define the public good, on the one hand, and recent pressures to make rational decisions that maximize net overall benefits, on the other. In short, much like the health commissioner in Wallkill, they are pulled in one direction by a desire to help and, in the other, by pressures to not waste public resources on low-priority problems. The clash of these models frequently helps generate their ambivalent response to the public.[20] Furthermore, bureaucratic organizational structures create fragmented patterns of work and responsibility that result in dehumanizing practices and promote overlap, confusion, gaps in offered response, and poor coordination among different agencies working in the same community. Agencies may also be subject to "regulatory capture," biased in favor of one side of a controversy, most often corporate and not citizen interests.[21]

Furthermore, as we have seen, how government officials communicate their evaluation of a situation determines the public's reaction. No situation is more feared by an official than the creation of panic. Thus we can understand the pressure on my health commissioner to play down risk despite justification for concern. Such officials walk a tortured path between arousing public fear and quelling it, both potentially in conflict with the facts as understood. Heather Tosteson, of the Centers for Disease Control, advocates that officials become sensitive to the psychology of this situation. Citizens may expect scientists to validate their beliefs by proving exposures or effects. Once confirmed, their fears become more controllable. Others expect scientists to conclude that all is safe so that everything can return to normal. In either case, toxic victims need the scientists to give them back some sense of control.[22]

Officials must also make decisions under uncertainty. Tosteson observes that uncertainty is as trying for the scientist as for the layperson. Beyond uncertainty over what actually has happened, scientists lack confidence due to the newness of the environmental science they practice and its highly politicized nature. "When studying the effects of toxic exposures at sites, scientists face all the areas of scientific uncertainty that the community experiences. . . . In this context, scientists can experience the high level of social distrust of the communities as an additional, and painfully personal, assault on their professional credibility."[23]

It is a given that, in a toxic incident, somebody has to determine the operational standards for risk, and whoever does is likely to take the brunt of criticism. Given the large number of unknowns in a toxic exposure incident, it is a thankless task to bear responsibility for bringing clarity and certainty to the situation. With the announcement of exposure, citizens look to government experts to inform them and to fix the problem. For an official to guess at the answers demanded may be rash, to hold back cautious. But at some point, citizens unappreciative of caution expect officials to have the answers. Invariably, this places the regulators in a no-win situation. Michael Reich cites a former EPA official, Steven Jellinek, on this point. "The regulator must make decisions about chemicals 'in the midst of pervasive uncertainty.' Since the regulator does not have 'the luxury' of putting off decisions until certainty arrives, there exists an 'inevitability of being wrong' sometimes."[24] Karl Reko quotes an EPA official at Times Beach feeling the pressures of regulatory bind after residents peppered him with questions and demands for solutions to their problems, "I could not give straight answers because there was no solution. We were taking the blame for everything that had, or had not, been done, and it was unfair."[25]

In sum, officials face the complex task of discerning the fine line between danger and false alarm. In some cases, standards are set and must be applied. In other cases, no clear standards exist. Nagging issues persist even when standards are available. For example, the health commissioner at the Wallkill meeting, in assessing the community threat, undoubtedly also had to weigh a host of considerations that are highly salient and concrete to a bureaucrat. His conflict was genuine. He was addressing an inherently gray question: How risky is exposure to small quantities of organic chemicals below the standard? He neither wanted to be responsible for failing to warn people of the risk nor for the consequences of a clear warning. Among the latter concerns were the fears of overcommitting his agency, overstepping his authority, causing "undue alarm or panic," becoming committed to the expenditure of unavailable funds, varying from the policy of the state health department, or taking on legal liability. He may have been uncomfortable pointing to the need for steps such as the provision of a totally new water source that he thought would be very difficult to achieve. His problem, in short, was how to simultaneously tell people that their water was unsafe and that he would do nothing about it—without their becoming understandably concerned.

The Consequences of Citizens' and Regulators' Binds

Citizens' and regulators' binds interact synergistically, making it highly unlikely that alarmed citizens will understand and accept regulators' decisions as rational. As a result, the very people the regulators attempt to help increasingly vilify them, making officials the scapegoats in situations that they didn't create. Any action these officials take is likely to be "wrong" according to one of their constituencies. Harris reports the outcomes of regulator's bind for health officials:

> In their battles for better sanitation, decent housing, milk pasteurization, and maternal and child health services, health departments had generally enjoyed the support of citizen reform groups. To find themselves now labeled by environmental activists of the 1980s as the enemy was a stunning reversal of history and a shattering blow to their self-perception as the champions of the public interest. The subsequent generation of officials has not been so naive, expecting to be confronted by public pressure and even opposition.[26]

These encounters are just as stressful for regulators as they are for toxic victims. For example, it is common for the public to force officials to confront all their limitations in public with little wriggle room. Take, for example, the "water trap" that officials routinely confront. During a public meeting, the official is offered a drink from a glass or jar of slimy water from a local resident's faucet. Few comply, although it is a rhetorical situation and no response is correct. Like embarrassing questions such as, "Would you let your family live in my house?" "Would you send your own children to school here?" or "Do you think it is safe for us to remain here?", the water trap invites the regulator to act distrustfully by refraining from taking on the same risks that citizens live with. More extreme confrontations also occur. One state official described his fears to me. At a point when he was already sleepless fearing "mob" retaliation for stringently regulating Al Turi landfill, he was almost lynched by an out-of-control mob of angry farmers for not shutting down a waste site called Merion Blue Grass Sod Farm. Everybody was after him.

Officials may carry a reservoir of anger and resentment from such pressures. At a statewide conference for toxic victims that I attended, an exercise intended to create a better understanding between regulators and citizens went awry after a New York State health official verbally attacked the audience until they responded to him in an equally hostile way. This official unconsciously played out the dialectic with citizens that characterizes their mutual binds. It is not surprising that David Tester, a therapist, treated a number of regulators who were greatly distressed by their inability to respond effectively to the public during their encounters.[27]

Levine sheds light on the coping strategy of officials who maintain a professional manner in the face of citizen anger.

> The person who conducted the meeting on that cold, gloomy morning in December mentioned later that he felt proud he had been able to remain cool, "to talk like a machine," despite the anger of the Love Canal residents displayed when he read the DOH announcement. Task force members expressed similar feelings more than once when they conducted or even were present at meetings with residents who seemed so unreasonable. Privately, the officials congratulated each other on not giving anything away, on not conceding anything to the residents. In public, they said they saw "no evidence," or said "I don't know," and argued that the people were given answers, but "like spoiled children," just did not like the answers they received.[28]

ATSDR's Tosteson further explains this defensive response. Facing combined pressure, insecurity, and rejection from angry citizens, scientists tend to overreact, compounding problems of communication by escaping into the safe turf of science.

> Scientists cope with the uncertainty they face professionally by becoming more emotionally detached from those they are studying, more insistent on method, more concerned with professionalism . . . and more insistent on remaining within what *is* certain for them, their own belief system. Scientific doubt, then,

becomes a form of certainty because it insists on the primacy of scientific method. . . . Scientists will often express and insist on the limits of scientific certainty in ways that heighten the uncertainty of the community.[29]

By playing the role of objective scientist, these officials try to place themselves outside the social context of the contamination victims. Answers within the value system of science are projected onto the community, as if the community shared these values. "Thus," Tosteson writes, "they refuse to provide an adequate context or interpretive frame to permit the community to understand what actions they can take to reduce the level of threat they feel, a threat compounded of not only scientific uncertainty but also of broader social and philosophical uncertainty."[30]

The essence of the regulators' bind, therefore, involves the fact that the required decisions are inherently complex in ways for which modern science is ill equipped. And these weaknesses are laid bare by the process. As the community confronts professional norms of behavior, citizens often test trustworthiness with questions and actions for which there is no right response, yet they cannot be treated as purely rhetorical either. The regulators realize that they cannot do their jobs without the trust of the community, but the more they do their jobs, the more likely it is that their actions will invite distrust, not only despite their efforts but often because of them.

What are the major sources of the disabling dialectic that exists between toxic victims and regulators? It is evident that the process of communication between these groups is flawed. Furthermore, they hold different paradigms for defining acceptable risk, placing them in basic conflict.

Communicational Distortion in the Institutional Context

A major source of stress and controversy is the form taken by regulatory communication. As threatened communities attempt to cope with exposure, information becomes a vital commodity. This is particularly true when the situation is novel and great uncertainty is experienced by individuals and communities alike. However, government agencies tend to maintain strict control over information.[31] This strategy reinforces the initial dependence and helplessness of citizens as well as their eventual distrust of the agencies.

Furthermore, regulatory communication tends to differ from the expectations for valid communication used in everyday life as judged by four criteria suggested by Jürgen Habermas: the clarity of the communication, its basis in fact, its believability, and its appropriateness. The failure of either or both parties to meet even one of the four criteria may result in the parties breaking off communication, arguing over unresolved issues, or adopting a mode of action aimed at forcing the issue in some way. All too often, regulators fail to communicate clearly, their assumptions are questioned, they lose people's trust, or their responses fall short of citizens' expectations for what is called for by the situation.[32] Partially as a result, citizens often use attention-getting strategies, such as the slimy-water trap noted above, inappropriate action by the standards of many officials. Citizens may also be unclear, inaccurate, or unbelievable.

Given citizens' lack of preparation for the situation, it is understandable that they may have difficulty communicating effectively. Government officials should not have the same excuse. When institutional communication to toxic victims fails to meet these criteria, the result is distorted communication, defined by Claus Mueller as "all forms of restricted and prejudiced communication that by their nature inhibit a full discussion of problems, issues and ideas that have public relevance."[33] Distorted communication takes three forms.

First, *directed communication* occurs when government policy structures language and communication. For example, in toxic incidents, regulations guide the definition of "the problem," the rights of victims, and the responsibilities of agencies to respond. The language of regulation dominates much of the exchange. Furthermore, this language relies heavily on the vocabulary and methods of science and engineering. Experts speak to legalistic regulatory requirements, which, if met, make the action approvable, even if it may be unacceptable in a broader social context. Thus a waste facility that meets the engineering criteria listed in the regulation deserves a permit, under regulatory rationale, even if the community is threatened in myriad ways not covered by the regulation. By meeting the listed criteria, the facility is deemed "safe." Citizens' concerns are therefore rendered "irrational," at least within the rationale of the regulation.

A clear example of directed communication was the effort by the Reagan and Bush administrations to use cost as the basis for judging risk.[34] Reagan ordered that regulatory policies be cost-effective in that they should offer more benefits in risk reduction than their cost in societal resources. The resulting approach was based on the view that "the purpose of government intervention is to achieve efficient risk taking and risk bearing, not necessarily to reduce risk. We reject the conventional wisdom that risk is always bad, and that it should be eradicated from the face of the earth."[35] The tool for achieving this policy was "cost-benefit analysis," used as the central calculus of government despite its limitations for meaningfully comparing risks, its questionable underlying value assumptions, and its emphasis on cancer as opposed to other health risks.[36]

Using this calculus, "comparative risk assessment" played a central role in EPA's own internal reviews of risk from 1983 onward. The approach took its final shape in the 1992 U.S. budget, setting the stage for the "neo-Reaganomic" attack on environmental regulation that occurred in the 1990s.[37] The budget presents a cost-benefit analysis for fifty-three health and safety regulations, concluding that environmental risks are much smaller than other threats to human health. For example, costs are estimated at $100,000 per averted death for passive restraint/seat belt standards for automobiles affecting more than six thousand lives per million exposed. In contrast, with one exception, the least expensive environmental regulations are in the $3.4 million to $5.7 million per averted death range and the most expensive as high as $19 billion to $92 billion per averted death. For example, the hazardous waste listing for wood preservatives was estimated to affect less than one person per million exposed at a cost of $5.7 trillion per averted death.

Similar calculus underlies the risk assessments used in Superfund to weigh trade-offs between different cleanup strategies and to demonstrate acceptable risk for a proposed hazardous facility. In this way, dangers are linguistically transformed into neutral numbers that can be "managed" (i.e., directed) in contrast to people's lives, the management of which we would never knowingly tolerate. In a 1989 interview, late Assistant Surgeon General Vernon Houk dismissed the scientific validity of risk assessment: "It's got to be something that's come down from the mountains with Moses on tablets. There is an illusion of precision. Risk assessment as now practiced is about as effective as a five-year weather forecast at best. At worst, it's just voodoo!"[38] The social validity of risk assessment is equally suspect. Thus Michael Heiman notes that, while risk assessment sounds like a macho process in which the daring decide what they will risk, in reality officials determine what the public will risk. Accordingly, it might more accurately be called "death assessment" or more precisely "retardation, hormone deficiency, immunization failure, and impotency assignment."[39]

Second, *arrested communication* occurs when some groups cannot engage in political communication because they lack the linguistic ability to do so. For example, the average citizen lacks the technical expertise to participate in many of the specialized decisions that follow from toxic exposure. Thus David Harris, a government official, blames "scientific illiteracy" for distorting regulator/citizen interactions.[40] If citizens had a better grasp of the scientific and technical issues involved, he argues, they would be better able to understand the reasoning employed by regulatory experts.

A contradictory view, held by grassroots leaders, is that citizens are capable of mastering complex environmental concepts, but that government agencies impede their acquisition of information.[41] The use of expert consultants by citizens' groups can compensate for this imbalance in background (see Chapter 6).

There is a likely relationship between findings that poor, minority, and unempowered populations have been disproportionately exposed to environmental hazards and broader issues of arrested communication. Limited access to education and literacy may selectively and disproportionately disempower some groups to discern dangers and to take protective action.

Third, *constrained communication* involves actions by private or governmental groups to seek their own self-interest by structuring and limiting public communication. This form of distortion invites distrust more than any other. Government officials constrain communication when they delay, give false reassurances, withhold information, take inadequate actions, mishandle testing, argue among themselves, act secretively, draw arbitrary boundaries, use insensitive or incomprehensible language, deny citizens' perceptions and fears, hide behind scientific reasoning for political decisions, and appear to be clueless. These responses may be genuine or may be unintentional faux pas. But they are also used as techniques strategically to distort an issue and undermine public involvement.

Adeline Levine illustrates strategic distortion in her description of the Thomas Commission, the panel of five prestigious scientists named by the governor of New York in 1980 to impartially evaluate conflicting scientific data about the health effects of Love Canal. Belying its credibility, Levine notes that the commission's finding of no evidence of acute health effects rested on no firm evidence whatsoever, citing only a single preliminary and general study. Levine also deconstructs the finding of no evidence of chronic health effect:

- A key study showing peripheral nerve damage at conventional levels of significance was dismissed for failing a more stringent test recommended by EPA statisticians.
- Evidence of possible cytogenetic effects was similarly dismissed by relying on negative reviews of the work and ignoring supportive reviews.
- Beverly Paigen's findings of excess miscarriage rates and other effects at Love Canal were dismissed through unsubstantial attacks on the author and the method and its political importance. A favorable federal review of the work was disregarded, and no evidence of deficiencies was presented.
- And the commission even dismissed the New York Department of Health's own data showing significant miscarriage rates and low birth weight infants in wet areas of the canal, cited by two New York governors to justify their policies at the canal.
- Dismissal of such effects as cancers and chloracne (a dermatological condition related to dioxin or other chlorinated compound exposures) lacked citation of supporting evidence.

Moreover, the commission ignored government's failure to undertake large, well-designed, and well-funded studies of the canal, did not properly cite its sources, and refused to answer inquiries about evidence. Conflicts of interest also undermined the independence of the review. Given that the New York State Department of Health regulated four of the five institutions where panel members served as administrators, it was not surprising that the commission's findings, in Levine's words, "provide a balm and a rationale for the DOH behavior."[42] Despite these shortcomings, the findings of the Thomas Commission were widely publicized in the media without questioning and even used in advertisements by Hooker Chemical dismissing health issues at Love Canal. It is instructive that, despite Levine's clear critique, the influence of the Thomas Commission lives on, as revealed in the recent work of Alan Mazur, who concludes that health effects from Love Canal were never proven.[43]

As illustrated, the distortion of regulatory communication is rooted in the inherent contradiction of agencies being nonindependent scientific entities. Such agencies combine severe institutional limits in inquiry with a method based on the objective search for truth. As a result, they can operate with a double standard, holding others' work to the highest expectations for scientific research while proceeding in a shoddy manner themselves. Similarly, government officials experience conflict in filling such roles as "public servant," "bureaucrat," "scientist," "technocrat," "fulfiller of public needs," "promoter of private enterprise," and "regulator of compliance with public laws." As the Thomas Commission illustrates, their performance is often further complicated by a politicized context.

Distortion and the Communication of Bad News

Perhaps no better situation illustrates the disabling consequences of government's own problems of directed, arrested, and constrained communication than the presentation of test data to toxic victims. For example, sometime after the new central water system in Legler restored a semblance of normalcy to the residents, a housewife opened her mail to discover the results of air quality tests in her basement. An impersonal letter from the New Jersey Department of Environmental Protection implied that a dangerous situation existed but offered little information for assessing the risk. She was so upset that, her husband recalled, "When I came home, I found my wife shaking; she was drinking." The wife added,

> *I couldn't calm down. Look what was in there! [pushing a list of chemicals toward me] Reading this and thinking about it, it bothers me as much as the water problem, almost more. We don't know what's going on. We understand that these are dangerous chemicals, but not how dangerous they are. We want to talk to somebody who isn't involved.*

Toxic victims frequently require a source of information independent of government if trusted interpretations are to be made. Lacking such, this family was left in a panic situation. They worried for weeks about the results but made no attempt at clarification. My glance at the state's letter indicated that the couple had misread some of their results. Despite a standard invitation to call if there were any questions, the overriding message of the letter so effectively made it seem like a one-way communication that the couple had not even considered phoning. Moreover, based upon the water contamination incident, they no longer trusted government. Barriers to effective communication were thus evident in the receiver and the sender.

Miscommunication of test results also occurred in the response to several dioxin incidents by the Missouri State Division of Health.[44] The department's study of the incidents occurred in a highly charged atmosphere. Under great pressure, the study directors created inaccurate expectations about the speed of the study and its ability to identify health effects from dioxin contamination. This set up a later crisis when, with the study incomplete, the agency was forced to release preliminary results. Study group members considered two factors in deciding which results to release. First, they wanted to avoid later accusations that data had been withheld. Second, like health officers working at Love Canal, they wanted family physicians to interpret the significance of a test result for a given individual.[45] As a result, they released all findings exceeding the norm as well as all abnormalities identified, even those known to be unrelated to dioxin exposure.

As a result, despite agency intentions to be open, their communication was distorted through violation of appropriateness, clarity, truthfulness, and authenticity. The simplified summary of results exaggerated adverse health findings by listing all abnormalities. Adding to the confusion, it employed general statements (e.g., "abnormal blood chemistry") rather than specific results (e.g., "elevated cholesterol [293]"). Actual results were buried in a complex laboratory report. Residents receiving these results in the mail became highly alarmed when they found themselves listed as abnormal on an apparent test for dioxin contamination. Contrary to the agency's assumption, many lacked access to a physician who would or could help them interpret the results. Rather than appreciating the intended full disclosure, residents felt either deceived or patronized by the simplified information.

Further miscommunication in Missouri occurred when the EPA varied from the mitigation strategy used at previous local dioxin sites. Rather than evacuate residents at Castlewood, officials decided to leave residents in their homes during remediation. Internally, EPA justified the decision due to the relatively low levels of contamination and the delays foreseeable in any attempt at permanent relocation. Although they took great pains to describe the planned remediation to the public, EPA made little attempt to discuss the reasons for selecting this approach. The result was to make "a perfectly reasonable decision seem arbitrary and capricious." This led to what Miller describes as "a series of acutely frustrating encounters in which residents ask the wrong questions and officials respond with the wrong answers."[46] Thus rather than explaining that the decision not to include a particular street in a sampling program was due to soil conditions minimizing the likelihood of contamination, an EPA official merely noted that the street hadn't been selected for sampling, violating norms for complete communication.

Differing Paradigms of Risk Between Citizens and Regulators

Controversy is inherent to the relationship of toxic victims and their institutional context because of differences in the way citizens and technocrats view risk. The "technocratic paradigm" of risk uses a scientific and technical rationale in making decisions for citizens. Basic to the modern concept of regulation is an implicit assumption that the dominant segments of society—government and the business community—must be protected from adverse impact. The technocratic paradigm thus employs risk estimates that equate "caution" with steps that least threaten the private sector. Experts must certify the legitimacy of claims by the victims of corporate pollution. For controlling risks, the marketplace is preferred to regulation.[47]

By way of illustration, here is a technocrat's perspective on nuclear wastes.[48]

The real problem is where and how do we dispose of nuclear wastes. This problem requires the organized efforts of technical experts. The political aspects of this problem stem from the fact that nobody wants the dump in their own backyard. The political problem is sustained by activists who alarm a misinformed public. DOE can correct some of these perceptions through its public relations activities, but in the end . . . the federal government will need to exert its authority over the states. . . . The bottom line is, will DOE be allowed to do its job or not?

The contrasting "democratic paradigm" takes the victims' perspective in estimating the probability of technological hazards. "Safety" is valued over profit; prevention is triggered by suggestive if not conclusive proof. Most importantly, those bearing the impacts are given an active voice in determining acceptable risk and in making decisions. This paradigm fits naturally with the public's grassroots and lay epidemiological response to contamination. Here is a contrasting "democratic" perspective on nuclear waste disposal.[49]

The fundamental issue is the relationship of the American citizenry to the institutions of power. . . . DOE claims scientific expertise, but the way it operates violates the ideals of science itself, ideals that call for open discussion, dialogue, and debate within a community of people free from the dominance of any outside power (such as DOE). . . . What is required is to hold such institutions of power accountable in ways not dominated by these institutions themselves. To dismiss such demands as "unrealistic" is to give up most the fundamental ideals of a democratic society.

It is not surprising that regulatory agencies proceed with the problem-solving approach characteristic of the technocratic paradigm. In contrast, the democratic model is readily adopted by toxic victims. These paradigms are in direct opposition. On one hand, a technological imperative derides the ignorance of those standing in its way. In response, participatory democracy attempts to function in the absence of trust.[50] In their dialectic, there are major differences between the roles of victim and regulator, between the ways that citizens and scientists/experts think, and, in particular, in the ways these two sets of actors define acceptable risk. These, of course, are not separate topics, but highly interconnected.

The Role: Professional Versus Victim

The difference between the psychological environments of citizen and regulator is captured in two examples. First, Levine reports of a Love Canal incident that "the state health officials thought they were offering help in this dreadful situation in a way that was reasonable, concerned, and within the department's legitimate purview and capabilities. In the words of a young man pointing to his pregnant wife, however, 'The damage is done! My wife is eight months pregnant. What are you going to do for my baby? It's too late for my child.'"[51]

Second, we encounter the "tyvec suit paradox," recounted in community after community where it is considered safe for residents to live in their homes in contaminated communities while workers testing or removing the hazardous wastes from their yards don protective clothing made of chemically resistant plastics and air-filtered helmets. This paradox was evidenced, for example, during the Chemical Control fire in Elizabeth, New Jersey. Thousands of barrels of toxic materials exploded and the Relocated Bayway neighborhood was totally blocked off, trapping residents. As one resident described the incident to me:

> *Nobody came and gave us a warning. The only way you can get out is to swim across that river. How's you going to get out when the streets was closed? Nobody could come in and out. And then finally one guy comes with his car, real*

*fast. EPA man. He jumps out of his car and opens his trunk. And he's putting his
mask on. I says, "Hey, where the hell is ours?" And he had everything for himself. Well, where's our stuff? And they told us not to go outside. And then you
know what? Your house was closed, your windows was closed. Do you know, the
bedding, the sheets, and the pillowcases was burning your face that night. How
did it get into the house? All that—your face was burning! If you wet with your
tongue, your lips was burning.*

As both of these examples suggest, for vigilant victims of toxic exposure, the
threat is near. It is in their homes, their neighborhood, their air, their water, their
bodies, and their children's bodies. This proximity makes the threat "real." It may
be invisible, but it is pervasive. They see it everywhere. It is no longer just part of
their physical environment; it has entered their perceptual environment as well. It
is not just out there in an out-of-sight-out-of-mind way. It is *here!*

In contrast, for government officials or experts, the threat is a faraway abstraction. Although they may be responsible for averting danger, they can be content to
do so in an "objective way"—after all, they are not personally involved, so why
should it be a subjective experience? They may visit the site for inspections, suit-
ably protected, but then they leave. At home that night, they can relax from their
work. Given their technical and scientific training, they may easily intellectualize
the problem. In fact, treating it as a *problem* has already packaged it for them conceptually. Unlike victims fearing a silent killer stalking their family, regulators face
a work problem that must be solved to the greatest degree possible given available
resources.

Accordingly, differences in the immediacy and meaning of the experience for
officials and citizens are at the root of the communications gap between them.
Although officials are professionals attempting to do a job according to the guidelines describing their responsibility, citizens are often in the role of victim, responsible for the well-being of families and threatened by newly discovered facets of the
environment. Victims have come to understand the environment as an ambient, a
surround. Officials and experts still treat it as an objective realm quite apart from
themselves. In short, the two groups approach their encounter from quite different
perspectives.

Perhaps these differences surface most clearly in their answers to the question of
what risk is acceptable for a given community. A rule of thumb (not a universal) is
that a given hazard is most acceptable to those farthest away and thus least vulnerable. In most cases, the regulators are more distanced than the residents—not only
by their professional role but also by the lack of proximity of their homes and
degree of exposure to the site. And, when they visit, they can don their tyvec suits.

Differences Between the Lay Public and Experts/Scientists

That expert and public opinion diverges is an axiom Paul Slovic and various colleagues have established over the past two decades.[52] In a recent examination of the issue, responses to a 1989 public survey about the siting of a high-level nuclear waste facility was compared to a sample of nuclear waste professionals responding to the same questions.[53] The result was a crude but instructive comparison of public and expert/industry opinions about both risk and stigma. Both groups agreed that there were potential economic benefits of the facility in terms of local employment opportunities. However, the relative agreement ended here. Specifically:

- The public overwhelmingly assumed that the U.S. nuclear program had caused and would cause local health problems, while the experts assumed it had not and would not.
- Experts more often recognized the potential to make the repository safe, in terms of properly handling radioactive materials, preventing groundwater impacts, weathering a hurricane or earthquake, and preventing an accident or sabotage.
- Three-quarters of the public indicated distrust for the Department of Energy, against half the nuclear professionals.
- The public had much greater expectations that a dump would stigmatize the identity of the host area. The groups held divergent imagery about a repository. Negative images held by the public overwhelmingly reference the dangers of high-level nuclear waste and the effort to dispose of it in a repository. In contrast, negative images held by nuclear experts cite only one risk category, transportation of wastes, as highly negative. Experts instead fear social risks, overwhelmingly abhorring the NIMBY dynamic and public fears opposing the repository.

What accounts for these differences in expert and lay thought? One possible explanation is that experts and citizens draw on different sources of information. Experts draw their information from research done according to the methods and norms of science. In contrast, citizens draw heavily on the media for their knowledge. Both sources have well-understood biases in reporting risk information. For example, newspapers overreport some causes of death (i.e., murder, accidents, and disaster), even while they underreport other causes (i.e., disease).[54]

Citizens and experts also hold divergent paradigms, as cited above. Perhaps as an expression of their alienation from the democratic response of the public, risk technocrats have a tendency to rationalize their place in democratic society as an "elite" status, legitimated through quantitative analysis and scientific expertise. Experts see their perspective as rational against public irrationality. This is precisely the wrong response for them to find common ground with the public.[55] Stephen Kaufman's studies of New Jersey's Lipari landfill captured the resulting tensions between official and citizen, respectively.

> These meetings were unreal—they would last for hours and involve hundreds of concerned people asking questions about health, technology, whatever, with really irrational tones. People would attribute any health concerns to the toxic exposure.

> We went to this meeting and there was this guy who wasn't receptive to our questions—explaining things, was very antagonistic. He basically told my wife she was an idiot.[56]

This view that the public is irrational permeates technocratic thought. Robert DuPont, a consultant hired in the 1980s to find a way to explain antinuclear sentiment, dismissed the public's "nuclear phobia" as the "ultimate irrational fear," constituting a clinical state of phobia. After Chernobyl, Russian and Western scientists described the terror of victims and the public as "radiophobia." And to Russian scientists siting facilities for the disposal of chemical weapons, opposition indicates "chemophobia." Sociologist Robert Cameron Mitchell observes that such labels allow advocates to reject hazardous facility opponents as "emotional and uninformed, influenced by the scare tactics of activists and by media hype." Stephen Hilgartner further deconstructs as pejorative terms such as "cancerophobia" and "chemophobia." He notes the political utility in the use of the term "phobia" to suggest an irrational and pathological fear. Implied is that risks are minuscule, beneath the need for concern, and that critics of industrial hazard lack credibility. Such language allows the problem to be redefined away from chemical exposure and toward unjustified fears. The threat, in this technocratic reformulation, is public perception and not contamination of the environment.[57] W. R. Freudenburg and S. K. Pastor examine technocrats' selective use of the work of cognitive psychologists on linguistic heuristics (culturally shared mental shortcuts used to address complexity) to justify the view that members of the public make poor decisionmakers, revealing that experts also use heuristics and their decisions are hardly infallible.[58] The fact is that experts themselves are often wrong in their assessments, with the result that "the dichotomy between 'real' and 'perceived' risk is less 'real' than is often assumed."[59]

Expert elitism is therefore unwarranted. Perhaps the greatest indication of this fallibility is the 1975 Reactor Safety Study, instrumental to civilian nuclear power and an early example of risk assessment prepared for the Nuclear Regulatory Commission by a team of sixty experts under the direction of MIT's Norman Rasmussen. Just four years before the Three Mile Island accident and a little more than a decade before Chernobyl, the "WASH-1400" study concluded that nuclear power plants are about 10,000 times less likely to produce fatal accidents than many nonnuclear activities and 1,000 times less likely to produce high-cost damage. Furthermore, the chance of fatal injury to a nearby resident due to a nuclear reactor accident was estimated at 1 in 5 billion per year, compared with 1 in 4,000 for a car accident and 1 in 10,000 for a fall. In sum, the study concluded that risk from the operation of nuclear plants is "very low" in comparison to both natural and human-caused disaster.[60] In his review of such expert error, Freudenburg notes that scientific judgments of technology err over human and social factors and when guesswork is required in the face of limited evidence. In contrast, although citizens may be misinformed in their actions, they have a greater ability for prudence.[61]

Errors can also be socially institutionalized. Michael Gerrard compared the risks associated with three regulatory systems for preventing toxic contamination. CERCLA, or Superfund, focuses on the cleanup of already contaminated sites, RCRA (Resource Conservation and Recovery Act) the management of current hazardous materials, and HTMA (Hazardous Materials Transportation Act) the transportation of hazardous materials by truck, rail, ship, and plane. Gerrard notes that HTMA-regulated actions cause more than 100 deaths per year, one or two orders of magnitude greater than deaths due to CERCLA- or RCRA-regulated activities. Despite its significance for actual risk, HTMA is hardly known, perhaps, Gerrard conjectures, because it involves familiar activities, such as hauling fuel, witnessed by people on a daily basis. In turn, CERCLA receives dramatically more attention than RCRA despite RCRA's importance for preventing future waste problems. As a striking indicator of social attention to these three statutes, Gerrard reports that a poll of attorneys found more than 3,000 specializing in CERCLA litigation, a little more than 1,000 on RCRA cases, and only five working on HTMA. Freeze argues that such imbalances require a fine tuning of the entire environmental regulatory system.[62]

The point is that laypersons and experts have different sources of information and both are subject to error. The fact that they think such different thoughts raises the possibility of a difference in their very way of thinking. Consider the distinction that cognitive psychologist and educational visionary Jerome Bruner made between psychologists and educators—between those trying to understand mind using what he calls a "computational" perspective and those using a "cultural" approach. Computationalists are concerned with how information is processed and emphasize how "finite, coded, unambiguous information about the world is inscribed, sorted, stored, collated, retrieved, and generally managed by a computational device following specifiable rules." Surrounding reality is defined by data. As they work from their findings back to reality, computationalists move in a manner that Bruner describes as "inside out." We can posit that technocrats tend to be computationalists. They want proof before drawing conclusions.

In contrast, democrats are more likely to adopt what Bruner terms a "cultural approach," finding meaning in the cultural context, often through discourse and reflection. Unlike the objective application of information processing, cultural meanings are inherently fuzzy—not only subjective but intersubjective. Meaning is derived from the overall context of contamination and its significance in a given cultural setting. This setting guides the interpretation of facts in an "outside in" direction.[63] Thus judgments of what is "safe" are not based ipso facto upon some rigid table of standards, but made in consideration of vulnerable loved ones exposed to a potential threat. This difference becomes important as we examine in more detail the question of acceptable risk.

Conflicting Definitions of Acceptable Risk

Conflicting definitions of acceptable risk are evident in the above contrast in the ranking and evaluation of risks by citizens and experts, in the controversial use of relative risk thinking, in the ambiguity of standards that purport to provide a clear line of risk, and in the contrast of actual decisionmaking rules within the technocratic and citizen paradigms.

Type I Versus Type II Error. In 1989, the building formerly housing the Psychology and Statistics Departments at the State University of New York at Buffalo attained a bleak notoriety. One of the worst clusters of Hodgkin's disease (a relatively rare form of lymph cancer) ever found was identified in the building's occupants.[64] A practical question demanding a clear answer was raised: Was it safe to allow further occupancy of the building?

The New York State Department of Health failed to find an obvious environmental cause for the cluster. Instead they gave an alternative explanation. The higher socioeconomic status and education levels of graduate students and faculty placed them in a population known to be at risk for the disease. Moreover, a few victims also had a positive family history of the disease. In short, victims probably would have developed the disease anyway no matter where they were. By blaming the victims, the DOH rationalized that the building was safe. A health official even encouraged the opening of a daycare center in the building.

Psychologist and epidemiologist Janice Hastrup, whose research originally identified the cluster, took the citizens' side and deconstructed the DOH's tautological reasoning.[65] The fact that no other buildings at the university (whose occupants were of similar socioeconomic and educational backgrounds) showed anything like the cluster's ten-fold increase in the disease refuted the population risk argument. Victims matching known risk factors were simply most vulnerable. And, absent proof of an elevated rate of a familial risk in the building population, it was premature to blame personal risk factors. Disease clusters rarely produce answers when the causes are not known. The failure to find proof of an environmental cause did not mean that there was none. The building could not be deemed safe.

Illustrated here are the interpretative biases of citizens versus those of government and industry experts. A useful analogy can be drawn to the statistical concept of the Type I and Type II error. Put simply, for the classical scientist a Type I error is "an error of rashness," when one concludes that an effect occurred when in fact it did not. Conversely, a Type II error is "an error of caution," when one disregards a real effect because of insufficient proof. The norms of science are weighted to guard against spurious conclusions that might erroneously support theory; it is assumed that a theory which is truly predictive will be able to survive a stringent test. Accordingly, scientists strongly bias their work in favor of committing Type II errors and avoiding Type I errors. In the context of toxic exposure, a conservative judgment for a government or industry expert means caution in concluding that a place is *unsafe*.[66]

Because a determination of significant contamination may result in costly demands, reliance on scientific purism can serve as a convenient excuse for avoiding action, as seen in the Hodgkin's case. Likewise, at Love Canal regulatory interpretation of risk was clearly affected by the concern over who would pay to remedy the hazard.[67] Such pressures incline an agency to favor "optimistic interpretations."[68]

In contrast to such "Type II conservatism," potential or established victims of toxic exposure are likely to evidence a "Type I conservatism." From the concerned citizens' perspective, it is caution, not rashness, to risk an error in defining a place as dangerous; overreaction to a potential threat is generally preferable to underreaction. Thus citizens tend to pay particular attention to "worst case analyses," in contrast to the focus on "best case analysis" by industry experts and regulators.[69] These differing views about risk reflect opposite normative frameworks for defining an "appropriate" response; they also reflect contrasting perceptions of truth.

A perfect example of the incompatibility of these views is seen in the use of the word "significant." To a scientist, a significant threat is one in which a statistically improbable trend or cause and effect relationship is shown to occur. Normally, such findings must demonstrate less than one chance in twenty of occurring randomly to be termed significant. Of course, this basis for judgment is rarely explained to toxic victims, who encounter comments about "significance" and "nonsignificance" without understanding why the terms were chosen. The distortion involved in using these terms can be seen when they are applied to something of keen interest, such as a person's water test results. What is not significant to the regulator may be very much so to the resident. These differences in defining conservative risk are a major source of conflict over how to address contamination, as Levine found at Love Canal.

> Most residents wanted to leave open the definition of how much harm had been done to their environment and to their health. They wanted the decisions about essential help left flexible, so that appropriate help could be offered to fulfill needs as they became apparent. The officials wanted the definition of harm to be narrow, to fit the resources they had available, so that some tasks could be successfully accomplished, accounted for, and pointed to. In a situation with so many unknowns, the people wanted to feel that the available help would be sufficient to meet their needs, even if some of their needs could not yet be anticipated; the officials wanted to define some aspects as *known* and to address their attention to these. Just as they were to fence in a defined area around a construction site when the underlying chemical leachates might be flowing far beyond, so they wanted to define and bound the problem to be solved, even though it lay within the problem that in fact *existed.*[70]

The resulting risk dynamic is likely to lead to a perceived mutual loss of trustfulness on the part of both regulators and citizens. The citizen is viewed as a "screamer" by the regulator for reacting to risks that are not scientifically established; the regulator is seen as "callous, corrupt or incompetent" by the citizen for denying the risk. In a sense, the citizen views the chemical as guilty until proven innocent, while the official sees the chemical as innocent until proven guilty.[71]

Relative Versus Absolute Risk.   The inverse of acceptable risk is to define adequate safety. Here again, citizens and officials are likely to differ. Unlike citizens exposed to PCBs, concerned with the potential effects of their "absolute" exposure, officials are more likely to weigh the "relative" risks of differing health threats in judging how much attention to pay to a particular PCB exposure. The regulator is willing to allow "reasonable acceptable risk," while the citizen seeks to prevent all "unnecessary risk."[72]

We have already encountered relative risk in the 1992 U.S. budget and in the Reactor Safety Study. A further illustration comes from a New York State Department of Health report which informs the reader that the risk of death from drinking two liters of water per day contaminated with organic chemicals is relatively small.[73] This level of exposure to PCE (tetrachloroethylene) would produce twenty-two cancer deaths for every 100,000 people exposed for a seventy-year lifetime. PCBs would cause 1.6 cancer deaths under similar conditions. In contrast, the lifetime risk of death due to motor vehicle accidents is an impressive 1,750 per 100,000, and the risk of respiratory cancer alone for someone smoking just one pack of cigarettes per day is an even more dramatic 4,000 in 100,000.

Given such comparisons, a public health officer can hardly be blamed for holding the view that smoking and driving are much greater threats to the public than consuming minute quantities of PCB or PCE. According to scientific definitions of significance, the priorities are clear, as noted by Harris.

> It would come as no surprise were public health officials to report high levels of frustration as they encounter relentless pressures for the commitment of scarce resources to combat ill-defined environmental hazards, but little popular enthusiasm for taking aim against the proven and terrible hazards of smoking, alcoholism, poor diet, lack of exercise, and failure to simply buckle up in the family car.[74]

While correctly highlighting socially tolerated risks, such risk comparisons can easily be used to rationalize exposures to small amounts of synthetic chemicals. Thus scientist Bruce Ames showed that the naturally occurring carcinogen aflatoxin, found in peanut butter, causes a much greater risk for children than alar, a ripening agent used on apples. Yet social outrage over alar threatened the apple industry while peanut butter remained unsullied over aflatoxins.[75] The same logic can be used to justify the siting of hazardous facilities as reflected in Robert Michaels's article comparing the risk of incinerators and peanut butter."[76] The politically (and economically) motivated use of conservative risk characterized the Reagan and Bush administrations' approach to toxic hazards. In particular, the U.S government has grounded its thinking about risk in the practice of cost/benefit analysis and comparative risk assessment newly reasserted under President G. W. Bush.[77]

Due to the involuntary, unnatural and intrusive, and unknown and unseen character of toxic exposure, victims are likely to reject statistically weighted risk comparisons that minimize their threat.[78] My cochair at a public meeting committed the faux pas of lecturing smokers for accepting a greater risk than entailed by drinking their polluted water. The audience loudly rejected her argument, seeing no relationship between what they chose to do and the contamination that was forced on them. More than a year later, they were still commenting about "the nerve" my colleague showed in raising this issue.

Accordingly, what is a relative risk to experts may appear as an absolute risk to citizens. It does not matter that the same citizens overlook (through denial, rationalization, or other distortions) an even greater threat from a source presumably under their control. Thus, the converse is also true. What is a significant threat to officials may be only a relative threat to citizens.

Standards as Absolutes.   A further twist on this question of absolute and relative risk involves standards that set maximum levels for some chemicals in the water, air, soil, or other media. Such action levels force officials to treat contamination as though there were a threshold for absolute concern. As a result, regulators discount as "insignificant" levels of contamination that fall below the "red line." Yet this legalistic response does not reflect the tentative scientific basis behind these standards. Thus as already noted, citizens in the Washington Heights section of Wallkill, New York, legitimately asked why PCE contamination in their water had to reach 50 ppb to be a significant risk when citizens of Vermont and Washington only needed 30 ppb to trigger government assistance.

As can be seen, the question of absolute and relative risk is reversed when standards exist. The victim, who applies an absolute criterion in judging the significance of contamination, uses a relative standard in assessing how much contamination is acceptable. The official, who sees risk as relative, uses absolute standards to define when contamination demands action. These contrary definitions of risk serve as the basis for the respective double binds of citizen and regulator.[79]

Precautionary Versus Regulatory Professional Views.   I conclude this discussion of different paradigms of risk by citing the extreme expressions of each perspective.

In January 1998, an interdisciplinary gathering, hosted by the Johnson Foundation at its Wingspread headquarters, concluded that risk assessment and regulatory decisionmaking have failed to be sufficiently protective, resulting in severe damage to human and environmental health. Acknowledging that human activities may involve hazards, the precautionary principle was proposed as an alternative. It states, in part,

> When an activity raises threats to human health or the environment, precautionary measures should be taken even if some cause and effect relationships are not fully established scientifically. In this context the proponent of an activity, rather than the public, should bear the burden of proof. The process of applying the precautionary principle must be open, informed and democratic and must include potentially affected parties. It must also involve an examination of the full range of alternatives, including no action.[80]

The precautionary principle is founded on six core concepts: preventative anticipation, care to not push ecological limits, consideration of economic externalities, shifting the burden of proof to change agents, recognizing an intrinsic natural right to suffer no ecological harm, and expecting debts to be paid for past ecological sins. The precautionary principle articulates the citizens' paradigm/Type I action rationale that characterizes the response to toxic victimization. Although advocates of the principle have argued that it needs to evolve, literally, "to seep through the pores of social change,"[81] contamination creates an oft repeated crisis demanding immediate decisions about precaution.

Institutional Contexts

The key institutional contexts associated with disabling dynamics vary for individual toxic incidents, but the dynamics are inherently similar from incident to incident. Although different levels of government are involved in every incident, one usually predominates. In Legler, the township was the key actor; for the Missouri dioxin sites, federal agencies played a central role; at Love Canal, the state was the main responder. Here we focus on the latter two contexts.

Times Beach: The Feds as Disablers

In the Times Beach dioxin contamination case, where federal agencies predominated, a major conflict occurred between the Centers for Disease Control and the Environmental Protection Agency. The CDC set risk levels at one part per billion. The EPA unsuccessfully attempted to raise the level to one hundred parts per billion, halving the number of "significant" instances of contamination.[82] Despite its ramifications for them, local citizens were shut out of the discussion. They were further excluded when then EPA director Ann Burford announced the long-awaited Times Beach buyout, addressing reporters face-to-face in a local hotel while residents were forced to listen to her speech through a glass wall that separated them.[83]

Love Canal: The State as Disabler

Of the many actors at Love Canal, the New York State Department of Health played a particularly disabling role, chronicled by Levine. The commissioner of health's dramatic August 1978 declaration of a health emergency, which advised evacuation of pregnant women and children under age two, created confusion from the onset. The order failed to clarify what was to happen to the rest of the family, who would pay for the evacuation, and whether others remaining were safe. That the DOH disregarded the need for such clarification was noted by an official's comment.

> The health department professionals were *scientists*, who did not worry about people's reactions to cautionary statements and recommended actions. They dealt with numbers—with data on physical conditions—and only with these. Political and social matters, the official stressed, were extraneous to the DOH work. The issues of how pregnant women and children would move to safe

places, how people might feel about recommendations from the state health commissioner not to go into their basements and not to eat food grown in their gardens, were not seen as the responsibility of scientists.[84]

Instead of dealing with people, the state focused on the technical site mitigation plan, which residents considered inadequate. Rather than residents' health, the predominant threat of concern to officials and politicians was political. They needed to attract federal funding for an expensive project while simultaneously minimizing costly precedents. After a change in federal guidelines for funding, the state formally downplayed the health issue, emphasizing the need to move people in order to conduct the remedial construction, which involved covering the landfill in order to limit the flow of leachate from the site.

Meanwhile, remaining Love Canal residents were expected to feel safe when their neighborhood was separated from the condemned area along the canal by only a fence and warning signs. Such precautions did not keep children from playing in the area; in fact, a supervised play program was held during the summer of 1978 on the school playground, which sat directly on the canal.

Residents' faith was further shaken when government representatives had open disagreements, made clearly unwarranted reassurances, issued incomprehensible test results, and by the inability of the health department to test all the blood samples it collected. The state appeared to be hiding behind excuses that more research was needed to prove health effects. Meanwhile it dismissed citizen-collected health data and denigrated the reputation of the scientist who did the research. The presence of dioxin in the neighborhood was initially denied. Findings of liver damage among children were handled suspiciously.

While residents were excluded from the decisionmaking, unnamed experts met at a distant location to advise the state. The subsequent Thomas Commission was additionally disabling because it maintained secretive control of information and excluded residents from its discussions. Its report was shaped by the governor's aides into a political tool for minimizing the problem. Rather than engender the public's trust, the commission generated additional questions regarding political interference in a pseudoscientific process.

The result of the Thomas Commission findings, widely cited by the chemical industry as well as by government, was the creation of a "semiofficial contemporary legend" about Love Canal. This legend discounted proven health effects from the canal and emphasized psychological damage due to "a. Fumbling bureaucrats, b. overzealous scientists, c. the mass media, d. corporate enemies, e. screaming housewives, f. rabid environmentalists, or g. any or all of the above." Accordingly, relocation occurred out of compassion or for the purpose of remedial construction, not because of a threat to health. In constructing this legend, state officials emphasized the uniqueness of Love Canal, hoping to rationalize the millions of dollars spent while minimizing the setting of precedents for other sites. Finally, the Thomas Commission became a model for the unified health reviews of hazardous sites now coordinated by ATSDR and state health departments, thus minimizing the chances for dissenting viewpoints to be publicly shared.[85]

Conclusion and Summary

In this chapter we have focused mainly on interaction between citizens and government professionals. While experts working for private consulting firms or directly for hazard-related companies also disempower citizens, their bias in favor of their employers is less disabling than is the same bias from professionals working for the government. Few citizens expect industry experts to come to the rescue of toxic victims. Their expectations are quite different for government officials.

The need to close the gap between regulators and the public they serve has emerged as a serious concern of government over the recent past. Several years after the first edition of this book was published, the New York State Department of Health in conjunction with ATSDR held a conference for its staff and some of their citizen clients on the theme of contaminated communities. Subsequently, ATSDR held a staff conference with leading technical and citizen experts to gather information for a manual for their field employees now in production. Having participated in these events, I was impressed with some noticeable changes in agency thinking. ATSDR psychiatrist Pamela Tucker, who has spearheaded the effort to make major changes in that agency's procedures, now leads workshops on stress reduction and psychological health in Superfund communities and for agency staff. A handbook on community stress has been prepared.

In April 2000, I joined Pam Tucker and her EPA colleague Pat Seppi to conduct a workshop in Edison, New Jersey, for government officials from the many agencies that respond to toxic disasters. The course, developed by Dr. Tucker, is called Possible Psychological Effects Related to Living near a Superfund Site. The session defined stress and discussed its occurrence and manifestation for the victims of acute and chronic contamination events, as well as the official responders' own stress. Officials from diverse state and federal agencies discussed how their own efforts contribute to community stress and shared different approaches for minimizing such consequences.

Nearby, in Manville, New Jersey, I also had the pleasure to witness an EPA Superfund cleanup at the federal creosote site that is organized around pro-community principles under the guidance of Seppi, a psychologist.

Such efforts of enlightened government officials to minimize the disabling dynamic confront major obstacles. The scientists and engineers who fill many of the key environmental agency posts are trained neither in communication skills nor sensitivity to their nuances. They are trained to break the physical aspects of

the situation down into "problems," but not to reconstruct these steps into an overall composite of the victims' whole experience. Many are tarnished by prior negative experiences. The nature of contamination problems, as seen above, creates
many pitfalls for even the most expert government communicator. Moreover, there
are only a few Tuckers and Seppis in a sea of thousands of agency personnel, complicating the task of changing agency behavior.

It is the nature of the dialectic of double binds that collaboration between government and citizens is confounded and communication between these parties is
easily strained. In the heat of controversy, divergent perceptions of the situation
and risk paradigms serve to solidify each party's existing belief system. Consensus
building tools to promote trust are generally absent from these interactions. The
victims add the weight of disappointment and abandonment by government to
their concerns over the exposure. The resulting frustration pressures victims to
break loose from passive dependency on government. Thus as Reich notes of the
Michigan PBB contamination, "The PBB case reminds us that to influence public
policy, individuals and groups must transform a private trouble into a public issue
and often into a public controversy."[86] As a result, the disabling response of government invites and demands that victims act on their own behalf. In the next
chapter I discuss this *enabling* process.

6

The Enabling Response: Community Development and Toxic Exposure

Earlier I defined a "contaminated community" as a residential area located within the identified boundaries for a known exposure to some form of pollution. In this chapter, I examine the social dynamics within such communities.[1]

Enablement Through Community Development

Community is often thought of as one of the victims of disaster.[2] However, a consequence of chronic, low-level contamination in many neighborhoods is the development, not the destruction, of community.[3] Grassroots groups emerge within the affected region. The commonality of this outcome is indicated by a study of twenty-one toxic sites that found that "*ad hoc* groups were formed, often quite rapidly, at every site studied with significant public participation."[4]

As a counterpoint to the *disabling* consequences discussed previously, this chapter explains how the development of community organizations serves to *enable* many toxic victims and describes the conditions under which community development is absent. Also examined is the networking of local groups into an impressive national social movement addressing concerns about toxic exposure.

As Figure 6.1 illustrates, grassroots participation results from a combination of occurrences conducive to at least temporary community consensus and cohesiveness: victims' normal lives are severely disrupted by the turbulent exposure incident, victims are isolated from their normal relational and institutional networks, individual families cannot solve their problems alone, and a group of proximate victims shares the same conditions.

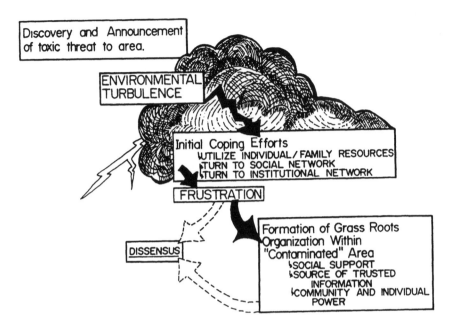

Figure 6.1   Directions to a Grassroots Response

In a society based on the autonomous nuclear family within an independent home, the family initially faces the news of contamination as a private challenge or problem. But it is a complex and confusing situation beyond the family's resources to control. Seeking to cope with this turbulence, the newly labeled "victims" turn to their social environments, specifically their "social network" (existing friends and relatives expected to offer support in the face of crisis) and "institutional network" (government agencies believed to be responsible for providing clarification and assistance to citizens in need).

Support from the social network is key to successful coping with a variety of stressful situations.[5] However, as noted, networks of relatives, friends, and coworkers frequently offer victims inadequate support. Government is also disappointing.

Because neither the relational nor the institutional network is likely to be of much help, toxic exposure results in a virtual isolation of victims from outside sources of support. As toxic victims discover that the channels they previously used for participation and problem solving are ineffective, they are forced to improvise alternatives. This isolation from key prior support networks combined with the geographic proximity of victims fosters the creation of a "spatial network," a community group corresponding to the boundaries of contamination. This grassroots effort is essential as individuals, families, as well as the newly defined community attempt to cope with toxic exposure.[6]

Negative encounters between the public and officials can serve to legitimize grassroots activity. At the Lipari landfill Superfund site in New Jersey, for example, the condescending response of officials made an angered public responsive to the efforts of community organizers.[7] And the routine focus of Superfund managers on technical site cleanup issues results in their insensitivity to public concern over health effects.[8]

Their common cause in the face of adversity gives toxic victims a shared identity superseding preexisting political, geographic, or social boundaries. They develop a "sense of community," which implies feelings of similarity, interdependence maintained by mutual support, and the sense that they are part of a structure that is larger and more stable than the isolated individual can ever have.[9]

This sense of community is openly expressed in communities confronting toxic exposure, as illustrated by the names for grassroots groups: HARP (Heights Area Residents Against Pollution), CHOKE (Citizens Holding Out for a Clean Environment), OUCH (Opposing Unnecessary Chemical Hazards), NOPE (Northern Ohioans Protecting the Environment), TWIG (Toxic Waste Investigative Group), DECALE (Deptford Citizens Against Landfills and Extensions), TRAPP (Tauton Residents Against Possible Pollution), SOCM (Save Our Cumberland Mountains), WARD (Warwick Against Radium Dumping), and scores of "concerned citizens" groups. These names display the fervor of community development inspired by residential contamination. Such groups serve as the basis for the enabling response to toxic exposure. They represent collective coping mechanisms that provide for local control through the participation of commonly affected residents.

Keys to Enablement: Leadership and Activism

The availability of talented leaders with time to spend is a prerequisite to organizing.[10] Commonly, U.S. toxic response organizations develop a relatively stable core of leaders who carry the organization. Group functioning requires a sufficient body of activist members to augment the leadership.

Who are these activists? Because of the diversity of communities facing pollution problems, participants represent the entire demographic spectrum. Although specific characteristics of activists differ from location to location, a national survey characterized typical members as being twenty-six to forty years old and homemakers. The leaders often had professional careers yet represented a diverse socioeconomic spectrum.[11]

A study of women in Washington State published at the time of the 1978 Love Canal disaster concluded that although women were more likely to be concerned about the environment and to take action to protect it, they were less likely than men to act publicly.[12] Over the ensuing fifteen years, however, that profile changed dramatically. The presence of local contamination threats forced women into leadership and active membership of the new toxics movement.

In fact, women tend to predominate in leadership positions of groups concerned with toxic exposure. According to Linda Price-King of the Environmental Health Network, 70 percent of the activists at the local level are women, and 30 percent at the national level.[13] This phenomenon reflects a number of factors. In the communities that tend to suffer most from toxic contamination—blue-collar, lower-middle-class, or poor areas—women tend to stay home and care for the children. They have established social networks available for quick action, and they are more likely to recognize patterns of ill health in the neighborhood. Men in the affected communities often work for polluting industries. They may see themselves as having failed in their role as protector of the home, or they may view as unmasculine the public admission of fears and concerns over health and safety. Finally, women may be a little more distanced from the dominant social paradigm of economic growth and therefore less willing to rationalize risks as necessary for economic well-being.[14]

Further insight into this gender difference comes from the work of Celene Krause, who interviewed women toxic activists in minority and blue-collar communities.[15] She was struck with the language used by her sources to describe their community struggles. Instead of speaking about the environmental issues that confronted them, victims spoke of the oppressive conditions that allow contamination. Furthermore, their subjective experience was shaped by tangible issues of the family—most notably illness and the fear of illness. At the same time, unlike black toxic activists who clearly see themselves as connected to the racial justice movement, working-class or lower-middle-class women in general did not relate their toxic activism to feminism or the women's movement, which has characterized women of higher social status.

Levine's intensive interviews with Love Canal activists shed further light on community involvement. Activists were most often found to have fairly recent roots in the neighborhood; they were neither old-timers nor new arrivals but had lived there long enough to develop an attachment to place (typically six to ten years). They tended to come from families with one wage earner (not a chemical worker) and young children, to own their homes, to have at least moderate incomes, and to be better educated and have smaller families than nonactivists. Activists tended to be under age forty. A similar profile is suggested by a review of groups at other sites.[16]

The development of such localized activism has occurred worldwide and has become a potent global force in the period subsequent to the Rio Conference on the Environment. The women's, environmental, and labor movements, and grass-roots toxic activists, have converged in a new global movement addressing universal concerns about the environment and the creation of a sustainable society.[17]

Key Benefits of Community Development

When a shared sense and practice of community occurs, a community group can serve as a "therapeutic social system" for a very stressed neighborhood. Such therapeutic communities help compensate for the stress of disasters by sharing information, warmth, and help; providing a means for rapid consensus about actions necessary to meet collective needs; and engendering a high degree of motivation among victims to work for common purposes.[18] The three key outcomes from the grassroots response to toxic exposure—social support, information, and power—are illustrated here by multiple case studies.[19]

Social Support

Social support provides reassurance and strength in the face of a shared predicament, helps disaster victims avoid the feeling of being abandoned, may help increase their accuracy in estimating danger, and is a key to successful coping with technological disaster.[20] Social support may be task-oriented or may focus on personal/emotional needs; its concern may be at the individual or the neighborhood level.[21] As toxic victims organize, they build relationships as well as an organization. In the absence of either external validation or correction of their fears, victims are forced to look to their neighbors for social support.[22]

As a "bedroom community," social interaction within Legler had been limited. But following the water problem, residents participated in the community organization, developed a sense of community, and engaged in "neighboring," defined by David Unger and Abraham Wandersman as "the social interaction, the symbolic interaction, and the attachment of individuals with the people living around them and the place in which they live."[23] The Concerned Citizens Committee helped people meet others with whom they shared what otherwise seemed to be a private experience, inaccessible to the understanding of nonvictims. People were reassured that they were neither crazy nor alone.[24]

Similarly, Levine writes of Love Canal:

> As time passed and discouraging incidents piled one on the other, residents felt more and more that no one but people undergoing the experience themselves

could understand them. Only fellow sufferers could share the feelings of uncertainty. As they confided in each other more and more, both privately and in public; as they worked together and participated in individual and group actions; as they interpreted their beliefs, their goals, their behavior; and as they thought and planned together for a better and happier future, free of Love Canal, they became essential supports for each other—a sort of large self-help group, a substitute for a strong, supportive, and ever-understanding family.[25]

Because activists are more absorbed in the issues, they become estranged from prior support networks and seek new "spatial" relationships with those sharing their ordeal. In contrast, nonbelievers and those least affected have less reason to become activists, to disrupt existing relationships, and therefore to seek new ones. Thus Love Canal activists came to rely on their community group for social support while those least involved continued to rely on their families and relatives. Activists exceeded nonactivists in losing friends as well as in finding new friendships. That activists underwent the greatest change from the incident is understandable; they tended to be the most heavily impacted by the disaster.[26]

A Source of Information

Neighbors, as they interact and offer social support to one another, share information about the neighborhood.[27] In Legler, such communication was minimal before the pollution crisis forced lines of intra-neighborhood communication to be opened. These networks then helped the community contend with an abnormal informational context characterized by an extreme degree of uncertainty.[28]

The Concerned Citizens Committee helped supply information to Legler residents at a time when they faced both a real confusion of facts and denial by responding government agencies of any responsibility for clarification. When respondents were questioned about their sources of information during the water crisis, they gave government and the press negative ratings. Government at all levels—the township and higher—was not seen as open or truthful. The press was seen as too dependent on the township government for information. Television was too sporadic in its coverage to be informative. Only the meetings of Concerned Citizens and its informal communications network were consistently seen by group members as being a reliable source of information. Suspicious occurrences and new facts were channeled immediately to the group's leadership. Perceptions were frequently verified with members of the executive board as rumors passed through Legler. The group's periodic meetings came to be seen as the one authoritative place where people could get straight answers to questions. In a parallel vein, the Love Canal Homeowners Association provided residents with information about chemical hazards, translation of scientific reports, and directions for filing relocation papers. Similarly, community organizations served as the primary sources of information in four communities in the Netherlands.[29]

A Source of Power

The development of community organizations tends to provide people with a new sense of power in the midst of an otherwise disempowering situation. The group serves as a collective means to achieve commonly shared individual goals while reversing some of the psychological damage inherent in the situation.

Community Power. As a source of collective power, the Concerned Citizens Committee in Legler helped people regain lost control.

> *We felt support. We were powerful enough not to have to take it. The township underestimated us "hicks." We made the township accountable.*

By forming a group that could wield power and be effective, residents could channel their frustrations constructively.

> *We helped each other not overreact. Some of us were going to township meetings with guns, we were that frustrated and angry. We felt like our arms were pinned back. We all channeled our frustrations into Concerned Citizens. Otherwise, there would have been vigilante violence.*

Most importantly, the group facilitated actions that families might not have been able to undertake individually. Media coverage was sought and coordinated. Most enabling of the group's activities, residents reported, was the lawsuit. When the lawyers hired specialists to address the issues facing the Legler neighborhood, the Concerned Citizens Committee attained a balance of power with experts representing government and the polluters.

In other instances, community groups recruited experts to work with them in an advisory role. The experts helped them understand the significance of new developments, plot strategy, and even take on adversaries directly. The Love Canal Homeowners Association made extensive use of such expertise, some volunteer and some government-sponsored. Particularly important was the work of a cancer researcher, Beverly Paigen, in helping to reinterpret government data, develop the capacity to collect additional information, and interpret this information credibly inside and outside the neighborhood.[30] In the Netherlands, mobilization of expertise has been shown to be a key to community power, allowing citizens to challenge official reassurances and to put forward alternative plans of their own.[31]

Community organizations may also create an infrastructure to support needed activities. Lois Gibbs notes that the office of the Love Canal Homeowners Association served as a base for community participation, stressing the importance for community organizations to provide such a setting.[32]

Through their collective activities and ability to attract resources, community organizations provide a means for attaining the power needed to address the complex issues resulting from toxic exposure. Leo Baas studied four Dutch communities that had little confidence in the solutions proposed by government.[33] In each case, community groups served their representative function well enough to earn overwhelming ratings of confidence from residents. These groups gained some control over community process by providing independent sources of information, criticizing technical investigations, and keeping authorities informed of local developments and the desired solutions.

For a community group to successfully influence policy, it must be able to put forward clear goals and develop good strategy.[34] The Concerned Citizens Committee in Legler was successful in meeting its two major objectives: installation of an alternative water system and victory in its lawsuit against Jackson Township. The Love Canal Homeowners Association succeeded in bringing political pressure to bear, resulting in a buyout of homes. Such success may not be uncommon. Thus Nicholas Freudenberg found that 83 percent of the community groups he sampled perceived themselves to be at least somewhat successful. Half reported the elimination or reduction of the hazard that was the group's main focus. Despite a possible sampling bias favoring successful groups, the influence of participation at the community level by toxic victims is clearly demonstrated.[35]

Over an extended time frame, a group's "success" may change many times. Thus, after twenty years failing to close Al Turi Landfill, Inc., in Goshen, New York, my organization, Orange Environment, Inc., won a permit denial for the landfill's expansion after long and contentious administrative hearings in 1999,[36] only to have yet another new permit proposal emerge shortly thereafter. For the activist, the experience is not unlike B horror movies: the source of the horror never dies, resurfacing just as the characters have relaxed into the complacency of normal life, or at least for the sequel. Depending on the point at which you queried me about Turi landfill, you might easily hit a point of victory or defeat without ever understanding the whole battle, over time, let alone the organization that waged it.

Individual Power. Community organizations help residents cope with what otherwise might be an unmanageable situation, buffering the individual and family from some of the ongoing stresses of dealing with government in seeking solutions to the crisis. A powerful grassroots organization provides its members a greater sense of security and efficacy. Rather than merely depend on government to meet their needs, residents use the organization as a vehicle to regain some control over the response to the situation. Thus, although government might leave them in the lurch, R. A. Stone and A. G. Levine note that residents' "own organizations would not consider the matter 'closed' as long as people were still having problems related to Love Canal." Psychologically, therefore, community organizations help victims regain a sense of control over their lives. Thus "if we assume that people feel better about themselves after they meet difficult challenges with action, we can speculate that the organized citizens' groups provided a means for people to feel more in control of events, even though active membership entailed a change in personal behavior that was surprising to the actors themselves."[37]

Toxic activism helps people recoup some lost psychological strengths. But it also produces personal growth, several examples of which were discussed previously. Leaders of Love Canal groups experienced enhanced self-control, self-worth, and personal efficacy.[38] There was an evident association between activism and positive individual change at Love Canal. Activists learned to assert their rights. Nonactivists reported many more negative outcomes but did not change their behavior.[39]

There is, of course, a relationship between this growth and the ability of the organized groups to achieve their desired ends. Thus power is heightened by the growing competence of the community group. Although some expertise is provided by consultants, at least equally as important is the learning evidenced by community leaders.[40] Therefore, the real importance of consultants to the citizens' groups may at times be less as technical experts than as educators. Individual learning translates to group power. The enhanced sophistication of citizens reflects the development of community organizations nationally.[41]

The Consensus/Dissensus Continuum

There are also limits to the development of community as a response to toxic exposure. Community development depends on the existence of an adequate level of "consensus," or agreement about the basic circumstances of exposure among residents of the contaminated area. The absence of consensus results in "dissensus," a situation with a high potential for conflict due to divergent definitions of the nature and origin of and response to the situation.[42] Unlike other disasters, toxic events present a complex challenge for consensus building, as seen here.

The Spatial Dimension

Dissensus marks the extracommunity boundaries around the contaminated area, in which diverse institutional, corporate, and social forces combine to cause government inaction and to stigmatize and blame victims. The very nature of contamination incidents challenges the economic foundations of society because industry is the villain. In fact, industry is the most common source of opposition to local organizations. An overall climate of conflict, uncertainty, and divergent pressures within the boundaries of contamination serve to divide neighbors, as found in one-third of the communities studied by Freudenberg. At the same time, extracommunity conflict and the resulting isolation serve as impetus for agreement among the exposure victims.[43] A shared view of the threat within the community promotes an emerging consensus allowing organized community response.

As in the Legler case, even incidents involving a fair degree of consensus are marred by conflict. Given the inherent uncertainties, elements of *both* consensus and dissensus are likely to be found to varying degrees in any toxic incident. Thus, within a given community, it may be useful to envision a continuum rather than a dichotomy between dissensus and consensus.

The Temporal Dimension

This mix of consensus and dissensus varies over the stages of toxic disaster. Community displaces family as the locus of decisionmaking and action only at certain points in a contamination incident, such as when organized community response is demanded at certain stages in the government effort to define solutions. If the goals that motivate collective action are eventually addressed, the grassroots organization may well lose its raison d'être, its members returning to more privatized concerns.[44] In other words, the group may literally put itself out of business by restoring the ability of private families to manage their own interests.

Furthermore, lifescape changes run counter to formation of community identity. Whereas successful neighboring requires an attachment to place,[45] feelings about home and environment are frequently inverted by the exposure experience. Thus the permanence of the new spatial network is undermined. Activism may take the form of a temporary community fighting for its own dissolution through government-sponsored relocation (as in the cases of Times Beach, Love Canal, and Centralia). Even if the physical environment is "repaired," further community development may be arrested. Community development may never broaden, despite the spatial networking, simply because many residents have lost their long-term commitment to the area. Thus in Legler, a substantial proportion of the residents whom I interviewed expressed a desire to move away if a successful lawsuit made it financially feasible to do so.

As a result, the community organizations that develop in response to toxic exposure differ from permanent community organizations seeking to maintain ongoing activities in a fairly stable environment. Instead, they resemble the kind of temporary organization described by Warren Bennis and Philip Slater that forms only for the duration of its problem-solving effort.[46] It is an irony that, due to the nature of the regulatory and legal process, these temporary organizations are often forced to address protracted issues, stretching way beyond the staying power of most transitory alliances.

Regulatory Stasis.   The temporary nature of grassroots toxic organizations is contradicted by the slow progress taken by contamination events through stages of solution. As already noted, U.S. implementation of long-term remedial measures at hazardous waste sites routinely has taken decades.[47] Of 1,405 sites on the National Priorities List in 1997, 489 had construction completed, almost as many had remedial construction under way, and the other third were at early stages in the process, either before, during, or just after remedial assessment. Many of these sites were listed in the early 1980s.[48] While, in Chapter 1, we saw the political volatility of Superfund progress, the point is that the life cycle of American community groups tends to be prolonged through a grueling period of study and evaluation. Groups become exhausted as they enter slow-moving and protracted stages of the incident during which continued mobilization becomes difficult to sustain.

Limping Litigation.   Lawsuits aimed at speeding the conclusion of the incident similarly tend to drag on beyond the coping resources of many victim groups. Litigation is undertaken in an unknown percentage of contaminated communities as a tool to address concrete needs, such as a new water source and medical monitoring in Legler, to assign responsibility, and/or to obtain damages for such consequences as loss of quality of life and enjoyment of the home, damage to health, and emotional distress. The popular book and movie *A Civil Action* well illustrates the challenges posed by a toxic tort.[49]

The search for an attorney is a challenge in itself. Plaintiffs must find and agree on a firm with which they feel comfortable and convince the attorney to take the case. This search is often time consuming. There may be false starts, failures, and firings along the way. Trusted local attorneys may lack the knowledge and resources to take on a case involving environmental law. Technical experts will be needed who have the ability to understand complex interdisciplinary issues, and the case may easily cost hundreds of thousands and more often millions of dollars to bring to trial. In the end, a larger national firm having staff and financial resources may need to be recruited. Plaintiffs (those bringing suit) may pay to pursue the cause of action, although most toxic torts are fee-contingent cases (the law firm will front the money and collect at the end of the trial if they prevail). Some lawsuits are broadened to represent a class or a group of individuals rather than specific plaintiffs.

After they finally launch their case, the plaintiffs face a difficult and adversarial period of disclosure, during which their privacy is systematically stripped away by hostile hands. Considerable effort may be needed to prepare information demanded by their attorney or by the defense, including answering of questionnaires or interrogatories. Their property may be invaded by experts, with placement of temporary or permanent test wells for long-term monitoring. Their bodies may be similarly poked and prodded. Their personal finances, medical and psychiatric records, documents, and life history may be intrusively reviewed.

Finally, under oath, they are questioned at deposition by defense attorneys intent on finding contradiction, omission, fabrication, or other ways of dismissing their testimony and claims, intimidating them, or building a rebuttal case. Such depositions may last for days. Plaintiffs are often unaccustomed to being questioned, to carefully weighing their words, fearing perjury yet also wary of saying something that will injure their case, and to having their comments recorded by a court reporter. Such depositions are a major source of stress, only surpassed by testimony at the trial itself. In a large group litigation or a class action law suit, a small sample of "lead" plaintiffs may be subjected to particularly intensive testing and questioning as representatives of the larger group of litigants. An initial trial may even focus only on the lead plaintiffs, paving the way for a settlement or establishing key legal points before a more comprehensive trial.

Years elapse before a case makes its way to trial, if it gets there at all. Protracted litigation may cause financial hardship, add enormous amounts of stress, and make major demands on time. The lawsuit may become a source of public conflict, as in Jackson, where litigation was against the municipality, or stigma, when others believe that people sue out of greed or a desire for notoriety. Considerable social pressure may be mounted during litigation—to raise money, blame litigants, threaten reputations, keep someone quiet, or obtain information.

Turning the case over to a law firm may relieve the victims of considerable responsibility, but often the lawsuit makes so many demands that the stress merely shifts from one type of situation to another. With lawyers now taking the lead, activist leaders may find it ironic that although they have given up control over the issue to advance their case, the demands on them have not correspondingly diminished. Frequently community members assist in gathering information in order to reduce costs. It is not uncommon for a law firm to have minimal contact with its clients during the life of a lawsuit, particularly at the beginning, during periods when the firm is focused on other cases, is tied up in arguing motions, or is gathering information. During these periods, plaintiffs may fear that nothing is happening, a fear that is sometimes justified. In the end, litigation may or may not succeed and, even if successful, it may not achieve the desired objectives. An initial verdict may invite a chain of expensive and time-consuming appeals.

Expectations that the lawsuit will rectify an injustice, assign responsibility, or remedy the situation are often unmet. Plaintiffs may feel that lawsuits failed to make them whole again. Often the periodic questioning during discovery, deposition, and trial forces plaintiffs to recall and reexperience difficult, unpleasant, and even traumatic situations. The experience may force families or friends to revisit troubling topics or may cause new interpersonal troubles. People often feel that their testimony was inadequate or unsuccessful and that they not only did not advance their own cause but let others down. On personal and collective levels, then, litigation is a trying and tricky time. It is hardly a panacea.

Conclusions

The point is that temporary organizations, created quickly in response to a toxic crisis, are most commonly forced to persist long beyond initial expectations. Such organizations are, in a sense, not voluntary. Moreover, they are grafted on top of the preexisting lives of active members and thus are themselves a source of continuing disruption. It is not surprising, therefore, that dissensus is found in grassroots groups. Recognizing the life cycle of community organizations is vital for identifying the points at which group members are most stressed.[50]

Finally, as reactive community groups succeed in responding to their original crisis, some are able to make the transition to becoming innovative and anticipatory organizations.[51] Such organizations may even play a role in the discovery and recognition of additional instances of contamination, acting as community watchdogs in preventing further threats.

Consensus and Dissensus in Legler

How community groups function in response to toxic exposure is subject to many influences, including the characteristics of the area, the residents, the political and geographic community, the specific toxic problem, the way the problem has been handled, and the characteristics of the members of the group.[52] These variables help determine the group's ability to create and maintain an operating consensus. The Legler case study highlights some of the dynamics surrounding the consensus/dissensus continuum.

Organizational Sources of Dissensus in Legler

Legler's Concerned Citizens Committee formed around a cluster of earlier residents who had fought having the landfill located in their section. These leaders began to network almost immediately after the water contamination was announced. They assumed a high profile and spoke at township meetings early in the incident. As issues crystallized and increased networking and attempts to share information occurred, the leadership expanded to include newer residents who, as a group, had been fairly isolated from long-term residents in the neighborhood.

Women here, as generally, formed the core of local activism; however, three of the seven key leaders in Legler, including the principal leader, were male. Because none of these men had demanding work schedules away from home (two were on disability and the third had the somewhat flexible schedule of a teacher), their available time may have been more comparable to homemakers than to nine-to-five employees. In other respects, the key activists of the Concerned Citizens Committee fit the profile of community leaders found at Love Canal.[53] They had young children, as did the majority of the group's constituents. The leaders reflected the group of residents who had come to Legler in the past ten or fifteen years. Like their counterparts at Love Canal, they had sunk roots but were not old-timers.

My interviews with the entire executive board and many members of the organization suggested that the brunt of the organization's work fell on a few key people (generally the executive board); most other residents attended general meetings but did little else. Therefore, it was not surprising that these leaders showed signs of extreme overload. Tellingly, while leaders reported being blamed by members for emergent problems, I found members consistently expressing positive regard for the leadership, citing their conscientiousness. That such support was not felt by executive board members suggests that it was not being communicated upward in the organization.

This outcome can partly be explained by the organizational structure of the Concerned Citizens Committee. Major roles in the organization were invested in the executive board. Particularly after concerns developed that a spy was feeding information to Jackson Township about the citizen group's plans, the executive board became highly secretive. As board members became less open, their isolation contributed to their feelings of abandonment.

Also contributing to leader burnout was the protracted course of the Legler disaster, which intimately involved the response of government. Initially, the Concerned Citizens Committee utilized broad participatory actions to capture attention and bring pressure to bear. But after the community entered the waiting period when decisions had been made but not yet implemented, the maintenance tasks required to keep the organization working toward its goals were handled best within the executive committee structure. Because they no longer were forced to go back to their membership for support, the leaders became increasingly isolated.

Conflict over Key Decisions

In Legler, the fact that an effective community organization emerged reflected an early consensus (at least among the approximately two-thirds of the Legler families who joined the group) about certain common problems, goals, and approaches. But conflict was never absent from the picture. Conflict outside Legler's borders contributed to internal disagreement. Within the organization, conflict occurred at key decisionmaking junctures when differing goals among members surfaced. Besides these task-oriented issues that related to the organization's attempts to meet its goals, conflict was also evident in the socioemotional relationships within the group. That friction was a result of interpersonal tensions that developed over time. Two key decision points served particularly to bring conflict to the surface.

Wells Versus City Water. Legler was a community that lacked homogeneity in certain key respects. Most important was the division between earlier and later settlers. Those who arrived in Legler during the first major wave of development in the 1960s and early 1970s, as well as their predecessors, valued the rural ambiance of the section and desired a high degree of seclusion and privacy from neighbors. They opposed further growth in the area. In contrast, most of the newcomers of the mid- to late 1970s sought a more suburbanized "coffee klatch" community with opportunities for social contact among neighbors. They sought "development-style" living and the growth of amenities in the immediate area. Obviously, the potential existed for a basic clash of values.

As the Concerned Citizens Committee took shape around a shared need to respond to the water crisis, the organization was nearly split due to disagreement over whether to fight for a central, municipally operated water district or new, deeper individual wells. Generally, long-term residents favored the replacement of wells; newer residents thought that a "city water" system would provide the same degree of safety they presumed existed in their prior (usually urban) homes. To the former group, wells were a sign of independence and rural living; city water was a sign of government interference, additional expense, and chlorinated water. To the latter group, wells were a big responsibility and very uncertain (as the pollution experience confirmed); city water was a service that could (and should) be provided by government.

This conflict was resolved when the option of individual wells became unattainable. Local government claimed that public money could not be spent to improve private property. Furthermore, assistance was available to the township for building the more expensive central district project but was not available for digging individual wells.[54] As a consequence, consensus was reestablished around the fight for city water.

To Sue or Not to Sue?   A second major area of conflict developed around the initiation of the lawsuit against Jackson Township. This issue divided the neighborhood, eventually determining who belonged to the Concerned Citizens and who did not. Although I had contact only with residents who were in the lawsuit, it became clear from the interviews that diverse reasons accounted for the failure of about one-third of the families to join the action. These reasons included inability to risk an initial retainer fee for the lawyers, general dislike of lawyers and lawsuits, and feared retaliation by the township against employees who sued or revocation of certificates of occupancy issued for their homes. Some felt that "you just can't win against city hall." Others had personality conflicts with leaders of the community group; still others had difficulty facing up to the problem at all. Finally, some may have believed that they could share in the benefits of a lawsuit without having to take the risks. Participation in the lawsuit was the source of division in the community, although this conflict ceased to be internal to Concerned Citizens after nonparticipants in the lawsuit left the organization.

Strains from Prolonged Mobilization

It is not surprising to find that conflict occurred as the group entered its third year without having met its objectives. Leaders, mobilized for an extended time, began to show signs of fatigue. This burnout surfaced in the form of personality conflict rather than disagreement over issues. Conflict may always have been present but was suppressed by the need for cooperation during crisis. But over time, feelings surfaced in arguments over meeting procedures, sharing of information, and the extensive media exposure of some leaders.

The disagreements over wells and the lawsuit involved crucial task-oriented decisions. In contrast, the issues of trust and interpersonal conflict were socioemotional in nature, revealing the kinds of cumulative tensions that evolve among a group of leaders under intense pressure. These conflicts surfaced after Concerned Citizens' success in getting a new water source lessened demand for members to pull together and hide extraneous conflicts. The lawsuit, the major continuing concern of the group, was almost totally in the hands of the lawyers. With those external pressures reduced, the leadership began to act like the diverse group of possibly incompatible individuals thrown together under high pressure that it indeed was. Thus, at a time when the leadership might have begun to relax, rising internal conflict within the group kept tensions at a boiling point.

These group conflicts were a normal response to extended stress. Prolonged disaster strains the cohesive forces holding a group together and results in disruption due to collective emotional disturbances, displacement, or mutual withdrawal, increased subgroup solidarity reflected in distrust of authority, charges of favoritism, and intensification of damages. Even a "therapeutic community" that pulls people together to face a disaster will split over questions of allocation of aid or resources and as fellow sufferers find their association less comforting and more painful over time as they continually remind one another of past crises. Finally, adding to organizational strain, in later stages of a toxic incident, personal rather than community issues become dominant, eroding strong ties of mutual interdependence found earlier.[55]

Consensus and Dissensus Elsewhere

Another strain from prolonged group effort is the battle for legitimacy. In the United States, government denial routinely forces community groups to confront officials, using the media and direct action to apply political pressure.[56] In contrast, community groups in the Netherlands are accepted into a semipermanent negotiation structure that provides a forum for communication with government. Although Dutch toxic victims still evidence distrust, the community group is readily accorded legitimacy. In both cases, the internal development of the organization is influenced by its government legitimacy.[57]

The Form of the Organization and Consensus

The form that a community organization takes can influence the development of consensus, as seen in an examination of three Dutch community organizations.[58] One organization, in Griftpark, used a decentralized, consensual approach. The second, in Volgermeerpolder, delegated authority to experts. The third, in Merwedepolder, utilized a highly centralized and hierarchical structure. The first group relied on direct actions in which all members could participate, such as public demonstrations. The other two groups emphasized the use of petitions and public meetings. The limitations of the latter approach for maintaining consensus were most evident in Merwedepolder, where dissenting members carried out direct actions outside of the group, occupying a town hall and cutting bridge cables. Implied is that the maintenance of consensus requires continuing opportunities within the group for members to directly participate in activities that express their concerns, fears, and frustrations.

Several community groups formed at Love Canal in response to the toxic incident that began there in August 1978. The most prominent was the Love Canal

Homeowners Association (LCHA). LCHA used media events to generate the political pressure necessary to force government action. Leaders attempted to speak for the community and were sometimes invited to government decisionmaking meetings. The group conducted its own epidemiological research with the expert help of a leading health researcher. And its efforts to expand an initial government relocation effort to the outer areas of the neighborhood eventually succeeded.[59]

The LCHA bridged two of the Dutch models, being run principally by a core of key members and yet frequently undertaking broad participatory actions. Lois Gibbs, the organization's president and dominant force, deliberately used direct action as a means of controlling dissenters within her organization.[60] These strategies changed over time. The expressive direct action used early in the incident gave way to more focused and instrumental activities (as evidenced by the attempt to halt remedial work at the canal by injunction).[61]

The Dissensus Community: Centralia, Pennsylvania

Toxic disaster may also produce a dissensus so fundamental that inter-neighborhood conflict undercuts a long-standing sense of community. This is precisely the situation described by Couch and Kroll-Smith.[62] Centralia, Pennsylvania, lacked both an overall consensus and the successful development of community groups representing different points of view. A beneficial therapeutic community was largely absent, and the level of stress was exacerbated by conflict. On the continuum, Centralia was truly on the dissensus side.

After an anthracite coal deposit beneath Centralia ignited in 1962 when burning trash was disposed of in a strip-mined area, an uncontrollable fire threatened the 1,000 mainly elderly and ethnically diverse residents with toxic gases, subsidence, and explosion. As the crisis continued into the 1980s, factions developed and disputes occurred over whether the fire was really under the town and in what direction it was moving, over the best method to fight the fire, and over health and safety questions. Some residents were not threatened; others feared subsidence, explosion, and exposure to gases such as carbon monoxide, carbon dioxide, and methane. Government failed to address this climate of uncertainty. The fire was not located, no strategy for fighting it was developed, and hazards were not defined. Existing confusion was exacerbated when standards for gas exposure were changed three times. In this instance, residents directed their anger at neither the fire nor government but toward the community. Violence was common. In contrast to the therapeutic communities found at Legler and Love Canal, "the primary stressor in Centralia is not the fire, but community conflict."[63]

Over a period of three years, seven different community groups developed, each representing factions in the general conflict over goals. Their differences are well illustrated by these contrasting definitions of the situation.[64]

> *Our message is clear. This town is in severe danger from an underground mine fire and each person in the town should acknowledge that danger and help us do something about it.*

> *We are being duped by the government and a handful of greedy people who want government to purchase their home so they can leave. There is no danger here (from the fire).*

Internal conflict has affected other communities without blocking the development of therapeutic community. Why, then, was Centralia so different? In Legler, internal conflict did not prevent the formation of one predominant community group that represented the bulk of the neighborhood. Similarly, at Love Canal, despite the presence of competing groups, the LCHA was the principal representative of the community. In neither neighborhood were all residents in agreement about the risks of exposure; however, community organizations were able to represent the shared interests of a substantial portion of the community.

Centralia differed in several ways from the other two communities. First, in Legler and Love Canal, the drawing of boundaries served to define the range of danger, to provoke anger for the way the boundaries were drawn, and to legitimate fears felt by residents living just outside the boundary who were at a disadvantage in receiving aid but felt threatened by their arbitrary separation from the danger zone. In contrast, in Centralia, boundaries were never firmly drawn delineating the endangered area. Second, the danger in Centralia was even less actualized and more uncertain than in the other cases. Finally, all Centralians were asked to agree on a common relocation strategy—a decision not forced on residents of the other two communities.

Kroll-Smith and Couch found that divisions within Centralia corresponded to existing cohesive neighborhoods that experienced different degrees of exposure to the fire and thus different levels of concern. Support for government-aided evacuation was logical for residents of the neighborhood adjacent to the fire. However, this strategy threatened neighborhoods less at risk whose residents wanted to stay in Centralia. Conflict resulted from an attempt to achieve consensus within a political community that was, in reality, several different communities of interest.

Given their insight, Kroll-Smith and Couch intervened to facilitate community discussion of the crisis. Neighborhood meetings were held rather than meetings of the entire community. The meaningful discussion of issues at this level of participation moderated the hostile atmosphere in the town.

As the Centralia example suggests, for community organization to be therapeutic there must be a shared sense of concern and a consensus around goals. Because "community" is such an elusive concept, dysfunctional attempts to create community support without consensus may occur. Decisionmaking structures representing both victims and nonvictims can hardly be expected to serve as a basis for social support, information, and power on behalf of the victims. The failure of a unified community response in Centralia, therefore, offers support for the thesis that isolation of those at risk is a prerequisite for the kind of community organization found in most toxic incidents.

Isolation Without Community

Beyond the continuum from consensus to dissensus rests the situation of contamination that affects only one or a few isolated families who must cope without collective local support. In my observations, pressures within isolated families appear to be comparable to those for families of grassroots leaders who become involved to the detriment of their private lives. An isolated family bears the full burden of work, demand for resources, and roles to play that in collective situations are provided by many, but are unable to share the constant pressure. Their sense that only fellow sufferers can understand their experience only underscores their isolation.

From the standpoint of managing its environmental turbulence, the isolated family suffers from a condition of "undermanning," signifying the presence of too few people to carry out required tasks.[65] The isolated family must learn to play a wide range of roles, adapting to the demands of dealing with government and the need for developing new competencies. Struggling with their crisis, isolated victims are particularly subject to the strains entailed in activism.

The isolated family's ability to command power and attain information is substantially compromised. Regulators and politicians are reluctant to define a private woe as a community concern. Lawyers have less incentive to provide contingent-fee services. Although media may see isolated victims as a "human interest" story, they are less likely to be "news." The importance of networking across incidents is paramount for such families, who otherwise easily become convinced, in their isolation, that their experience of suffering is unique.

Cooperation and the Dangers of Cooptation

Efforts to improve public involvement carry with them both promise and pitfalls for involved citizens. In the case of the Lipari landfill in New Jersey, citizens commented on three sets of RI/FS (remedial investigation and feasibility study) and RODs (records of decision). However, when the emergency action waste containment plan called for on-site treatment of wastes, residents felt that all of their input had been ignored. The EPA addressed this disenchantment by appointing a new on-site coordinator who possessed excellent community relations skills. The agency instituted new procedures providing more time for public comment, the opportunity to comment on draft documents, and a technical advisory grant for the hiring of an expert, and to set up an advisory oversight committee. When the New Jersey Department of Health undertook a health study, great effort was spent encouraging community collaboration and educating participants. The public's ownership of the study helped them accept results showing aberrance in expected leukemia rates and the birth of underweight children.[66]

However, community collaboration exacts "cooptation costs" following "the law of process momentum." Accordingly, the more fully engaged participants are in a collaborative process, the harder it becomes for them to represent their original interests and organizational points of view.[67] Particularly if there is real dialogue and involvement of all parties, representatives easily become members of the new group as well as their original one, perhaps without even recognizing any possible conflicts. As an "inside player," the representative, and perhaps his or her group, may shift their focus from the periphery to the center.

PALLCA, the community group mobilized around the Lipari landfill, is a good case in point of the consequences. The group prided itself in its mastery of technical documents and access to such elites as national environmental organizations and government officials. As a result, PALLCA failed to build a solid bloc of community support. By working with instead of opposing government, in the end, the group lost its legitimacy and the leadership split apart over differences in tactics.[68]

Concluding Comments on Enablement

Commonly, community develops out of the isolating nature of contamination events. At the same time, corrosive and conflictive elements are inherent in the situation, suggesting fluctuation across a continuum of consensus and dissensus. Following the social process model, similar dynamics can be expected at the societal level as are seen in the community.

Toxic Victims: A New Social Movement?

With thousands of communities responding to toxic threats across the United States, what are the cumulative effects of these grassroots efforts at a societal level of social process? Here I consider the nature of the toxic victims' movement, and its implications. Do toxic victims' organizations represent an extension of the existing environmental movement, or do they form the basis for a new social movement?

The Emergence of a National Movement

Technological controversy commonly follows three stages leading to a mass movement. First, a warning about the technology is brought to the public's attention. Second, a few people at the local level oppose the technology (as early Legler residents fought the local siting of the Jackson landfill). Or, after a contamination incident, controversy arises after the discovery of exposure has been announced. Finally, a mass movement develops as "the growing number of communities experiencing disputes serve as building blocks, all of a kind, which become linked together into a national coalition."[69]

A national toxic victims' movement, consisting both of exposure victims and those acting from anticipatory fear, has evolved precisely along these lines, building on the networking of groups concerned with local issues.[70] The movement developed quickly in the first decade after toxic incidents reached national prominence in the late 1970s. In the early 1980s, John O'Connor, then director of the National Campaign Against Toxic Hazards, observed more activity in this country on the toxics issue than on any other single issue.[71] The emergence of this successful movement occurred at the very point, Andrew Szasz notes, when other liberal causes were generally suffering at the hands of the Reagan onslaught.[72]

The organization of this movement varied from that of the traditional social movement in which hierarchical bureaucracies are created at a national level. Instead, the movement was highly decentralized and based on active participation and networking. With a few although notable exceptions, it avoided the development of national leaders.[73]

Although a decentralized structure puts opponents off guard, it suffers from limitations. The consensual view of national corporations allows for pooling of knowledge and resources. In contrast, in a movement of local defensive battles against these corporations, different local organizations easily repeat each other's mistakes. With heterogeneous constituencies, community groups concerned with toxic exposure have a comparatively harder time developing a collective vision and strategy.[74]

As it evolved, the toxics movement overcame the problems of decentralization while employing its strengths. Networking among groups sharing similar problems occurred spontaneously and as the result of deliberate organizing. In contrast to the ebb and flow of the national-scale movements affected by media coverage,[75] the emerging toxic victims' movement is "refueled" by the proliferation of new incidents that serve to broaden the grassroots base and to generate renewed media interest.

Furthermore, given their personal experience, members of the toxics movement are less likely to lose commitment. For them, the issues are not global and abstract but personal and concrete. The movement builds on these personal interests, creating collective action required to pressure government. The resulting media attention has served to make environmental protection a top priority for nonvictims, as well.[76]

The movement has superseded parochial concerns, moving beyond local threats, such as the siting of specific landfills and resource recovery plants, to address the generic issues in waste disposal and treatment that Lois Gibbs calls the "toxic merry-go-round." Instead of each community asserting "not in my backyard" or "take it somewhere else," these groups demand "not in anyone's backyard" and argue for on-site solutions to toxic problems.[77] As a result, the intersite conflict generated when waste is hauled from one place to another has been minimized, preserving the consensus required for the growth of the national movement.

A number of factors have helped spur the development of this national toxics movement, including the actions of facilitating organizations, supportive legislation, legal precedents, and continuing media coverage.

Facilitating Organizations. The creation of national organizations focused on the toxic victim's plight has helped give impetus to the movement. The Citizens Clearinghouse for Hazardous Wastes, Inc. (CCHW), now the Center for Health, Environment, and Justice (CHEJ), was founded in 1981 by Lois Marie Gibbs, former head of the Love Canal Homeowners Association. CHEJ/CCHW seeks to build a national toxics movement, as this mission statement indicates:

> At Love Canal, we proved that when neighbors band together, do their homework, and stand up for their rights, they can win! When we won at Love Canal and then moved on to form CCHW, we started a movement that has since become the fastest growing and most dynamic movement that this country has seen since the Civil Rights movement. In fact, the fight against irresponsible hazardous waste disposal *is* a civil rights movement.[78]

CHEJ/CCHW staffers have visited many hundreds of groups to provide consultation and training and have worked in some capacity with some 8,000 grassroots organizations and hundreds of traditional environmental groups. Thousands of community activists have attended CHEJ/CCHW training programs, including their leadership development conferences and continuing education programs for Organizers.[79]

The organization disseminates information through a periodic newsletter entitled *Everyone's Backyard,* quarterly action bulletins, other publications, and lots of
face-to-face contact. Covered topics include how to deal with government, experts,
and lawyers; environmental testing; stress and burnout; standards for hazardous
waste cleanup; and waste disposal methods such as incineration, deep-well injection, and landfills. Since 1988, a journal called *Environmental Health Monthly* has
been published. The *Leadership Handbook on Hazardous Waste* is a typical publication, written to be readily accessible by activists starting from scratch and with only
modest education. One-page handouts, such as one entitled "How to Get and Keep
People Involved," offer excellent suggestions, in this instance, to organize local
groups in a nonhierarchical manner through action committees whose heads form
an executive council.

Among various publishing efforts, Lois Gibbs was listed as lead author for the
1995 book *Dying from Dioxin: A Citizen's Guide to Reclaiming Our Health and
Rebuilding Democracy,* to which other board members of the organization contributed. Beyond a readable and very competent overview of the politics and science of dioxin, the book contains a cogent guide to organizing to stop dioxin production and to deal with the hazards.

Leadership programs for grassroots leaders are offered, along with an organizing assistance program that provides advice to dozens of local leaders every day, site
visits around the country, and specialized organizing efforts, for example, in the
South and for Hispanics. A technical assistance program helps local groups review
such documents as the plans for closure of Superfund sites. And innovations are
created through roundtable conferences to evaluate different issues. A landfill
moratorium campaign helped discredit this waste disposal method, and the
"McToxics" campaign played a key role in forcing the restaurant chain to reduce
and change its use of materials.[80]

Although their action bulletins provide a means for applying political pressure,
CHEJ/CCHW primarily serves as a support organization for smaller regional and
local organizations. For example, when local leaders are in Washington, D.C., they
lobby for their causes with CHEJ/CCHW assistance instead of having
CHEJ/CCHW lobby on their behalf.[81]

Perhaps the greatest contribution of the CHEJ/CCHW has been its role as a
meta-organization, pulling together local grassroots activists to offer psychological
as well as logistical and technical support. I recall the sense of cohesion in the room
when I attended the fifth anniversary convention of the Grassroots Movement
Against Hazardous Waste in May 1986. Some 400 community leaders gathered in
Washington, D.C., for twenty-six workshops on various topics. At the conference,
ten resolution committees developed objectives for the toxic waste movement over
the next five-year period. Although the movement has exponentially progressed

since that meeting, the 1986 conference was a good snapshot of how a national grassroots toxics movement was being consciously built.[82]

Another important player in the field is the Environmental Research Foundation. ERF describes itself as "a non-profit organization whose goal is to provide reliable, scientific information about environment and health." It is headed by Peter Montague, a former Princeton geographer whose research played a key role in the early critique of state-of-the-art landfill design. Montague publishes a newsletter called *RACHEL's Hazardous Waste News*. Available for a low-cost mail subscription or free electronically, *RACHEL's* has become the bible of the grassroots toxics movement and Montague's well-considered and researched opinions are its editorial page. Recent newsletters ranged broadly across such topics as how chemicals cause cancer, precautionary principles, unionization and the role of corporations, the impacts of biotechnology, the effects of television, mad cow disease, hazardous materials policy, sustainability, and the dumbing down of children.[83] Szasz points to this diversity of interests in concluding that the toxics movement has matured to a much greater scope of issues and concerns.[84]

Another national organization, the National Campaign Against Toxic Hazards, or the National Toxics Campaign, combined the efforts of two other national groups concerned with toxics issues—Citizens Action and the Clean Water Project. Until its demise in the early 1990s, the campaign waged a multiyear grassroots organizing effort on a state-by-state basis, building coalitions intended to wield political muscle. The campaign made source reduction its clarion call. Included in its declaration of "citizen's rights" were the rights to be safe from harmful exposure, to knowledge, cleanup, participation, compensation, prevention, protection, and enforcement. In the early 1990s, the national campaign was an early advocate for environmental justice issues and made them a key project issue. It was ended in 1993.[85]

The Environmental Health Network was yet another short-lived but influential national organization. A splinter group from CCHW, EHN was headed by Linda Price King, a veteran of Louisiana toxics battles and a former CCHW staff person. EHN was focused on the health consequences of contamination and how community groups could address them. Its express goal was to change the attitudes and prejudices of health scientists and to educate physicians and other health care professionals about the health consequences of toxic exposure. The annual conference of the EHN was a meeting place for the key experts on the health effects of contamination, as well as a diverse groups of whistle-blowers, toxic victims, sufferers of environmental illnesses, ill Gulf War veterans, and occupationally injured workers. It served as a major training ground for activists in the practice of popular epidemiology, offering training in the gathering and interpretation of data about local environmental illnesses.

EHN published critical reviews of government practice, such as the report *Inconclusive by Design: Waste, Fraud, and Abuse in Federal Environmental Health Research,* a critique of ATSDR practice coauthored with the National Toxics Campaign,[86] as well as a guidebook on how to work with environmental attorneys. It promoted the collection of health registries, a means for documenting subtle change over time in a large exposed population, as an alternative community health assessment process to the quantitative approaches to epidemiology employed by ATSDR and its state affiliates. Overall, EHN fostered popular epidemiology as an approach to community empowerment. Lacking the kind of broad-based membership and organizing capability of CCHW, EHN was totally dependent on soft money for support.[87]

Statewide coalitions are another vital link in these developing national networks. Although such groups vary widely in their form and activities, they represent an important step in building a grassroots movement. For example, the New Jersey Grassroots Environmental Organization grew out of a coalition of community organizations and has been an active vehicle of support for local groups in that state. NJGREO won funding and hired a full-time director, Madeline Hoffman.[88] Stringfellow acid pit activist Penny Newman, after a stint as the western coordinator of CCHW, founded the California-based Center for Community Action and Environmental Justice. CCAEJ focuses heavily on training activists.[89] The New York Toxics in Your Community Coalition branched off from an existing statewide environmental organization under the leadership of Ann Rabe, pioneering coalitions with organized labor.[90] Other statewide coalitions include the Arkansas Chemical Cleanup Alliance, the Louisiana Environmental Action Network, Vermonters Organized for Cleanup, and the Maine and New Hampshire People's Alliances. At a regional level, my organization, Orange Environment, Inc., illustrates the power of networking with issue-oriented local grassroots groups in Orange County, New York.

In contrast to these grassroots organizing and networking groups, the major national environmental organizations have traditionally focused on litigating and lobbying. However, during the Reagan-Bush years (1981–1993), with the environmental community forced into exile, grassroots and organizational networking took on a special importance. During this period, the Environmental Action Foundation published an excellent bimonthly paper, *Exposure,* for several years. Both Environmental Action and the Environmental Defense Fund sponsored regional networking conferences across the United States.[91] A number of organizations have also published manuals for toxic activists, including the Sierra Club, the National Wildlife Federation, and the League of Women Voters.

Efforts to move the grassroots movement into the political arena include the evolving presence of the American Green Party and presidential campaigns by such figures in the toxics movement as Barry Commoner and Ralph Nader. That such initiatives can influence the outcome of national elections was demonstrated in the 2000 presidential election.

Overall, the accomplishments of grassroots environmental activism include pressure to clean up pollution and prevent further contamination, improve environmental health, change corporate culture toward environmental responsibility, adopt prevention as a goal, create public support for a clean environment, and include the public in environmental decisionmaking.[92] The movement has also become a force for legislative change.

Legislative Impetus.   Faced with the novel demands of Love Canal, lawmakers found that federal law provided neither authority nor funding for government action to address such disasters. To fill this gap, Superfund (more formally, the Comprehensive Environmental, Response, Compensation, and Liability Act of 1980, or CERCLA) was enacted to clean up the nation's most severe toxic sites, resolving the barriers to fast action encountered at Love Canal.

Like all regulatory statutes, Superfund not only presents a process of implementation but additionally offers an "issue infrastructure," defined by Szasz as "that complex of knowledge, technology, and institutions that makes it possible for society to understand and cope with any issue."[93] There is a virtual lesson plan embodied in Superfund, which offers a systematic way to work through the problems of characterizing, rating, evaluating, and designing solutions for a hazardous waste site.

Despite its promise, Superfund has been widely viewed as a major disappointment. Under the original law, insufficient money was provided for site cleanup. Instead, short-term remediation was offered. And even with this limitation, only a few sites received attention, prompting Lois Gibbs to term CERCLA a "deliberate distraction by government," inviting competition among communities for limited funding.[94] Adam Stern of the Environmental Defense Fund described how hopes for Superfund to effectively address cleanup of contaminated sites gave way to frustration on the part of affected communities. Effective government action was blocked both by the inadequacy of technology and by political interference. This failure was particularly evident during the Reagan administration, when the EPA under Ann Gorsuch created scandals at such sites as the Stringfellow acid pits.[95]

Against $1.62 billion in the first five-year bill applied to work at 100 sites, the reauthorized Superfund bill passed late in 1986 made $8.5 billion available for cleanup of 375 sites over the subsequent five-year period. SARA (the Superfund Amendments and Reauthorization Act) featured important improvements over the original law, including provisions addressing victim compensation and the "right to know," an important tool for preventing toxic exposure. With strong environmental lobbying, it received wide congressional support. Pressure due to scandals helped override opposition from the Reagan administration to block industry taxation.[96] Since SARA, Congress has continued to appropriate funds for cleanups but it has not reauthorized Superfund; trust funds are being depleted since the 1995 cutoff of supporting industry taxes. A major congressional emphasis has been to recover less contaminated sites as Brownfields. In the active debate over Superfund's future, contentious issues include disagreements over the extent of cleanup required, the twelve year average delay, differences between Superfund and other federal cleanup programs, the costs, who pays, impact on small businesses that may be drawn into costly cleanups, and expensive litigation among Potentially Responsible Parties and insurers over liability issues.[97] Questions of program priority have also been raised, spurred by between 121 and 137 "Mega sites," costing over $50 million each to remediate, with the result that 80 percent of Superfund resources are being used at 20 percent of the sites.[98] An EPA Superfund advisory committee is working through to the end of 2003 on recommendations for program changes.[99] In any case, it has been predicted that the bulk of sites (93 percent) will have remedial activities completed by 2009.[100]

Addressing Uncivil Actions: Pressure Through the Courts.   The success of legal efforts to demand compensation and force remediation has also helped spur the grassroots environmental movement.[101] In this section I consider four relevant contexts for toxic litigation.

The Toxic Tort

The most prominent legal approach in contaminated communities is the "toxic tort." This form of civil lawsuit is evocatively named by combining a victim's deliberate harm or punishment (i.e., their "torture") with the damage to people, property, and/or the environment due to the toxicity of a product, process, or substance.[102]

The issue of psychological damage due to a human-caused environmental disaster was perhaps first clearly raised in a precursor to the toxic tort, namely, the litigation filed in the wake of the Buffalo Creek flood disaster in West Virginia. This case met both common tests used to limit claims of psychological injury: the damage was associated with clear physical harm and the cause was negligence violating the plaintiffs' rights to emotional well-being. The ruling that psychological harm would be considered contributed to a settlement.[103]

An explicit prototype for the modern toxic tort was the suit by Legler residents against Jackson Township over contamination from the municipal landfill (see Chapter 2).[104] Inspired by the Buffalo Creek suit, *Ayers v. Jackson Township* was planned by lead attorney Steven Phillips with the deliberateness of a military campaign. It featured the deployment of a wide array of experts to address issues that included groundwater contamination, toxicology and environmental health, property damage, and emotional distress and psychosocial impacts. The litigation established an important precedent requiring Jackson's insurers to back the municipality. Then, in 1983, after a lengthy trial, a New Jersey jury found that Jackson Township had created a "nuisance" and "dangerous condition" in operating the landfill in a "palpably unreasonable" manner and that the landfill caused contamination of the plaintiffs' water. The verdict awarded to 339 plaintiffs more than $15 million for emotional distress ($2 million), medical surveillance ($8 million), diminished quality of life ($5.4 million), and reimbursement for costs such as hooking up to the new water system ($200,000). Awards granted to individual plaintiffs varied according to their proximity to the landfill, length and amount of exposure, and age.

A 1985 appellate decision upheld the award for loss of quality of life but reversed the awards for emotional distress and medical surveillance. In 1987 the New Jersey Supreme Court upheld the quality of life award, reinstated the medical surveillance award, and confirmed the reversal of the emotional distress award. The decision set an important affirmative precedent on all three grounds, however, because the reversal on emotional distress was due only to a technicality in New Jersey law barring "pain and suffering" awards against government. In fact, the only limiting precedent involved the courts' refusal to grant damages for enhanced health risk, in part, because the risk could not be quantified and declared "reasonably probable" even if recognized as significant.[105]

A flood of additional toxic tort suits followed the filing of the Jackson case. But the public awareness of this type of litigation only became established after the release of two popular movies with high-powered stars. *Civil Action*, based on Jonathan Harr's compelling book, tells the story of the tort action filed on behalf of residents of Woburn, Massachusetts, who suspected an environmental cause for the childhood leukemia cluster plaguing that community. The litigation concerned whether this cause involved toxic contamination due to improper waste handling and disposal at local factories owned by Beatrice Foods and W.R. Grace. The related psychosocial impacts are well described by two of the experts in this case, Phil Brown and Ed Mikkelsen, in their book *No Safe Place: Toxic Waste, Leukemia, and Community Action*.[106]

These authors recount a classic case of "popular epidemiology." Facilitated by a local minister, parents of the sick Woburn children joined other local residents to form a local grassroots organization called FACE (For a Cleaner

Environment). By mapping the incidence of local leukemia cases, FACE was able to convince the Centers for Disease Control and Massachusetts officials to conduct a study of the community. Although the study failed to prove the existence of a leukemia cluster, the results inspired epidemiologists at Harvard to team up with FACE volunteers to conduct a more comprehensive study. This effort linked ingestion of water from two polluted wells and development of childhood leukemia and other diseases.

Meanwhile, thirty-three residents representing eight families had sued Grace and Beatrice in 1982, shortly after an EPA study found contamination in Woburn's groundwater. Represented by Jan Schlictmann and given heroic stature by Harr's story, FACE confronted a hostile judge. Schlictmann employed novel strategies involving groundwater study and medical causality in attempting to prove that subsidiaries of Grace and Beatrice dumped toxic chemicals, contaminated the groundwater, and caused the death and illness of residents. Although FACE successfully established Grace's (but not Beatrice's) responsibility for dumping chemicals in the first three intended phases of the trial, the case subsequently became hopelessly mired in a complex mix of settlements and appeals that demonstrate the difficulty of asking a civil court to resolve toxic disputes. Illustrative of this complexity was the ruling in *Anderson v. W.R. Grace and Co.* that plaintiffs could recover for emotional distress from subclinical damage to the immune system, but not due to family illness.[107] With hero attorney Schlictmann left penniless for his efforts and the victims unfulfilled in their search for justice, *Civil Action* is a cautionary tale about the prospects for toxic tort action.

A more upbeat legend is suggested by the subsequent movie *Erin Brockovich*, which recounts the tale of a highly successful toxic tort built around the tireless efforts of a novice paralegal. Given clear and compelling evidence, plaintiffs living near a Pacific Gas and Electric facility in Hinkley, California, who had been exposed to a particularly toxic form of chromium, were awarded $333 million in damages.[108] We see in these two popular movies both a best- and worst-case scenario for toxic tort litigation.[109]

My own experiences with toxic torts as an expert witness also suggests a wide disparity of outcomes. These stretch from the successful Legler case, described above, to other cases that accepted minimal settlements or failed entirely. Failures occurred because the defense was too well financed, plaintiffs or key witnesses were intimidated, a legal strategy failed, causal proofs were elusive, or because the defendant proved someone else was responsible for the incident. Tort litigation is a rocky road, indeed. Yet no other strategy provides the same engine for amassing information about impacts to the environment and victims, causes of the incident, and advocacy for those harmed.[110]

Environmental Citizen's Suits

Another useful legal tool are the citizen's suit provisions of the clean air and water acts that empower the public to act as "citizen attorneys general" to uphold environmental laws which government has failed to enforce.[111] Because these suits, if successful, recover fees from the defendant, such cases can be more easily financed. However, such suits are limited to forcing agency enforcement action or winning a remedy to the violation. Most important, they are not useful for recovering damages for the adverse impacts of the violations on behalf of the victims.

Civil Rights Litigation

Most litigation citing environmental civil rights injustice follows Executive Order 12898, discussed later in this chapter. Here we note a novel strategy for addressing contamination and related nuisances as violations of victims' civil rights. Attorneys Scott Thornton and Michael Sussman represent neighbors of a junkyard contaminated during an extended period of regulatory inaction. Reasoning that New York State law grants its citizens certain rights to environmental protection, they argue that these rights were denied plaintiffs by the government's failure to prevent harm. The U.S. District Court Northern District of New York, refusing dismissal, found that the agency's lack of regulatory action over a ten-year period could not be excused as merely "discretionary enforcement decisions." The case was, nevertheless, later dismissed and is now under appeal.[112]

NEPA Review and Adjudicatory Law

A fourth legal approach, intervention in the administrative permit approval process, also has promise for addressing the psychosocial impacts of "anticipatory" contamination. When approval triggers review under the National Environmental Policy Act (NEPA) or its state and local analogs, an environmental impact statement (EIS) is required when there is a potential for significant environmental consequences of the action. The EIS is intended to inform decisionmakers about potential impacts, the possibilities for mitigating them by altering the project, whether alternative approaches involve less impact, and such other considerations as its long-term and cumulative effects. They then can weigh the environmental, social, and economic impacts of the project in deciding whether to permit it.

Adjudicatory hearings occur when there are substantive disputes of fact over whether the project can meet regulatory requirements. These science trials are overseen by an administrative law judge (ALJ) and generally follow civil court protocol. The applicant for the permit, the regulating agency(ies), and any recognized public interveners can present evidence and offer and cross examine witnesses on issues potentially leading to permit denial or modification of the project. Based on the ALJ's findings, the agency commissioner makes a final decision as to whether to issue the permit. Although EISs rarely consider issues of psychological impact, these issues are even less common in the administrative review process. In effect, it is easier to identify the potentially adverse psychosocial effects of a project than to establish them as a basis for project denial or modification.

The most significant early test of the need to consider psychological impacts under NEPA occurred with the restart of the Three Mile Island (TMI) nuclear reactor I, on routine shutdown at the time of the 1979 accident at its sister plant, TMI II. A lengthy legal battle ensued after the Nuclear Regulatory Commission (NRC) denied a request by a Harrisburg grassroots group called People Against Nuclear Energy (PANE) that they consider stress due to the restart. In 1982, the U.S. Appeals Court for the District of Columbia found for PANE, the majority concluding that NEPA requires an examination of psychological health and that a regulatory decision such as that before the NRC constitutes an action under NEPA.[113] In his dissent, Judge Wilkey lamented that the decision would "let any special interest group effectively repeal an act of Congress if it could whip up sufficient hysteria."[114]

The court majority limited the scope of its decision, concluding that NEPA "does not encompass mere dissatisfactions arising from social opinions, economic concerns, or political disagreements with agency policies." As such, the court distinguished between "true psychological stress" caused by an action, such as post-traumatic anxiety and physical effects due to "fears of recurring catastrophe," and more routine "socioeconomic anxieties," such as middle-class homeowners' feelings about a proposed land use they found to be undesirable. The majority also found relevant the severity of the psychological effect, as well as its cognizability under NEPA. Finally, the court concluded that it need not "draw a bright line" distinguishing TMI from other instances because the TMI disaster "is, at least so far, the only event of its kind in the American experience."[115]

A more troublesome qualification occurred when the NRC and Metropolitan Edison, owner of the TMI plants, appealed to the U.S. Supreme Court. These appeals asserted that to trigger NEPA review, some physical effect had to be evident due to the restart of the TMI I reactor. No such trigger existed. Moreover, they argued that psychological harm can not be validly measured so as to be considered by a permitting agency. These arguments were rebutted by the American Psychological and Sociological Associations, who argued that Congress intended NEPA to review psychological impacts, citing numerous studies of stress due to the accident at TMI II as evidence of proximate psychological damage from restarting TMI I. APA also supported use of measurements of perception to assess psychological impact.[116]

The Supreme Court unanimously rejected PANE's arguments, Justice Rehnquist's decision concluding that the causal chain between risk perception and the restart of the TMI I reactor was too long. Specifically, Rehnquist wrote, "But a risk of an accident is not an effect on the physical environment. A risk is, by definition, unrealized in the physical world."[117] The accident at TMI II was considered to be irrelevant as a physical effect because it was a past action and occurred at a different plant than the one under review by the NRC.

The Supreme Court's ruling in the PANE case was not intended to exclude psychological impacts altogether from NEPA review. Rather, as Justice Brennan clarified in his concurring opinion, such impacts must be assessed in response to "direct sensory impact of a change on the physical environment," but not due merely to the "perception of risk." A clear causal link between an event and its psychological impact is established when psychological effects are seen as secondary or indirect consequences of an action, not merely as risks of a possible accident.[118] Of course, as we have seen throughout this volume, contamination events, even of an anticipatory nature, are more than ephemeral perceptions of risk. Rather, they involve the direct sensory impacts about which Brennan wrote.

Nevertheless, the PANE decision had a chilling effect on subsequent opportunities to consider psychosocial impacts in NEPA review. Freudenburg and Jones have challenged the wisdom of the higher court's reasoning, testing "the Supreme Court hypothesis" that stress measurements would be unable to distinguish those suffering from genuine psychological stress due to the restart of TMI I from those merely opposed to the facility. The Court presumed that facility opponents would also test with significant psychological stress, confounding the issue of who is psychologically damaged and who merely politically opposed. Freudenburg and Jones find no social science literature supporting the Court's view; what's more, their analysis of data on the siting of a Washington nuclear plant suggests no correlation between opposition and perceived stress. In refuting the Court's concern that social scientists cannot distinguish impact from concern, the authors suggest that the justices asked the wrong question. "The relevant question, in fact, may have to do not with the capabilities of social sciences, but with the capabilities of *courts,* particularly for dealing with the range of problems that appear to have accompanied many of the technological developments of recent decades."[119]

Freudenburg and Jones's assessment is certainly applicable to my own experience testifying to psychosocial impacts in permit hearings. My first effort, as a witness for the Town of Goshen, New York, in its 1980 opposition to the expansion of Al Turi Landfill, Inc., was derailed by inexperience—mine as a witness and the ALJ's in considering novel impacts. The ALJ had allowed a three-week recess of the hearing for me to conduct interviews with residents living near the landfill. Following the norms of social science, I offered confidentiality to my interview sources, not anticipating that I would be asked to divulge their names on the stand. My subsequent refusal to do so caused the ALJ to dismiss my testimony as hearsay. In fact, had he been forced to consider expert testimony from a social scientist and to weigh psychological effects in his decision, the ALJ was totally unprepared to do so.

My second chance to test this issue in administrative court came when CECOS applied for a sixth hazardous waste disposal site at its Niagara Falls compound in the 1980s. I took the stand on behalf of the "concerned citizens," an amalgam of opposed citizen organizations grouped by an ALJ unfamiliar and unsympathetic to psychological impacts (an issue forced on him by a siting board). With only a few weeks to prepare, I reviewed thousands of pages of media and regulatory documents, interviewed activists and a cross-section of local residents, and hired a survey research firm to conduct a phone survey randomly sampling 10 percent of local residents. I had robust evidence for my conclusions of psychological impact.

The CECOS case evidenced a dialectic pattern that I later described as the "expanding and limiting models" of expert testimony.[120] I had to make the case for impact, presenting evidence of damage to be expected were the facility to be built. In contrast, the two social scientists hired by CECOS to oppose and rebut my arguments merely had to cast doubt on my testimony, not prove anything on their own. They spoke with no one but CECOS employees and collected no data whatsoever. Their role was clearly *limiting* whereas mine was *expanding,* as these examples illustrate.

- Whereas I defined psychological impacts inclusively to involve effects on the behavior, cognitions, and emotions of those potentially exposed to an expanded hazardous waste facility, the CECOS experts tried to limit the definition of legitimate impact to one construct—stress—and to limit the valid measurement of stress to a few quantitative approaches.
- I projected potential outcomes by examining past and current effects and dynamics for impacts that might be reasonably generalized to the proposed waste facility. The applicant's experts ruled out the validity of any approach not measuring statistically significant differences between the population near the CECOS site and a control community. In the absence of this comparison, they asserted that it was impossible to prove impact.
- I interpreted my findings of strong, widespread opposition to the facility as clear evidence of community stress. The CECOS experts did not dispute the stress, but dismissed public concern as inaccurate, reflecting misinformation from biased media coverage. They argued that, as a state-of-the-art design, by definition, the proposed "secure chemical residue facility" entailed no risk. As a state-of-the-art facility, SCRF-6 by definition entailed no risk. Thus fears about the facility were *irrational* and *inappropriate*. These fears could be simply treated through educational programs and stress-reduction techniques.

The testimony of CECOS' experts unfortunately offered rationalizations for both the ALJ and the Commissioner of Environmental Protection to limit the impact of my testimony and, more generally, the weight of psychological impacts as a factor in the permit decision. Commissioner Jorling's ruling on psychological impacts echoes the NRC argument against PANE, embodied in the dissent of Judge Wilkey cited above. It is as clear a statement of the technocratic bias of government as one will ever find.[121]

> Though perhaps obvious, it is worth repeating that no activity is risk free. Apparently, the intervenors believe that as long as an activity is not risk free, it is rational to fear it. This is clearly not the case. . . . Regulatory agencies and society in general address questions of risk and make judgments determining a level of risk which is considered acceptable. Although these decisions necessarily have an element of subjectivity, they reflect societal values. If no risk were acceptable, every power plant, every factory and every gas station would have to shut down operations and the basis for our advanced technological society would come to a grinding halt. Through legislation and otherwise, society has made the decision that some level of risk is acceptable in exchange for the benefits of technology.
>
> The principal focus of this hearing has been on questions of whether the risk associated with the construction and operation of the facility is within acceptable limits. If such risk is shown to be unacceptable the project will not be approved. As a public policy matter, if the department were to deny an application for a facility after concluding that it met all regulatory criteria and that the risk of its construction and operation was within acceptable limits merely because of the fears in the host community, the agency would be abdicating its responsibility to administer the State's environmental programs which was vested in its control by the governor and legislature. Therefore, I conclude that any psychological impact caused by this facility cannot, standing alone, be grounds for denial of the applications.[122]

Jorling went on to conclude that, in any case, psychological impacts could be mitigated through permit conditions. However, in the end, not all ears were deaf to my findings. The permit was denied when the siting board refused to issue a Certificate of Environmental Safety and Public Necessity given its finding that the facility posed a potential risk to a large local population.

The CECOS and PANE decisions chilled subsequent adjudication of psychosocial impacts, despite the copious convergent social science literature and success in litigating these issues in civil court after *Ayers v. Jackson Township*. As the illuminating CECOS decision indicates, the real problem is not with proving valid adverse effects. Rather, in recognizing that psychosocial impacts affect health, enjoyment of property, and quality of life negatively, one legitimates a provable harm of such broad implication that those in authority fear *the impact of the impact* on facility siting.[123]

Media Coverage.   We have seen that information shapes the risk personality of the hazard. Media coverage generally serves to amplify risk, sometimes increasing concern for events that in fact have low probability of occurrence.[124] Media coverage and information released by government may also play down beliefs about the event, or information may simultaneously amplify and minimize the same belief for different observers holding divergent beliefs of what has occurred. Thus, for example, information that a chemical has been proven cancerous in animal tests can be interpreted divergently; one person concludes that it is a proven carcinogen, the other that its effects on humans are not yet established.

This influence makes relevant the substance and accuracy of coverage. The substance of news articles is frequently burdened by the journalistic norms for objectively dealing with topics shrouded in uncertainty. Thus stories often lack any critical grasp of the subject, mindlessly balancing different points of view according to form, regardless of their merit.[125] Studies have shown substantial levels of inaccuracy in coverage of risk-related events, including omissions of qualifying statements, methodological detail, and significant results necessary to fully understand what is happening.[126] Superseding these concerns, Mazur argues that the public impact of a hazardous site is established by its sheer quantity of coverage rather than substantive information contained in the stories.[127]

Beyond the melodrama and mystery inherent in disaster coverage lies the potential for creating new mythologies.[128] For example, Lee Wilkins observed that media coverage of the Bhopal accident focused on institutions as the actors and on individuals as the helpless victims, while totally ignoring the context or a critical view of how policies shaped the event.[129] Edelstein and Makofske detail a series of myths of geologic radon created by government policy and media coverage that greatly distorted response to this issue.[130]

Coverage, in turn, creates an "availability heuristic," where observers vicariously apply images associated in the media with one incident to others of a similar nature.[131] Such heuristics may employ fictional images, as when the movie *China Syndrome* influenced comprehension of the Three Mile Island accident or real events, as seen after Chernobyl and Love Canal.

Media coverage is often strategically valuable for community groups pressing their demands. Environmental protesters almost always benefit from publicity, Alan Mazur argues, regardless of the merits of their issue, to the extent that "protesters and journalists have a symbiotic relationship."[132] News coverage can cause self-fulfilling outcomes, as at Love Canal, where government was forced to respond to the climate of belief created by media and citizen groups. Government action and language then shaped subsequent meaning of the event, as Szasz observed.[133]

The administration's and Congress's efforts to get out in front of a fast-breaking story contributed to transforming Love Canal into *the Tragedy of Love Canal* and hazardous waste into *the Nation's Most Important Environmental Problem*. Love Canal was repeatedly, ritualistically, termed a public health "tragedy."

This example, in turn, suggests how environmental stories become national in scale.[134] To make this leap, the story must achieve coverage in a paper like the *New York Times*. And to keep its national prominence, it must be kept newsworthy by a continual flow of new information or it will drop from sight. Love Canal was sustained as a story not in large part because of its inherent interest but because Lois Gibbs was persistent and creative in generating news.[135]

Extensive media coverage has helped to build the American toxics movement. It has brought awareness of contamination into American homes, feeding a growing concern about toxic issues nationwide, captured by a variety of polls.[136] Such polls, themselves, inflame concern, helping to further augment and legitimate the grassroots protests that often generated the media coverage to begin with. Media modeling has also benefited the toxics movement. Andrew Szasz notes that the coverage of Love Canal literally spawned hundreds of similar groups around the country as people found their own feelings and situation reflected in the publicized events from Niagara Falls.[137]

A New Social Movement or an Extended Environmental Movement?

Toxic exposure is a politicizing and radicalizing experience.[138] At various levels, the safeguards and assumptions of a society fall away. Victims are forced to develop a more critical perspective than the one citizens bring to most decisions. Yet toxic victims are not often "sectarian" environmentalists, acting out of a faith in ecological principles, but rather citizens reflecting the central values of society, filled with faith in the goals of a consumptive and capitalistic society.[139] With toxic exposure, they receive an unsolicited de facto critical environmental education. Once their lives have been transformed by the incident, toxic victims are in a position to see what is nearly invisible for those for whom the system is still working.

A New Constituency.   The toxic victims' movement is an environmental movement whose constituency varies greatly from that of the classic environmental movement.[140] Ken Geiser noted that unlike the professionals, scientists, students, and civic activists who led the environmental movement of the 1970s, middle- and working-class people, who live in the areas affected by toxic hazards, are the foundation of the toxics movement. He further observes that

> this new movement is bringing forth environmental consciousness among people who were unlikely to think of themselves as "environmentalists." Because the movement is so tightly rooted in the immediate experience of people's community and family life, it has an urgency and a concreteness that is incredibly compelling. For these new "environmentalists," environment is not an abstract con-

cept. It is something which has already exposed them to hazards which are debilitating them and hastening their deaths.[141]

Commenting in a similar vein, Newark community leader Bob Cartwright underscored the difference between the abstract issues of the first Earth Day and a new environmental movement composed of people who are "stuck with a problem and take matters into their own hands."[142] This new constituency has a stake in issues such as the health of family members, the safety and value of homes, and regaining lost control and meaning in their lives.[143]

Labor Joins the Movement.   The early days of the grassroots toxics movement came at a point when the entire U.S. environmental movement was pitted against business and labor. My own New York state senator poured salt on this "jobs versus the environment" wound when he coined the popular phrase "eat an environmentalist for lunch." Indeed, many early contaminated communities were riven with conflicts between proindustry forces, including organized labor, that feared for the economic consequences of cleaning up the environment.

A classic example of this rift in the early 1980s involved the agonizing decision of whether to enforce stringent clean air regulations in Rushton and Tacoma, Washington, that would force the closure of the Asarco copper smelter, a local landmark and the principal local employer. The source of nearly a quarter of all national arsenic emissions through its fugitive and stack emissions, Asarco was the epicenter for the new arsenic emission standards, which EPA was under court order to set. On one hand, community studies found high levels of arsenic in local soils and also in the blood of regional school children. On the other hand, some 650 jobs were on the line. In considering whether to set a separate standard for Asarco, in 1983 EPA created an innovative community dialogue about risk, the "Tacoma Process." At three public workshops, EPA encountered widely divergent perspectives on the plant. In a very split community, most people perceived the smelter as a threat and wanted it closed. In contrast, workers wanted to preserve their jobs. Still others advocated a compromise involving both jobs and clean air, tying closure of the plant to a move from industrial to technology-based industry. EPA promulgated the standards and, indeed, Asarco opted to close the plant in the mid-1980s.[144]

This corrosive issue was still evident a decade later, when I spent many weeks in the community studying the Superfund cleanup of the Asarco plant. Former workers still congregated in their traditional haunt, an old greasy spoon on one side of the street, while clean air advocates still congregated at their headquarters in the vegetarian café just across the way. Anyone who ate at both restaurants witnessed that tensions between workers and environmentalists were still potent. This was a town where they just might eat an environmentalist for lunch.

But times have changed. Labor and environmental forces have realized common cause around world trade, economic justice, and environmental safety. Some labor unions have stepped to the fore to protect their workers, a logical development given workers' well-documented vulnerability to environmental exposures.[145] In the new millennium, job safety and environmental compliance have become virtually synonymous.

"Traditional" Versus "Toxic" Environmentalists. The above developments help explain Lester Milbrath's findings that one-fifth of the U.S. population has abandoned the predominant American worldview to become "vanguards" for a "new environmental paradigm" that espouses limits to growth, participation, risk minimization, appreciation of nature, and global consciousness. Another fifth adheres strongly to the old tenets, putting material wealth before a clean and safe environment. The remaining segment of the population consists of "environmental sympathizers," appreciating the need for change but not knowing how to achieve it. They are sympathetic to the environment while still subscribing to material wealth and other values of the "center."[146]

Are toxic victims adherents of the new paradigm? Or are they simply individuals within the marketplace, raising the banner of "not in my backyard" merely to protect their private self-interest? Is there any environmental or ecological consciousness behind their positions? Unlike the more sectarian environmental public interest groups, their concerns are not global but specific and immediate. They seek personal protection, compensation for loss, and the ability to return speedily to the normative consumptive American lifestyle. They assert the rights of individuals to avoid toxic exposure. And they join together out of necessity, not voluntarily because of shared ideals.[147]

According to this analysis, one would expect to see major value differences between sectarian environmentalists and toxic victims newly radicalized but still cognitively part of the dominant growth paradigm. Lois Gibbs observed that there is indeed tension between what she termed the "yogurt" and the "Bud" elements. Although she sees both sharing the same ends, the traditional environmentalists and the grassroots community activists vary in their methods. The latter know how to "street fight"; the former are given to compromise before the community activists would seek it.[148]

Gibbs reports instances of traditional environmentalists identifying with regulators distrusted by toxic victims. There was the League of Women Voters chapter that told an inner-city organization that, since their community was already so contaminated, it was the best site for new waste facilities. Traditional environmentalists echoed regulators in their attempts to avoid hysteria by being cautious in the release of information. And there are environmental experts whose use of jargon distances them from community people, such as the staff member of a national environmental organization whose lengthy lecture on Superfund contingency I attended. It was apparent to me that most of the audience of community people had not understood the term but were reluctant to ask what it meant.

Strategic goals and approaches may differ as well. According to Gibbs, environmental organizations attempt to work through the system: speaking to Congress, seeking to negotiate with business and government as equals, and making only "feasible" demands on government. Thus, environmental groups told California toxic activists that it was infeasible to get expert assistance that was funded by Superfund. They persisted anyway, and succeeded.

In contrast to these characteristics of conventional environmentalists, toxic victims use a grassroots approach based less on lobbying than on threatening unhelpful politicians with defeat. These new environmentalists are not afraid to cause hysteria and use it to garner power, seeing information sharing as an important tool regardless of the concerns raised. Rather than develop goals according to what can feasibly be attained, community groups reject compromise and go after what they believe they need and deserve. Community activists take pride in their refusal to accept waste projects, arguing that those proposing facilities should put them in their *own* backyards.

Several years ago, Lois Gibbs told a gathering of New Jersey toxic victims a story that dramatically illustrates the tension between toxic and traditional environmentalists. The scene was a Louisiana hazardous waste site hearing. Citizens set up an aquarium filled with contaminated drinking water from their wells. They loudly announced that the fish they were about to place in the tank would be dead by the end of the hearing. When the environmental officials and traditional environmentalists protested, the crowd began to chant, "Kill the fish." Gibbs explained that this was not hysteria but the protective action of parents. "If we have to kill the fish to make the point, we'll do it. We're sacrificing our children." She later ended her talk noting that the traditional environmentalist would not have done what needed to be done—kill the fish. Gibbs reasoned that this story is not a rejection of an ecological perspective because "People are part of ecosystems too." Toxic victims might graduate to a broader ecological perspective, but only after they have been able to get their own needs met. Thus, she explained, when an issue such as the celebrated dam-delaying snail darter becomes the focal point of the environmental concern, it illustrates to victims that environmentalists are unwilling to come to grips with harder political issues suggested by dead babies in a toxic waste case. The former is viewed as a safe issue, not of major political significance; but the latter issue raises major questions of responsibility that are difficult to address.[149]

As it matures, the toxic victims' movement has entered ever wider coalitions with other groups having related concerns (such as firemen and workers). Some multi-issue advocacy groups have evolved from single-issue groups.[150] Freudenberg suggested that the movement's future lies in a battle for two fundamental rights, "the right to live in an environment that does not damage health and the right to participate in making decisions about the environment in which one lives."[151]

Environmental Justice as a New, Overarching Frame

The U.S. environmental movement has historically been seen as a white, middle-class affair.[152] The new grassroots environmental movement, although highly diverse, initially appeared rooted in mostly white communities of toxic victims. Historically, however, blacks had organized in some contaminated communities prior to 1980 and even formed coalitions with white environmental and labor groups around environmental concerns.[153]

Evolution of a Movement

When I met Bob Bullard in 1984, he had already spent some five years documenting toxic exposure "on the other side of the tracks." Institutionalized racism was evident in his findings from both urban and rural areas of the South. In Houston, a city of fast growth and no zoning, a de facto zoning pattern placed all five of the city's municipal landfills and six of eight incinerators in African American neighborhoods. In rural all-black Triana, Alabama, pollution of the local environment garnered relatively little media coverage or government assistance compared with the attention paid to white communities suffering contemporary contamination issues, such as Love Canal and Times Beach. In short, African Americans were more likely than whites to confront polluting industries and contamination and less likely to receive recognition and assistance.

Bullard notes that this vulnerability was due to blacks' dependence on jobs in the manufacturing sector and their historic lack of politically oriented community organization, rendering them "the path of least resistance." Now recognized as toxic victims, African Americans, as well as other minorities, were pushed to enter an environmental movement that they previously had avoided. Bullard's work inspired African American involvement in the burgeoning toxic victims' movement.[154]

Around the time Bullard was doing his early research, the racial issues connected with the siting of hazardous waste facilities first captured national attention. In 1982, a disposal site for PCBs was permitted in a poor minority community in

Warren County, North Carolina. Residents there joined forces with the Commission for Racial Justice of the United Church of Christ to conduct a nonviolent civil disobedience campaign against the facility. Some 500 arrests ensued.[155]

In response to this public protest, Congressmen James Florio and Walter Fauntroy requested that the General Accounting Office, Congress's research arm, examine the "correlation between the location of hazardous waste landfills and the racial and economic status of the surrounding communities." Focusing on four landfills disconnected from industrial facilities in eight southeastern states in EPA Region IV, GAO concluded:

> Based on 1980 census data at three of the four sites . . . the majority of the population in census areas . . . where the landfills are located is Black. Also, at all four sites the Black population in the surrounding census areas has a lower mean income than the mean income for all races combined and represents the majority of those below the poverty level.[156]

These findings, in turn, spurred the Commission on Racial Justice to undertake a more comprehensive study of the racial composition of communities near hazardous waste sites. Their statistical study of commercial hazardous waste sites found the existence of "clear patterns which show that communities with greater minority percentages of the population are more likely to be the sites of commercial hazardous waste facilities. The possibility that these patterns resulted by chance is virtually impossible." Looking at closed and abandoned hazardous disposal sites, the commission similarly found "an inordinate concentration of uncontrolled toxic waste sites in Black and Hispanic communities, particularly in urban areas."[157]

The way was now clear for the environmental justice movement to emerge as a second-generation civil rights movement. A loose-knit alliance of civil rights and environmental leaders from both the grassroots and national levels emerged to lead this new movement, focusing on the fair application of procedures, geographic discrimination in the siting of noxious facilities, and social equity in siting. Nearly 1,000 activists from across the South gathered in Atlanta in 1988 for a presidential forum on the environment. The next year, the Gulf Coast Tenants Association organized "the Great Louisiana Toxics March Through Cancer Alley," from Baton Rouge to New Orleans.[158]

Besides the United Church of Christ, other African American leaders and organizations were joining forces to recognize what Benjamin Chavis had termed *environmental racism* as a fundamental violation of the civil rights of minorities. By 1990 the environmental justice movement was emerging as a decidedly separate movement from the grassroots environmental movement spearheaded by

Lois Gibbs and other leaders originating from contaminated communities. The latter was a movement of grassroots groups from diverse localities that had gradually developed networks and national leadership. In contrast, the "EJ" movement was able to step up to the bat with heavy hitters already in place at the national scale, both in terms of existing civil rights organizations and charismatic advocates already in prominent leadership positions. It is not surprising that within a decade the environmental justice movement had gathered so much steam that it appeared to be taking over the leadership role of the grassroots environmental movement.

These differences were also evident at the grass roots level in the ecohistory of contaminated communities. In particular, there are important cultural differences between the white blue-collar neighborhoods that leaders such as Gibbs came from and the cultural context of black toxic activism.[159] White working-class culture is imbued with a strong belief in democracy that is contradicted by the circumstances surrounding contamination. Thus white women activists undergo a transformation, overcoming their new feelings of disempowerment and disablement to emerge as assertive and competent individuals. This is a new situation for them, often leading to major changes of personhood, family relationships, and even marital status. Indeed, more than a transformation, it is a revelation. In contrast, trust of democratic process was stripped from black culture long ago. Women in the black community have long assumed an activist role with regard to race and justice. The battlefields of civil rights were their training ground as toxic activists. Thus the frame of race is easily laid over toxic contamination issues that emerge from the same oppressive power structure as have other historic challenges. Similarly, Native American women readily use their history of suppression, annihilation, loss of sovereignty, and theft of land as a cognitive frame. Thus the realignment of the grassroots toxics movement reflected not just organizational actors but also divergent experiences of contamination.

Over the decade of the 1990s, accommodations were made on all sides to bring unity to the battle for environmental justice. The Citizens Clearinghouse for Hazardous Wastes was renamed the Center for Health and Environmental Justice. And Lois Gibbs was being invited to participate in forums on environmental justice. The narrowed focus of the environmental racism movement was being broadened back to the inclusive scope of the original grassroots environmental movement, built around a consensus for environmental equity. The clarion call in the movement is for the rights of all people to avoid toxic exposure, for the cleanup of abandoned waste sites, and for a reduction in the production and use of hazardous chemicals.[160]

Formal recognition in the environmental policy process for the movement for environmental justice was an outcome of dialogue between citizens, national environmental organizations, and federal agencies, most notably the Agency for Toxic Substances and Disease Registry and EPA, and later the National Institute for Environmental Health Sciences. Key early events were a 1990 conference at the University of Michigan of organizers, academics, and regulators which resulted in EPA's formation of a working group on environmental justice, as well as the Minority Health Conference and the First National People of Color Leadership Summit, both held in 1991. The latter event attracted nearly 1,000 delegates from across the United States and its protectorates. As a result of the summit, both the Indigenous Environmental Network and the Southern Organizing Committee were formed.[161]

The summit issued a "Call to Action" to address what was termed "environmental genocide," proclaiming seventeen principles of environmental justice that included such diverse fundamental rights and principles as the following:

• the sacredness of Mother Earth
• mutual respect and freedom from bias and discrimination
• sustainable use of the earth
• universal protection from nuclear and toxic hazards and the right to clean air, land, water, and food
• self-determination of all peoples
• cessation of hazards production and containment and detoxification of existing hazards by producers
• participation as equal partners in decisionmaking
• employment in a safe and healthy work environment
• compensation, reparations, and health coverage for victims
• violations of environmental justice counting as violations of international law
• codification of rights of native peoples
• rebuilding of cities and rural areas to promote natural and cultural integrity and access to resources
• informed consent and a stop to medical experimentation on minorities
• opposition to harmful multinational corporate operations
• opposition to military occupation, repression, and exploitation
• education for cultural diversity and environmental values
• lifestyle change to minimize consumption and protect the health of nature

The summit also served to forge a link between the big ten environmental organizations, until then disconnected from minority communities, and the local minority activists whose community efforts had not been previously seen as environmental in nature.[162]

Evidence for Environmental Racism

Evidence of environmental racism supporting the work of Bullard, the United Church of Christ, EPA, and GAO accumulated from many sources, including release of incriminating government documents and work in a new field in the social sciences involved with the demographic analysis of environmental injustice.

Documented Bias.   The early EJ movement was bolstered by discovery of several incriminating government documents. One was an internal EPA memo plotting a public relations campaign to neutralize the "politically explosive" issue of environmental racism before the big, powerful environmental organizations were attracted to the topic. The memo's release by the Southwest Organizing Project's Southwest Network for Economic and Environmental Justice, a group of minorities and native peoples, compelled EPA into a dialogue on environmental justice and to target prosecution of environmental violations in minority communities.[163]

An even more eye-opening confirmation of institutionalized environmental racism surfaced in 1984 in the form of a report prepared by Cerrell Associates for the California Waste Management Board. Cerrell had been contracted to identify sites where waste incinerators could be located with minimal opposition. Recommended sites had these demographic attributes: a rural, blue-collar workforce already engaged in hazardous employment, having a low level of education, low income, limited English-speaking competency, Catholic, and living in a Republican area. In short, this siting report was targeting Hispanic areas of the state to host unwanted hazardous facilities. A similarly fascinating report on the selection of sites for a low-level radioactive repository in North Carolina included results of a windshield survey of the candidate locations. Sites described by such adjectives as "houses fairly wealthy" and "affluent" were dropped from consideration. Locations described as "minority-owned" and "depressed" were kept in. Michael Heiman correctly characterizes these siting efforts as "at best 1 percent science."[164] The rest was blatant environmental racism.

Demographic Research.   A sampling of the social science literature generally confirms the existence of environmental racism. Phil Brown's literature review on race and income concludes that race is the dominant factor determining environmental injustice.[165] Contaminated sites on the Superfund National Priority List were more likely to be located in areas with minority populations (although not necessarily lower-class neighborhoods).[166] And Superfund sites in communities with higher minority populations were less likely to have records of decision (necessary for cleanup to begin) than those with fewer minorities.[167]

However, it may not be possible to meaningfully separate race and class, as suggested by a Texas study in which hazardous waste siting was found to be correlated with poverty and rural, low-density locations but not with race. Tellingly, minorities moved into the area *after* facility siting.[168] In a Florida study of proximity to potential sources of pollution that found inequity in exposure for African Americans and Hispanics, proximity to Toxic Release Inventory sites was initially related to income and class. However, these relationships were most persistent for blacks, showing just how closely race and income are intertwined.[169]

Other studies suggest different variables besides race and class as a basis for bias. For example, an analysis of social vulnerability in southeastern states to fugitive toxic releases found that population density, rather than race and class, was the best underlying predictor of risk.[170] Other studies find no bias. For example, air pollution in Texas was found to most strongly affect middle-class residents who live near their jobs, not the poor and minorities.[171] A second GAO study in 1995 failed to find a pattern of environmental racism in the distribution of nonhazardous landfills.[172]

Overall, demographic studies are highly subject to methodological issues that influence whether and what kind of discrimination is found. Thus data from Georgia and Ohio did not reveal discrimination in the siting of specific waste facilities, but rather in overall toxic exposure.[173] And the GAO similarly concluded from its early meta-study of the environmental injustice literature that identifying locational bias for hazardous waste facilities depended on such variables as type of facility, the questions asked by the researchers, sample size, the geographic delineation of the contaminated community, and the research methods employed.[174]

Michael Heiman notes that environmental racism may be a more appropriate descriptor for environmental injustice in some places than others; the specific pattern of discrimination differs according to region. Furthermore, discrimination may be very subtle and not easily accessible to analysis. For example, discrimination may occur due to the choice of language used by an agency during its information sessions, unequal treatment in managing the Superfund process in different communities, use of such free market approaches as emissions trading (which may rationalize higher levels of pollution in poorer and minority areas), and the assumptions built into risk assessments and standard setting (given that some people are more susceptible than others).[175]

Bullard argues that environmental injustice is deeply embedded in the technocratic regulatory paradigm.[176]

The dominant environmental protection paradigm reinforces rather than challenges the stratification of *people* (race, ethnicity, status, power), *place* (central cities, suburbs, rural areas, unincorporated areas, Native American reservations), and *work* (e.g., office workers are afforded greater protection than farm workers). The paradigm exists to manage, regulate, and distribute risks. As a result, the dominant paradigm has (1) institutionalized unequal enforcement; (2) traded human health for profit; (3) placed the burden of proof on the "victims" and not on the polluting industry; (4) legitimated human exposure to harmful chemicals, pesticides, and hazardous substances; (5) promoted risky technologies, such as incinerators; (6) exploited the vulnerability of economically and politically disenfranchised communities; (7) subsidized ecological destruction; (8) created an industry around risk assessment; (9) delayed cleanup actions; and (10) failed to develop pollution prevention as the overarching and dominant strategy.

Lack of informed consent is also a major factor in environmental injustice.[177] Its absence would easily be invisible to research studies seeking to document discrimination yet be very visible to affected residents. Similarly, the most fundamental underlying cause of bias appears to be totally missed by demographic research, namely, the disabling nature of environmental regulation which has ensured that the least powerful receive the most environmental harm. By the very nature of our social dynamics, poorer, less educated, less informed, and marginalized and stigmatized people receive what those with more choices do not want.

Tools for Preventing Injustice

Community groups adopting an "environmental justice frame" have typically made claims for accurate information, a timely and honest hearing, full involvement in shaping future directions of the community, compensation from wrongdoers, and an end to environmental racism.[178] More specifically, the 1987 Commission for Racial Justice report called on the U.S. president to issue an executive order directing government agencies to consider the racial impacts of their decisions and policies. By 1992, legislation on environmental justice had been introduced in Congress under the leadership of Congressman John Lewis and Senators Al Gore and Max Baucus. Supported by EPA's 1992 report, *Environmental Equity: Reducing Environmental Risk for All Communities*, the core of this legislation was later embedded in President Clinton's Executive Order 12898 of February 1994 entitled "Federal Actions to Address Environmental Justice in Minority Populations and Low-Income Populations."

As part of its consideration of potential adverse environmental impacts under the National Environmental Policy Act, Executive Order 12898 reinforces Title VI of the Civil Rights Act of 1964, which prohibited discrimination in federally funded programs. Specifically, Executive Order 12898 requires the identification of disproportionately high and adverse human health and environment effects on minority and low-income populations. Under the order, agencies are required to analyze impacts to human health in light of cumulative and multiple environmental exposures. The resulting impact statements are to assess such factors as risk, risk communication needs, dietary and resource consumption impacts, cultural resources, community health data and occupational exposures, and the community's priorities for environmental cleanup.

Executive Order 12898 required U.S. agencies to incorporate environmental justice issues into their compliance with the National Environmental Policy Act. In its guidance on environmental justice issued in April 1998, EPA defined environmental justice as "The fair treatment and meaningful involvement of all people regardless of race, color, national origin, or income. . . . Fair treatment means that no group of people . . . should bear a disproportionate share of the negative consequences resulting from industrial, municipal or commercial operations or the execution of federal, state, local, or tribal programs and policies." Cooperation among environmental agencies was to be achieved through an interagency working group.[179]

EPA regions have issued interim guidelines for implementing the agency's EJ policy. For example, the Region II policy calls for data to be collected on "communities of concern" for comparison with larger "reference areas," such as census blocks. To be deemed an "EJ community," the community of concern would have to have both a significantly higher percentage (i.e., a relative difference greater than 25 percent) of minority and/or low-income residents and also have a significantly greater "environmental burden" according to a profile of "environmental load" (i.e., measuring the burden or load from specific environmental sources, from cumulative area-wide sources, and/or due to uneven application of government authority).[180]

An early test of Executive Order 12898 occurred when Shintech applied for a permit to build a vinyl plastics facility in a predominantly African American and impoverished area in Convent, Louisiana. Greenpeace and Tulane University's Environmental Law Clinic cowrote a complaint against Shintech, which was filed with the U.S. Environmental Protection Agency. The complaint was an end run around Louisiana's pro-project governor and environmental agency, and resulted in retaliation when the funding of Tulane's law clinic was threatened. Despite the promise of jobs from the facility, a Greenpeace poll revealed that a little more than half the residents of the parish in which the plant was to be sited opposed Shintech and nearly three-quarters believed that the plant would harm the environment. Two-thirds doubted that the promise of jobs would be fulfilled. EPA administrator Carol Browner eventually denied the permit.[181]

Less successful was another Louisiana case, a planned uranium enrichment plant applied for under the name Louisiana Energy Services and proposed in 1989 for a site in Claiborne Parish located between two poor minority communities. On behalf of a grassroots group called CANT (Citizens Against Nuclear Trash), Robert Bullard testified about discriminatory aspects of the siting process, showing that the selection was racially biased. As a result, the Atomic Safety and Licensing Board ordered the Nuclear Regulatory Commission to investigate, threatening that a finding of no bias would lead them to require a further study of discriminatory impact of the facility. In an agency decision reminiscent of *PANE v. Metropolitan Edison*, the NRC overturned the lower ruling. They concluded that NEPA is neither a tool for addressing racial discrimination nor a civil rights law requiring litigation of such bias. More generally, the legal weight of environmental justice is just being tested, but with few clear patterns clearly established at this time. To date, courts have determined that effect, rather than discriminatory intent, is sufficient to establish harm under EPA's environmental justice regulations.[182]

Native Americans and Environmental Injustice

There is also a growing recognition of the environmental injustices that Native Americans and other native peoples have suffered. In my years of working on the issue of radon gas exposure, I repeatedly encountered data justifying the conclusion that radon is the second leading cause of lung cancer behind cigarette smoke. This conclusion rested firmly on a data set collected from a human population, uranium miners from the four-corners area of the western United States. Never acknowledged in the radon literature, however, was the fact that these 400 dead and other diseased miners who had been exposed to radon came from a population of some 3,000 Navajo men who served as the principal uranium mining workforce from 1940 through 1980. In all, between 1,200 and 2,500 mines were located on or near the Navajo reservation and run, through government contract, by large corporations—Kerr-McGee, United Nuclear, and Exxon.

Environmental injustice occurred in all aspects of this "radioactive colonization" (to use Ward Churchill's term). Although some 40 percent of U.S. uranium resources were not on native lands, 80 percent of uranium mining and 100 percent of uranium processing occurred and the bulk of the country's 191 million tons of radioactive waste was deposited on reservation lands. The Navajo reservation was expropriated for the national defense and nuclear energy market. Miners operated with absolutely no safety equipment or protection, working in unventilated mines, drinking water from inside the mines, and eating their meals there. Occupational standards were delayed for nearly thirty years despite clear scientific data about the consequences of exposure. Pearson notes that among the factors discouraging protective action was the fact that the miners were socially marginal. It was only after there were sufficient numbers of deaths and attendant publicity that occupational safety standards were set. Moreover, the workers were never informed of the hazards they faced on the job. Crucial data on disease incidence was hidden from them. Wives and families were also exposed to uranium brought home on clothes and as objects of curiosity. Children played in the mine and mill buildings and tailings. The Navajo reservation was heavily contaminated from mine wastes, runoff, and the tailings left over from the four uranium processing mills that made "yellow cake" from the uranium ore.[183]

Beyond the health impacts, there were serious cultural implications for the Navajo's continuing bond with the land. For example, one Navajo elder was isolated socially after the uranium mining hazards became known, since her traditional hogan and lands rested in a contaminated area. Others did not wish to visit her, but she remained bound to her ancestral lands.[184] Other instances of contamination on native lands may lead to relocation. When an oil well discharged a rolling foglike gas cloud of hydrogen sulfide onto the inhabitants of the Blueberry Reserve in Canada on July 16, 1979, they were quickly evacuated without serious injury. However, most believed that had they remained, deaths would have resulted. Subsequently, the Cree and Beaver Indians in the community petitioned the Canadian Supreme Court to injunct the reopening of the well. The bands were no longer willing to live near this known hazard, and relocation of the village was sought if the well reopened.[185] For natives, such alienation from the land is a serious psychosocial impact, illustrated by Shkilnyk's description of the Grassy Narrow Ojibwa. The tribe suffered an undesired forced relocation due to a combination of nonenvironmental reasons and mercury contamination resulting from the timber industry. Although the Natives in no way caused the pollution, from a traditional perspective, the poisoning of their home was interpreted as a punishment for some unidentified misbehavior, contributing to the subsequent precipitous social decline of the reservation's inhabitants. In such instances, environmental stigma for a Native American can be seen as a cultural stigma as well.[186]

Sustainability as a Metaenvironmental Justice Issue

Internationally, the toxic waste movement has expanded beyond the industrialized nations as third world countries attempt to address the exportation of toxic products, pesticides, wastes, the manufacturing processes, and other vestiges of world trade and the global economy. In the aftermath of the Bhopal disaster, for example, environmental meetings and groups in India, Japan, Zimbabwe, Malaysia, Indonesia, Thailand, and Kenya commemorated the victims and planned actions to prevent further tragedies.[187] Likewise, in the wake of the Seveso accident, the European Union issued directives on cross-boundary toxic incidents. And the Rio Conference on the Environment—the Earth Summit—in June 1992 set Agenda 21, which considered chemicals issues and waste management.[188] Although the Rio event was intergovernmental, perhaps of greatest interest was the extensive involvement of nongovernmental organizations worldwide at Rio and in subsequent efforts. The work of these NGOs broadens the environmental justice networks to global dimensions.

Increasingly NGOs have crisscrossed the "north–south" divide between the resource-exploiting and resource exploited portions of the globe with cooperative networks. Although sometimes viewed as imperialistic in their interventions to dictate solutions for local problems having global significance,[189] overall, first world organizations have learned to work hand in hand with third and fourth world activists. Their allegiances help local and indigenous actors reach the international legal and political stage and affect their own national political response to environmental issues. By the 1990s, first world efforts to address human rights issues, which were closely linked to the grass roots, and efforts to change environmental policy by the World Bank, United Nations, and national and multinational corporate entities fused into one effort. The key change driving cooperation during this period was the activism of local grassroots groups worldwide in opposing the consequences of top-down development. These groups were energized by the Bruntland Report, the U.N. Commission on Environment and Development call for sustainability to become an overarching theme for future global economic development, recognizing that the achievement of sustainable development requires both contemporary and cross-generational equity.[190]

In these ways, networks linking the heroic efforts of local victims to regional and national leaders and organizations gain global connections. Victimization due to resource exploitation, long-distance manufacturing and food production, and cross-boundary dumping and waste trade invites meta-linkages that enable people in localities across the globe by pulling them under an environmental justice umbrella.[191] The global sustainability movement is built from these linkages of local action and global thinking.

Interestingly, many in the sustainability movement reject the conventional environmental movement. Inherently focused on finding a balance between ecological, economic, and social spheres, sustainability activists operate in a metaenvironmental justice framework, concerned with changing inequitable conditions between humans and other species, people in different parts of the globe, and the prospects for future generations.

Conclusion: A Radical Environmental Populism

Overall, the environmental justice movement, according to Szasz, embodies the traditions of American populism, in this case a "radical environmental populism." Local groups begin their political education fighting a local undesired facility. But as they come in contact with national organizations, they are quickly inculcated into the movements' radical agenda for social change based on a firm belief in social justice and an environmental platform based on forging a consensus in favor of pollution prevention and source reduction as a means to avoid dumping in anyone's backyard. Szasz elaborates:[192]

> When the problem was conceived of as "our contaminated community," the cause was "that landfill" or "that careless chemical firm." When the problem was conceived of as hazardous industrial waste, generally, the cause of the problem was Waste Management, Inc., Browning-Ferris, the disposal industry, polluting firms, do-nothing state and federal officials. As the movement grew and addressed an ever larger set of problems, the cause came to be defined very broadly, in terms of a whole system of technology and chemical production, driven by profit, unchecked by a government that serves private wealth rather than public interest.

In these ways, issues of justice and the need to fundamentally change the whole material relationship of consumer and capitalist society emerge in the broad consciousness of formerly noncritical participants in modern/postmodern society.[193] We return to this theme in the next chapter.

7

The Societal Meaning of Pollution

All major environmental issues involve dilemmas. They reflect problems for which no panacea exists; there are costs to any possible choices. To choose a compromised path, rationalized in some artificial trade-off matrix, only perpetuates the inherent conflicts involved in the dilemma to begin with. Breaking out of this dilemma requires an alternative approach that might be called "third path analysis." In this chapter, I explore the dilemma of contamination in depth, seeking a third path. I begin by framing modern Western culture as a culture of contamination.

Denial and the Culture of Contamination

The culture of contamination rests on at least four pillars of denial: the water closet model, mal-consumption, technological optimism, and normative complicity. I will review each in turn.

The Water Closet Model

Perhaps inspired by our ease in flushing human wastes mysteriously "away," we tend to view our waste stream as easily transferred downstream to become someone else's worry.

By way of illustration, throughout much of 1987, a barge carrying 3,000 tons of Islip, Long Island, garbage plied the Gulf of Mexico looking for a nation, state, or country that would accept the waste for disposal. Nobody wanted it. For a while, there were reports that the waste would be disposed of in my hometown of Goshen, New York, at Al Turi Landfill, Inc. What struck me as odd was that the public outcry could be so loud against this particular pile of trash when two major landfills in town daily accepted roughly as much tonnage, half of it imported from outside the county, including from towns near Islip. There was clearly something special about the Islip barge garbage. It was no longer your average garden-variety trash. The barge garbage was no longer anonymous. It had been stigmatized. In acquiring an identity, the garbage threatened in turn to stigmatize the place that took it in. Moored in New York City, awaiting the outcome of a court battle over whether its load could safely be burned, the barge even became a tourist attraction. Its eventual incineration became the best available means of not only destroying the garbage but obliterating its identity as well.

It is ironic that fast-food wrappers discarded by teenagers in Islip, New York, should travel thousands of miles on a barge laden with garbage. The irony is not only that the trip failed to identify a disposal site but that needless wastes are generated to begin with and that we then think that distant others will take over responsibility for the consequences. Thus, an essential element of the story is that the waste was being exported to begin with. *Not only did no one else want Islip's waste, but Islip did not want its own waste.* Long Island had come to recognize that landfilling is a threat to the sole source aquifer beneath its sandy (and thus permeable) soil. Since this aquifer is the principal source of drinking water, it must be protected. Although the effort to safeguard the island's groundwater was a step in the right direction, the waste had now emerged as a major potential threat to my own source of drinking water some three hours' drive to the northwest.[1]

The point is that increasingly distant disposal sites allow us maximum freedom to degrade materials to a state of spent utility. Developed nations have even targeted third world countries as our next generation of dumping grounds, selling hazardous products in their markets, exporting banned pesticides for poor farmers to use, sending waste materials overseas for disposal, and relocating hazardous industries to locations where there is little environmental or worker regulation.[2] Export of wastes allows us to employ an "out of sight, out of mind" approach to the issue. The larger society is thus complicit in waste siting against the wishes of the receiving locality. The garbage barge is not such a bad idea, it seems, as long as it is heading the other way. Wastes are for export only.

Mal-Consumption

What is the meaning of pollution, not just *for* society but *about* society? It has been several decades since Vance Packard described in his prescient *The Waste Makers* the myriad pressures on post–World War II Americans to increase their consumption and waste way beyond their actual needs and to adopt a culture of obsolescence.[3] Indeed, the growth economy rests on such practices as a basis for generating demand. The fallacy of the resulting throwaway society is clarified by economist Herman Daly's three commonsense guidelines for a sustainable society:[4]

- Are we employing renewable resources to the maximum amount allowed by their rate of renewal?
- Are nonrenewable resources used only when absolutely necessary, and then in the most limited and efficient way possible?
- Are we producing pollution beyond the assimilative capacity of the environment?

The Islip garbage barge epitomized the essence of the throwaway society. Its mixture of municipal solid wastes revealed an abject squandering of both renewable resources (those quickly regenerated by natural process) and nonrenewable (essentially irreplaceable) resources. These wastes were concentrated at volumes exceeding nature's ability to break them down. As a source of environmental degradation, the barge embodied all the impacts associated with indiscriminate global resource exploitation, mining, refining, and production, the embedded ecological costs of transportation, the consumptive craving that a film a few years back cleverly called "affluenza," and the myriad impacts associated with garbage disposal. It, therefore, expressed the core attributes of our lifestyle and values. We waste, contaminate, and stigmatize as part of the business-as-usual functioning of modern society.

Technological Fixes and the Engineering Fallacy

Early last century, in a period of disillusionment with politicians and their inability to cope with a world of increasing complexity, Americans came to revere engineers' awesome insight into the world of hard facts. Although the "technocrats," the political movement that sought to elevate engineering to formal leadership in American society, failed as a political party, reverence for the engineer's ability to solve problems became wedded to the American way. In a world of revolution, expanding technology, and bewildering change, we looked to the steady engineer's hand to design progress.[5]

Along with this transformation came an unfortunate piece of baggage, what I call the "engineering fallacy." This fallacy involves the assumption that problems can be solved unto themselves, isolated from the complicating factors and uncertainties of an overly complex world. By narrowing the problem, we make it controllable (on paper at least); one speaks of solutions, since the thing to do with problems is to solve them. But what of problems that defy solution? Too often we assume that they are solved, only to realize later that they have reemerged, demanding new solutions. In this way, the era of indiscriminate dumping gave way to landfilling, or discriminate dumping. When landfilling subsequently came to be recognized as an abject failure, dumping gave way to new fads of incineration and deep-well injection.[6] With each shift, society is convinced that it has "solved" the problems of municipal and hazardous waste when in fact these technological fixes only end up as the engineer's next challenge. The engineering fallacy illustrates a key point: *contamination reflects a fundamental defect in our process of social learning.*

Escape from the trap of solving problems that only generate new ones requires a shift to a new kind of learning. Gregory Bateson noted that in order to understand the context of any problem, we must engage in "meta-learning," exploring deeper underlying levels of foundational thought behind our initial learning. Meta-learning requires the acquisition of skills for learning how to learn. By exploring the context within which problems occur, we can see that the problem not only exists in its own right but reflects something more basic. Indeed, a meta-analysis of contamination and waste would reveal origins and causes in our patterns of resource exploitation, processing, transport, manufacture, consumption, and disposal. Our failure to understand the basic laws of living on the earth and the requirements involved in sharing it with 6 billion plus others is evident.

Meta-learning is an important tool for individual learners, but it is an even more urgent requirement for societies. The Club of Rome aptly pointed out years ago that most learning blindly maintains societies. Such maintenance learning does not require meta-analysis, and even discourages it. In contrast, the Club of Rome touted what it called "innovative learning." Innovative learning rests on two foundations—anticipation of the consequences of actions and broad participation in making decisions of how to proceed. A society employing innovative social learning would develop practices aimed at long-term anticipation with broad involvement of diverse publics.[7]

Unfortunately, innovative learning to learn is decidedly not on the educational agenda of a society enraptured with the control of the engineer's hand, the predictability of deductive thought, and controlled variables. The bulk of our educational process is focused on maintaining modernity. The approach of the engineer is to find better technical fixes for problems that might actually require systemic reevaluation. These barriers to innovative learning appear even in the social practice that most closely emulates the Club of Rome's prescription, environmental impact assessment. Pioneered in the U.S. National Environmental Policy Act of 1970, EIA is a tool for anticipating the consequences of planned actions and, after public participation, weighing impacts in making decisions.

Impact assessment requires a comparison of the alternatives to whatever action is being assessed. However, this tool for innovative learning is routinely defined in a way that maintains the status quo. For example, instead of considering alternatives that would remove the need for a proposed landfill expansion, such as materials recovery, reuse, waste avoidance, and lowering consumption, the alternatives analysis routinely focuses only on optional locations for the landfill or alternative ways of building it. The impact statement might not even include a comparison of other technologies for waste disposal. In the instance of power plant siting, no consideration is routinely given to whether conservation combined with use of renewable energy might remove the demand for the plant. Although I have twice successfully raised these issues in administrative proceedings, the engineering perspective usually prevails. Alternatives analysis thus fails as a social learning tool; unsustainable approaches continue, and the opportunity for meaningful change is lost.

Beyond modernity's faith in technological fixes and its absence of critical social learning, the engineering fallacy reflects the influence of powerful vested interests. These interests are driven by power and profit, and by the control of technical elites over complex areas of technological enterprise. Echoing President Eisenhower's warning about the "military-industrial complex," the engineering fallacy serves the ends of what Lewis Mumford called *authoritarian* (as opposed to *democratic*) technics.[8] Given their complexity, fragility, and danger, our engineered systems demand authoritarian control and decision structures resistant to innovative learning, anticipatory analysis, admission of dilemmas (unsolvable problems), or truly alternative approaches, as well as to the involvement of a questioning, critical, or opposed public. Authoritarian impulses were heightened by our post–9/11 awareness of vulnerability.

A prime example is permitting the nation's High Level Nuclear Waste Repository (HLNWR) at Yucca Mountain, Nevada. This site is intended to contain the most hazardous of all wastes, the many tens of thousands of metric tons of high-level nuclear waste that will remain dangerous for tens to hundreds of thousands of years. A legacy of our civilian and military nuclear history, nuclear wastes create the same self-fulfilling prophecy found with all authoritarian technics: having already created the hazard, we are forced to solve the "problem" of disposal. As one of the most challenging moral-technical dilemmas of our challenged time, decisions about nuclear wastes demand discourse. Yet the degree of complexity, hazard, and risk predispose us to a highly authoritarian and technocratic process of problem solution.

Congress opened this issue to democratic participation through the Nuclear Waste Policy Act of 1982, ensuring public involvement in the U.S. Department of Energy's search for candidate deep repository sites in stable rock capable of isolating wastes from water for millennia. Even in short circuiting the siting process to select Yucca Mountain, the Nuclear Waste Policy Act Amendments of 1987, recognized the independent perspectives of states, tribes, and the public.[9]

The HLNWR plan is vulnerable to deep anticipatory and participatory analysis. Physicist-philosopher K. S. Shrader-Frechette used meta-analysis to thoroughly deconstruct the project on both technical and moral grounds. Such doubts are shared by the public. Riley Dunlap and colleagues found Americans to strongly fear and oppose the siting of a high-level nuclear waste facility and distrust the Department of Energy to run it properly. These authors found the HLNWR project unlikely to meet the test of critical and democratic review that Congress intended. In fact, Paul Slovic's team discovered public trust in the HLNWR to be so low that they saw little choice but to postpone the project in favor of interim monitored retrievable storage, a conclusion shared by the above authors, as well.[10]

Technocrats at the Department of Energy used the engineering fallacy to prevent a fully democratic review in the manner noted previously. Thus Gerald Jacob observed, "The technical definition of the problem reasserted the influence of technocrats and engineers by narrowing conflicts to small technical issues. Similarly, focusing on location effectively constricted and suppressed conflict."[11] When siting issues are defined in terms of technical choices, broader social choices are excluded from public discourse, a point elaborated by Riley Dunlap, Michael Kraft, and Eugene Rosa.

> Defining a problem as scientific or technical sets the stage, arranges the props, and casts the actors who are "qualified" to take part in its solution. Because citizens lack an understanding of the scientific details of complex technological problems, they are pushed off the stage of key decision making—viewed by some insiders, if not publicly, as idiots, at least as unqualified to make informed judgments.[12]

A key point here is that the risk of the facility, as evaluated by professional risk assessors, is certain to vary from risk as perceived by the public. This divergence does not, as is so often implied, indicate that the public is subjective, self-interested, and emotional, whereas the professionals are objective, expert, and accurate. Rather, in determining risk, the public assesses different factors than the technocrat does. To the technocratic mind, a high-level nuclear waste repository might appear to be the solution. To the citizen, it is the next permutation of the problem. Dunlap, Kraft, and Rosa perceptively conclude, on the basis of their findings, that the depth of public opposition makes it impossible to site this facility in a democratic manner. In ominous response, the first Bush administration's energy plan codified the authoritarian nature of such projects, acting to reduce public input into energy and waste facility siting. The younger Bush now appears to be following in these footsteps.

In sum, the engineering fallacy represents a limiting approach to social learning that includes voluntary or forced deference to technocrats. The engineering fallacy reflects a broader culture of ecological denial. It is not that we trust technology; rather, our legacy of authoritarian, or "hard," choices makes us routinely dependent on technocrats and technological fixes, and thus we may have no choice but to put our faith in them.[13]

Social Pressure and the Polluting Consensus

How does society enforce adherence to the contaminating paradigm? The prescient Norwegian playwright Henrik Ibsen in his 1882 play, *An Enemy of the People,* recognized that environmental problems are most fundamentally social and not merely engineering issues. The protagonist, Dr. Thomas Stockman, physician at the baths in a resort city, discovers bacterial pollution in the water. He realizes that the contamination, traced to upstream tanneries, may explain a pattern of illness among the patrons of the baths. When Stockman develops a plan for a new water system to abate the pollution, he initially receives the overwhelming support of homeowners and the press, both of whom see him as an expert acting in their best interests. Given that his brother is mayor, he naively assumes that he will be able to move ahead and address the problem smoothly. But it is not long before political interference arises: from big investors in the baths, who want the issue kept quiet for fear of stigma, and from politicians (including his brother) with public support, put off by the cost of Stockman's solution. The bottom line is that none are willing to pay for the repairs, the losses during the construction period, and the decrease in tourism due to stigma.

As a public official, Stockman is caught in a bind. Is his duty to those who control his job or to the protection of public health? Now faced with overwhelming community pressure to conform to the general definition of "good," Stockman has a disturbing realization. The people collude with the establishment. They define their welfare in terms of economic well-being, not in terms of public health. This collusion involves a greater desire to bury the bad news than to bury the pollution. The problem will go away if knowledge of the pollution goes away! Stockman's plan for solving the problem has inadvertently touched the very nerve of the culture, transforming him from hero to villain. The source of "pollution" is no longer the tanneries that contaminated the water; it is now Stockman himself!

But Stockman can no longer see the problem at the level of analysis used by his fellow townspeople. For him, it is not a matter of making a trade-off between costs and benefits because mitigating the pollution is too expensive. To Stockman, the issue is that the majority eschews wisdom. By opting for short-run profit while accepting risk to others, the town's residents reinforce the legitimacy of the order that created the pollution problem to begin with. A community consensus exists behind the status quo, and Stockman will not be given a veto, even if he is correct. Pollution is less of a threat to the existing order than unemployment, high taxes, and reduced profits. To put it bluntly in the words that a crude politician once threatened me with: "Don't shake the grapes."

In the contemporary world, the same kinds of social pressures are often mobilized to discourage whistle-blowers, witnesses, or keen observers from labeling an area contaminated. For example, take the Irish farmer from Ballydine who believed that hydrochloric acid mists released from a plant operated by Merck, Sharp, and Dohme caused illness in both local cattle and his family. For years, his neighbors applied severe social pressure on the farmer to abandon this view. His family was shunned and demonized. And he received no support from local and national farmers' associations fearful that the issue would stigmatize their products.[14] This story closely parallels the social dynamics I observed in the late 1980s among farmers downwind of the Hanford Nuclear Reservation who feared that their crops would become worthless were the presence of local radioactive contamination to be publicized. Whistle blowers there were shunned.

The Meta-Issue: A Culture of Contamination

Stockman's experience highlights the meta-issue—why have we come to accept contamination as a necessary cost of the good life? Said another way, why have we come to accept the polluting life as good? Given its intrinsic challenge to our core assumptions, it is no wonder that people deny the meaning of contamination. We accept pollution's existence by adopting the engineering fallacy—that pollution simply needs to be "cleaned up." Landfills or other technological systems can be designed to *securely* contain hazards; pollution is merely a technological problem waiting to be solved. This is societal denial!

Rarely do we admit that pollution results from our wasteful society, from actions in which we collude. We often balk at the costs of preventing pollution, while assuming that sufficient resources will exist to carry out the much more costly and difficult exercise of cleaning it up after the fact. Routinely these costs are merely transferred to the next generation.[15] Because it is harder to quantify the costs of toxic exposure than the costs of preventing it, we allow it to continue. We are complicit in this choice, much as Stockman's townspeople colluded to preserve the status quo. How then do we shift to innovative learning and understand the deeper social, psychological, and cultural conflict raised by the "crisis" of pollution?

Instances of meta-learning are found in the "de facto education" of contamination's victims. Their turbulent redefinition of the parameters of life, lifestyle, and lifescape tests their faith in the American Dream. The dominant social paradigm—promising as it does a world of technological progress, economic growth, and personal satisfaction—is much harder to take for granted. It has been opened to challenge. Former naive trust in others and in the system gives way to anger, resentment, and a sense of having been wronged.

In the absence of an alternative paradigm, toxic victims are left to deal with toxic exposure in ways that continue their participation in the system that caused the pollution. Toxic activists seek "cleanup" and other engineering solutions. They press for health testing as a way of gaining some control over the problem. And they demand compensation for victims as an economic accounting for losses. All of these demands are necessary and vital, but they serve to institutionalize and legitimate as a problem what might otherwise be viewed as a fundamental crisis and thus a challenge to our modern industrial way of life.

The Rise of Neo-Ludditism

The paradigm of Western thought, what some call "the dominant social paradigm," holds at its core a fundamental optimism about technology in "a society that recognizes that physical risks are unavoidable in the production of wealth." One of the most striking shifts evident in this paradigm over the past fifty years is an emergent rejection of technological risk.[16] We are left with hybrid moderns who are as dependent on and devoted to technology as ever. But they selectively reject technological hazards due to involuntary environmental exposure and intrusion. This rejection is evident in the dynamics of NIMBY and local environmental resistance.

Rejecting a Contaminating Culture: Local Environmental Resistance

Even as our participation in the broader culture of contamination characterizes our behavior toward the environment globally, there has been an explosion of local actions on behalf of place. "Local environmental resistance" is the defense of place against the siting of stigmatized facilities. These include landfills, hazardous waste disposal sites of all types, resource recovery plants, various sludge and septage facilities, sites for disposing of dredged materials, nuclear waste disposal sites, nuclear facilities of all types, potentially hazardous industries, and microwave towers, and power lines.[17] Whether local environmental resistance is regarded as a national phenomenon or as a collection of isolated and unique parallel events in thousands of communities, its consequences are felt simultaneously at all levels of social process.

Local environmental resistance is more commonly referred to as the "not in my backyard," or NIMBY, syndrome. NIMBY is hardly a value-free term. Corporate and government officials use it as a pejorative synonym for narrow selfishness, speaking of the NIMBY syndrome as something of a social disease, a rabid and irrational rejection of sound technological progress. In contrast, community advocates portray NIMBY more sympathetically, as the response to an ill-conceived plan or LULU (locally undesirable land use), changing the focus from the resisters to what is resisted. NIMBY may also connote conscientious concern, as a fight for democratic rights more properly termed NIMBI ("now I must become involved").[18]

This divergence in meaning signifies the dynamics of local environmental resistance. On the one hand, technical experts espouse a world determined by state-of-the-art science and engineering; on the other, citizens holding local expertise demand safe and healthy communities. The resulting not-in-my-backyard battles pit government and industry against grassroots environmental and community groups. Often such battles balance the potential of enormous profit for an outside corporation against those fearing for the loss of local common values. This conflict illustrates the worst side of capitalism: the exploitation of locality for the benefit of the market.

On its part, government exercises its responsibility to solve perceived social problems according to the engineer's fallacy. Tens of millions of tons of toxic substances enter the environment as unwanted waste every year, beyond the flow of toxic wastes.[19] Thus the most overused cliché in environmental management—The waste must go somewhere! As waste disposal acquired a priority position on municipal agendas across the United States, public opposition became the central concern. Rules enshrined in regulation and law that permit facilities against local interest and opposition violate norms of civility as understood by the alarmed members of the community. Some state and federal waste-siting procedures explicitly curtail public participation to expedite permitting.[20]

Clearly NIMBY is a perceptual, and thus inherently psychological, phenomenon triggered by three dynamics: anticipatory fear, local disempowerment, and cultural contamination.

First, *anticipatory fear* underlies public opposition to stigmatized facilities. Local environmental resistance reflects a desire to protect one's locality or backyard from unwanted change, desecration and destruction, and from becoming a source of danger. Local environmental resistance, therefore, shares many of the same characteristics of realized toxic exposure—fears, stigma, stress, disablement, and community mobilization. People fear the kinds of lifestyle and lifescape impacts that might accompany future toxic exposure. The occurrence of actual instances of local environmental resistance is an even more reliable indicator than public surveys of the fact that toxic exposure is viewed as a threat.

This wariness of potentially hazardous facilities is a legacy of the publicized experience of toxic victims over the past decades. Moreover, one of the clearest messages conveyed by past toxic disasters such as Legler and Love Canal is the abject failure of prior state-of-the-art disposal practices. In fact, some 80–90 percent of our hazardous waste disposal sites are recognized as unsafe. For every waste disposal technology available, an array of environmental and human health hazards has been identified.[21] Knowledge of past failures illuminates the engineering fallacy and contributes to an overall level of "contagious distrust," dispelling illusions of "secure" disposal sites and creating a general disbelief in the ability of engineers to create and maintain safe facilities. Seeing how disruptive toxic exposure is to its victims, when the external threat of pollution becomes personalized, the prospective victims are reasonably motivated to take precautionary action.

Local environmental resistance is also a response to threatened *local disempowerment*. The siting of stigmatized and hazardous facilities is inherently an issue of power. The locality can become a pawn in the power relationship with outside governmental and/or private forces or it can resist. Disabling dynamics wrest away collective as well as personal control that local resistance seeks to counteract.

Finally, local environmental resistance is a response to our *contaminated culture*. Our revulsion to contamination reflects empathy for its victims as well as the fact that we ourselves participate in stigmatizing them. The stigma derives from the fact that they have been contaminated, physically and socially, as well as from their powerlessness to prevent this victimization. In "blaming the victim," we attribute volition to the victims and conclude that they are at fault for allowing this to happen.[22] This rationalization that victims somehow deserve their "fate" not only diminishes our view of them while making their plight acceptable, but it also inspires a desire to not emulate their victimization.

Our participation in the contaminating culture complicates this power relationship, for if *they* are the victims, in many ways, *we* are the victimizers. Thus, even as they mobilize to fight a compartmentalized threat in their own community, local opponents themselves collude in the necessity for pollution everywhere in myriad ways. Resisters may themselves profit from polluting activities through investments in corporate enterprises whose identity they may not even know. They consume large quantities of products produced and packaged in ways that maximize pollution and waste but at incremental and seemingly innocuous levels. They treat their lawns with poisons, imitating the manufactured perfection of Astroturf. Their achievement of the American Dream is intimately wedded to the economic and technological system that produces pollution. Thus the stigma and blaming reflect an abstraction and denial of our role as victimizers. The essence of NIMBY is straightforward. The message is clear. People are left with what amounts to a territorial instinct. Pollution will occur. Victims will suffer. The challenge is to avoid being one of the victims.

Case Studies of Community Opposition

In my view, the human reaction to perceived threat is not easily reduced to simple formulations. In identifying the psychosocial underpinnings of local environmental resistance, I do not imply that there are not also technically rational bases for opposing potential hazards. The following case studies illustrate siting battles over proposed waste disposal facilities derived from my own research, observation, and involvement. These case studies form a foundation for a subsequent discussion of the psychosocial and rational bases of the NIMBY response.

Case 1: Merion Blue Grass Sod Farm[23].   Early in 1979, local farmers noticed heavy truck traffic into Merion Blue Grass Sod Farm at the edge of the fertile "black dirt" area of Orange County, New York. Soon foul odors wafted from the site, impairing neighboring farmers' ability to work their fields and enjoy their homes. Town officials learned that the New York State Department of Environmental Conservation (DEC) had granted a temporary operating permit to a private firm, Nutrient Uptake, to fertilize sod with sewage and septic wastes. Anticipating no adverse environmental impacts, the DEC had neither required an environmental impact statement nor notified the town. Citizens were denied any opportunity to participate in the decisionmaking process.

When the temporary permit expired, the DEC called for an adjudicatory hearing to review the application for a long-term permit. Local communities and citizens could declare themselves parties to the hearing. Many did so. In fact, the town and its citizens were virtually unanimous in their opposition. Local farmers expressed many concerns about the sludge operation. They feared that word of the waste disposal would reach their customers, stigmatizing their crops. They were revolted by the human wastes and believed it would contaminate food crops and threaten their health, the contamination spreading through the soil, air, groundwater, and surface water. The hearings ran throughout the summer and early fall of 1979. I attended most of the sessions, watching angry, frightened farmers fight to regain control over their community from a disabling regulatory process. Among my observations were the following:

- The impressive sludge expert flew in from Boston for the day to testify about how well the project was designed. Pointing at the map to what he supposed was to be a sludge lagoon, he prompted the man next to me to jump up screaming, "That's my house! They're going to dump sludge on my house!" Next his testimony about the attributes of various sod grasses was sagely contradicted by farmers in the audience. The ability of the facility's berms to isolate wastes from the flood-prone Wallkill River was similarly questioned. The expert did not appreciate these hostile challenges, complaining to me, "How dare these uneducated farmers interfere in an issue about which they lack competence! I'm the expert."
- The hearing was designed to minimize participation by residents. The sessions were held in daytime during the prime summer growing season, making it a

real sacrifice for farmers to attend. Lawyers and experts for the sod farm and several municipalities were seated in front, directly facing the hearing officer and stenographer and forcing the public to sit toward the rear. These lawyers tried to control the proceedings with dramatic objections and other legal maneuvers; the hearing judge had to continually remind them that this was not a courtroom. The frustrated public, forced to remain quiet during lengthy direct and cross examinations of experts by the lawyers, would at times explode in anger, only to be admonished by the judge to show respect appropriate in a courtroom.

- Little opportunity was granted for citizens to be heard and little credibility given when they were. Whereas testimony from technical experts was carefully weighed in the DEC's decision to approve the facility, the local expertise of the farmers was essentially ignored, as I ascertained by examining the hearing record to see what information served as the basis for the various factual conclusions.[24]

The hearing proved to be an inadequate means to involve the public. There was little attempt to ensure that either the experts' arguments or the hearing procedures were clear and understandable. There was little to engender the residents' trust. Evident in statements by the judge, the lawyers, and the experts was the assumption that what technical experts said was "truth," while citizens held only private "opinions." Partially as a result, the hearing, like the facility, was never accepted as appropriate or legitimate by the community.

When word spread that the DEC had granted Nutrient Uptake permission to construct and operate the sludge disposal facility, farmers resisted, blockading the entrance to the site with their tractors. The failure to stop the facility left the farming community despondent. A crucial community leader died of cancer depressed over her failure. Activists continued to monitor the site for evidence needed to close it. When the DEC-appointed monitor spent his working hours at a nearby striptease club, he was "exposed" as a no show (and later prosecuted for submitting time sheets). However, despite questions over dumping of illegal wastes, other unpermitted practices, and permit violations, it was six years before the DEC finally forced the operation to close, suing in civil court to revoke the permit after repeated enforcement actions against the operators failed. In the end, virtually every anticipatory fear expressed by the citizens had come true. Wastes had flowed over the berms into the Wallkill River. Groundwater was contaminated with cadmium. Undocumented hazardous wastes were disposed of at the site. Five million gallons of sludge were "temporarily" stored in lagoons. And much more than the planned volume of wastes was received. The sod farm was eventually remediated at taxpayer expense under the state's Superfund program. As a final twist, a housing subdivision was apparently built directly over the former waste pits with no disclosure to home buyers. Residents report finding contaminants in the soil and drinking water.

Case 2: Al Turi Landfill, Inc.   Al Turi Landfill, Inc., is located in Goshen, New York.[25] The landfill is a private operation linked to organized crime by government hearings in the early 1980s.[26] In the summer of 1980, hearings were held before an administrative judge from the New York DEC to review an application and draft environmental impact statement for a proposed expansion of the facility. On behalf of the town of Goshen, which intervened to stop the project, I undertook a study of the social impacts of the expansion. I conducted group interviews with nearby residents sampled according to proximity using concentric rings drawn outward from the landfill site. My approach was to assess impacts from the existing adjacent landfill, operating for more than a decade, in order to project future effects of the proposed expansion. The proximity of the Orange County Landfill further suggested the likelihood of cumulative impacts.

Although farming was the predominant surrounding land use, some 1,000 people either lived or worked within an 8,000-foot radius around the proposed landfill.[27] Farm families drawn to the area because of its rich soil had roots as far back as two hundred years. A number of nearby residents were also professionals, who, having escaped the highly developed areas much closer to New York City for the privacy and isolation of a country home, often commuted to jobs an hour or more away. Other area residents, clustered in a small development, had made residential choices more dependent on quality of schools and proximity of jobs. All of the residents evidenced low mobility.

Residents had diverse concerns about the landfill. Farmers worried about their herds and vegetables, not just their families. They were acutely aware that anything that affected the large amounts of water they drew from their wells could affect their dairies. Other residents focused on family impacts, particularly related to their children's safety and health. Truck traffic, smells, and dirt invaded their privacy and isolation. The threat of water contamination undermined hopes that they had found a clean environment in which to raise their children free of environmental hazards.

As I interviewed residents living at various distances from the facility, I discovered that certain fears about the long-term consequences of the landfills did not correlate with proximity. The closest neighbors had documented concrete, daily impacts of the operation of the existing landfill that caused substantial erosion of their lifestyles. But even residents living as far as a mile from the site, who could neither see, smell, nor hear it, experienced fear. The fear was based principally on the expectation that the landfills would pollute both the adjacent Wallkill River and the Southern Wallkill Valley aquifer, source of their well water.

People generally knew of the DEC's discovery of a "contravention of ground-water standards" at the old landfill. They were uncertain how the pollution would move underground and believed that the expansion would add to the existing contamination. Discussions of expected leachate generation from the new "high-tech" landfill exacerbated concerns over what was leaking from the existing "old-fashioned" landfill. If pollution occurred, residents feared their health would be threatened and they might be forced to move, as was happening at that very time in Love Canal, which residents knew about from media coverage.

Residents gathered to plot strategy for opposing the proposed landfill and worked closely with the town of Goshen in these efforts. Although they failed to stop the landfill, a citizens' group created from the effort persisted as a multi-issue organization for a decade, serving as the precursor for a permanent county environmental watchdog organization, Orange Environment, Inc., which took the subsequent lead in opposing Turi landfill's operations. I served as president of both organizations. After twenty years of opposition, OEI successfully blocked Turi from receiving a permit in 1999 for a third expansion, successfully proving in administrative hearings that the owners of the landfill were not fit to hold a New York State permit, given their criminal and compliance records.[28] Subsequently, a subsidiary of the French multinational Vivendi considered seeking a permit for the same expansion denied Turi with an option to buy if successful. OEI is again mobilized to intervene.

Case 3: High-Level Nuclear Waste at the Richton Dome[29]. The Richton salt dome in Mississippi was one of the sites under initial consideration for the nation's first high-level nuclear waste repository. Salt domes are an extremely stable geological environment, thought by some experts to provide ideal settings for nuclear waste during the tens of thousands of years or more that the wastes will have to be isolated in order to prevent the escape of harmful radiation.

The Richton dome is in a rural but populous area some fifty miles upriver from the Gulf Coast. Among concerns was the potential relocation of some residents in the small and close-knit community of Richton, particularly frightening to elderly residents who depended on their neighbors for assistance and their church for security. Furthermore, publicity about a nuclear accident at the Tatum dome in the 1960s led to fear about radioactive contamination and distrust of government's ability to safely handle hazardous facilities. There were concerns about future health problems due to the project. Opponents claimed that the area's entire population would be at risk in the event of an accident and that radioactive materials would leach into waterways, threatening the vital coastal fishing industry. Their worst fears were portrayed when a newspaper cartoon pictured the repository destroyed by an earthquake, fish along the Pascagoula River dying of radiation burns, and residents of southern Mississippi ordered to evacuate.

Projected impacts included traffic hazards all along the network of road connections to the nation's nuclear facilities. Locals particularly feared accidents on narrow, winding country roads, where nuclear haulers would have to compete with log trucks. Adverse impacts were expected from both short-term boom-bust growth during construction and long-term induced growth. The slow-paced decisionmaking process created a period of uncertainty during which planning was difficult for individuals and families, as well as the community. And, even if the project was abandoned, Richton would remain in "perpetual jeopardy" of another hazardous waste project being attracted to so "ideal" a site.

State and local groups organized to oppose the facility. Politicians were pressured to lead the attack. One congressman was said to have held up a piece of radioactive rock and declared "You can hold it in your hand; it is completely safe." But, after gauging public reaction, he astutely declared a short time later, "This project will go forward over my dead body."

Residents were angry at the defensive manner of DOE officials and questioned their competence. One resident claimed that she had spent eight years studying DOE documents, years that she would rather have spent with her grandchildren, and that DOE experts could not match her local expertise.

I read that trash. They say that the wind doesn't come our way. Well, I know which way the wind comes; I don't think that the DOE is God Almighty.

The project both threatened and evidenced stigma. Arrival in Richton was greeted with large signs opposing the DOE project. One Richton official shared fears that opponents would stigmatize the town and scare away potential residents. Similarly, visible opposition in the coastal areas threatened to stigmatize the very fishing industry that residents feared would be contaminated. In ecohistorical context, the federal designation of Richton as a candidate repository was viewed locally as an intrusion from Washington intended to punish Mississippi for past sins, a continuing stigma going all the way back to the U.S. Civil War, some 120 years earlier, by which the state was still viewed by northerners as "the rectum of the United States."[30]

Case 4: The Vernon Radium-Contaminated Soil Site.   In 1981 radium-contaminated soil was discovered in several Essex County, New Jersey, communities where uranium mill tailings from a defunct luminescent watch and dial plant had apparently been used as fill for housing lots.[31] Houses built atop the soil evidenced harmful levels of ionizing radiation from the radium and from radon gas decay. The New Jersey governor issued an executive order aimed at expediting the cleanup of the neighborhood.[32] With assistance from EPA, a pilot project was undertaken to remove the soil from beneath several Montclair homes, whose families were relocated to small apartments during the excavation project. Neighboring residents remained in their homes while various protective measures were tried. Once removed from the ground, the contaminated soil was placed in thousands of metal drums that were then "temporarily" stacked outside the homes until a permanent disposal site could be found.

But locating even an interim disposal site proved to be more difficult than the DEP had anticipated. The nearby city of West Orange rejected a plan to store barrels there. Some drums were moved for storage to Kearny, New Jersey, before public pressure stopped the transfer. The remaining 5,000 barrels were left stacked in the yards of the Montclair homes. Meanwhile, operating nuclear waste disposal sites in Nevada and Washington rejected the soil, in part because it was not radioactive enough to warrant using precious room in these facilities. But their rejection stemmed also from the politics of nuclear waste disposal—Nevada and Washington were indicating their displeasure at being saddled with most of the nation's nuclear disposal problem. Pressured to act on the governor's executive order, the DEP revised a siting study it had hastily commissioned, selecting a Vernon, New Jersey, quarry in the far north of the state on the New York border as a disposal site for the soil.

In the summer of 1986, the DEP informed Vernon-area politicians of the decision. The quarry would be taken (by eminent domain if necessary) and united with adjacent parkland and the Appalachian Trail. On-site soil would be blended with the radium-contaminated material and used to reclaim the quarry. The resulting soil mix would contain radium and radon at levels in line with existing background radiation for the Vernon area. From the DEP's perspective, it was a perfect solution—a major waste disposal problem would be solved, a scarred quarry made beautiful, and no resulting net hazard created. Using extraordinary powers granted by the governor, the DEP moved to quickly executed its plan. DEP officials viewed the project as totally benign; the material was "just *dirt*." They quickly discovered that the rural and suburban residents of northern New Jersey and southern New York did not agree.

Vernon politicians were shocked. The decision had been made without their knowledge or participation. They viewed the project as an intrusion from Trenton, a message that their area was so peripheral that it should take wastes that no one else wanted. They also rejected the DEP's use of the governor's order to waive a siting procedure that would guarantee them some say in the outcome. A powerful political coalition formed around a consensus that Trenton had violated the democratic tradition.

Once the radium-contaminated soil disposal proposal was made public, the news drew a strong response from citizens. Organizers had no trouble recruiting volunteers willing to stop the project. Within two weeks of their announcement, DEP representatives faced a hostile crowd of more than 3,000 people at the local high school. The prospect of violence forced the regulators to arrange for an escape route from the high school auditorium. As officials presented a glossy slide show about the project, the audience became increasingly angry. When the displaced Montclair residents were cited as a reason for moving quickly with the project, the audience, as a unit, broke into a caustic "aaw." One DEP official repeatedly referred to the soil mix with the words, "It's just dirt," each time driving the crowd to a near frenzy. The mayor of Vernon and a group of citizen leaders had to intervene to prevent an eruption. And then the most impressive scene of the meeting occurred. Following scores of ranting politicians, only one citizen rose to speak—but she spoke on behalf of the entire crowd. Already citizens were sufficiently unified to allow their views to be represented in this fashion. The resulting "organization" was termed the No-Name Group. The Vernon mayor also convened a "yellow-ribbon panel" to review the case.

Citizens raised a series of concerns about the project, including fears that the radium might leach into a major aquifer and contaminate downstream areas in New York State. Both farmers and residents became concerned. The New York Department of Environmental Conservation agreed that the risk crossed the state border. Extensive organizing in New York nearly matched the level of concern revealed in New Jersey. Both communities began to think of themselves as part of "the Valley." Large fund-raising events were held, such as a rock concert featuring area entertainers, called Vernon Aid. Citizens, towns, counties, and New York State entered an array of court cases against the New Jersey DEP, tying the project in legal knots.

Perhaps most telling, hundreds of citizens on both sides of the border joined small affinity groups to learn nonviolent protest techniques. Citizen leaders claimed that 1,000 people could be called on short notice to block trucks bringing the soil, fomenting a major political defeat for the governor. Although the DEP won the right in court to use the site for temporary storage, fear of direct action was instrumental in forcing New Jersey to back down. Some six months after its initiation, the project was abandoned.

During the short-lived crisis, there were reports of reluctance to purchase nearby land. Anticipatory fear about the escape of radium was rampant, with "Hell No We Won't Glow" and "Keep the Soil Out of Our Valley" signs and bumper stickers appearing everywhere. The level of mobilization was itself a major impact. New social networks were a major gain.

In the wake of the Vernon fiasco, the DEP formed the New Jersey Radium/Radon Advisory Board to guide its decisionmaking. However, in June 1986, the DEP repeated its Vernon siting blunder almost identically when it tried to move the radium-contaminated soil south to Jackson Township, near Legler. The citizen response mirrored the one in Vernon, again blocking relocation of the barrels. Subsequently the DEP offered financial incentives to willing community hosts for the soils. During this period, the Mexican government blocked a plan to export the materials there. In 1987, test barrels of the soil were shipped to Oak Ridge, Tennessee, to be mixed with highly radioactive material, thereby qualifying it for disposal at Hanford, Washington.

This did not end the nightmare but only disposed of materials excavated during the experimental remediation of sixteen homes. Meanwhile, beginning in early 1987 hundreds more families in several Essex County communities were informed of dangerous radium contamination beneath their homes, an advisory insensitively thrown on their doorsteps. The Centers for Disease Control expanded the warning beyond indoor radon, telling residents not to eat vegetables from their gardens or allow children to play in the dirt. The enormous cost and questionable feasibility of soil excavation, transportation, and disposal for the soil beneath homes forced the DEP and its advisory board to explore options other than excavation. But because residents had already come to believe that nothing less than excavation would protect them, EPA restored it as the preferred solution, beginning the cycle all over again. With some 700 homes currently listed as contaminated, estimated costs associated with the cleanup are projected to run into the hundreds of millions.[33] The dialectic of double binds between citizen and regulator continues. Nobody wins.

The Psychosocial Basis for NIMBY

A major lesson can be derived from each of the four case studies discussed above. The Merion Blue Grass Sod Farm case taught me that the decisionmaking process itself is a source of victimization. The Al Turi Landfill, Inc., case taught me that anticipatory fear can be learned from experiences in other communities. The Richton, Mississippi, case demonstrated the importance of stigma in a siting controversy. And the Vernon, New Jersey, case proved that an enabling response to disabling conditions can result in a broad-based and powerful sense of community. With these cases in mind, we can draw on many of the key concepts already discussed to explore the psychosocial reasons for NIMBY defense.

Stigma.   Facilities identified as "hazardous" are inherently stigmatizing and thus undesirable. They are likely to be seen as threatening a community directly, by virtue of physical hazards, and indirectly, by virtue of a "courtesy stigma" whereby the community also becomes stigmatized because of its direct association with the hazard.[34] Thus, as seen in all four case studies, stigma is both an attribute of the hazardous project and a potential adverse impact of the project on the community.

Courtesy stigma is inherently tied to image, since image is what is harmed by stigma. Areas known for scenic tourism, growing wholesome food products, or providing a safe residential environment are all vulnerable to the devaluing of image. Accordingly, fear of stigma is likely to be a motivating force in the community's reaction to the proposed hazardous facility. And one can logically infer a direct relationship between fear of stigma and the degree to which a hazardous facility threatens the community's projected image.

The very nature of siting controversies emphasizes this courtesy stigma. As more people know more about the project, more harm is done. Thus, as the controversy becomes highly publicized, the community acquires an increasing stake in successfully stopping the facility. Ironically, were the project developed quietly with little public awareness, "anticipatory" stigma would probably be minimized (although "realized" stigma might be a possible outcome of later accidents or contamination).

Health Threat and Anticipatory Fear.   Anticipatory fear develops from concern about the future hazards associated with a facility. As discussed in earlier chapters, health concern, particularly in regard to children, motivates a vigilant response that prompts the prospective victim to rehearse the worst outcomes possible from the facility. People vigilant about threats to their families and homes are likely to prefer mobilizing to stop a proposed facility before it is built instead of waiting to react to a dangerous condition brought about by the facility's operations. This is particularly true for women and for people generally expecting to exert control over hazards.[35]

Inversion of Home and Territoriality.   Threat to the sanctity of home as a psychological refuge and an economic investment results in "territoriality," or the defense of space. By extension, those feeling "ownership" over their community may exhibit a collective territorial defense.[36]

Loss of Control and Disablement.   Their inability to prevent an unwanted change in the community challenges residents' sense of well-being. Facility impacts serve as reminders of their impotence, causing possible feelings of depression, helplessness, and disability. Active prevention of facility siting is a way to maintain a sense of control. Such activism is most evident when residents are not newcomers, have a strong sense of community, think they have a chance of winning, and fight collectively.[37]

Stress and Lifestyle Infringement. A facility may be expected to disrupt affected residents' everyday lives. Anticipating traffic, odors, pollution, litter, noise, and other direct physical impacts, residents have ample reason to oppose the facility.[38]

Victimization and the Loss of Trust. Siting also causes feelings of violation. Through site selection, government chooses certain residents to be the victims of any adverse impacts caused by the operation. Even a private facility requires government permits. Government is blamed when the rights of nearby residents go unprotected, often inviting distrust in the way it handles siting cases. Furthermore, facility siting can be seen as an outside intrusion involving a reckoning over past disputes.

Enablement and Vigilance. Local environmental resistance involves citizen vigilance in observing events, exploring alternatives, and evaluating decisions. As they gain knowledge, citizens become competent to analyze the technical aspects of siting controversies. In exercising oversight, they often find government officials lax in their enforcement of regulations. The more that vigilant citizens learn about a hazardous project, the more likely they are to appreciate its undesirable characteristics. Absent a major benefit associated with the facility, it is a losing proposition. Thus, opposition to stigmatized facilities is a proactive response, as opposed to the reactive response of toxic victims who have already suffered exposure. Residents respond to their anticipatory fears rather than to realized ones. In organizing to block the facility, they protect identity, health, home, lifestyle, and personal control, and they avoid victimization. Avenues of participation are created. Seen from this perspective, NIMBY is an enabling process.

The Rational Basis for Local Environmental Resistance

The deconstruction of the engineering and science justifying the safety of a facility is the first rational basis for local environmental resistance. When experts and expert documents testify to "truths" that do not jibe with local experience or that make specious claims, serious doubts are created. The prospective victims of a hazardous facility also pose a series of critical contextual questions that bear on the perceived legitimacy of the siting process. Three questions tend to be particularly central to the rationality of the NIMBY response. Have I been heard? How will I be affected? Why me?

Are My Concerns Being Heard and Addressed? The anxiety of community members about a proposed facility is aroused when they cannot participate directly in a decision that may greatly affect them. Siting decisions are routinely made by government officials or by special siting boards charged with meeting the needs of the larger community. Local concerns raised at public hearings often receive less weight than technical and political considerations. As a result, the citizen feels devalued, as a Canadian activist explained to Audrey Armour.[39]

> When you are an environmentalist, I discovered, you become a lesser person because you care. When you have to stand before boards and you're just a citizen and not an expert, not much weight is put on your testimony. We felt that the more we got involved, the harder it became to be involved in a democratic process. We were allowed our democratic right to speak. But at the end of the first hearing, we didn't feel that it was fair and impartial.

Armour further cited a Canadian government letter about a facility hearing that referred to the people of the town "twenty-three times as objectors, opponents and complainers." Clearly, this is how the citizens were viewed by government officials. In fact, an analysis of DOE high-level nuclear waste facility hearing records for instances of NIMBY instead found opponents to be generally well-informed in addressing technical issues of importance.[40] If citizens are able to make cogent input into the siting process, then why are their views not heard?

The first explanation is the divergence between experts and citizens in using qualitative versus quantitative reasoning. Citizens' perceptions of the truth often vary from the "facts" as understood by experts. Citizens often raise moral issues rather than arguments of fact over technical issues. Deciding how much risk of cancer someone should be subjected to is a fundamentally different question than how to best gather data about a leaking hazardous waste site. And the "goodness" of a particular facility is a different consideration than is the projected performance of its technical systems. Experts frequently fail to distinguish such moral appeals from purely emotional assertions. Although both are qualitative, moral arguments draw their rationale from generally accepted principles. The need for both questions about the "goodness" of a principle and the "correctness" of information is often lost on government technocrats.[41] As experts seek a calculus for reducing social concerns to numbers, they find the issues raised by opponents of hazardous facilities to be hard to quantify, simplifying or even omitting them in their ratings. Citizens' subsequent rejection of the legitimacy of quantification reflects this gulf between pseudo-objective and pseudo-subjective arguments.[42] Everyone except "the suits" sees through the subjectivity of objectivity. Perhaps all see this, but the suits don't admit it.

Paul Slovic has contrasted cognitive models for interpreting health risks according to both scientific toxicology and the "intuitive toxicology" of laypeople. Assumptions differed about what is toxic, the relationship of dose and effect on health outcomes, the ability to generalize from animals to humans, and the cause and effect relationships between chemical exposures and human health problems. For example, while laypeople believe that any exposure to a toxic substance or carcinogen is dangerous, for professional toxicologists, a sufficient "threshold" dose is required to find consequences.[43]

Such differences need not mean that citizen input is less correct or veridical than expert testimony. Slovic, Fischhoff, and Lichtenstein's classic analysis of biases and errors in risk perception found experts to be just as subject to cognitive errors or "heuristics" as laypeople were. However, there were fundamental differences in the types of errors made. Laypeople employed the availability heuristic, a bias toward seeing as most likely events that are easiest to imagine or recall. They also exhibited personal optimism, an unfounded belief that "it won't happen to me." On their part, technical experts evidenced denial of uncertainty, assuming, for example, that hazardous environments are safe. Both experts and laypeople were overconfident in their judgments and held on to opinions, once formed, in the face of disconfirming information. There are also differences in the types of evidence used to influence opinions. Experts are more likely to rely on statistical evidence while laypeople use inference, both potentially faulty approaches.[44]

A second reason for discounting citizen input is the bias for technical over local expertise. Holding social origin and education comparable, the key difference may be less in how technical and lay experts think than in the substantive knowledge technical experts have at their disposal. However, in-depth knowledge affords experts no special advantage in going beyond the available data or into realms outside their expertise. Indeed, the price for acquiring such depth of field may be a reduction in breadth of understanding. Given the complex interdisciplinary nature of contamination issues, context-rich local wisdom may be as applicable to a given problem as is technical expertise.[45]

Technical experts have certainly evidenced fallibility.[46] Brian Wynne recounts the plight of Cumbrian sheepherders in the United Kingdom in the wake of fallout from the Chernobyl accident. Believing this to be a short-term problem, government scientists encouraged the farmers to hold on to the sheep until the contaminants cleared up. Their prediction that it would take only three weeks for radioactive cesium to dissipate from herds was based on scientific tests on the behavior of radiocesium conducted in clay soils, where the contaminant bound to the soil and became inactive. The Cumbrian hill country, however, is not characterized by clays. In its predominant soils, cesium remained active, reaching plant roots and thus recontaminating the grazing animals. Contrary to the expert opinion of government scientists, if kept to their pasture, the contamination of the herds was hardly a short-lived problem.

As a temporary ban from the market was extended indefinitely, the local economy was devastated. Not only were farmers denied income from selling their sheep, but now they had to pay for imported feed to keep their herds alive. To ease their plight, officials modified the ban to allow the sale of the sheep, expected to clear of contamination once relocated to uncontaminated pasture. However, this plan failed for reasons of environmental stigma. To be sold, the sheep had to be clearly marked by dye as unfit for human consumption. The dyed sheep were "blighted" on the market and brought rock-bottom value. Demand even dropped for uncontaminated sheep from the region.

Now a shift to local expertise occurred. Forced to think for themselves, farmers theorized that the contamination might not be from Chernobyl at all, but rather from what had been previously the world's worst civilian nuclear disaster, the 1957 accident at the Sellafield Nuclear Reprocessing Plant, just upwind from Cumbria. Secrecy over that disaster had already caused public distrust of Britain's government and scientists. Now experts and officials hotly denied any contribution of Sellafield to the post-Chernobyl contamination of the sheep. In doing so, they also denied the validity of the farmers' knowledge of the lands they had lived on for a lifetime and the indigenous knowledge passed down for many generations. These official denials stopped, however, after tests revealed that, indeed, half the cesium could be backdated to the Sellafield incident. Wynne concludes that experts are not as objective as they claim, nor is the public as subjective as it is often considered to be.[47]

Similarly, Alan Irwin cites the battle of British farm workers against use of the herbicide 2,4,5-T. Abstract expert proclamations about safety contradicted the farm workers' direct local knowledge of the variability and complexity of actual field conditions, operating circumstances, and social factors during the spraying of pesticides. In response, the farm workers engaged in "popular epidemiology," collecting their own survey data on health outcomes and successfully proving harm in the experts' own scientific language.[48]

A third reason citizens may not be heard is that they have a very different conception of risk than does the regulator, as discussed in Chapter 5. For example, citizens defined air pollution largely in terms of its effects (e.g., odor, haze, and other visual characteristics, sore throats, breathing problems, and other health symptoms) while experts focused on the chemical composition and technical causes of the pollution.[49] This difference in definition of the problem makes it likely that the citizen and the regulator/expert will talk past each other.

Illustrated here are useful distinctions made by Timmerman between two universes of thought, one the "instrumental rationality" employed by a calculating bureaucracy and the second the "coherent rationality" of a mutualistic community. Risk is thought about differently within these two universes, and different issues are salient. While the former uses technical criteria to create abstract rules, the citizens' rationality uses generally held tenets of acceptability to suggest two "trump rights." First, "an absolute right not to have one's own health jeopardized for someone else's good without one's permission." And second, "an absolute right not to be forced to put someone for whom one is responsible into jeopardy."[50] Similarly, one can distinguish between a "thin" description of risk, based on estimated probability and magnitude of harm, and "thick" risk description, considering such factors as voluntariness, equity of sharing the risk, familiarity, whether those bearing the risk benefit, and whether the risk can be eliminated rather than merely reduced.[51] Citizens expect a thick review. Thus NIMBY is a problem of both perceived risk and conceived risk.

How Will This Project Affect Me?   Many direct and secondary impacts potentially associated with a hazardous facility can be anticipated. Generally corresponding to the impacts earlier noted for actual toxic exposure, such expected effects serve as further grounds for rational opposition. Citizens assume that if an impact is possible, it *will* occur. Experts, employing the engineer's fallacy, make the opposite assumption. They expect that facility designs will work as planned and therefore problems are unlikely to develop. Thus mitigations will not be undertaken unless citizens forcefully raise concerns over adverse outcomes.[52]

Studies of high-level nuclear waste siting by Slovic and colleagues further clarify differences between experts and citizens in anticipating impacts.[53] When similar questions were asked of attendees at a conference of the American Nuclear Society and members of the general public, the latter held portents of disaster at about twice the rate as the experts.

- Whereas 31 percent of the images of a high-level nuclear waste repository suggested by nuclear professionals were negative (against 20 percent neutral and 49 percent positive), 68 percent of the public's images were negative (against 10 percent neutral and 22 percent positive).
- Although only 8 percent of the nuclear professionals rated future health problems among those living near nuclear facilities as highly likely, 55 percent of public respondents had this expectation.
- Among professionals, 15 percent foresaw stigma associated with the nuclear "dump," against 30 percent for the public.
- Only 32 percent of professionals thought an accident in waste handling was highly likely, against 72 percent of the public.

- Among members of the public, 33 percent thought that the repository would be effective in preventing contamination of groundwater, against 77 percent of professionals.
- Although 79 percent of the public survey shared the concern that an earthquake or volcano might release radioactive material, only 32 percent of the nuclear professionals agreed.

A key issue of comparison had to do with the level of trust found in the facility. Although the public lacked trust in the Yucca Mountain repository site, experts were more likely to believe that the site can be properly operated.[54]

Why Me?

Equity in exposure to hazards is a final issue likely to influence citizen reaction to stigmatized facilities.[55] Inequity is likely to be perceived when one is either asked to bear the risks for others without sharing the benefits or faces disproportionate threat, even if some form of benefit is shared. With these conditions, it is unlikely that the siting of a facility will be seen as fair and just. There are several dimensions to this inequity.

The "Reverse Commons" Effect. A popular analogy for the pollution of our planet has been the "tragedy of the commons," whereby what all hold in common is destroyed by the private pursuit of self-interest.[56] But the private property of others is often affected too. Although we generally look to government to protect the public commons, the "owners" are most often responsible for protecting their private domain. NIMBY commonly involves the clash of this individual responsibility with government actions or government-sanctioned actions purportedly on behalf of the common good.

When facilities are sited for *concentrating* wastes (the term "disposal" is actually inaccurate), there is a different twist in the tragedy of the commons theme. This "reverse commons effect" occurs when impacted parties are asked to bear disproportionate risks for society. The general good is served at their expense. Therefore, the willingness of individuals to sacrifice their own interests is called into play.

Saturation, Distribution, and Power.   John Seley and Julian Wolpert suggest that equity issues arise from three general locational considerations in siting hazardous facilities.[57] First, there are the actual impacts of the facility on people and the community, including the duration of the impacts, the scale of the project, and the sensitivity of the location. They note that a community saturated with facilities may have less impact sensitivity to a proposed project than an area having few facilities. Yet to take advantage of such adaptation is to create equity impacts.

There are also distributional effects that determine whether the facility makes the host community better- or worse-off in relation to the rest of society. Within the community, some may profit from the facility while the general costs are borne by the public. Thus Seley and Wolpert ask,

(1) Are the costs borne by one group in order to spare larger groups (or society as a whole)?

(2) Is one group's equity more important than another's (that is, should we assume a compensatory or distributive role for equity)?[58]

Finally, equitability is affected by power dynamics. Thus, as people become more vocal in opposing a certain facility, the siting effort is likely to shift toward a more powerless community.

The political nature of siting inspired Timmerman to comment that "hazardous waste management has become one of the central stages (or 'battlegrounds') upon which a series of moral dilemmas (or 'battles') are being played out." At the crux is the view that all people, whether equal or not, deserve equal and proper consideration so that none are forced to accept conditions that force them to abandon their sense of equal worth.[59]

Who Bears the Risks?   Although siting a facility usually involves generating criteria for identifying the "best" sites, the most "feasible" sites are actually chosen. Thus, as the previously discussed Cerrell report demonstrated, patterns in hazardous facility siting reflect the general power dynamics of the society.

In the mid-1980s, a representative of a then major waste disposal company, Service Corporation of America (SCA), addressed an environmental conference that I attended. In response to my question, he explained that the optimal sites for hazardous disposal facilities were urban centers such as Newark, New Jersey (home of SCA's Earthline facility). Residents of such cities, he explained, benefited from working in chemical factories located there; they should accept the risks of chemical waste disposal.

Although there are many flaws to this logic,[60] it points to the kinds of rationalization used in facility siting to create an inequitable pattern of toxic exposure. Similarly, Robert Bullard identified "institutional racism" in the siting of hazardous facilities in black neighborhoods in urban areas of the South, such as Houston.[61] The General Accounting Office, in a 1983 report, found the same pattern in eight southern states. For three of four hazardous facilities studied, the majority of local residents were black. Furthermore, at least one-quarter of the population in the four communities had an income below the poverty level, with the impoverished population being almost entirely black.[62] Similarly, Greenberg, Anderson, and Rosenberger found that hazardous sites were located in areas where people were poor and marginal (younger, older, black, or foreign). They caution that the siting of these facilities may have been due less to political reasons than to proximity to plants generating the wastes.[63] Thus, rather than blatant discrimination, biases in siting may involve a subtle process of inequity that Bullard described. As with the SCA official's comment, we see here the rationality of environmental injustice.

Concerns with equity and distributive justice have been magnified with the birth of the environmental justice movement, described in Chapter 6. In a way unimaginable at the time of the first edition of this volume, the force of the civil rights movement has become focused on issues of discriminatory siting. Although it is premature to assume that there will be an overnight shift in the ways that environmental decisionmaking occurs, there are significant hurdles put in place by the Clinton administration to ward off blatant acts of environmental injustice and racism. There are several important components of this shift. First, there is an already referenced body of information that demonstrates a probable discriminatory pattern in U.S. siting practices against minorities and the poor. Second, the controversy raised by this data has contributed to a new consciousness among minority groups of the toxic legacy in their communities, tied to a resolve to not allow it to continue. Third, in response to both the proofs of discrimination and the new politics of environmental civil rights, the Clinton administration required all agencies to put in place policies to prevent violations of environmental justice in their practice. Offices of environmental justice now exist at the EPA and other agencies. On its part, EPA offers special funding to EJ groups to organize and act at the community level. Finally, as noted previously, Executive Order 12948 offers a uniform policy with legal standing to prohibit systematic governmental decision-making that embodies environmental injustice. The order requires government agencies and communities to undertake both the social analysis and the cumulative effects assessment necessary to determine whether an environmental justice threshold exists for a project and whether its approval and implementation would constitute a violation. This mandate has an important implication for the impact issues discussed in this volume. The mandate to protect environmental justice presents a new framework for making psychosocial community impact assessment and cumulative effects research into mainstream tools for preventing environmental victimization under the National Environmental Policy Act (NEPA).

Despite past patterns of discrimination in siting issues, toxic victimization under the rubric of environmental justice should not generate government policy paralleling Affirmative Action in hiring. Rather, EJ must establish the rights of all people to protection from unwanted environmental exposures. It should mandate careful psychosocial and cumulative studies of any population to assure an understanding of past exposures and effect (the ecoenvironmental history) and to anticipate future consequences, taking such information into account in decisionmaking. In considering past injustices to the least empowered and most harmed, it must avoid creating new patterns of injustice.

Action is required to prevent a continuation of the existing discriminatory patterns of victimization. Often these patterns are social, not just environmental. For example, when the Marathon Oil refinery in Texas City, Texas, suffered from a 1980s hydrofluoric acid spill, a cloud of toxic gases was released over the city. A large government housing project immediately next to the plant was populated by mostly African Americans. Lacking cars, yet located at the epicenter of the accident, residents of the project were forced to run down the street chased by the gas cloud. Government housing assistance had reified environmental injustice in the community long before this near reenactment of the Bhopal disaster occurred. As already discussed, social stigma laid the foundation for environmental stigma. Environmental stigma then further reified the social stigma.

Conclusion: Institutionalized Irresponsibility

The corollary of having a few bear the burden for the many is that most people can escape having to take responsibility for the ecological consequences of their wasteful practices. As wastes are increasingly hauled to more distant locations because of poor local planning and the failure to site local facilities, the problems addressed in this book are only moved elsewhere.

But why should communities take wastes from other areas? Why would people truly want someone else's wastes in their backyard? It is interesting that those who condemn NIMBY pay little attention to what might be called YIYBY (yes, in *your* backyard), the tendency of people to want to foist their wastes off on others. When people don't have to come to grips with their own waste problems, there is little pressure for conservation, recycling, waste cycling, cleanup, and waste reduction. When wastes go somewhere else, there is no impetus to be responsible for the consequences of one's actions. This is a moral issue. Perhaps the fallacious concepts of "waste disposal" and YIYBY are really the problem, not NIMBY or local environmental resistance.

In sum, NIMBY is a complex response. It represents reaction to the inherent stigma and induced anticipatory fear associated with projects. And it articulates citizens' frustrations over the manner in which projects are sited and environmental decisions are made. NIMBY stems in part from the failure of regulators to take seriously the psychosocial impacts of facilities. Because these concerns are unlikely to be subject to mitigation and negotiation, the citizen rightly sees the siting question as an all-out, win-or-lose battle. In a rationalized siting process, citizens are robbed of their power when the discourse of technical experts is the basis for decisions and citizens' concerns are viewed as private and subjective. The result is that citizens often must go outside the process, to the political or legal spheres, if they are to "win." The difference between communities that can mobilize political influence and those that cannot is evident where local resistance is most successful.

Changing the Culture of Contamination

A response to the contaminating culture, local environmental resistance has also become a force for changing it, emerging as a vital tool for ecosocial change and an antidote to the engineering fallacy. Here we see a series of embedded cultural contradictions disclosed by an examination of NIMBY.

It is important to note that local environmental resistance, in its frequent NIMBY form, hardly stems from radical ecological origins. Rather, its etiology is based on a combination of modern middle-class values of home and property and postmodern fears about the health consequences of contamination. It begins as a legitimate, enlightened act of private self-interest.

Based on the nuclear family as an individual entity seeking its own benefit, our society rests on a firm belief in private property. Home as property serves as a means to separate ourselves from the competitive world. It is a material means of accumulating both wealth and status. And it is an expression of the degree of control we possess over the earth and other humans. Threats to property are, therefore, deeply psychological in nature. Herein lies a dilemma. On the one hand, our beliefs in individualism, in the right to property and profit and in the ethical acceptability of acting solely in one's own best interests, foster acceptance of polluting activities. On the other hand, these beliefs also explain our strong opposition to collective technocratic solutions to the problems caused by our selfish behavior. We have a clash of self-interests.[64]

In isolation, NIMBY can be a tool for avoiding responsibility and forcing it elsewhere. If we don't want these wastes, someone else will have to take them. At the same time, as a defense of place and community, local environmental resistance involves a community level collective self-interest, as well. Thus local environmental resistance is simultaneously an act of ultimate responsibility and irresponsibility.

NIMBY as a Force for Ecosocial Change

This chameleon nature of NIMBY changes character as it moves beyond the individual, family, and community levels of social process to the societal level. As a

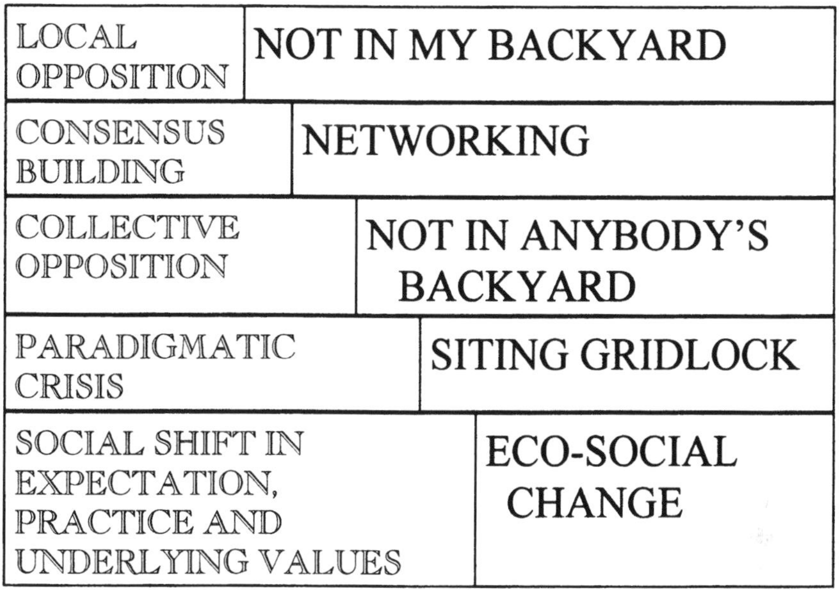

LOCAL OPPOSITION	NOT IN MY BACKYARD	
CONSENSUS BUILDING	NETWORKING	
COLLECTIVE OPPOSITION	NOT IN ANYBODY'S BACKYARD	
PARADIGMATIC CRISIS	SITING GRIDLOCK	
SOCIAL SHIFT IN EXPECTATION, PRACTICE AND UNDERLYING VALUES	ECO-SOCIAL CHANGE	

Figure 7.1   Social Learning Promoted by NIMBY

social trend, NIMBY has yet another implication. Waste reduction, composting, recycling, source separation, and the avoidance of unnecessary plastic packaging, as well as other conserving steps, will occur not just if they are profitable but to avoid the social and economic costs of siting landfills and incinerators.[65] With its evolved norms of "nobody's backyard," local environmental resistance has emerged as an advocacy process for meta-learning, with the potential to address the issues rather than shift them to someone else.[66] Accordingly, as Figure 7.1 illustrates, NIMBY is a force for radically altering the paradigm of environmental degradation.

How has this shift been evidenced? The key environmental legislation of the 1970s, principally the Resource Conservation and Recovery Act (RCRA), was premised on a "cradle-to-grave" control of the waste stream that aimed at curtailing the practice of illegal dumping and improper disposal common at that time. Waste was to be "manifested" to a specific disposal site and its arrival confirmed. A major siting initiative throughout the 1980s and 1990s intended to meet the resulting need for permitted "state-of-the-art" disposal facilities was undermined by the fact that no one was allowing suitable graves to be dug. Within one year of the Love Canal incident's achieving national notoriety, the General Accounting Office documented a new pessimism about siting among industry and government. The industry already perceived public opposition as its number one problem, and finding a solution to this problem quickly became its preoccupation.[67] As a case in point between 1985 and mid-1989, siting of some forty incinerators was blocked across the United States.[68] The last hazardous waste landfill built in the United States was completed in 1976, appropriately in Last Chance, Colorado.[69] The waste market was caught in a "scissors" effect. Public pressure forced government to enact increasingly stringent regulations, creating a demand for more waste disposal sites. Yet public opposition to these facilities made the supply of these sites even scarcer. As a result, the price of waste disposal increased dramatically. In the early 1980s, land disposal of wastes cost as little as $15 per ton; by 1986, it had risen to $250 per ton. Incineration had gone to $500–$1,500 per ton.[70]

Facility siting had become an incredible challenge. The result was an amazing dialectic between technocrats and local environmental resisters. The technocrats define siting as a problem, advancing engineered solutions for resolving various threats, even if such solutions are only temporary. They rationalize the solutions using environmental and economic criteria. But then they confront their major challenge: the tendency of neighbors to "irrationalize" their decisions by considering worst-case scenarios and detecting weaknesses in the plans. Since hazardous technologies by definition are not subject to mitigation for worst-case scenarios, they cannot be "rationally" sited from the perspective of those who would suffer should problems arise. In siting, what is rational for the many is irrational for the few.

Siting thus became a modern ceremony for selecting victims for sacrifice. Having eschewed human sacrifice on the altar as uncivilized, we have yet instituted a more modern form of slow death by cancer that, silently dreaded by all, appears to be acceptable if due to general background sources or personally caused pollution. But when a specific source of externally caused danger becomes apparent, barring economic incentives, we are likely to express our opposition.

To overcome resulting gridlock, government tries to disable citizen participants and create bureaucratic avenues to assure successful siting. Citizen activists are now branded as terrorists for their opposition to facilities. But ironically, the focus on NIMBY obscures a parallel response by polluters to claim "Not in my smokestack." While NIMBY is viewed as base greed, the work of political action committees, industrial lobbying groups, elite influence, and public relations persuasion of the consumer is viewed as enlightened self-interest. The "problem" is again the victim, not the polluter! The majority solves the problem by creating yet another definable "minority." The corporate-governmental complex uses totalitarian methods to pacify resistance to facilities necessary for the overall "good" of the high-consumption, high-profit society.

As a decentralized phenomenon, isolated groups of victims or facility opponents have little chance of changing this dynamic. The very "backyard" nature of the crisis invites isolation. People only recognize crises threatening themselves;

other people's problems are exactly that. "Backyarders" in this way collude in the social dynamic that victimizes them. The potential for demanding social change occurs when such groups network and organize around national coalitions such as the Center for Health, Environment and Justice/Citizens Clearinghouse for Hazardous Wastes. Their principle of "not in anybody's backyard" suggests the same core issues that Dr. Thomas Stockman inadvertently raised. But a society cannot isolate a movement in quite the way that Stockman, an individual, was. Thus the movement has the potential to force fundamental societal change, whereas Stockman faced ostracism.

As parallel, networked, and integrated local actions imposed selective Ludditism over our choice and deployment of polluting technologies, the technological optimism of modernity was lost. NIMBY—as a cumulative effect of simultaneous local battles often only loosely networked into a larger social movement—has significantly affected normative "state-of-the-art" engineering approaches to problem solving. Postmoderns want the progressive assistance technology affords, but without the costs it imposes on its victims. Consequently, social wisdom has been reimposed over technological choice. Although laws and regulations have helped codify some of this shift, these are a secondary outcome. The primary force has been fear of community opposition and the sheer difficulty of obtaining permits. Siting battles have significantly curtailed the use of high-risk and centrally controlled technologies in the United States,[71] forced a shift away from waste disposal toward waste cycling and prevention, and made the siting of facilities perceived to be hazardous or stigmatizing difficult at best. Similarly, the evolution of new industrial norms,[72] industrial ecology, pollution prevention, waste exchange, and the effort to avoid hazardous waste generation reflect the point at which corporations were forced to abandon the assumption of easy and inexpensive waste disposal. And the precautionary principle, already ingrained in Europe, is emerging as a new model here as well.[73]

NIMBY as a Force Discouraging Desired Innovation

It may be premature to view local environmental resistance as a panacea. As a social force for reasoned technology, just as it is used to resist bad technologies, community opposition may also be used to defeat or slow efforts to institute changes in a sustainable direction. This effect is readily seen, for example, in the many NIMBY battles against community residences for the disabled. It is sometimes also evident with regard to environmental facilities.

In my home area, I have watched local opposition defeat or hamper several potentially desirable environmental projects. One involved a plan to compost food wastes as part of a nursery operation in an agricultural district. Opposition to this plan may have been inspired by its proximity to the Merion Blue Grass Sod Farm site discussed above, reflecting the extreme legacy of distrust caused by this eco-historical debacle.

Another instance involved a plan to earn funds for rebuilding the port of Newburgh, New York, by importing Hudson River dredge spoils by barge and transferring the material to train cars for transit to a disposal site. The project was abandoned after opponents claimed incorrectly that the project would expose the largely poor and minority population living near by and working in the port to dangerous PCBs. Terming prospective victims as guinea pigs and the project as environmental racism, they alarmed the public and provided ammunition for political opportunists. Meanwhile, the mayor and many leading citizens, themselves African American, charged that the real environmental injustice was the lost opportunity for the poor and minority community to revitalize its port, create economic opportunity and jobs for unskilled laborers, and restore use of the river for commerce. Already investments in Newburgh were lost to the social stigma of poverty, race, and decay. Now the environmental stigma of dredge spoils blocked a major hope for economic revitalization. [74]

Some beneficial projects survive community opposition. This appears to be the case for the Pencor-Masada waste-to-ethanol project, which my nonprofit organization has long supported but some local opponents challenged bitterly. A bold effort to recover some 95 percent of the waste stream by producing the clean fuel ethanol from organic waste components, this pioneer commercial-scale plant is being sponsored by the city of Middletown, New York. The project developed in response to Orange Environment's successful battle against county landfills and vision for a county solid waste plan based on waste cycling and recovery. For us, it is the solution. Some immediate neighbors, however, raised concerns and with the aid of the conventional waste industry threatened by the project, they spent hundreds of thousands of dollars on inflammatory advertisements, expert reports, and legal challenges. Although they succeeded in arousing some public concern, their legal efforts failed. Orange Environment now faces the challenge of reuniting the community through a Citizens Action Committee able to monitor and oversee the plant's compliance and providing reassurance through opportunities for direct public participation. [75]

Conclusion: NIMBY as a Force for Social Change

Although local environmental resistance can discourage needed innovation at times, it has, overall, played an important social editing function. Risky technologies and undesired projects have been removed from the technocratic agenda because they were socially unacceptable. NIMBY serves as a countervailing force to the technological juggernaut. [76]

Cultural Immunity:
Last Defense of the Contaminating Culture

In Chapter 1, we briefly considered the notion of "reflexive modernity" as developed by European theorists, best represented by the work of Ulrich Beck.[77] I have already presented my own corroborating view that modernity represents a culture of contamination that is responsible for toxic victimization. Beck depicts the postmodern person as living in a "risk society," in which questions of risk insinuate themselves into all facets of life—through the air we breathe, the water we drink, the food we eat, through procreation and health, and through transportation and shelter. As a result, people are continually confronted with new kinds of risk choices and trade-offs, becoming burdened with unprecedented responsibilities for determining what is safe and what hazardous in the face of inherent uncertainty. In contrast to the trust in technological systems that characterized modernity, in the risk society, aversion to risk becomes the postmodern preoccupation.

Cultural Immunity and the Refutation of the
Risk Society: Apathy as Anomaly[78]

The plight of toxic victims and ecological resisters discussed throughout this volume is a perfect example of the "immiseration" predicted by Beck in his thesis of the risk society.[79] Toxic victims and anticipatory activists (ecological resisters and NIMBYs) offer an antidote to a poisoning society through local responsibility, intracommunity organization, intercommunity networking, and technological conservatism. Their efforts are not "the problem" of modernity, as technocrats allege, but a meaningful and corrective response.

The really intractable problem of the modern era is the prevailing social denial, numbness, and complacency that permit and promote the polluting pathology. This NUMBY syndrome, and not NIMBY, is the villain in the culture of contamination. NUMBY represents a challenge to the idea that people have now entered a postmodern "risk society" marked by an obsession with environmental, technological, and other hazards caused by modernity itself. Instead, modern people are often blind not only to the problems they cause but to the consequences as well.

Thus, contrary to the risk society, evidence collected from local communities indicates that the majority—the outsiders, disbelievers, or nonvictims—continue to enjoy a cultural immunity from contamination, a perceptual blinder that allows people to stay the course of modernity. Rather than the predicted societal shift away from the expectations of modernity and toward the new reflexive consciousness of the postmodern risk society foreseen by Beck, the empirical evidence reveals that modernity continues to retain its tight grip over the daily reality of life.

Modern people are extremely resistant to the idea that they themselves are threatened by contamination. A global and abstract awareness of environmental pollution problems does not loosen this grip. Rather, as we have seen throughout this book, a personal confrontation with the contamination of place and person is required to make such abstractions real and to challenge a perception of personal immunity to ecological threat.

We can see the enduring strength of this immunity to environmental threat from the very experience of contamination. Cultural immunity to contamination is first suggested by the violent readjustment demanded of its victims. We have considered how the environmental and psychosocial turbulence of contamination is required to wrench people from the private sphere of modern everyday life. Several dimensions of this "turbulence theory" of transformation are informative for our understanding of cultural immunity.

First, modernity creates an insulating sphere through workaholism, consumerism, privacy, and isolation in the nuclear family, extreme time pressure, media seduction, the need to relax and forget, and the disconnection from community, polity, and nature. The normative lifestyle and lifescape do not recognize the possibility of contamination. Lifestyle subsumes a set of activities built around the core tenets of the lifescape: the assumptions of health, personal control, secure home, benign environment, and trustworthy social context (discussed in Chapter 3). In the course of ordinary contemporary life, most people are concerned with home, family, work, entertainment, and their immediate social circle but not environmental risk—unless a particular hazard intrudes into their lives in a visible and believable fashion.

Second, contaminated communities are hardly unknown. Quite to the contrary, the media have saturated the public with the stories of victims, making Love Canal, Woburn, Hinkley, and other examples more vernacular than esoteric. But these familiar tragedies are bounded. They happen to others, not to oneself. Repeatedly, toxic victims report previously seeing themselves as immune from such catastrophe: "This was something that could happen to someone else, but I never thought it would happen to me."

Third, in the dynamic between insiders and outsiders, those victimized have a clear position. They want the problems to be solved. Nonvictims, however, are ambivalent. While opinion polls indicate awareness, concern, and a willingness to pay the costs of prevention and cleanup, these attitudinal intentions intrude relatively little into the cocooned and compartmentalized reality of their everyday life. The frame of reality for lifestyle and lifescape is disconnected from the abstract sense of what should be. As a result, people live in a way that supports the pollution habit without even seeing the contradiction. Even a transformation in values may not translate into a new way of life. Lacking even basic ecological literacy, people may fail to link abstract environmental problems and personal culpability and vulnerability. Pollution is seen as an abstract "issue"—a problem to be solved—and not as an ambient or personal threat demanding attention and resulting from one's own actions.

Fourth, risk is suspect as a naive construct. An insurance term expropriated for rationalizing dangerous technological activities, "risk" was not traditionally a vernacular concept. Despite the alleged "risk society," risk still has not entered common everyday language precontamination. Furthermore, the term has rarely surfaced in my interviews with toxic victims, postcontamination. Instead, victims adopt an all-or-none view of environmental "threat" that does not accept tradeoffs of costs and benefits, declarations of safety due to risk assessments, compromises due to greater public goods, or any of the other machinations of risk professionals. Risk has emerged in social science jargon, research, and theory. However, the fact that conferences, professional organizations, government documents, books, and journals are devoted to *risk* suggests a professional rather than a popular adoption of the construct and its subsequent projection onto the masses.[80] Risk is the way officials and experts think. In itself it is abstract, neither personal nor ambient. The threat, not its risk, is what chills the spine.[81]

Finally, the subjects of toxic exposure believe they have been unfairly victimized; contamination is unjust, and if justice were to prevail, they would not have deserved their unfortunate fate. By extension, outsiders remain reasonably secure in their lifescape assumption of control and a just world. They see themselves as effectively immune to such disasters. Furthermore, the uncertainty experienced by victims is not what others wish to emulate.

Therefore, despite the readily available media images of contaminated communities, people are ill prepared for the prospect of becoming toxic victims. Rather, it catches them by surprise. It is only after a clear discovery, announcement or demonstration of contamination, making toxic exposure a personal issue, that we find an acceptance of exposure and a resulting sense of victimization and immiseration. Even then, some nonbelievers will deny the contamination.[82] The persistent hold of modern values suggests that the "dominant social paradigm" of the industrial society has not been replaced despite evidence of widespread belief in the ideals of a "new environmental paradigm."[83]

In conclusion, Beck's thesis that risk has crept into everyday existence is belied by my interviews with more than a thousand people in diverse community settings. Rather than orienting life around risk, people remain in an individual and economic paradigm, at least until forced out by turbulence. Contrasted against the empirical evidence, the risk society formulation overstates risk aversion. It applies within contaminated communities. Contaminated communities are risk societies. But, as prior chapters suggest, outsiders do not understand the plight of contamination victims precisely because they do not *share* this plight. Their lifescape is still rooted in modernity, not in the risk society. If the latter were true, the wider public would be empathetic and understanding toward victims; environmental stigma might be moderated. People would also not be so severely shocked when they themselves become recognized as victims of contamination.

Turbulence theory suggests that people have to be shaken out of the private sphere in which operative modernity insulates them from the environment. Even when contamination is publicly recognized as a dominant attribute of place, most individuals treat it as an abstraction, a marginal, minority, and private experience for some unfortunate few. People's concerns are with their home, family, work, entertainment, and immediate social circle—but not with risk from the environment—unless risk turbulence intrudes and catapults them into the postmodern mind-set of the risk society by removing their protective sense of immunity.

Accordingly, we can see an integral relationship between cultural immunity and *othering*—the differentiation between self and other. The fact that Americans appear not to live in a risk society, but rather the "normal" world of modernity, offers an explanation for why outsiders don't understand the experience of contamination. The insider/outsider boundary is effectively one between those shaken involuntarily from Eden by the turbulence of contamination and now grappling with immediate and personalized threat and those blithely living their normal lives, having the luxury to put off worrying about abstract and remote problems. Many impacts on victims reflect the stigmatizing or differentiating marks of contamination due to this differentness. The risk society is not a reality for the majority of people, who continue to deny the potential for their being affected by contamination and who continue to collude in the contaminating worldview.

NUMBY is a deep challenge for democracy. Can one institutionalize public involvement absent threat? Or must fear prod participation? Must cultural immunity be stripped away in order to mobilize social change to end the contaminating society? And, if it is, can people en masse cope with knowledge of the hostile ambient reality? These questions pose challenges for a social transformation to a third stage of modernity.

Sustainability as the Third Stage of Modernity

In this volume, we have focused on bounded contamination. Even without considering the whole range of adverse ecological changes introduced by the modern era, we have established the conclusion that, *by making our world increasingly uninhabitable, the contaminating society is unsustainable.* The risk society, as a second stage of modernity, is an involuntary result of this sustainability crisis that begs for the definition of a successor paradigm. Neither option—normal modern life nor toxic victimization—represents a viable future direction. Therefore, our concern in this final section is to define a third path, circumventing as best we can the toxic mine field, to reach an alternative third stage of modernity. Following numerous threads in recent thought that have informed my teaching and activism for the past decades, I term this third stage *sustainability*.[84]

I wish to posit sustainability as representing an emerging global vision for this new era. Sustainability reflects a new balancing of economic, social, and environmental spheres so as to achieve three equalities of life.

- *Contemporary human equality* involves equity of all people across the globe to live healthy and quality lives. Beyond environmental justice, inequity here reflects the ecological and social consequences of the overconsumption of the rich and the desperation of the poor.
- *Cross-generational human equality* provides equity between this and future generations such that our mode of existence does not foreclose the ability of future generations to live healthy and productive lives.
- *Interspecies equality* reflects equity in the rights of all living things and viable earth systems to thrive. From a purely anthropocentric perspective, we are dependent on these systems for our own survival.

The transition to sustainability is an inviting escape from the self-induced hazards of the modern era. The rub is that achieving sustainability means addressing issues of persistent environmental hazard that are modernity's legacy to future generations. We may delight in the wonders of pyramids that have lasted thousands of years, art works and buildings that have lasted hundreds of years, but no legacy compares to that of toxic and particularly radioactive contaminants that will connect us to the future tens if not hundreds of thousands of years hence.[85] To ignore this nasty bit of leftover reality would render sustainability as mere utopianism. Beyond addressing existing pollution, a sustainable world will have to find ways not to further magnify this burden.

Moreover, our lifestyle and lifescape mount a challenge for a transition to sustainability. We have seen that our normal ways are resistant to self-reflection and change. But even the contaminated lifescape, grasping as it does for alternatives, is focused on how to restore normalcy and get back what was lost. In short, while it is clear that contamination alerts victims to the anomalies of modern life, it may not motivate them to foment broad ecosocial change. Moreover, the lifescape changes from contamination have ambivalent implications for the transition to sustainability. Health pessimism may create a strident focus on avoiding future hazards, although it may also lead to a sense that "I've already been exposed, what do I have to lose now?" We have seen the power of defense of the home for limiting new threats, although NIMBY may also deter sustainable changes. Fear of the larger environment may motivate environmental activism or lead to a sense of hopelessness. Loss of control, likewise, may inspire empowerment or lead to complacency. And the legacy of distrust from contamination may hamper future consensus or inspire all parties toward new ways of communicating and thinking. Even given these possible limitations, this altered lifescape is probably more fertile ground for change than is the certainty of the unchallenged modern life. Secure in the paradigm, people are not open to change. However, such vested interest in the status quo are often redefined by exposure, giving old stakeholders a new stake.

The transition to Sustainability requires new innovative approaches to social learning that will institutionalize and make culturally normative the practice of both anticipatory and participatory learning, discussed earlier in this chapter. While this volume is hardly the place to explore this transition in depth, several relevant themes emerge from our review of contamination. These are the need to build proactive transitional institutions, the need to build collaborative cross-sectoral processes, and the need to integrate the existing regulatory framework with transitional and transformative planning strategies.

Turning the Corner from Reactivity to Proactivity

The goal of sustainability requires a shift from reactive to proactive empowerment. While reactive empowerment comes in the face of a threat, proactive empowerment is voluntary and desired. Reactivity is driven by crisis management and discourages optimizing approaches. And because the toxic legacy demands reaction, there is often no clear playing field for proactivity. Thus contexts for proactive empowerment generally must be deliberately created.

Empowerment has four interactive dimensions.[86] It can be *formal*, reflecting opportunities for participation allowed by institutions; *intrapersonal*, reflecting the actors' feelings of personal competence; *instrumental*, reflecting the actual ability of actors to participate and influence decisionmaking; and *substantive*, reflecting the ability to reach decisions that solve problems or result in desired outcomes. While our framework of environmental regulations in the United States has created clear niches for reactive empowerment, if only to a modest level of efficacy, the proactive landscape is largely uncharted.

NIMBY, local environmental resistance, grassroots organizations and networks, and other tools of the risk society have proven useful for deconstructing modernity. But reactive, short-term, one-issue groups are rarely transformed into proactive building blocks for new sustainable relationships. My own experience may be instructive of the potential for doing so. Orange Environment, Inc., the New York nonprofit organization I have headed for a score of years, was formed during a land use controversy and has since often engaged in local environmental resistance. As a county-scale watchdog organization, our model is somewhere between that of the traditional environmental organization and the emergent grassroots group. In fact, one of our key goals is to promote grassroots efforts in local communities. Our own battles have been carefully chosen to help move Orange County toward sustainable outcomes. Thus, in closing the two working landfills and blocking several incinerator proposals, we consciously worked toward a solid waste program based largely on waste recovery and materials cycling. Our work has directly enabled the City of Middletown to plan the aforementioned waste-to-ethanol plant that will recover more than 95 percent of the waste stream while generating clean-burning fuel.

Although most are reactive, some government regulatory programs have a proactive focus, empowering residents to monitor community hazards. For example, SARA (Superfund Authorization and Reauthorization Act) Title III deputizes the general public to indirectly regulate industries that keep hazardous materials on site. However, the process is often underutilized and local emergency preparedness committees (LEPCs) are often more absorbed in the technical demands of their roles than in public mobilization.[87] SARA also seeks to educate and empower the community for the long and complex regulatory process involved in contaminated site cleanup.[88] Efforts by the Chemical Manufacturers Association and the Good Neighbor Project go beyond such laws to create community contracts.[89] Protective oversight projects directly involve the community in ongoing dialogue about hazardous facilities through Citizen Action Committees (CACs) and parties-of-interest processes. By institutionalizing mobilization, they may reempower a contaminated community or make local resistance proactive.[90]

Take, as a case in point, the citizen action committee that Orange Environment is helping create for the Orange Recycling and Ethanol Production facility, our sixth CAC project. A voluntary effort, not mandated by permits, this CAC will only work if it achieves real ongoing citizen oversight and active involvement by the facility owner, the main regulatory agencies, other involved agencies, and the key community stakeholders. The CAC must simultaneously promote the effectiveness of the facility, its permit compliance, and its being a good neighbor. All stakeholders concerned with the consequences of the plant must be invited while preserving an atmosphere of constructive cooperation.

Such oversight processes face numerous challenges. Politics may interfere, as occurred in Orange Environment's collaborative initiative for the port of Newburgh.[91] A further challenge is to attract sufficient public participation. Orange Environment chairs the CAC mandated for the RSR battery recycling plant in the town of Wallkill. There are many potentially hazardous industries in Wallkill and this CAC addresses only one of them. Because citizen oversight takes so much time and effort, only the most motivated participants attend unless there is a problem at the plant. As a result, it is often difficult for the CAC to find local citizens to participate. Still another obstacle to CAC success is the regulatory drain they cause for understaffed agencies. While officials of the permitting agency can productively use CAC meetings to solve problems at a facility, promoting permit compliance, the time demands are a major burden for officials already required to frequent evening meetings. Were all permitted facilities to have CACs, agencies would have no way to staff them. We have overcome some of the resulting agency resistance to CACs by having an on-site monitor paid for by the facility represent the agency. One final challenge, noted earlier, is the problem for an independent watchdog organization to closely cooperate with the object of surveillance without having the resulting openness at times border on collusion.

Fortunately, the proactive landscape is not barren. The first earth summit inspired the global networking of NGOs, nongovernmental organizations that help citizens translate their local knowledge and activism into greater control over their lives, health, and environment. Resulting Agenda 21 projects are found across the world, although rarely in the United States. This shift toward proactivity reflects a global movement toward the third stage of modernity—the effort to establish an environmentally, socially, and economically sustainable society.

Building a Sustainable Consensus

Sustainability demands collaborative participation and decisionmaking around a common shared vision.[92] Such cooperation can be expected on issues where varied stakeholders hold similar interests. But can consensus occur around such conflicted issues as hazardous facility siting or other stigmatized or threatening projects?

Allow me a brief digression to consider the observation of Couch and Kroll-Smith that although community solidarity is undermined in exposure situations, it is likely to be enhanced in siting disputes.[93] You may recall that in Chapter 6, I examined the first part of this proposition, comparing my own conclusion that contamination unites victims with the perspective that exposure is corrosive and divisive. I reconciled these views by noting that both dynamics occur to varying degrees in the communities I have studied. It is likely that, at some point in time, either dynamic may predominate, at others both are simultaneously true, and, in many cases, they may have a synergistic relationship, as when social rejection by outsiders leads insiders to band closer together.

I similarly question Couch and Kroll-Smith's conclusion that siting disputes unify. As the instances shown above indicate, local environmental resistance is indeed a force for rallying people to the defense of place and community. At the same time, factions of a community often disagree over siting issues. Local governments and tax reduction advocates may weigh the potential for host community benefits, tipping fees, and prospective tax payments as a basis for considering projects rejected by others. Some may advocate paying legal fees to fight a project when others would oppose litigation. Labor unions and business groups may be attracted to promises of employment opportunities, local purchase of materials, or secondary spin-off benefits to the economy. Residents who view a proposed facility as being "far away" may react differently than those who perceive themselves to be close or somehow threatened. In short, it is simplistic to conclude that cohesion is assured by a siting dispute, just as it is wrong to assume that exposure causes conflict. Instead, both siting and exposure incidents result in simultaneous dialectics of conflict and cohesiveness—bringing the proximate affected "at-risk" community together while simultaneously splitting the community of victims from the larger community.

This dialectic of community conflict and cohesion is crucial to addressing core issues of contamination salient to sustainability. Stakeholders with very divergent positions in the battles over resource and risk equity must somehow be brought together around reformulated questions that, at least in theory, present win-win opportunities rather than conflicts. In this new dialogue, it is not sufficient for any of the many sides to say no. Rather, they must negotiate new scripts for how to move ahead. In the ideal, the creative search for such "third approaches" is optimizing. Science and engineering are mobilized in the service of sustainable solutions rather than growth and profit. Citizens shift from blocking threatening change toward facilitating sustainable change. Sustainability demands that neither technical nor local expertise prevail, but that there be a wise integration of the two.

Required is a discursive or intensive communicative approach to building community understanding and perhaps consensus.[94] For example, in the wake of the *Exxon Valdez* accident, a variety of cathartic, healing, and redirecting efforts were held for and by residents of the Alaskan city of Cordova. As Picou reports, the native village of Eyak, located in Cordova, hosted Alaskan natives from Prince William Sound in a talking circle, a traditional village sharing exercise. Held in January 1996, the two-day event included spiritual ceremonies and open discourse through which most attendees made a public statement. In this way, participants addressed relationships with the group, with Exxon, with cultural spirits, and with self. Following Couch, Picou notes that it is impossible for a contaminated community to recover; instead, it must go through a process of transformation. The talking circle helped forge a transformative direction for a harmed community, modeling a successful community effort and the importance of native culture in coping with life. Although conflict was expressed during this ceremony, it provided a path to greater harmony, support, and collaboration.[95]

Other instances of successful community decisionmaking exist. In Rushton, Washington, I witnessed a planning charette conducted by Asarco's consultants to involve local residents in developing a vision for redevelopment of the site of the closed smelter. Beyond issues involving the cleanup of the site, the charette addressed the development of Rushton's only open space.

For the port of Newburgh project, mentioned previously, I designed a "collaborative process" with colleagues on the mayor's advisory committee. All stakeholders, including the port owner, would join in creating a shared vision for the port, oversee preliminary studies of port projects, and then jointly monitor construction and operations. The process brought the diverse advisory committee together and received strong public support in its two public sessions before it was eventually blocked by politics and parochialism.

Liberating the Regulatory Framework:
Sustainability and the Need for Transformative Methodologies

Sustainability's social learning requirements demand moving beyond experiments in citizen participation and stakeholder partnerships toward a transformative methodology. For example, Alan Irwin's "citizen science" process involves self-critical, self-aware, and open discourse between scientific and local experts. Responsive to the uncertainties and limitations encountered in any local application, Irwin's approach forces mutual growth: citizens develop new competencies and scientists confront novel problems encountered only in localized contexts. Both are thus simultaneously informed through this social learning process.[96]

In developing the collaborative process for the port of Newburgh, I had the opportunity to design an approach for doing citizen science. There was need for a tool with which the collaborative stakeholder committee might forge a sustainable vision and plan for the port while also providing an environmental assessment for potentially hazardous port projects.[97]

I have long admired the National Environmental Policy Act (NEPA), passed by Congress in late 1969 and signed by President Nixon on New Year's Day 1970. More than any other single piece of legislation, NEPA marked the beginning of the environmental era. The goals of sustainability converge remarkably with the language of NEPA. The legislation proclaimed a national consensus on the responsibility of the current generation to protect the environment for generations to come. In framing a balance between social, economic, and environmental values, NEPA calls for long-term as well as short-term consideration of the consequences of our actions. Cumulative effects, not artificially isolated events, are to be studied. Alternatives are to be comparatively analyzed. Adverse effects are to be mitigated. Irreversible and irretrievable consequences and energy costs of actions are to be understood. Induced growth is to be considered, along with other types of secondary and radiating effects. Concern for health is legitimized.[98]

NEPA offered more than lofty goals, however. In what was termed its "action-forcing mechanism," NEPA introduced the environmental impact statement as a tool for anticipating potentially significant adverse effects of planned actions. This tool is an interdisciplinary form of research that draws on the sciences, social sciences, and design arts in affording decisionmakers information with which to weigh the environmental, social, and economic costs and benefits of the action in making their determination. About half of the states in the United States passed state environmental policy laws (SEPAs) that to varying degrees create more localized mandates for environmental review. New York's State Environmental Quality Review Act (SEQR) is one of the strongest SEPAs.

It was evident that a series of specific projects planned for the port of Newburgh would require SEQR review. This need raised the opportunity to design a new form of impact assessment that I termed *SPIA*, or sustainability planning and impact assessment. Employing the legal mandate of SEQR, impact assessment would be transformed from a reactive instrument to a proactive tool for sustainability planning. Involved parties and agencies would first agree to an alternative approach to meet their SEQR requirements. A dialogic planning effort would then bring together stakeholders to oversee a study exploring the need, alternatives, consequences, and cumulative effects associated with the project. "Third path" visions would be invited.

SPIA offered four advantages as a collaborative tool. First, like NEPA (or SEQR), the SPIA would take a hard look at the consequences of intended actions before they were approved, thus allowing for mitigation, choice of other alternatives, or a decision not to act. Second, unlike NEPA or SEQR, the SPIA would be undertaken by the open collaborative process, not project developers or the lead agency, which would build a consensual framework for scoping, methodology, choice of consultants, review of work, and eventual decisions. Stakeholders would become co-collaborators in the study through the collaborative process.

Third, coming early in the process, SPIA allows the characteristics and needs of the community to shape the project. The Newburgh study was to be generic in scope, providing a thorough baseline study of port conditions encompassing all the known potential changes to the port and community and framing later project-specific assessment efforts.

Finally, the SPIA would be a sustainability planning document, building on community visioning efforts and the input of various stakeholder groups. The study would examine potential scenarios for port development and use, taking into account such cumulative impact issues as the fit between port development and the residential, commercial, and waterfront areas and activities existent and desired.

The study would measure indicators of sustainability as a baseline and promote alternative projects and mitigations that would maximize sustainable outcomes for both the port and city. Equity of impacts, both positive and negative, would also be encouraged.

This first test application of SPIA never got launched due to political conflict and the controversy surrounding the intended use of the port to transship stigmatized materials. However, as an application of Citizen Science, SPIA is a promising transformative tool, combining both anticipatory and participatory learning steps for proactively addressing the legacy of past contamination while protecting the future. I am actively planning future tests of the approach.

Conclusion

The legacy of environmental contamination discussed in this volume represents a serious obstacle to the social transformation to a sustainable post-modernity. It prevents us from envisioning a fresh start toward a new era based on ecological balance and care. It is a sobering realization for the change agents amongst us. And, here, I have restricted my consideration mostly to the American version of a globally repeated pattern of local community contamination and not the issues of global climate change, stratospheric ozone holes, and other global/regional dynamics that also demand our attention. Although such unbounded threats are perceived differently, they represent a whole other dimension to our negative environmental legacy.

Against the cultural immunity that allows most to live as if business were as usual, toxic victims demonstrate the psychological trauma associated with environmental turbulence. Coping in that changed perceptual environment demands a dramatic reconfiguration of life expectations and deconstruction of Modern normalcy. It takes but one glimpse inside this Risk Society fully realized to know this is not the way we want to go. But how do we proceed differently?

First we must realize that our "solutions" to environmental problems are often rhetorical, leaving behind substantial problems, causing new problems, and leaving in place practices that caused the problems to begin with. The result is that we pass along substantial baggage for future generations. Finding the third path toward sustainability requires innovative learning, involving a shift from reactivity toward a proactive stance on the future, from mindless social maintenance to a critical self awareness, from living for today to anticipatory planning and ethics, and from antipathy to the active development of institutional mechanisms for public involvement. If the problems of contamination are not solvable, per se, at our level of social maturity, then we must create a society wise enough to grapple with them.

Toward this end, this book opens up the potential for understanding the alienation of insiders from outsiders, permitting sensitivity to the plight of victims and replacing the outsiders' "it can't possibly happen to me" with a "there but for the grace of God go I." In the end, all that separates the toxic victim from the outsider is a combination of denial, luck and time. We share the same environment at large but, for victims, threats are visible and palpable while, as outsiders, ours remain abstract and undefined. Toxic victimization is the visible edge of what is happening to all of us. We must learn to respond supportively to victims, but not because they are so dramatically different from us. Rather, we are they.

NOTES

Chapter One

1. Defoe 1960, p. 40.
2. Ibid., p. 37.
3. Markham 1994; Dalton 1973.
4. Tarr and Jacobson 1987.
5. Maltoni and Selikoff 1998.
6. Maltoni and Selikoff 1998.
7. Tarr and Jacobson 1987, pp. 324–325; the citation related to the Civil War is from Kirkwood 1876 and the quote within the quote comes from a 1905 article by Leighton, pp. 29–41.
8. See, for example, Eckholm 1982.
9. See Colborn et al. 1996.
10. Garrett 1994. See also the excellent discussion by Kroll-Smith and Floyd 1997.
11. Variations in estimates of contamination reflect the inherent difficulty of producing accurate numbers (GAO 1997). Nevertheless, the figures cited all point to a dramatic and widespread phenomenon (Freeze 2000; Faber 1998, Szasz 1994, Ottum 1983, Ridley 1987, Office of Technology Assessment 1983; Robertson 1983; Hewitt 1981; and Toth 1981).
12. Lewis 1992.
13. See, for example, Kroll-Smith and Floyd 1997.
14. Wendroff 1990.
15. www.hq.usace.army.mil/cecw/fusrap.
16. See Petterson 1988.
17. Slovic 1990.
18. See Brown 1980; Levine 1982; Fowlkes and Miller 1982; L. Gibbs 1982a; Shaw and Milbrath 1983; Tarr and Jacobson 1987; Mazur 1998.
19. New York State Department of Health 1998. In the mid-1990s, posing as a potential home buyer, I visited the Love Canal Resettlement Authority and browsed the large selection of homes available under this controversial program.
20. See, for example, Sorenson et al. 1987; Goldsteen and Schorr 1991.
21. Harr 1995. See also the superb study prepared for this litigation by Brown and Mikkelsen 1999, 1990.
22. See, for example, Miller 1984; Reko 1984.
23. This social disaster is powerfully captured by Kroll-Smith and Couch 1990.
24. See Lee Clarke's excellent *Acceptable Risk* (1989).
25. See, most importantly, Shrivastava 1987; Wilkins 1991; also Pearce and Tombs 1998; Bogard 1989; Kurzman 1987; Morehouse and Arun 1986; Appen 1986; Edelstein 1995.
26. See, for example, Marples 1988; Edelstein 1995.
27. For the most comprehensive examination of the human impacts of the *Exxon Valdez* accident, see Picou et al. 1997.
28. See, for example, Silbergeld, Gordon, and Kelly 1993.

29. EPA Superfund report on Federal Creosote. www.epa.gov/region02/superfund/site_sum/0204097c.htm.

30. Stoffel et al. 1991. Note that I address unbounded contamination in a companion volume entitled *Poisoned Places*.

31. GAO 1997.

32. Levine 1982.

33. See Couch and Kroll-Smith 1985; Barton 1969; Erikson 1976; Janis 1971.

34. Portions of this and the following section were written for my contribution to the ATSDR *Psychological Stress Handbook*, forthcoming.

35. Wilkins and Patterson 1990.

36. For a thorough review of uncertainties, particularly relating to medical uncertainty, see Vyner 1988.

37. See Freeze 2000; Shrader-Frechette 1993.

38. Kroll-Smith and Couch 1993b. Kroll-Smith and colleagues (Spring 2000) more recently have argued that we must not look just at facts of contamination or the subjective meaning attached to it but rather at a "symbolic realist" blend of both.

39. See Edelstein and Makofske 1998; Edelstein 1999.

40. See Edelstein 2000, 1993b.

41. Douglas (1991, p. 46) underscores the inappropriateness of the term "risk," observing that the word "danger" would serve as well. In politics, she notes that risk becomes a "menacing thing. . . . But it is not a thing, it is a way of thinking, and a highly artificial contrivance at that."

42. Kasperson et al. 1988.

43. Slovic et al. 1980, Beck and Frankel 1981; Roger 1975.

44. For the case of radon, see Edelstein and Makofske 1998, from which this table is taken. See also Edelstein 1991. The mirex example is drawn from my consulting report to the law firm Murray and Murray in the case *Bettis v. Nease* (Edelstein 1999). See also my forthcoming *Poisoned Places*.

45. See Edelstein and Makofske 1998.

46. See Baum et al. 1983; also Kushnir 1982; Milbrath 1984.

47. Perrow 1984. Vaughan (1989) demonstrates how NASA's decision to launch the *Challenger* shuttle was influenced by the competitive environment of the agency, its organizational characteristics, and its regulatory environment, all applicable factors in the decisionmaking of polluting industries.

48. Wynne 1980, pp. 185, 189. These ideas echo also through the works of Lewis Mumford 1964a,b.

49. See Erikson 1976. The famous 1889 Johnstown flood was also human-caused (see McCullough 1968).

50. See Edelstein and Makofske 1998.

51. Purcell, Clarke, and Renzulli 2000.

52. Edelstein 1991; Edelstein and Makofske 1998.

53. See Slovic et al. 1982, 1980.

54. See Edelstein 1988; Edelstein and Makofske 1998.

55. Edelstein 1999b; Public Health Service 1997, Tables 7–8, pp. 18, 20.

56. See Barton 1969; Miller 1964; Wallace 1957; for an alternative approach, see Finsterbusch 1987.

57. See Miller 1984; Baum et al. 1983.

58. See De Boer 1986; Miller 1984; Vyner 1988.

59. Barton 1969.

60. Baum et al. 1983.

61. See Levine 1982; Fowlkes and Miller 1982; Baum et al. 1983; Miller 1984; Couch and Kroll-Smith 1985.

62. See Barton 1969 for natural disaster; Baum et al. 1983; Edelstein 1982 for toxic disaster; and Baum 1987 for a thorough contrast of the two.

63. Baum et al. 1983.

64. Bogard 1989.

65. See, for example, Baum et al. 1983; Edelstein 1982; L. Gibbs 1982a; Levine 1982.

66. www.epa.gov/unix0008/sf/cerc.html.

67. Declassifying sites may not always remove community concerns for the sites, only the prospects for assistance. For the latest Superfund data, see M. R. Greenberg, American International Group, letter of May 1991, as cited by Mazmanian and Morell 1992; letter from Max Dodson, EPA Superfund program, Region 8, March 4, 1997.

68. As a further swing of what Freeze (2000) aptly termed "the environmental pendulum," President George W. Bush announced on February 23, 2002 that he would further reduce the number of sites remediated under Superfund and shift the source of funding from industry taxation to the general taxpayers (Seelye 2002).

69. See, for example, Mazmanian and Morell 1992.

70. See Erikson 1994 and 1991; Beck 1995; 1992, p. 27; Beck et al. 1994; and Giddens 1990.

71. Freudenburg 2000, p. 114.

72. Wynne 1996.

73. See Beck 1992, p. 27.

74. Parallel to Glaser and Strauss's (1967) "grounded theory," this work began with careful case study analysis, that, once formalized, was retested and reconceptualized, being stretched and shaped according to detailed observations from additional case material. I have found the theory of environmental turbulence, as a field research guide, to be reliably descriptive and predictive. However, every case has idiosyncratic details that make it unique in important ways. In applying the theory, it is therefore necessary to examine the context and specific case characteristics for new lessons. See also Chapter 2.

75. Edelstein 1985.

76. Shkilnyk 1985.

77. For an application of the social process model in a community contamination study, see Soliman 1996.

78. The classic exposition of quality of life was presented by Campbell 1981.

79. Lifescape fills a niche that I found no other construct to address, namely, the invisible assumptions underlying daily life. The construct draws on Lewin's concept of lifespace (Lewin 1936), and Berger and Luckmann's (1966) work on the social construction of reality. Lifescape assumptions are midrange paradigms. They are highly personal, influenced by personal experience and lifestyle. Yet they are also social norms as well, in the sense suggested by Kuhn (1962; see also Harmon 1976; Janoff-Bulman and Frieze 1983).

80. On the dominant social paradigm, see Olsen et al. 1992; Milbrath 1989, 1984; Pirages 1978; Devall and Sessions 1985; Orr 1994.

81. Pearlin et al. 1981; Monat and Lazarus 1977; Baum et al. 1981; Beck and Frankel 1981; Evans and Cohen 1987; Janis and Mann 1977; Lazarus 1964, 1966; Lumsden 1975; and Rogers 1975.

82. See Janis and Mann 1977.

83. See Sonnenfeld 1966.

84. In the first instance, from Edelstein et al. 1975; in the second, from Kroll-Smith and Couch, private communication regarding Centralia, Pennsylvania.

85. In the first instance, Fowlkes and Miller 1982, p. 82; in the second, Evans and Jacobs 1981; see also Preston et al. 1983; Wohlwill 1966.

86. Dohrenwend and Dohrenwend 1974.

87. Baum et al. 1990; Gatchel and Newberry 1991.

88. See Cutherbertson and Nigg 1987.

89. See Edelstein 2000a, 1993, 1992, 1991–1992, 1991, 1987, 1984, 1981. The theory of environmental stigma draws on the works of Goffman 1963; Ryan 1971; and Jones et al. 1984.

90. Based on the work of Janis 1971.

91. Smith et al. 1986, discussing Biegel and Berren 1985.

Chapter Two

1. See Edelstein 2000.

2. For example, Baum, Gatchel, and Schaeffer 1983; Gatchel and Newberry 1991.

3. See Edelstein 1989.

4. I usually match my qualitative work with that of a clinical psychologist doing quantitative comparisons on standardized measures. As a result, statistical and logical validity can be combined (Gibbs 1986, 1981; Hastup, forthcoming). Other collaborators have done clinical screening interviews, neuropsychological assessments, and psychiatric examinations. For other efforts at triangulation, see Kroll-Smith and

Couch 1990; Couch, Kroll-Smith, and Wilson 1997; Brown and Mikkelsen 1997; and Baum, Gatchel, and Schaeffer 1983.

5. Unless noted, all information pertaining to the Legler case study and all quotes are drawn from the original consulting report that I prepared in 1981 for the Kreindler & Kreindler law firm for use in *Ayers v. Jackson Township* (Edelstein 1981b).

6. In 1981 Legler was demographically similar to the rest of Jackson Township, whose population of 25,000 was almost entirely white, about equally divided between men and women, and heavily skewed in age toward younger residents. The modal income range in Jackson in 1970 was between $10,000 and $14,999. At that time there was an average of 3.79 people per household. In 1979 all units built were single-family dwellings (Ocean County 1981).

7. "Cancer Alley" was a term that came into general use in the New York metropolitan area in the mid-1970s. It referred to the industrial center and northern section of New Jersey, where elevated levels of cancer had been identified by the National Cancer Institute (see Greenberg 1986; Greenberg et al. 1980).

8. New Jersey Department of Public Health 1993; EPA, May 6, 2000.

9. For the idea of direct impacts, see Edelstein 1980.

10. Shusterman et al. 1991, p. 25.

11. Edelstein 1998b.

12. See, for example, Gibbs et al. 1997; Staples 1996; Evans and Jacobs 1987; Weinstein 1982; Cohen and Weinstein 1981; Glass and Singer 1972; Reim et al. 1971.

13. See Edelstein et al. 1975.

14. Edelstein 1998b.

15. See Division of Epidemiology and Disease Control 1980.

16. New Jersey Department of Health 1993; EPA CERCLIS Report for Jackson Township Landfill.

Chapter Three

1. See Fowlkes and Miller 1982.

2. Kroll-Smith and Couch 1993.

3. Because nearly all Legler adults under forty had children in the home, parental age and the presence of children were highly correlated.

4. Fowlkes and Miller 1982; Levine 1982; re denial, also see Vissing 1984; Francis 1983; Evans and Jacobs 1981.

5. Fowlkes and Miller 1982, pp. 101, 104.

6. Fowlkes and Miller 1982; Stone and Levine 1985.

7. Fowlkes and Miller 1982, p. 96; note the fit with work on social paradigms by Milbrath 1989 and Olsen et al. 1993.

8. See also Kroll-Smith and Couch (1990). Cuthbertson (1987), in her study of asbestos contamination in Globe, Arizona, differentiated between four exposure archetypes: the hazard endangered (the half of the residents believing in the threat from asbestos), the hazard disclaimers (those dismissing the threat or their vulnerability), the hazard ambivalent, and the hazard tolerant. Similarly, in *Radon's Deadly Daughters*, I distinguish between the apathetic subpublic, who either are uninformed or see exposure as irrelevant to their lives; the fearful subpublic, so scared of exposure that they deny it; the vigilant subpublic, actively on guard against exposure; the pragmatic subpublic, motivated only by economics to address exposure; and the victimized subpublic, who believe they have already been exposed and potentially harmed (Edelstein and Makofske 1998).

9. These factors were also confirmed in a series of New England studies. See Hamilton 1985a,b; Ottum and Updegraff 1984.

10. See Gibbs 1989.

11. See Weinstein 1989, 1984, 1982a.

12. Ablon 1981, p. 7.

13. Berman and Wandersman 1990.

14. See, for example, Colbern 1996; Gibbs 1995.

15. See Levine 1982.

16. Campbell 1981, p. 210; see also Dowenrind and Dowenrind 1974.

17. Arthur Frank, *At the Will of the Body: Reflections on Illness* (New York: Houghton Mifflin, 1991), p 39.

18. Creen 1984, p. 52. See also Freudenberg 1984a; Fowlkes and Miller 1982; Levine 1982.

19. Gill and Picou 1998.

20. Vyner 1988.

21. Doctors played key roles in recognizing potential environmental causes in Bloody Run in Niagara Falls (Brown 1980) and Woburn (Brown and Mikkelsen, 1990).

22. Kroll-Smith and Floyd 1997.

23. Kroll-Smith and Floyd 1997; Fowlkes and Miller 1982.

24. One rare exception was the Harvard research project in Woburn, Massachusetts, which successfully linked exposure to solvents and leukemia (DiPerna 1984).

25. Levine 1982. Mazur (1999) disputes that there was any health justification for relocation.

26. Lay or popular epidemiology (Brown 1987; Brown and Mikkelsen 1990) exemplifies local knowledge and practical epistemology (Geertz 1983; Kroll-Smith and Floyd 1997).

27. See Hallman and Wandersman 1995.

28. Wandersman et al. 1989.

29. Gill and Picou 1991.

30. Gibbs 1982, 1986.

31. See Fowlkes and Miller 1982.

32. Division of Epidemiology and Disease Control 1980, p. 11.

33. See Hatcher 1982.

34. Edelstein 1999b; Rouse et al. 1990.

35. McGee 1996.

36. Van Uexkull 1984; see also Hornborg 1996.

37. Ittelson 1970.

38. See von Uexkull 1984; also Bateson 1972; Slater 1974.

39. Koffka 1935, pp. 27–28.

40. See Wolfenstein 1957.

41. Abram 1996.

42. Kameron 1975, p. 3.

43. Edelstein 1994.

44. Kameron 1975; Marx 1964.

45. McKibben 1989.

46. These observations about Triana, Alabama, were gathered while I was consultant to the law firm of Hogan, Smith, Alspaugh, Samples & Pratt, P.C.

47. Dyer et al. 1992.

48. Picou and Gill 1996; Picou et al. 1992.

49. Dyer 1993.

50. Rodin et al. 1992; Palinkas et al. 1992, 1993a,b.

51. Jorgensen 1995, p. 7.

52. The ensuing battle against Exxon's demands for raw notes from these studies was an epic, albeit unsuccessful, defense of academic research (see Picou 1996b).

53. Jorgensen 1995, pp. 2, 93.

54. Shkilnyk 1985.

55. See Heider 1958; Kelley 1972; DeCharms 1968.

56. Gibbs 1989; Janoff-Bulman 1986; Janoff-Bulman and Frieze 1983.

57. Creen 1984, p. 53.

58. See Bruner 1995, pp. 35–37.

59. Baum et al. 1991; Davidson et al. 1986.

60. See Gibbs 1989.

61. These indicators were significantly co-correlated, as well (Fleming et al. 1990).

62. See also M. Gibbs 1986, 1982.

63. Janis 1971.

64. Wolfenstein 1957, p. 153; also Janoff-Bulman and Frieze 1983.

65. See Lerner 1980; also Peterson and Seligman 1983; Janoff-Bulman and Frieze 1983.

66. See Kulik and Mahler 1987; and Weinstein 1982. What happens in the absence of such optimism? Vaughan and Nordstrom (1989) found, in their study of farm workers, that those who felt little control over negative health effects of pesticide exposure worried less than those having a greater sense of control.

Seemingly, there was no reason to worry about something if you felt you could not affect it anyway (see also Vaughan 1993).

67. This topic was covered in Edelstein 1986. See also Hayword 1976; Goffman 1971; Fitchen 1989.

68. See also Ruesch and Kees 1956; Cooper 1971; Edelstein 1973.

69. Altman and Chemers 1980; Becker 1977.

70. Perin 1977, p. 129.

71. Rapoport 1969.

72. Altman and Chemers 1980.

73. Preston et al. 1983.

74. This example is drawn from a manuscript tentatively titled *Hazardous Hollows: Contamination of Place in the Rural Appalachians* and is based on fieldwork done in 1992.

75. See Fried 1963; Erikson 1976.

76. See also Hayword 1977.

77. Ocean County 1981.

78. See Janet Fritchen 1989.

79. See Fowlkes and Miller 1982; Levine 1982 for the former; and Reko 1984 for the later case.

80. Reko 1984, p. 41.

81. See Fried 1984, 1982.

82. Gill 1986; Gill and Picou 1991; Kroll-Smith and Couch 1990; Shkilnyk 1985. Such community research rightfully goes back to Herbert Gans's description of an ethnic community in Boston that was lost due to redevelopment (1962) and Kai Erikson's classic description of the loss of community after the Buffalo Creek flood (1976). See also Cuthbertson and Nigg 1987; Erikson 1994; Brown and Perkins 1992.

83. Reko 1984, p. 31.

84. Reko 1984, pp. 49–50.

85. This case was prepared for Michael Gordon, Esq., in 1983.

86. Levine 1982.

87. Kroll-Smith 1995.

88. See Campbell 1981.

89. Barton 1969.

90. Edelstein 1988a; Finsterbusch 1987; Goldsteen and Schorr 1991.

91. Smith et al. 1988. Two-thirds blamed government and others for failing to prevent the flooding that dispersed the dioxins throughout the community.

92. Miller 1981.

93. Throughout this discussion, for Love Canal, see Levine 1982; Fowlkes and Miller 1982; L. Gibbs 1982a; Stone and Levine 1984; Paigen 1982; and Shaw and Milbrath 1983; for Times Beach, see Reko 1984 and Miller 1984.

94. ICF 1981.

95. Miller 1984.

96. Miller 1984, p. 2.

97. See, in particular, Fowlkes and Miller 1982.

98. Miller (1984, p. 3) quoting from the *St. Louis Post-Dispatch*, November 14, 1983.

99. Miller 1984; Stone and Levine 1984.

100. Barr 1981, p. 125.

101. Harris 1984, p. 429.

102. Drotman et al. 1983.

103. Reich 1983, p. 309.

104. See Shaw and Milbrath 1983.

105. Fowlkes and Miller 1982, p. 119.

106. Miller 1984.

107. Miller 1984, p. 4.

108. Brickman et al. 1982.

109. See Thornton and Edelstein 1999.

110. Although now more substantial, Superfund technical assistance grants remain insufficient to provide enough expertise to monitor the remedial investigation process.

111. Reich 1983, p. 306.

112. Coyer and Schwerin 1981.

113. In the Washington Heights section of Wallkill, New York, government agencies suspected that a neighborhood laundry was the source of tetrachloroethylene found in residential wells for months before discovering the real polluter.

114. See Fowlkes and Miller 1982; Paigen 1982; Francis 1983.

115. Paigen 1982, pp. 31–32.

116. See Vissing 1984.

117. What Hollander (1958) called "idiosyncrasy credits."

118. Michael Edelstein, *Poisoned Places*, forthcoming.

119. Freudenburg 1991, p. 15; see also Goldsteen and Schorr 1991; Miller 1984.

120. Edelstein 1988a.

121. See Edelstein 1993a, 1991–1992, for a discussion of trust and stigma related to hazardous sites.

122. See Easterling and Kunreuther 1990b; Goldsteen and Schorr 1991.

Chapter Four

1. See M. Gibbs 1982.

2. See Stone and Levine 1985.

3. Smith et al. 1986; Gatchel et al. 1985.

4. Gatchel and Newberry 1991, p. 1976.

5. See Lazarus and Launier 1978.

6. Hatcher 1982.

7. See also Stone and Levine 1985.

8. See Botkin et al. 1979.

9. L. Gibbs 1998, 1982a; see also Levine 1982.

10. See Janoff-Bulman 1986; Janoff-Bulman and Frieze 1983.

11. Edelstein 1982.

12. Janis 1971 discusses stress and insomnia.

13. Gibbs 1982. Knowledge of later studies rests on private communication from Margaret Gibbs; see also Gibbs 1986.

14. Markovitz and Gutterman 1986; see also Gruber 1985.

15. Foulks and McLellen 1992.

16. Davidson et al. 1986.

17. Fleming at al. 1991; Fleming and Baum 1984.

18. Rehner et al. 2000.

19. Davidson et al. 1986; Baum, Cohen, and Hall 1993.

20. Bowler et al. 1990.

21. Markowitz and Gutterman 1986; see also Gibbs 1989.

22. Smith et al. 1986, 1988.

23. Gibbs 1989.

24. Gibbs 1989; Lazarus 1966.

25. Gleser et al. 1981.

26. Bachrach and Zautra 1986.

27. Stone and Levine 1984.

28. Collins et al. 1983.

29. Gibbs 1989.

30. Bowler at al., 1998, p. 80.

31. Shusterman et al. 1991; Lipscomb et al. 1991; Neutra et al. 1991.

32. Rubonis and Bickman 1991.

33. Davidson et al. 1986, p. 59.

34. Smith et al. 1986, 1988.

35. Davidson et al. 1986; Gatchel et al. 1985; Schaeffer and Baum 1984; Baum et al. 1983; Fleming et al. 1982.

36. Green et al. 1990a,b. Titchener and Kapp (1976), describing the same incident, note some of the dynamics contributing to these results: "Former feelings of self-assurance, sociability, trust in neighbors, and enjoyment of community activities disappeared." For a discussion of trauma, see Erikson 1976.

37. Lipscomb et al. 1991.

38. Gill and Picou 1991; see also Gill 1986.

39. Picou and Rosenbrook 1993.

40. Davidson et al. 1986; Gatchel and Newberry 1991.

41. Baum, O'Keefe, and Davidson 1993, 1990, pp. 1649, 1651; Fleming et al. 1982.

42. McGee 1996; see Edelstein and Wandersman 1987.

43. Lifton and Olson 1976, p. 8; see also Hallman and Wandersman 1992.

44. Rehner et al. 2000.

45. Ginzburg 1993.

46. Gibbs 1982.

47. Rehner et al. 2000.

48. Private communication; see also Gibbs 1986.

49. Tucker 2000; Kahn and Scher 2000; Rogge 1995; Hoff and McNutt 1994; Ellis et al. 1992.

50. See also Ellis et al. 1992.

51. Wilkins and Patterson 1990, 1987; Heider 1958. A provocative instance of the fundamental attribution error is the idea that contamination is caused by a specific perpetrator, called under Superfund the "potentially responsible party" or "perp." Presumed guilty, the polluter may be held accountable for millions of dollars in cleanup costs even if disposal at a waste site was legal and even mandatory. This blaming dynamic prevents a general recognition of the ways that all Americans contribute to the problem (Gerrard 1998; Freeze 2000).

52. See Edelstein 1993a, 1989a.

53. Becker 1997.

54. In Jackson, Mississippi, where heads of households hired the cheapest exterminators who then illegally sprayed parathion, spousal and self-blame were common (Rehner et al. 2000).

55. Stress due to involvement occurs for all activists. Thus Holman (1981, p. 147) suggests that "up to a point, community involvement helps a person improve his or her performance of marital roles; however, as the involvement begins to take increasing amounts of time, marital role performance declines and there is a concurrent drop in marital satisfaction."

56. At Love Canal, Stone and Levine (1985) found that coping resources, such as higher income and educational levels, helped to buffer some residents from stress impacts.

57. Kleese 1982, p. 3.

58. See also Levine 1982.

59. Freedman 1981.

60. L. Gibbs 1982a, p. 53.

61. L. Gibbs 1982b, pp. 10–11.

62. Freedman 1981, p. 624.

63. L. Gibbs 1982b, pp. 10–11.

64. Freedman 1981, p. 624. Levine (personal communication) did not confirm these suicides.

65. Stone and Levine 1985.

66. Solomon 1986; Fleming and Baum 1986; and Gottlieb 1981.

67. See Solomon 1986; Unger and Wandersman 1985.

68. See also Levine 1982.

69. See also Stone and Levine 1985.

70. See also Stone and Levine 1985.

71. See also Fowlkes and Miller 1982.

72. See also Levine 1982.

73. Barton 1969.

74. Marples 1988, p. 145; see also Edelstein 1995.

75. Becker 1997.

76. Goffman 1963.

77. Freudenburg and Jones 1991; Kroll-Smith and Couch 1993b.

78. Fowlkes and Miller 1982, p. 98.

79. Conversation with Steve Kroll-Smith and Stephen Couch, August 1984; Kroll-Smith and Couch 1990.

80. As contrasted to the "consensual adaptation" found after natural disasters (Cuthbertson and Nigg 1987).

81. Cuthbertson 1987, pp. 83, 177.

82. Edelstein 2000.

83. McGee 1996.

84. Stone and Levine 1985.

85. See Stone and Levine 1985; Fowlkes and Miller 1982.

Chapter Five

1. Levine 1982, p. 74.

2. Illich 1977.

3. Illich 1999.

4. Habermas's 1970 treatment laid the foundation for the "risk society" argument (Beck 1992). See also Irwin 1995.

5. Bateson 1972, pp. 236–237.

6. For more examples of believer/nonbeliever dynamics, see Edelstein and Makofske 1998; Kroll-Smith and Couch 1990; Fowlkes and Miller 1982, 1987.

7. Reich 1983; Coyer and Schwerin 1981.

8. See Creen 1984; Levine 1982; Paigen 1982; also Freudenberg 1984a.

9. Van Eijndhoven and Nieuwdrop 1986.

10. Residents of Washington Heights were eventually given the opportunity to join a newly formed water district at their own expense.

11. Reich 1983; see also Reich 1991.

12. See Shaw and Milbrath 1983; Fowlkes and Miller 1982; L. Gibbs 1982a; Mazur 1998; and Levine 1982.

13. See, for example, Melief 1986.

14. Based upon my consulting report, Edelstein 1992b.

15. Based on research for the law firm Riddell, Williams, Bullitt, and Walkinshaw for *Branin v. Asarco*, 1994–1995.

16. See Lewis et al. 1992.

17. Tucker 2000.

18. See Levine 1982; Mazur 1998.

19. Kramer 1997, p. 30.

20. Fiorino 1989, commenting on the work of Reich 1985.

21. See Reich 1983; Coyer and Schwerin 1981.

22. Tosteson 1995a,b.

23. Tosteson 1995b, pp. 5–6; also Tosteson 1995a.

24. Reich 1983, p. 303.

25. Reko 1984, p. 40.

26. Harris 1984, p. 428.

27. Tester 1982.

28. Levine 1982, p. 98.

29. Tosteson 1995b, p. 6.

30. Tosteson 1995b, pp. 6–7.

31. Paigen 1982.

32. Habermas 1979; see Forester 1980; Edelstein 1986–1987.

33. Mueller 1973, p. 19.

34. Edelstein and Makofske 1998, pp. 233–235, 240–245; CBA has re-emerged under President G. W. Bush.

35. Beltzer 1991, p. 2.

36. Goldstein 1989; Stevens 1991a,b; Wartenberg and Chess 1992; Center for Risk Analysis 1991; Schrader-Frechette 1991; Gutin 1991; Colborn et al. 1996; Freudenberg 1988.

37. See Edelstein and Makofske 1998, pp. 241–244.

38. I interviewed Houk during his campaign to downgrade dioxin as a risk and found the above comments an interesting contrast.

39. Heiman 1996, pp. 409–410.

40. Harris 1984.

41. Freudenberg 1984a.

42. Levine 1982, p. 165. Levine also discusses the active role in commission meetings by DOH and Governor's staff.

43. Mazur 1998.

44. Miller 1984; note this source for continuing references to Times Beach in this chapter.

45. See Fowlkes and Miller 1982.

46. Miller 1984, p. 22.

47. Dickson 1981. See also Polanyi 1944 for the history of regulation and Mumford 1964 for fundamental insights.

48. Bella et al. 1988, p. 37.

49. Bella et al. 1988, p. 38.

50. See, for example, Slovic 1993.

51. Levine 1982, p. 36.

52. See, for example, Slovic et al. 1980.

53. Flynn et al. 1993b.

54. Combs and Slovic 1979.

55. See Fiorino 1989.

56. Kaufman 1995, pp. 43, 45 respectively.

57. Mitchell 1984; Hilgartner 1985.

58. Freudenburg and Pastor 1992.

59. Freudenburg 1988, p. 44; see also Fischoff et al. 1982; Fiorino 1989.

60. NRC 1975.

61. Freudenburg 1988.

62. Recall that transportation was the only issue raised by experts in the nuclear repository study reported above. Gerrard 1998; Freeze 2000.

63. See Bruner 1996, pp. 1–13.

64. Eight cases were diagnosed among the faculty, staff, and graduate students (against less than one case to be expected from a population of this size). Additional (not fully tallied) cases occurred among undergraduates taking classes in the building.

65. Dr. Janice Hastrup, personal communication to author, November 4, 2000.

66. See Scott and Wertheimer 1962, pp. 204–205, for the statistical use of the Type I/II distinction; for applications to acceptable risk, see Edelstein 1981b; Levine 1982; Paigen 1982; and Brown and Mikkelsen 1997.

67. See Fowlkes and Miller 1982; L. Gibbs 1982a; and Levine 1982.

68. See Van Eijndhoven and Nieuwdorp 1986.

69. See Van Eijndhoven and Nieuwdorp 1986, p. 6.

70. Levine 1982, p. 66.

71. See Levine 1982; Brown 1980.

72. Drawn from an unpublished paper by Daniel Wartenberg and Theodore Goldfarb, p. 2.

73. Kim and Stone 1980.

74. Harris 1984, p. 430.

75. Ames et al. 1987. The natural versus synthetic character again proving key to risk personality.

76. Michaels 1988.

77. See, for example, Lasch et al. 1984; Marshall 1982. Also Shrader-Frechette 1985.

78. See Vyner 1984; Edelstein 1982; and Levine 1982.

79. See Shrader-Frechette 1985 for a sound deconstruction of cost-benefit analysis.

80. Susan Maret, private communication. See the Web page of the Science and Environmental Health Network; for a historical discussion, see O'Riordan and Cameron 1994. See also Rachel Environmental News.

81. O'Riordan and Cameron 1994, p. 297.

82. Miller 1984.

83. Reko 1984.

84. Levine 1982, p. 40.

85. Levine 1982, p. 168.

86. Reich 1983, p. 309.

Chapter Six

1. For an expanded version of the early part of this chapter, see Edelstein and Wandersman 1987. The final section of the chapter has also appeared as Edelstein 1984–1985.

2. See Erikson 1976; Barton 1969; Wallace 1957.

3. Edelstein 1982; L. Gibbs 1982b; Levine 1982; ICF 1981.

4. ICF 1981, p. 34.

5. Sowder 1985; Gottlieb 1981.

6. See also Baas 1986; De Boer 1986; Van Eijndhoven and Nieuwdorp 1986; Stone and Levine 1985; Freudenberg 1984b; Creen 1984; Shaw and Milbrath 1983; Edelstein 1981; L. Gibbs 1982b; Levine 1982; ICF 1981.

7. Kaminstein 1995.

8. Powell 1988.

9. Sarason 1974.

10. ICF 1981.

11. Freudenberg 1984b.

12. McStay and Dunlap 1978.

13. Brown and Ferguson 1995.

14. See ICF 1981; Shaw and Milbrath 1983; L. Gibbs 1982b; Milbrath 1984; Krause 1993, 1994.

15. Krause 1994; see also 1993. See also Di Chiro 1998.

16. Stone and Levine 1985 for Love Canal; also ICF 1981.

17. Brown and Masterson-Allen 1994; Brown and Ferguson 1995.

18. Barton 1969; see also Sowder 1985.

19. See Baas 1986; De Boer 1986; Van Eijndhoven and Nieuwdorp 1986; L. Gibbs 1985; Stone and Levine 1985; Edelstein 1981; and L. Gibbs 1982b.

20. See Schacter 1959 on the first point; Wolfenstein 1957 on disasters; and for technological disaster, M. Gibbs 1986; Sowder 1985; Baum et al. 1983.

21. See Unger and Wandersman 1985; see also Baas 1986; M. Gibbs 1986.

22. Creen 1984; see also Baas 1986.

23. Unger and Wandersman 1985, p. 141.

24. Edelstein 1981.

25. Levine 1982, pp. 185–186; also L. Gibbs 1982b, 1985.

26. Stone and Levine 1985.

27. Unger and Wandersman 1985.

28. See Fleming and Baum 1985; Freudenberg 1984a; Edelstein 1982; Levine 1982; and Slovic et al. 1980.

29. L. Gibbs 1982b; Baas 1986.

30. See Fowlkes and Miller 1982; L. Gibbs 1982a; Levine 1982.

31. Van Eijndhoven and Nieuwdorp 1986.

32. L. Gibbs 1982b.

33. Bass 1986.

34. Milbrath and Shaw 1983.

35. N. Freudenberg 1984a.

36. www.dec.state.ny.us/website/ohms/decis/alturid.htm.

37. Quotes are, respectively, Stone and Levine 1985, pp. 158, 173. See also Edelstein 1981; Levine 1982.

38. Shaw and Milbrath 1983.

39. Stone and Levine 1985.

40. Stone and Levine 1985.

41. Freudenberg 1984a; Shaw and Milbrath 1983.

42. See Quarantelli 1988 for a thorough discussion of longitudinal dynamics in emergent grassroots organizations.

43. Freudenburg 1984a.

44. De Boer 1986; ICF 1981.

45. Unger and Wandersman 1985.

46. Bennis and Slater 1968; see also Katz and Kahn 1978.

47. The Dutch process is much quicker (de Boer 1986).

48. EPA, "Superfund Cleanup Figures," December 14, 1999. For current data see www.epa.gov/super-fund/whatissf/mgmtrprt.htm.

49. Harr 1995.

50. A workshop on family stress by the Center for Health, Environment, and Justice that I attended early in 1987 used the life cycle of the community organization as a basis for projecting the type of stress toxic victims are likely to experience. Interactions of individual, family, and organizational dynamics were charted for different points in the evolution of a toxic incident in order to identify key issues for coping with each stage. Participants representing community groups from across the country then compared notes on the most effective coping strategies for organizational leaders, their families, and their groups.

51. See Botkin et al. 1979. Such groups represent an important tool for social learning.

52. See Edelstein and Wandersman 1987.

53. See Stone and Levine 1985.

54. ICF 1981.

55. Lang and Lang 1964; Barton 1969; De Boer 1986.

56. E.g., L. Gibbs 1982a,b; Levine 1982.

57. Baas 1986; Van Eijndhoven and Nieuwdorp 1986; ICF 1981.

58. Van Eijndhoven and Nieuwdorp 1986.

59. E.g., L. Gibbs 1982a; Levine 1982.

60. L. Gibbs 1982b.

61. Levine 1982. Levine took exception to this last point, suggesting that actions of the LCHA were always instrumental.

62. Kroll-Smith and Couch 1990; Couch and Kroll-Smith 1985; Kroll-Smith and Garula 1985; Kroll-Smith and Couch 1984.

63. Kroll-Smith and Couch 1984, p. 6.

64. Kroll-Smith and Couch 1984, p. 7.

65. Wicker 1979.

66. Kaufman 1995.

67. Conversely, parties engaged in a conflictive process find it harder to consider emergent shared new perspectives because their original divergent interests and views are reinforced.

68. Kaminstein 1995.

69. Mazur 1981, p. 93.

70. ICF 1981.

71. John O'Connor, private conversation with author, May 21, 1984.

72. Szasz 1994.

73. Blumer, cited by Perry et al. 1976; Freudenberg 1984b.

74. Freudenberg 1984b.

75. Mazur 1981; Molotch and Lester 1975.

76. Morrison 1983; Milbrath 1984.

77. CCHW 1985.

78. CCHW 1985, p. 1.

79. Lois Marie Gibbs, private conversation with author, May 15, 1984; updated on December 10, 1987, and periodically since. See also CCHW 1985. The Center for Health, Environment, and Justice, Inc., can be reached at P.O. Box 6806, Falls Church, VA 22040. E-mail: chej@chej.org. Web site: www.chej.org.

80. Lois Marie Gibbs, private conversation with author, December 10, 1987.

81. CCHW 1985.

82. CCHW 1986.

83. www.rachel.org.

84. Szasz 1994.

85. John O'Connor, private conversation with author, May 21, 1984; *Exposure* 1984; Moore and Head 1993.

86. Lewis et al. 1992.

87. See Novotny 1998.

88. Madeline Hoffman, private conversation with author, May 1986.

89. Di Chiro 1998.

90. Ann Rabe, private conversation with author, May 1986.

91. Adam Stern, private conversation with author, May 15, 1984.

92. See Cable and Cable 1995; Freudenberg and Seinsapir 1992.

93. Szasz 1994, p. 139.

94. Lois Marie Gibbs, private conversation with author, May 15, 1984.

95. Adam Stern, private conversation with author, May 15, 1984. See also Landy 1986; Bowman 1984; Davis 1984; Novick 1983; Hill 1984.

96. Szasz 1994; Crawford 1986.

97. Mark Reisch, "Report IB10011: Superfund Reauthorization Issues in the 106th Congress." Congressional Research Service. October 30, 2000. http://www.ncseonline.org/NLE/CRSreports/Waste/waste-28.cfm?&CFID=7927406&CFTOKEN=18237364#_1_.

98. Bruce Means, EPA, "The Mega Site Issue." June 2002. http://epa.gov/oswer/SFsub.htm

99. The Superfund Subcommittee of the National Advisory Council for Environmental Policy and Technology http://www.epa.gov/superfund/news/nacept.htm.

100. Kate Probst, "Superfund: Past and Future," Resources for the Future, report to EPA, June 2002. http://epa.gov/oswer/SFsub.htm

101. See Morrison 1983.

102. See Picou 1996; Hartsough 1989.

103. See Savitsky and Hartsough 1986; also Hartsough and Savitsky 1984.

104. Steven Phillips, private conversation with author, December 15, 1986.

105. Steven Phillips, private conversations with author, December 15, 1986, and December 10, 1987. Also *Ayers et al. v. Township of Jackson* (A–83/84), decision of the New Jersey Supreme Court, May 7, 1987. See Judge Handler's partial dissent in the above matter for a critical discussion of the court's distinction between "significant" and "reasonably probable" risk.

106. Brown and Mikkelsen 1999.

107. See Llewellyn and Freudenburg 1989; Grossman and Vaughn 1999.

108. www.masryvititoe.com/Erin.htm.

109. The Brockovich case is less informative on psychological impact, however, since this issue was not argued. However, in *Sterling v. Velsicol,* a contemporary case involving pollution of groundwater in Hardeman County, Tennessee, the plaintiffs were awarded damages for emotional distress due to increased risk of cancer and fear of future cancer, in addition to other awards. This decision was modified on appeal (Brown and Mikkelsen 1999, 1990; Llewellyn and Freudenburg 1989).

110. It is appropriate to note the emerging restrictions on expert testimony that may influence consideration of psychological impacts in toxic torts. Through the initial history of toxic torts and related litigation, expert testimony was governed by the liberal *Frye* and Rule 702 standards, which stated, respectively, that expert testimony must fall within the normative acceptance of a field appropriate to the judgment rendered and/or must advance the understanding by jurors of the issues at trial. In the 1993 Supreme Court *Daubert* ruling, the *Frye* standards were replaced by a sharpening of the Rule 702 standard. Trial judges were given enhanced responsibility as "active gatekeepers" for determining what constitutes relevant and reliable evidence. Criteria for this judgment included whether a theory or technique has been or can be subjected to testing, peer review, and publication and whether the methods are generally accepted in the discipline and supported, at least minimally, in the community. Although initial thought was that *Daubert* would help relax limits on allowed testimony, in fact, it has often been used to restrict expert input. For relatively novel arguments, such as those relating to psychosocial impact, such screens represent a series of hoops that expert witnesses are made to jump through in order to testify. (See Kroll-Smith and Jenkins 1996; see also Eggen 1994.)

111. See Thornton and Edelstein 1999.

112. U.S. District Court, Northern District of New York, 99-CV-1449, *Leland v. Moran et al.,* Justice David Hurd, April 13, 2000. Also 235 F Supp 2nd 153.

113. Jordan 1984; *People Against Nuclear Energy v. NRC 1982,* 1352; see also Marshall 1982.

114. *People Against Nuclear Energy v. NRC 1982;* see also Marshall 1982.

115. *People Against Nuclear Energy v. NRC 1982,* 1352; see also Jordan 1984; Marshall 1982.

116. See my review of these issues in Edelstein 1989a.

117. U.S. Supreme Court 1983. See also Edelstein 1989; Sorensen et al. 1987; Llewellyn and Freudenburg 1989; Hartsough 1989; Hartsough and Savitsky 1984; and Jordan 1984. Note the influence of *PANE v. NRC* on the Department of Energy's siting guidelines for the environmental review of the high-level nuclear waste repository printed in the Federal Register on December 6, 1984. The DOE wrote, in part, "The DOE recognizes that the risk of new technologies involving hazardous materials may be perceived to be greater by the general public than it is by technical experts. . . . Perceived risk, however, is not an appropriate topic for general repository-siting guidelines; it is a subjective condition that cannot be fairly com-

pared among sites. . . . Past experience with other new technologies suggests that the anxieties of the public may be alleviated as the technology is seen to be effective and its benefits become more apparent." Overall, the DOE views fear as mitigable, to be alleviated, in part, by an open review process.

118. U.S. Supreme Court 1983. See also Edelstein 1989; Jordan 1984; Sorensen et al. 1987; Llewellyn and Freudenburg 1989; Hartsough 1989; and Hartsough and Savitsky 1984.

119. Freudenberg and Jones 1991, 1162–1163.

120. Edelstein 1989a; see also Picou 1996.

121. Jorling 1990.

122. Note similarities to the DOE guideline discussed above.

123. Savitsky and Hartsough 1986; Hartsough and Savitsky 1984. Llewellyn and Freudenburg (1989, p. 205) ascribe the reluctance of agencies to consider such impacts to three factors: distaste for social science, narrow agency interests, and narrow specialized disciplinary training and practice.

124. Wilkins and Patterson 1990.

125. Nelkin 1987 offers clear examples of this practice.

126. Singer and Endreny 1993.

127. Mazur 1989.

128. Wilkins and Patterson 1990.

129. Wilkins 1986; Wilkins 1987.

130. Edelstein and Makofske 1998.

131. Slovic et al. 1980; also Molotch and Lester 1975; Mazur 1981.

132. Mazur 1989, p. 127.

133. Szasz 1994, p. 52.

134. See Mazur 1991, 1989; Molotch and Lester 1975.

135. Mazur 1991.

136. See Morrison and Dunlap 1985; *Sunday Star Ledger* (Newark, New Jersey), March 11, 1984; *Times Herald Record* (Middletown, New York), February 6, 1984; Freudenberg 1984a.

137. Szasz 1994.

138. Hamilton 1985b; Molotch and Lester 1975.

139. See Douglas and Wildavsky 1982; also Milbrath 1984.

140. See Morrison and Dunlap 1985; ICF 1981.

141. Geiser 1983, p. 3.

142. Bob Cartwright, presentation to the New Jersey Grass Roots Environmental Organization, April 18, 1984.

143. Freudenberg 1984a.

144. Krimsky and Plough 1988.

145. Sheehan and Wedeen 1993; Hofrichter 1993.

146. Milbrath 1984.

147. See Douglas and Wildavsky 1982.

148. Lois Marie Gibbs, private conversation with author, May 15, 1984.

149. Lois Marie Gibbs, private conversation with author, May 15, 1984 and presentation to the New Jersey Grass Roots Environmental Organization, April 18, 1984.

150. See Freudenberg 1984a.

151. Freudenberg 1984b, p. 261.

152. Morrison and Dunlap 1985; Cutter 1981.

153. Hurley 1995.

154. Bullard 1984; Bullard 2000, 1998, 1994.

155. Commission for Racial Justice 1987.

156. GAO 1983, pp. 1, 3. Note that the fourth landfill was run by SCA.

157. Commission for Racial Justice 1987, p. 23.

158. Ferris and Hahn-Baker 1995.

159. Krause 1994, 1993; see also Di Chiro 1998.

160. See Hyman 1996a.

161. Bullard 2000; Ferris and Hahn-Baker 1995.

162. Grossman 1994; see also Miller 1993.

163. Moore and Head 1993.

164. Cerrell Associates 1984; Heiman 1996, pp. 404–406.

165. Brown 1995.

166. These findings could be in part an artifact of the heavy concentrations of minorities in large urban areas.

167. Zimmerman 1993. Note that this finding may be confounded by length of time on the NPL. Thus earlier NPL sites are most likely to have seen action on cleanup and were less likely to be located in minority-dominated communities.

168. Yandle and Burton 1996.

169. Pollock and Vittas 1995.

170. Rogge 1996.

171. Napton and Day 1992.

172. GAO 1995.

173. Kriesel et al. 1996.

174. GAO 1995.

175. Heiman 1996.

176. Bullard 2000, pp. 115–116.

177. Wigley and Shrader-Frechette 1996.

178. Capek 1993.

179. EPA, April 1998; see also Gaylord and Bell 1995. Quote is from EPA 1998, 1.1.1.

180. EPA, June 1999, pt. 1.

181. www.greenlink.org/public/issues/justice/98i02805.html.

182. Gerrard 2001; see also Gerrard 1999.

183. See Dawson 1992; Johnston and Dawson 1994; Eichenstaedt 1994; AP 2000; Pearson 1980; and Churchill 1993.

184. Dawson 1992.

185. Ridington 1980.

186. Shkilnyk 1985; see also Erikson 1994.

187. Abraham 1985.

188. Sitarz 1994.

189. Kiefer and Benjamin (1993) point to the conflict between a local Ecuadoran organization, the Ecuadoran Amazon Campaign, and two American NGOs, Natural Resources Defense Council and Cultural Survival, over how to negotiate with Conoco oil over their drilling for oil in natural and indigenous-peopled regions.

190. See World Commission on Environment and Development 1987.

191. Johnston 1994.

192. Szasz 1994, pp. 80–81.

193. See Faber 1998.

Chapter Seven

1. With closure of the world's largest landfill, Staten Island's Freshkills, New York City's wastes have been seeking a new home. Given the reception to the Islip garbage barge, you can imagine the resistance encountered to the city's wastes.

2. Norris 1982.

3. Packard 1960.

4. Daly and Cobb 1992.

5. Akin 1977.

6. Abelson 1985; Montague 1984.

7. Bateson 1972; see also Botkin et al. 1979. Jacob's (1990) contextual approach to the Nuclear Waste Policy Act is an example of the kind of metacritique advocated by Bateson.

8. Mumford 1964a,b. Lovins 1977 and Commoner 1988 extend Mumford with discussions of "soft" versus "hard" energy and waste paths, respectively.

9. See Jacob 1990; Dunlap et al. 1993.

10. Shrader-Frechette 1993; Dunlap et al. 1993; Slovic et al. 1991. Conceptually the MRS is the opposite of a permanent repository. The MRS unit is visible, "temporary," monitored as if it were expected to leak, and local to the existing sources of high-level radioactive materials. However, as I observed with a MRS siting in Maine, this alternative hardly ends fears for safety. In fact, the dispersed but now visible hazard is likely to become a source of widespread concern.

11. Jacobs 1990, pp. 139–140.

12. Dunlap et al. 1993, p. 316.

13. Szerszynski 1999 cites Wynne to the effect that modern people have a fatalistic trust in institutions. Their statements of trust may serve as "directive declarations" reminding those in power to act responsibly because the safety of others depends on their performance. For the dependents, such expressions of trust may be the only proactive way to exercise control over the situation.

14. Maguire 1996.

15. See Freeze 2000.

16. See Milbrath 1984, 1989; Olsen et al. 1993. The wording here is from Milbrath's instrument for measuring adherence to the DSP.

17. Superficially similar resistance is also found regarding socially stigmatized facilities, including low-income housing, trailer parks, and community residences for the handicapped, incarcerated, substance abusers, ill, emotionally ill, or aged (see Edelstein 1987).

18. MacDonald 1984; Isaacs 1984; Cornwall 1984, p. 9; Hayes 1984, p. 16.

19. Anderson and Greenberg 1982; Purcell 1982.

20. Weller 1984; Timmerman 1984a,b. My experience with the Article X Power Plant Siting Process suggests another variant: The public is openly welcomed to participate so long as the hard critical meta-questions are excluded from consideration.

21. Freeze 2000; Anderson and Greenberg 1982.

22. See Ryan 1971.

23. This case is based on my field notes and a review of the hearing record and commissioner's decision from the permit hearings for a sludge spreading facility at Merion Blue Grass Sod Farms held in Wawayanda, New York, in 1979. The case is described more fully in Edelstein 1986–1987.

24. These conclusions were drawn from a content analysis of the hearing record and the commissioner's decision.

25. Based on Edelstein 1980, a report prepared for hearings before the New York State Department of Environmental Conservation on behalf of Goshen, New York.

26. Hinchey 1986.

27. A large state hospital immediately adjacent to the landfill accounted for the bulk of the population.

28. For the administrative law judge's findings of February 11, 1999, see the Web site of the New York State Department of Environmental Conservation. For Orange Environment, see www.orangeenvironment.com. For a description of OEI's parallel battle to stop the expansion of Orange County landfill, see Thornton and Edelstein 1999.

29. This case is based on Edelstein 1985, prepared for the Mississippi Department of Transportation.

30. The site was delisted when Congress abruptly abrogated the Nuclear Waste Policy Act to focus only on the Yucca Mountain Nevada site. See Jacobs 1990; Shrader-Frechette 1993.

31. This case is drawn from firsthand observation, review of DEP documents, interviews with a number of key informants, and Orange Environment's involvement in opposing the Vernon site.

32. Executive Order 56, Governor Thomas H. Kean, December 4, 1983.

33. Edelstein 1991. See the EPA Superfund reports for Montclair, Glen Ridge, and West Orange, New Jersey. Similar documentation exists for most of the sites referenced in this volume. www.epa.gov/superfund/sites/rodsites/0200997.htm.

34. See Goffman 1963.

35. Stallen and Tomas 1985.

36. Gerrard 1996 explored some of these themes.

37. Bachrach and Zautra 1985.

38. See also Cook 1983.

39. Cited in Armour 1984, p. 103; see also Lee 1984, citing Daneke.

40. Kraft and Clary 1991 found the DOE's lack of credibility to be the greatest cause of citizen opposition.

41. Timmerman 1984a.

42. Timmerman 1984b; see also Mazur 1981.

43. Slovic 1990b. Academic and government experts viewed chemicals as more dangerous than did toxicologists working for industry.

44. Slovic et al. 1980.

45. Fischhoff et al. 1982, p. 253.

46. See, for example, Gerrard 1998.

47. Wynne 1996. See also the Merion Blue Grass Sod Farm case described earlier and in Edelstein 1985–1986; Schlove 1995.

48. Irwin 1995.

49. Evans and Jacobs 1981.

50. Timmerman 1984b; 1984a, p. 38.

51. Gerrard 1998, p. 731, citing Schroeder 1993.

52. Regarding the fallacy of mitigation, see Bogard 1989; about citizen action toward mitigation, see Mazur 1981.

53. Flynn et al. 1993.

54. See Pijawka and Mushkatel 1992.

55. See Kasperson 1983.

56. Hardin 1968.

57. Seley and Wolpert 1983.

58. Seley and Wolpert 1983, p. 85.

59. Timmerman 1984a, p. 2.

60. Among the flaws: those living near factories may not work in them; even if they do, they may not be the major beneficiaries; density surrounding the facility will be high, putting more people at risk; workers and nearby residents already bear the risks associated with manufacture and should not also bear additional risks from disposal.

61. Bullard 2000.

62. GAO 1983.

63. Greenberg et al. 1984.

64. It is important to reflect on these values, given their near universality today. Communism left its own legacy of pollution problems rivaling those in the West (see Peterson 1993). Both systems embodied the commodification of nature (see Polanyi 1944).

65. Of course, there may be local opposition to a good facility (see Edelstein 2002b). And otherwise good facilities may generate adverse impacts (see Stuglia 1998).

66. A key indicator of acceptance of the not in anybody's backyard norm is that the public now supports on-site treatment of hazardous waste, particularly when a permanent solution is offered to the site's problems (Zimmerman 1989).

67. Szasz 1994.

68. Commoner 1990.

69. Szasz 1994 attributes this outcome to grassroots activism. Other factors were depression in the waste industry caused by a poor economy and the efforts of industry to avoid the costs of waste disposal by generating less waste (Gerrard 1998).

70. Szasz 1994, p. 145.

71. This war is far from over. After public opposition blocked siting of a new generation of nuclear plants, new technocratic rules imposed were intended to streamline siting and remove the public's veto. Similar dynamics have occurred with communications technologies, such as cell and microwave towers, and with power lines and nonnuclear power plants.

72. See Sandman 1990.

73. The election of 2000 embodied nuances of this dynamic when Al Gore, as the rightful heir to environmental concern, became associated with technocratic (as opposed to grassroots) environmentalism, inviting challenge from Ralph Nader, running as the Green Party candidate for president and opponent of what he has termed "toxic violence."

74. See Edelstein 1999a, 2001b.

75. See Edelstein 2001b and forthcoming 2003. Of course, as the Merion Blue Grass Sod Farm case showed, seemingly beneficial projects may cause local harms that outweigh the goods. Similarly, in a review of California recycling facilities, Rachel Struglia (1998) concludes that such facilities can cause environmental racism, victimize local communities, and harm the environment.

76. Recall the DEC commissioner's decision in the CECOS hazardous waste landfill application, quoted in Chapter 5, which acknowledged the power of community opposition by dismissing testimony on adverse psychological effects, arguing that the recognition of the legitimacy of those impacts would undermine meeting the societal need for facility siting.

77. Beck 1992, 1995; Beck, Giddens, and Lasch 1994. Although European theory relating to contamination seems largely to have focused on societal levels of social process, American empirical studies of con-

tamination cited throughout this volume tend to focus on individual, family, institutional and/or organizational, and community levels of process.

78. The discussion of cultural immunity draws heavily on Edelstein 2000.

79. Beck 1992, p. 51.

80. Edelstein 1993, pp. 60–64.

81. Jasinoff thinks that risk is becoming a more convivial concept. Like the song lines of the Aboriginal dream time, in which the song is believed to precede the actual event, she argues that risk has been redefined from a real and physical phenomenon measurable only by experts to a culturally embedded historical experience equally accessible to expert and layperson.

82. Fowlkes and Miller 1982.

83. See Olsen, Lodwick, and Dunlap 1992; Milbrath 1984.

84. See World Commission on Environment and Development 1987; Daley and Cobb 1992; Roseland 1995; Pirages 1996; Maser 1996; Schroyer 1998.

85. Details inspired by a comment by Freeze 2000.

86. Rich et al. 1995.

87. Rich et al. 1993; Hadden 1991, 1989.

88. Folk 1991.

89. Lewis 1993. See also www.enviroweb.org/gnp.

90. See Aranoff and Gunter 1992b; Rich et al. 1995.

91. See Edelstein 1999a.

92. See Susskind et al. 1999; Schneekloth and Shibley 1995.

93. Couch and Kroll-Smith 1994.

94. Eder 2000.

95. Picou 2000.

96. Irwin 1995.

97. See, for example, Edelstein 1999a, Edelstein forthcoming 2003.

98. Canter (1996) notes that around one hundred countries have adopted some form of NEPA.

BIBLIOGRAPHY

Abelson, Philip M. 1985. "Waste Management." *Science*, June 7, p. 1145.

Abram, David. 1996. *In the Spell of the Sensuous.* New York: Vintage.

Abraham, Martin. 1985. *The Lessons of Bhopal: A Community Action Resource Manual on Hazardous Technologies.* Penang, Malaysia: International Organization of Consumers Unions, September.

Adeola, F. O. 1995. "Demographic and Socioeconomic Differentials in Residential Propinquity to Hazardous Waste Sites and Environmental Illness." *Journal of the Community Development Society* 26, 1: 15–40.

———. 1994. "Environmental Hazards, Health, and Racial Inequity in Hazardous Waste Distribution." *Environment and Behavior* 26, 1: 99–126.

Agarwal, A., J. Merrifield, and R. Tandon. 1985. *No Place to Run: Local Realities and Global Issues of the Bhopal Disaster.* Knoxville, Tenn.: Highlander Research and Education Center.

Akin, William E. 1977. *Technocracy and the American Dream.* Berkeley: University of California Press.

Albrecht, S. L., G. A. Robert, and S. Amir. 1996. "The Siting of Radioactive Waste Facilities: What Are the Effects on Communities?" *Rural Sociology* 61, 4: 649–673.

Altman, Irwin, and Martin Chemers. 1980. *Culture and Environment.* Monterey, Calif.: Brooks/Cole.

American Psychological Association. 1982. Briefs of Amicus Curiae. U.S. Supreme Court, October term.

Ames, Bruce, Renae Magaw, and Lois Swirsky Gold. 1987. "Ranking Possible Carcinogenic Hazards." *Science* 236: 271–280.

Anderson, Henry. 1985. "Evolution of Environmental Epidemiologic Risk Assessment." *Environmental Health Perspectives* 62: 389–392.

Anderson, R. F., and Michael R. Greenberg. 1982. "Hazardous Waste Facility Siting: A Role for Planners." *APA Journal,* Spring, pp. 204–218.

Aranoff, Marilyn, and Valerie Gunter. 1994. "A Pound of Cure: Facilitating Participatory Processes in Technological Hazard Disputes." *Society and Natural Resources* 7: 235–252.

———. 1992a. "Defining Disaster: Local Constructions for Recovery in the Aftermath of Chemical Contamination." *Social Problems* 39: 201–221.

———. 1992b. "It's hard to Keep a Good Town Down: Local Recovery Efforts in the Aftermath of Toxic Contamination." *Industrial Crisis Quarterly* 6: 83–97.

Armour, Audrey, ed. 1984. *The Not-In-My-Backyard Syndrome.* Downsview, Ontario: York University.

Asia Pacific People's Environment Network (Appen). 1985. *The Bhopal Tragedy: One Year After.* Penang, Malaysia: Friends of the Earth.

Associated Press. 2000. "Navajo Miners Never Warned Work Could Kill Them." *The (Middletown, New York) Times Herald-Record,* August 2, p. 25.

Baas, Leo. 1986. "Impacts of Strategy and Participation of Volunteer-Organizations of Involved Inhabitants in Living-Quarters on Contaminated Soil." In Henk Becker and Alan Porter, eds., *Impact Assessment Today,* 2:835–842. Utrecht, The Netherlands: Jan van Arkel.

Bachrach, Kenneth, and Alex Zautra. 1986. "Assessing the Impact of Hazardous Waste

Facilities: Psychology, Politics, and Environmental Impact Statements." In A. H. Lebovits, A. Baum, and J. E. Singer, eds., *Advances in Environmental Psychology,* pp. 71–88. Hillsdale, N.J.: Erlbaum.

———. 1985. "Coping with a Community Stressor: The Threat of a Hazardous Waste Facility." *Journal of Health and Social Behavior* 26: 127–141.

Baker, Brian. 1988. "Perception of Hazardous Waste Disposal Facilities and Residential Real Property Values." *Impact Assessment Bulletin* 6: 47–54.

Barr, Mason, Jr. 1981. "Environmental Contamination of Human Breast Milk." *American Journal of Public Health* 71, 2: 124–126.

Barton, Alan. *Communities in Disaster.* Garden City, N.Y.: Doubleday, 1969.

Bassett, Gilbert, Jr., and Ross Hemphill. 1991. "Comments on 'Perceived Risk, Stigma, and Potential Economic Impacts of a High-Level Nuclear Waste Repository in Nevada.'" *Risk Analysis* 11, 4: 697–700.

Bateson, Gregory. 1972. *Steps to an Ecology of Mind.* New York: Ballantine.

Baum, Andrew. 1987. "Toxins, Technology, and Natural Disasters." In *Cataclysms, Crises, and Catastrophes: Psychology in Action,* pp. 9–53. Washington: American Psychological Association.

Baum, Andrew, Lorenzo Cohen, and Martica Hall. 1993. "Control and Intrusive Memories as Possible Determinants of Chronic Stress." *Psychosomatic Medicine* 55: 274–286.

Baum, Andrew, and India Fleming. 1993. "Implications of Psychological Research on Stress and Technological Accidents." *American Psychologist* 48, 6: 665–672.

Baum, Andrew, Raymond Fleming, and Jerome Singer. 1983. "Coping with Victimization by Technological Disaster." *Journal of Social Issues* 39, 2: 117–138.

Baum, Andrew, Robert Gatchel, and Marc Schaeffer. 1983. "Emotional, Behavioral, and Physiological Effects of Chronic Stress at Three Mile Island." *Journal of Consulting and Clinical Psychology* 51, 4: 565–572.

Baum, Andrew, Mary O'Keeffe, and Laura Davidson. 1990. "Acute Stressors and Chronic Response: The Case of Traumatic Stress." *Journal of Applied Social Psychology* 20, 20: 1643–1654.

Baum, Andrew, Jerome Singer, and Carlene Baum. 1981. "Stress and the Environment." *Journal of Social Issues* 37: 4–35.

Beach, Hugh. 1990. "Perceptions of Risk, Dilemmas of Policy: Nuclear Fallout in Swedish Lapland." *Social Science and Medicine* 30, 6: 729–738.

Beck, Kenneth, and Arthur Frankel. 1981. "A Conceptualization of Threat Communications and Protective Health Behavior." *Social Psychology Quarterly* 44, 3: 204–217.

Beck, Ulrich. 1995. *Ecological Enlightenment: Essays on the Politics of the Risk Society.* Atlantic Highlands, N.J.: Humanities.

———. 1992. *Risk Society: Towards a New Modernity.* Newbury Park, Calif.: Sage.

Beck, Ulrich, Anthony Giddens, and Scott Lash. 1994. *Reflexive Modernization: Politics, Tradition, and Aesthetics in the Modern Social Order.* Stanford, Calif.: Stanford University Press.

Becker, Franklin. 1977. *Housing Messages.* Stroudsburg, Pa.: Dowden, Hutchinson & Ross.

Becker, Steven. 1997. "Psychosocial Assistance after Environmental Accidents: A Policy Perspective." *Environmental Health Perspectives* 105–106: 1557–1563.

Been, Vicki. 1994. "Locally Undesirable Land Uses in Minority Neighborhoods: Disproportionate Siting or Market Dynamics." *Yale Law Journal* 103, 6: 1383–1422.

Bela, David, Charles Mosher, and Steven Calvo. 1988. "Technocracy and Trust: Nuclear Waste Controversy." *Journal of Professional Issues in Engineering,* pp. 27–39.

Bennis, Warren, and Philip Slater. 1968. *The Temporary Society.* New York: Harper & Row.

Berger, Peter, and Thomas Luckmann. 1966. *Social Construction of Reality: A Treatise on the Sociology of Knowledge.* New York: Anchor.

Berman, Steven, and Abraham Wandersman. 1990. "Fear of Cancer and Knowledge of Cancer: A Review and Proposed Relevance to Hazardous Waste Sites." *Social Science and Medicine* 31, 1: 81–90.

Bhagat, D. 1985. "A Night in Hell." In Lawrence Surendra, ed., *Bhopal: Industrial Genocide?* Hong Kong: Arena.

Biegel, A., and M. Berren. 1985. "Human-Induced Disasters." *Psychiatric Annals* 15, 3: 143–150.

Blocker, T. Jean, and Douglas L. Eckberg. 1989. "Environmental Issues as Women's Issues: General Concerns and Local Hazards." *Social Science Quarterly* 70: 586–593.

Bogard, William. 1989. *The Bhopal Tragedy: Language, Logic, and Politics in the Production of a Hazard*. Boulder: Westview.

Botkin, J. W., M. Elmandrja, and M. Malitza. 1979. *No Limits to Learning: Bridging the Human Gap*. New York: Pergamon.

Bowler, Rosemarie, Christopher Hartney, and Long Hun Ngo. 1998. "Amnestic Disturbance and PTSD in the Aftermath of a Chemical Release." *Archives of Clinical Neuropsychology* 13, 5: 455–471.

Bowler, Rosemarie, D. Mergler, G. Huel, and J. E. Cone. 1994. "Aftermath of a Chemical Spill: Psychological and Physiological Sequelae." *Neurotoxicology* 15.

Bowman, Ann. 1984. "Intergovernmental and Intersectoral Tensions in Environmental Policy Implementation: The Case of Hazardous Waste." *Policy Studies Review* 4: 230–244.

Brickman, Philip, Vita Carulli Rabinowitz, Jurgis Karuza Jr., Dan Coates, Ellen Cohn, and Louise Kidder. 1982. "Models of Helping and Coping." *American Psychologist* 37, 4: 368–384.

Brown, Barbara, and Douglas Perkins. 1992. "Disruptions of Place Attachment." In Irwin Altman and Setha Low, eds., *Place Attachment: Human Behavior and Environment: Advances in Theory and Research*, pp. 279–304. New York: Plenum.

Brown, Michael. 1980. *Laying Waste: The Poisoning of America by Toxic Chemicals*. New York: Pantheon.

Brown, Phil. 1995. "Race, Class, and Environmental Health: A Review and Systematization of the Literature." *Environmental Research*. 69: 15–30.

———. 1992. "Popular Epidemiology and Toxic Waste Contamination: Lay and Professional Ways of Knowing." *Journal of Health and Social Behavior* 33: 267–281.

———. 1987. "Popular Epidemiology: Community Response to Toxic Waste-Induced Illness in Woburn, Massachussetts." *Science, Technology, and Human Values* 12: 78–85.

Brown, Phil, and Faith Ferguson. 1995. "Making a Big Stink: Women's Work, Women's Relationships, and Toxic Waste Activists." *Gender and Society* 9: 145–172.

Brown, Phil, and Susan Masterson-Allen. 1994. "Citizen Action on Toxic Waste Contamination: A New Type of Social Movement." *Society and Natural Resources* 7: 269–286.

Brown, Phil, and Edwin Mikkelsen. 1997. *No Safe Place: Toxic Waste, Leukemia, and Community Action*. Berkley: University of California Press.

Bryant, Bunyan, ed. 1995. *Environmental Justice: Issues, Policies, and Solutions*. Washington, D.C.: Island.

Bryant, Bunyan, and Paul Mohai, eds. 1992. *Race and the Incidence of Environmental Hazards: A Time for Discourse*. Boulder: Westview.

Bullard, Robert. 2000. *Dumping in Dixie: Race, Class, and Environmental Quality*. Boulder: Westview.

———. 1996. "Environmental Justice: It's More Than Waste Facility Siting." *Social Science Quarterly* 77, 3: 493–499.

———. 1993. *Confronting Environmental Racism: Voices from the Grassroots*. Boston: South End, 1993.

———. 1984. "The Politics of Pollution: Implications for the Black Community." Paper presented at the annual meeting of the Association of Black Sociologists, San Antonio, Texas, August.

Bullard, Robert, ed. 1994. *Unequal Protection: Environmental Justice and Communities of Color*. San Francisco: Sierra Club, 1994.

Bullard, Robert D., and B. H. Wright. 1992. "The Quest for Environmental Quality: Mobilizing the African-American Community for Social Change." In R. E. Dunlap and A. G. Mertig, eds., *American Environmentalism: The U.S. Environmental Movement, 1970–1990*, pp. 39–49. New York: Taylor & Francis.

Burton, Ian, Robert Kates, and Gilbert White. 1978. *The Environment as Hazard*. New York: Oxford University Press.

Cable, Sherry, and Charles Cable. 1995. *Environmental Problems/Grassroots Solutions: The Politics of Environmental Conflict*. New York: St. Martin's.

Camacho, David, ed. 1998. *Environmental Injustices, Political Struggles: Race, Class,*

and the Environment. Durham, N.C.: Duke
University Press.

Campbell, Angus. 1981. The Sense of Well-Being
in America. New York: McGraw-Hill.

Canan, Penelope, and George Pring. 1988.
"Strategic Lawsuits Against Public
Participation." Social Problems 25:
506–519.

Capek, S. M. 1993. "The Environmental Justice
Frame: A Conceptual Discussion and an
Application." Social Problems 40: 5–24.

Carson, Rachel. 1962. Silent Spring. Boston:
Houghton Mifflin.

CCHW [Citizen's Clearinghouse for Hazardous
Wastes, Inc.]. 1986a. "The Five Year Plan of
Action." Everyone's Backyard 4, 3: 5–8.

———. 1986b. "Annual Report for 1985."
Unpublished report.

Cerrell Associates, Inc. 1984. Political Difficulties
Facing Waste-to-Energy Conversion Plant
Siting. California Waste Management
Board Technical Information Series. Los
Angeles: California Waste Management
Board.

<CHEJ.org> (Center for Health and
Environmental Justice).

Churchill, Ward. 1993. Struggle for the Land:
Indigenous Resistance to Genocide Ecocide
and Expropriation in Contemporary North
America. Monroe, Me.: Common Courage.

Clark, Lee. 1989. Acceptable Risk? Making
Decisions in a Toxic Environment. Berkeley:
University of California Press.

Cohen, Sheldon, and Neil Weinstein. 1980.
"Nonauditory Effects of Noise on
Behavior and Health." Journal of Social
Issues 17, 1: 36–70.

Colborn, Theo, Diane Dumanoski, and John
Peterson Myers. 1996. Our Stolen Future:
Are We Threatening Our Fertility,
Intelligence, and Survival? A Scientific
Detective Story. New York: Penguin
Dutton.

Collins, Daniel, Andrew Baum, and Jerome
Singer. 1983. "Coping with Chronic Stress
at Three Mile Island: Psychological and
Biochemical Evidence." Health Psychology
2, 2: 149–166.

Combs, Barbara, and Paul Slovic. 1979.
"Newspaper Coverage of Causes of
Death." Journalism Quarterly 56: 837–843,
849.

Commission for Racial Justice. 1987. "Toxic
Wastes and Race in the United States: A
National Report on the Racial and Socio-

Economic Characteristics of Communities
with Hazardous Waste Sites." Cleveland:
United Church of Christ.

Commoner, Barry. 1990. Making Peace with the
Planet. New York: Pantheon.

———. 1988. Remarks by Barry Commoner. In
Carl E. Van Horn, ed., Breaking the
Environmental Gridlock: The Report on a
National Conference, pp. 40–49. New
Brunswick, N.J.: Eagleton Institute of
Politics.

Cook, J. 1983. "Citizen Response in a
Neighborhood Under Threat." American
Journal of Community Psychology 11:
459–471.

Cooper, Clare. 1971. "The House as a Symbol of
Self." Working Paper no. 120. Berkeley:
Institute of Urban and Regional
Development, University of California.

Cornwall, George. 1984. Comments cited in
Audrey Armour, ed., The Not-In-My-
Backyard Syndrome, 8–10. Downsview,
Ontario: York University.

Couch, Stephen, and J. Stephen Kroll-Smith.
1994. "Environmental Controversies,
Interactional Resources, and Rural
Communities: Siting Versus Exposure
Disputes." Rural Sociology 59, 1: 25–44.

Couch, Stephen, and J. Stephen Kroll-Smith.
1985. "The Chronic Technical Disaster:
Toward a Social Scientific Perspective."
Social Science Quarterly 66: 564–575.

Couch, Stephen, and J. Stephen Kroll-Smith, eds.
1991. Communities at Risk: Community
Responses to Technological Hazards.
Worster: Peter Lang.

Couch, Stephen, J. Stephen Kroll-Smith, and
John P. Wilson. 1997. "Toxic
Contamination and Alienation:
Community Disorder and the Individual."
Research in Community Sociology 7:
95–115.

Couto, Richard A. 1985. "Failing Health and New
Prescriptions: Community-Based
Approaches to Environmental Risks." In C.
E. Hill, ed., Current Health Policy Issues
and Alternatives: An Applied Science
Perspective, pp. 53–70. Athens: University
of Georgia Press.

Covello, Vincent. 1988. "Testimony of Dr.
Vincent T. Covello on the Psychological
Impacts of SCRF 6." Unpublished testimo-
ny in support of the application of CECOS
International, Inc., for the proposed

Secure Chemical Residue Facility no. 6, application 90–85–0551.

Coyer, Brian Wilson, and Don Schwerin. 1981. "Bureaucratic Regulation and Farmer Protest in the Michigan PBB Contamination Case." *Rural Sociology* 46, 4: 703–723.

Crawford, Mark. 1986. "Toxic Waste, Energy Bills Clear Congress." *Science* 234: 537–538.

Creen, Ted. 1984. "The Social and Psychological Impact of Nimby Disputes. In Audrey Armour, ed., *The Not-In-My-Backyard Syndrome,*" pp. 51–60. Downsview, Ontario: York University.

Cuthbertson, Beverly. 1987. "Emotion and Technological Disaster: An Integrative Analysis." Ph.D. diss. Arizona State University.

Cuthbertson, B. J., and J. M. Nigg. 1987. "Technological Disaster and the Nontherapeutic Community: A Question of True Victimization." *Environment and Behavior* 19: 462–483.

Cutter, Susan. 1981. "Community Concern for Pollution: Social and Environmental Influences." *Environment and Behavior* 13: 105–124.

Dalton, Edward. 1973. "Combating Disease and Pollution in the City." In Donald Worster, ed., *American Environmentalism: The Formative Period, 1860–1915*, pp. 133–149. New York: Wiley.

Daly, Herman, and J. B. Cobb Jr. 1992. *For the Common Good: Redirecting the Economy Toward Community and Environment and a Sustainable Future.* Boston: Beacon.

Davidson, Laura M., and Andrew Baum. 1986. "Chronic Stress and Posttraumatic Disorders. *Journal of Consulting and Clinical Psychology* 54: 303–308.

Davidson, Laura M., India Fleming, and Andrew Baum. 1986. "Post-Traumatic Stress as a Function of Chronic Stress and Toxic Exposure." In Charles Figley, ed., *Trauma and Its Wake*, 2:57–77. New York: Brunner/Mazel.

Davidson, Laura, Linda Weiss, Mary O'Keeffe, and Andrew Baum. 1991. "Acute Stressors and Chronic Stress at Three Mile Island." *Journal of Traumatic Stress* 4, 4: 481–493.

Davis, Joseph. 1984. "Superfund Contaminated by Partisan Politics." *Congressional Quarterly* 42: 615–620.

Dawson, Susan. 1992. "Navajo Uranium Workers and the Effects of Occupational Illnesses:

A Case Study." *Human Organization* 51, 4: 389–396.

———. 1993. "Social Work Practice and Technological Disasters: The Navajo Uranium Experience." *Journal of Sociology and Social Welfare* 20, 2: 5–20.

De Boer, Joop. 1986. "Community Response to Soil Pollution: A Model of Parallel Processes." In Henk Becker and Alan Porter, eds., *Methods and Experiences of Impact Assessment*, pp. 187–200. Special issue of *Impact Assessment Bulletin* 4, 3–4.

DeCharms, R. 1968. *Personal Causation.* New York: Academic.

Defoe, Daniel. 1960. *A Journal of the Plague Year.* New York: New American Library.

Devall, Bill, and George Sessions. 1985. *Deep Ecology: Living as If Nature Mattered.* Salt Lake City: Peregrine Smith.

DiChiro, Giovanna. 1998. "Environmental Justice at the Grass Roots: Reflections on History, Gender, and Expertise." In Daniel Faber, ed., *The Struggle for Ecological Democracy: Environmental Justice Movements in the United States*, pp. 104–136. New York: Guilford.

Dickens, Charles. N.d. *Hard Times: For These Times.* New York: Books Inc.

Dickson, David. 1981. "Limiting Democracy: Technocrats and the Liberal State." *Democracy* 1, 1: 61–79.

DiPerna, Paula. 1984. "Leukemia Strikes a Small Town." *New York Times Magazine*, December 2.

DOE. 1984. Rules and Regulations. *Federal Register.* 49/236, December 6, 1984, 47747.

DOE. <www.fusrap.doe.gov/geninf/wahtis.html>

Dohrenwend, B. S., and B. P. Dohrenwend. 1974. *Stressful Life Events: Their Nature and Effects.* New York: Wiley.

Douglas, Mary. 1992. *Risk and Blame: Essays in Cultural Theory.* New York: Routledge.

Douglas, Mary, and Aaron Wildavsky. 1982. *Risk and Culture.* Berkley: University of California Press.

Drotman, D. P. 1983. "Contamination of the Food Chain by PCBs from a Broken Transformer." *American Journal of Public Health* 73: 302–313.

Dunlap, Riley, Michael Kraft, and Eugene Rosa, eds. 1993. *Public Reactions to Nuclear Waste: Citizens' Views of Repository Siting.* Durham, N.C.: Duke University Press.

Dunlap, Riley, Eugene Rosa, Rodney Baxter, and Robert Cameron Mitchell. 1993. "Local Attitudes Toward Siting a High-Level Nuclear Waste Repository at Hanford, Washington." In Riley Dunlap, Michael Kraft, and Eugene Rosa, eds., *Public Reactions to Nuclear Waste: Citizens' Views of Repository Siting*, pp. 136–174. Durham, N.C.: Duke University Press.

Dyer, Christopher L. 1993. "Tradition Loss as Secondary Disaster: Long-Term Cultural Impacts of the Exxon Valdez Oil Spill." *Sociological Spectrum* 13, 1: 65–88.

Dyer, C., D. Gill, and S. J. Picou. 1992. "Social Disruption and the Valdez Oil Spill: Alaskan Natives and a Natural Resource Community." *Sociological Spectrum* 12, 2: 105–126.

Easterling, Doug. 2001. "Fear and Loathing of Las Vegas: Will a Nuclear Waste Repository Contaminate the Imagery of Nearby Places?" In James Flynn, Paul Slovic, and Howard Kunreuther, eds., *Risk, Media, and Stigma*. London: EarthScan.

Easterling, Douglas, and Howard Kunreuther. 1990a. "The Vulnerability of the Convention Industry to the Siting of a High Level Nuclear Waste Repository." Unpublished paper at the Wharton Risk and Decision Process Center, University of Pennsylvania.

<tmr>. 1990b. Siting Strategies to Install Trust and Legitimacy: The Case of Radioactive Waste Repositories." Paper presented to the symposium on Hazardous Materials/Wastes: Social Aspects of Facility Planning and Management, Toronto, Ontario, Canada, October 2.

Eckholm, Eric. 1982. *Down to Earth*. New York: Norton.

Edelstein, Michael R. Forthcoming. *Poisoned Places*. Cambridge, Mass.: Perseus.

———. Forthcoming 2003. "Sustainable Innovation and the Siting Dilemma: Thoughts on the Stigmatization of Projects Good and Bad." *Journal of Risk Research*.

———. 2002. "Contamination: The Invisible Built Environment." In Robert Bechtel and Arza Churchman, eds., *The Handbook of Environmental Psychology*, pp. 559–588. New York: Wiley.

———. 2001a. "Crying Over Spoiled Milk: Contamination, Visibility, and Expectation in Environmental Stigma." In James Flynn,

Paul Slovic, and Howard Kunreuther, eds., *Risk, Media, and Stigma*. London: EarthScan.

———. 2001b. "Innovation and the Siting Dilemma: Thoughts on the Stigmatization of Projects, Good and Bad." Paper presented at the New Perspectives on Siting Controversy conference, Glumslov, Sweden, May 17–20.

———. 2000. "'Outsiders Just Don't Understand': Personalization of Risk and the Boundary Between Modernity and Postmodernity." In Maurie Cohen, ed., *Risk in the Modern Age: Social Theory, Science, and Environmental Decision-Making*, pp. 123–142. New York: St. Martin's.

———. 1999a. "The Challenge of Implementing Sustainable Planning in a Troubled American City." In Maria Tysiachniouk and George McCarthy, eds., *Towards a Sustainable Future: Environmental Activism in Russia and the United States: Selected Readings*, pp. 37–60. St. Petersburg, Russia: Publishing Group of the Institute of Chemistry, St. Petersburg State University.

———. 1999b. "Psychosocial Impacts Associated with the Contamination of the Middle Fork of Little Beaver Creek." Report prepared for the law firm Murray & Murray for *Bettis v. Reutgers-Nease*, January 7.

———. 1998a. "Environmental Contamination and Housing." In William Van Vliet, ed., *The Encyclopedia of Housing*. Thousand Oaks, Calif.: Sage.

———. 1998b. "Preliminary Report: Psycho-Social Impacts Associated with Tullytown Landfill for New Jersey Residents in the Florence Township Area." Report prepared for the law firm Shabel & Shabel, April 19.

———. 1995. "Disaster Revisited: Bhopal and Chernobyl–What are the Lessons?" In William J. Makofske and Eric Karlin, eds., *Technology and Global Environmental Issues*, pp. 305–336. New York: HarperCollins.

———. 1993a. "When the Honeymoon Is Over: Environmental Stigma and Distrust in the Siting of a Hazardous Waste Disposal Facility in Niagara Falls, New York." In William Freudenburg and Ted Youn, *Research in Social Problems and Public Policy*, 5:75–96. Greenwich, Conn.: JAI Press.

———. 1993b. "Public and Private Perceptions of Risk." In Thomas Burke, Nga Tran, Jane Roemer, and Carol Henry, eds., *Regulating Risk: The Sciences and Politics of Risk,* pp. 60–64. Washington, D.C.: International Life Systems Institute Press.

———. 1992a. "NIMBY as a Healthy Response to Environmental Stigma Associated with Hazardous Facility Siting." In Gary Leitch, ed., *Hazardous Material/Wastes: Social Aspects of Facility Planning and Management,* pp. 413–431. Winnipeg, Manitoba: The Institute for Social Impact Assessment.

———. 1991–1992. "Mitigating Environmental Stigma and Loss of Trust in the Siting of Hazardous Facilities." Yucca Mountain Studies Series, U.S. Department of Energy.

———. 1991. "Ecological Threats and Spoiled Identities: Radon Gas and Environmental Stigma." In Stephen Couch and J. Stephen Kroll-Smith, eds., *Communities at Risk: Community Responses to Technological Hazards,* pp. 205–226. Worster: Peter Lang.

———. 1990. "The Psychological Basis for the 'NIMBY' Response." In John Andrews et al., eds., *Proceedings of the Fourth National Environmental Health Conference: Environmental Issues—Today's Challenge for the Future,* pp. 271–278. Washington, D.C.: U.S. Department of Health and Human Services, Public Health Service.

———. 1989a. "Psychosocial Impacts on Trial: The Case of Hazardous Waste Disposal." In Dennis Peck, ed., *Psychosocial Effects of Hazardous Toxic Waste Disposal on Communities,* pp. 153–176. Springfield, Ill.: Charles Thomas.

———. 1989b. "Final Project Report to the New Jersey Department of Health: The New Jersey Ozone Notification Program Evaluation." Prepared on behalf of the Ramapo Institute for Environmental Studies. February 15.

———. 1988a. "Water, Water Everywhere, But Not a Drop to Drink: The Case of Groundwater Contamination in Jackson, N.J." In Mick Charles and John Kim, eds., *Crisis Management,* pp. 65–84. Springfield, Ill.: Charles Thomas.

———. 1988b. "The Psychosocial Impacts of the Proposed SCRF no. 6 of the CECOS Hazardous Waste Disposal Facility." Unpublished testimony and report prepared for the law firm Milbank, Tweed,

Hadley & McCloy on behalf of the Concerned Citizens Organizations before the New York State Department of Environmental Conservation hearings on the application of CECOS International, Inc., for the proposed Secure Chemical Residue Facility no. 6, application 90–85–0551.

———. 1988c. *Contaminated Communities: The Social and Psychological Impacts of Residential Toxic Exposure.* Boulder: Westview.

———. 1987. "Toward a Theory of Environmental Stigma." In Joan Harvey and Don Henning, eds., *Public Environments,* pp. 21–25. Ottawa, Canada: Environmental Design Research Association.

———. 1986–1987. "Disabling Communities: The Impact of Regulatory Proceedings." *Journal of Environmental Systems* 16, 2: 87–110.

———. 1986. "Toxic Exposure and the Inversion of Home." *Journal of Architecture and Planning Research* 3: 237–251.

———. 1985. "Psychosocial Impacts on the Community" and "Modeling Mississippi." Reports prepared for the Center for Social Impact Assessment as part of the socioeconomic impact study of the proposed Richton, Mississippi, High-Level Nuclear Waste Repository, Mississippi Department of Transportation.

———. 1984–1985. "Social Impacts and Social Change: Some Initial Thoughts on the Emergence of a Toxic Victims Movement." *Impact Assessment Bulletin* 3, 3: 7–17.

———. 1984. "Stigmatizing Aspects of Toxic Pollution." Report prepared for the law firm Martin & Snyder for *Cito v. Monsanto.*

———. 1983a. "Contaminated Children: Toxic Exposure in Jackson, New Jersey." *Childhood Quarterly.* January.

———. 1983b. "The Social Impacts of Residential Exposure to Toxic Waste." *Social Impact Assessment* 79–80, April–May.

———. 1981a. "Answer to the Editor's Question, 'What Does an Environmental Psychologist Find Interesting About Toxic Wastes'?" *Design Research News* 11, 3 (March).

———. 1981b. "The Social and Psychological Impacts of Groundwater Contamination in the Legler Section of Jackson, New

Jersey." Report prepared for the law firm Kreindler & Kreindler for *Ayers v. Jackson Township*.

———. 1980. "The Social Impacts of Al Turi Landfill, Inc." Testimony prepared for the Town of Goshen, New York, for administrative hearings before the New York State Department of Environmental Conservation.

Edelstein, Michael, Joel Kameron, Matina Colombotos, and Syrrel Lehman. 1975. "Psychological Impact of Traffic and Attendant Factors of Air Pollution, Noise, and Safety." In Richard Graham and Steven Posten, eds., *An Applied Natural Resource Inventory of the Borough of Paramus, New Jersey*. Paramus: Paramus Environmental Commission.

Edelstein, Michael R., and Deborah A. Kleese. 1995. "The Cultural Relativity of Impact Assessment: Native Hawaiian Opposition to Geothermal Energy Development." *Society and Natural Resources* 8: 19–31.

Edelstein, Michael R., and William Makofske. 1998. *Radon's Deadly Daughters: Science, Environmental Policy, and the Politics of Risk*. Lanham, Md.: Rowman & Littlefield.

Edelstein, Michael R., and Abraham Wandersman. 1987. "Community Dynamics in Coping with Toxic Exposure." In Irwin Altman and Abraham Wandersman, eds., *Neighborhood and Community Environments*, pp. 69–112. Human Behavior and the Environment, vol. 9. New York: Plenum.

Eder, Klaus. 2000. "Taming Risks Through Dialogues: The Rationality and Functionality of Discursive Institutions in Risk Society." In Maurie Cohen, ed., *Risk in the Modern Age*, pp. 225–248. London: Macmillan.

Eggen, Jean Macchiaroli. 1994. "Toxic Torts, Causation, and Scientific Evidence After *Daubert*." *University of Pittsburgh Law Review* 55: 889–955.

Eichstaedt, Peter. 1994. *If You Poison Us: Uranium and Native Americans*. Santa Fe, N.M.: Red Crane.

Ellis, Derek. 1989. *Environments at Risk: Case Histories of Impact Assessment*. New York: Springer-Verlag.

Ellis, Priscilla, Sarah Greenberg, Bianca Cody Murphy, and Jonathon Ruessow. 1992. "Environmentally Contaminated Families: Therapeutic Considerations." In Benina

Gould and Donna DeMuth, eds., *The Global Family Therapist: Integrating the Personal, Professional, and Political*, pp. 69–81. Boston: Allyn & Bacon.

EPA. 1999a. "Superfund Cleanup Figures." December 14.

EPA. 1999b. "USEPA Region 2 Draft Interim Policy on Identifying EJ Areas," June, pt. 1.

EPA. 1998. "Final Guidance for Incorporating Environmental Justice Concerns in EPA's NEPA Compliance Analysis." April 1998.

EPA. 1992. "Environmental Equity: Reducing Environmental Risk for All Communities." Washington, D.C.

EPA. <www.epa.gov/superfund/whatissf/mgmtrpt.htm>.

EPA. <www.epa.gov/superfund/sites/rod-sites/0200997.htm>.

EPA, CERCLIS. 2000. *Report for Jackson Township Landfill*. May 6.

EPA, CERCLIS. 1999. *Report for Midway Landfill*. December 14.

Erikson, Kai. 1994. *A New Species of Trouble: Explorations in Disaster, Trauma, and Community*. New York: Norton.

———. 1991. "A New Species of Trouble." In Stephen Couch and J. Stephen Kroll-Smith, eds., *Communities at Risk: Community Responses to Technological Hazards*, pp. 12–29. New York: Peter Lang.

———. 1976. *Everything in Its Path*. New York: Simon & Schuster.

Evans, Gary, and Sheldon Cohen. 1987. "Environmental Stress." In Daniel Stokols and Irwin Altman, *Handbook of Environmental Psychology*, 1:571–611. New York: Wiley.

Evans, Gary, and Stephen Jacobs. 1984. "Air Pollution and Human Behavior." *Journal of Social Issues* 37 (1981): 95–125.

Exposure. 1984. January-February.

Faber, Daniel. 1998. "The Struggle for Ecological Democracy and Environmental Justice." In *The Struggle for Ecological Democracy: Environmental Justice Movements in the United States*, pp. 1–26. New York: Guilford.

Faupel, C. E., C. Bailey, and G. Griffen. 1991. "Local Media Roles in Defining Hazardous Waste as a Social Problem: The Case of Sumter County, Alabama." *Sociological Spectrum* 11 : 293–319.

Ferris, Deeohn. 1995. "Environmentalists and Environmental Justice Policy." In Bunyan

Bryant, ed., *Environmental Justice: Issues, Policies, and Solutions*, pp. 66–75. Washington D.C.: Island.

Finsterbusch, Kurt. 1987. "Typical Scenarios in Twenty-Four Toxic Waste Contamination Episodes." Paper presented at the annual meeting of the International Association for Impact Assessment, Barbados, June.

Fiorino, Daniel. 1989a. "Environmental Risk and Democratic Process: A Critical Review." *Columbia Journal of Environmental Law* 14: 501–547.

———. 1989b. "Technical and Democratic Values in Risk Analysis." *Risk Analysis* 9, 3: 293–299.

Fischhoff, Baruch, Paul Slovic, and Sarah Lichtenstein. 1982. "Lay Foibles and Expert Fables in Judgments about Risk." *American Statistician* 36, 3: pt. 2, pp. 240–255.

Fischoff, Baruch, Ola Svenson, and Paul Slovic. 1987. "Active Responses to Environmental Hazards: Perceptions and Decision Making." In Daniel Stokols and Irwin Altman, *Handbook of Environmental Psychology*, 2:1089–1134. New York: Wiley.

Fitchen, Janet. 1989. "When Toxic Chemicals Pollute Residential Environments: The Cultural Meanings of Home and Homeownership." *Human Organization* 48, 4: 313–324.

———. 1985. "Cultural Factors Affecting Perception and Management of Environmental Risks: American Communities Facing Chemical Contamination of Their Groundwater." Paper presented to the annual meeting of the Society for Applied Anthropology, Washington, D.C., March.

Fitchen, Janet, Jenifer Heath, and June Fessenden-Raden. 1987. "Risk Perception in Community Context: A Case Study." In Brandon Johnson and Vincent Covello, eds., *The Social Construction of Risk: Essays on Risk Selection and Perception*, pp. 31–53. Boston: Reidel.

Fleming, India, and Andrew Baum. 1985. "The Role of Prevention in Technological Catastrophe." In Abraham Wandersman and Robert Hess, eds., *Beyond the Individual: Environmental Approaches and Prevention*, pp. 139–152. New York: Haworth.

———. 1984. "Stress in Residents Living Near a Toxic Waste Site." Paper presented to the Eastern Psychological Association, Baltimore, Md.

Fleming, India, Mary O'Keeffe, and Andrew Baum. 1991. "Chronic Stress and Toxic Waste: The Role of Uncertainty and Helplessness." *Journal of Applied Social Psychology* 21, 23: 1889–1907.

Fleming, Raymond, and Andrew Baum. 1986. "Social Support and Stress: The Buffering Effects of Friendship." In Valerian Derlega and Barbara Winstead, *Friendship and Social Interaction*, pp. 207–226. New York: Springer-Verlag.

Flynn, J., W. Burns, C. K. Mertz, and P. Slovic. 1992. "Trust as a Determinant of Opposition to a High-Level Radioactive Waste Repository: Analysis of a Structural Model." *Risk Analysis* 12: 417–429.

Flynn, James, and Paul Slovic. 1993. "Nuclear Wastes and Public Trust." *Forum for Applied Research and Policy* 8: 92–100.

Flynn, James, Paul Slovic, and Howard Kunreuther, eds. 2001. *Risk, Media, and Stigma*. London: EarthScan.

Flynn, James, Paul Slovic, and C. K. Mertz. 1993. "Decidedly Different: Expert and Public Views of Risks from a Radioactive Waste Repository." *Risk Analysis* 13, 6: 643–648.

Folk, Ellison. 1991. "Public Participation in the Superfund Cleanup Process." *Ecology, Law Quarterly* 18: 173–221.

Forester, J. 1980. "Critical Theory and Planning Practice." *APA Journal*, July, pp. 275–286.

Foulks, Edward, and Thomas McLellen. 1992. "Psychologic Sequelae of Chronic Toxic Waste Exposure." *Southern Medical Journal* 85, 2: 122–126.

Fowlkes, Martha, and Patricia Miller. 1987. "Chemicals and Community at Love Canal." In Brandon Johnson and Vincent Covello, eds., *The Social Construction of Risk: Essays on Risk Selection and Perception*, pp. 55–78. Boston: Reidel.

———. 1982. "Love Canal: The Social Construction of Disaster." Report to the Federal Emergency Management Agency.

Francis, Rebecca S. 1983. "Attitudes Toward Industrial Pollution, Strategies for Protecting the Environment, and Environmental-Economic Trade-Offs." *Journal of Applied Social Psychology* 13: 310–327.

Frank, Arthur. 1991. *At the Will of the Body: Reflections on Illness*. N.Y." Houghton Mifflin Company.

Freedman, Tracy. 1981. "Leftover Lives to Live." *Nation* 232, 23: 624–627.

Freudenberg, Nicholas. 1984a. "Citizen Action for Environmental Health: Report on a Survey of Community Organizations." *American Journal of Public Health* 74, 5: 444–448.

———. 1984b. *Not in Our Backyards.* New York: Monthly Review Press.

Freudenberg, Nicholas, and Carol Steinsapir. 1992. "Not in Our Backyards: The Grassroots Environmental Movement." In Riley E. Dunlap and Angela Murtig, eds., *American Environmentalists: The U.S. Environmental Movement, 1970–1990*, pp. 27–38. Philadelphia: Taylor & Francis.

Freudenburg, William. 2000. "The 'Risk Society' Reconsidered: Recreancy, the Division of Labor, and Risks to the Social Fabric." In Maurie Cohen, ed., *Risk in the Modern Age: Social Theory, Science and Environmental Decision-Making*, pp. 107–122. New York: St. Martin's.

———. 1991. "Risk and Recreancy: Weber, the Division of Labor, and the Rationality of Risk Perception." Paper presented to the American Sociological Association, Cincinnati, August 24.

———. 1988. "Perceived Risk, Real Risk: Social Science and the Art of Probabilistic Risk Assessment." *Science* 242: 44–49.

Freudenburg, W. R., and Timothy Jones. 1991. "Attitudes and Stress in the Presence of Technological Risk: A Test of the Supreme Court Hypothesis." *Social Forces* 69, 4: 1143–1168.

Freudenburg, W. R., and S. K. Pastor. 1992. "NIMBYs and LULUs: Stalking the Syndromes." *Journal of Social Issues* 48: 39–61.

———. 1991. "Public Response to Technological Risks: Toward a Sociological Perspective." *Sociological Quarterly* 33: 389–412.

Freudenburg, William R., and Ted I. K. Youn, eds. 1993. *Research in Social Problems and Public Policy.* Vol. 5. Greenwich, Conn.: JAI Press.

Fried, Marc. 1963. "Grieving for a Lost Home." In L. J. Dahl, ed., *The Urban Condition*, 151–171. New York: Basic.

Gans, Herbert. 1962. *The Urban Villagers: Group and Class in the Life of Italian-Americans.* New York: Free Press.

GAO. 1997. "Superfund: Times to Complete the Assessment and Cleanup of Hazardous Waste Sites." <www.gao.gov>.

———. 1995. "Hazardous and Nonhazardous Waste: Demographics of People Living Near Waste Facilities." <www.gao.gov>.

———. 1983. "Siting of Hazardous Waste Landfills and Their Correlation with Racial and Economic Status of Surrounding Communities." <www.gao.gov>.

Garrett, Laurie. 1994. *The Coming Plague: Newly Emerging Diseases in a World Out of Balance.* New York: Farrar, Straus, Giroux.

Gatchel, Robert J., and Benjamin Newberry. 1991. "Psychophysiological Effects of Toxic Chemical Contamination Exposure: A Community Field Study." *Journal of Applied Social Psychology* 21: 1961–1976.

Gatchel, Robert, Marc Schaeffer, and Andrew Baum. 1985. "A Psychophysiological Field Study of Stress at Three Mile Island." *Psychophysiology* 22, 2: 175–181.

Gaylord, Clarice, and Elizabeth Bell. 1995. "Environmental Justice: A National Priority." In Laura Westra and Peter Wenz, eds., *Faces of Environmental Racism: Confronting Issue of Global Justice*, pp. 29–39. Lanham, Md.: Rowman & Littlefield.

Geertz, Clifford. 1983. *Local Knowledge: Further Essays in Interpretive Anthropology.* New York: Basic.

Geiser, Ken. 1983. "The Emergence of a National Anti-Toxic Chemical Movement." *Exposure* 3 (February): 7.

Gerrard, Michael. 2001. "Environmental Justice and Local Land Use Decisionmaking." In Patricia Salkin, ed., *Trends in Land Use Law from A to Z*, pp. 125–155. Chicago: American Bar Association.

Gerrard, Michael, ed. 1999. *The Law of Environmental Justice: Theories and Procedures to Address Disproportionate Risks.* Chicago, Ill.: American Bar Association.

———. 1998. "Demons and Angels in Hazardous Waste Regulation: Are Justice, Efficiency, and Democracy Reconcilable?" *Northwestern University Law Review* 92, 2: 706–749.

———. 1996. "Territoriality, Risk Perception, and Counterproductive Legal Structures: The Case of Waste Facility Siting." Paper presented at the annual meeting of the

Society for Risk Analysis, New Orleans, December 10.

———. 1994. *Whose Backyard, Whose Risk: Fear and Fairness in Toxic and Nuclear Waste Siting*. Cambridge: MIT Press.

Gibbs, Lois Marie. 1998. *Love Canal: The Story Continues <el>* Gabriola Island, B.C., Canada: New Society.

———. 1995. *Dying from Dioxin: A Citizen's Guide to Reclaiming Our Health and Rebuilding Democracy*. Boston: South End, 1995.

———. 1985. "The Impacts of Environmental Disasters on Communities." Citizens Clearinghouse for Hazardous Wastes, reprint, 1985.

———. 1982a. *Love Canal: My Story*. Albany: State University of New York Press.

———. 1982b. "Community Response to an Emergency Situation: Psychological Destruction and the Love Canal." Paper presented at the American Psychological Association, Washington, D.C., August 24.

Gibbs, Margaret. 1989. "Factors in the Victim That Mediate Between Disaster and Psychopathology: A Review." *Journal of Traumatic Stress* 2, 4: 489–511.

———. 1986. "Psychological Dysfunction as a Consequence of Exposure to Toxics." In A. Lebovitz, A. Baum, and J. Singer, eds., *Health Consequences of Exposure to Toxins*, pp. 47–70. Hillsdale, N.J.: Erlbaum.

———. 1982. "Psychological Dysfunction in the Legler Litigation Group." Report to the law firm of Kreindler & Kreindler for *Ayers v. Jackson Township*.

Gibbs, Margaret, and Susan Belford. 1988. "Toxic Threat, Coping Style, and Symptoms of Emotional Distress." *Paper presented to the American Orthopsychiatric Association Annual Meeting, San Francisco, March*.

Gibbs, Margaret, Susan Staples, and Randolph Cornelius. 1997. "Factors Relating to Neighborhood Satisfaction Near a Small Developing Airport." Paper presented to the Environmental Design Research Association, Montreal, Canada, May.

Gill, Duane. 1986. "A Disaster Impact Assessment Model: An Empirical Study of a Technological Disaster." Ph.D. diss., Texas A&M University.

Gill, Duane A., and J. Steven Picou. 1998. "Technological Disaster and Chronic Community Stress." *Society and Natural Resources* 11: 795–815.

———. 1991. "The Social Psychological Impacts of a Technological Accident: Collective Stress and Perceived Health Risks." *Journal of Hazardous Materials* 27, 1: 77–89.

Gilroy, John Martin, ed. 1993. *Environmental Risk, Environmental Values, and Political Choices: Beyond Efficiency Trade-offs in Public Policy Analysis*. Boulder: Westview.

Ginzburg, Harold. 1993. "The Psychological Consequences of the Chernobyl Accident: Findings from the International Atomic Energy Agency Study." *Public Health Reports* 108, 2: 184–192.

Glaser, Barney, and Anselm Strauss. 1967. *The Discovery of Grounded Theory: Strategies for Qualitative Research*. Chicago: Aldine/Atherton.

Glass, D., and J. Singer. 1972. "Behavioral Aftereffects of Unpredictable and Uncontrollable Aversive Events." *American Scientist* 60: 457.

Glendinning, Chellis. 1990. *When Technology Wounds: The Human Consequences of Progress*. New York: Morrow.

Gleser, G. C., B. L. Green, and C. Winget. 1981. *Prolonged Psychological Effects of Disaster: A Study of Buffalo Creek*. New York: Academic.

Goffman, Erving. 1971. *Relations in Public*. New York: Harper & Row.

———. 1963. *Stigma: Notes on the Management of Spoiled Identities*. Englewood Cliffs, N.J.: Prentice-Hall.

Goldsteen, Raymond, and John Schorr. 1991. *Demanding Democracy After Three Mile Island*. Gainesville: University of Florida Press.

Gottlieb, B. 1981. *Social Networks and Social Support in Community Mental Health*. Beverly Hills, Calif.: Sage.

Green, Bonnie, Mary Grace, Jacob Lindy, Goldine Gleser, Anthony Leonard, and Teresa Kramer. 1990. "Buffalo Creek Survivors in the Second Decade: Comparison with Unexposed and Nonlitigant Groups." *Journal of Applied Social Psychology* 20, 13: 1033–1050.

Green, Bonnie, Jacob Lindy, Mary Grace, Goldine Gleser, Anthony Leonard, Mindy Korol, and Varolyn Winget. 1990. "Buffalo Creek Survivors in the Second Decade: Stability of Stress Symptoms." *American Journal of Orthopsychiatry* 60, 1: 43–54.

Greenberg, Michael. 1986. "Does New Jersey Cause Cancer?" *Sciences,* January-February, pp. 40–46.

Greenberg, Michael, Richard Anderson, and Kirk Rosenberger. 1984. "Social and Economic Effects of Hazardous Waste Management Sites." *Hazardous Waste* 1: 387–396.

Greenberg, Michael, Frank McKay, and Paul White. 1980. "A Time-Series Comparison of Cancer Mortality Rates in the New Jersey-New York-Philadelphia Region and the Remainder of the United States, 1950–1969." *American Journal of Epidemiology* 3, 2: 166–174.

Greenberg, Michael, Dona Schneider, and J. Martell. 1994. "Hazardous Waste Sites, Stress, and Neighborhood Quality in the USA." *Environmentalist* 14, 2: 93–105.

Greenberg, Michael, and Daniel Wartenberg. 1991. "Communicating to an Alarmed Community About Cancer Clusters: A Fifty State Study." *Journal of Community Health* 16: 71–82.

Greenlink. 1998. "Governor Foster's and Shintech's Attempts to Buy-Off Communities Backfire; Times-Picayune Poll Shows Shintech Has Credibility Problem." January. <www.greenlink.org/public/issues/justice/98i02805.html>.

Gregory, Robin, Paul Slovic, and James Flynn. 1996. "Risk Perceptions, Stigma, and Health Policy." *Health and Place* 2, 4: 213–220.

Gregory, Robin, James Flynn, and Paul Slovic. 1995. "Technological Stigma." *American Scientist* 83: 220–223.

Gricar, Barbara Gray, and Anthony Baratta. 1983. "Bridging the Information Gap at Three Mile Island: Radiation Monitoring by Citizens." *Journal of Applied Behavioral Science* 19, 1: 35–49.

Grossman, Karl. 1994. "The People of Color Environmental Summit." In Robert D. Bullard, ed., *Unequal Protection: Environmental Justice and Communities of Color,* pp. 272–279. San Francisco: Sierra Club.

Grossman, Lewis, and Robert Vaughn. 1999. *A Documentary Companion to a Civil Action.* New York: Foundation.

Gruber, Sheila. 1985. "Terrible Impact: Residents Suffer Psychologically from Living Near Toxic Site, Study Reveals." *Ann Arbor News* (Michigan), February 10, p. A17.

Guidotti, Tee, and Philip Jacobs. 1993. "The Implications of an Epidemiological Mistake: A Community's Response to a Perceived Excess Cancer Risk." *American Journal of Public Health* 83, 2: 233–239.

Gunter, Valerie, and Barbara Finlay. 1988. "Influences on Group Participation in Environmental Conflicts." *Rural Sociology* 53, 4: 498–505.

Habermas, Jürgen. 1979. *Communication and the Evolution of Society.* Boston: Beacon.

———. 1970. *Toward a Rational Society.* Boston: Beacon, 1970.

Hadden, S. G. 1991. "Public Perception of Hazardous Waste." *Risk Analysis* 11: 47–57.

Hadden, Susan. 1989. *A Citizen's Right to Know: Risk Communication and Public Policy.* Boulder: Westview.

Hallman, William. 2000. "Perceived Risk, Stigma, Sense of Community, and Residential Satisfaction in Communities Near a Hazardous Waste Landfill." Unpublished manuscript.

Hallman, William, and Abraham Wandersman. 1995. "Present Risk, Future Risk, or No Risk? Measuring and Predicting Perceptions of Health Risks of a Hazardous Waste Landfill." *Risk: Health, Safety, and Environment* 261: 261–280.

———. 1992. "Attribution of Responsibility and Individual and Collective Coping with Environmental Threats." *Journal of Social Issues* 48, 4: 101–118.

———. 1989. "Perception of Risk and Toxic Hazards." In Dennis Peck, ed., *Psychosocial Effects of Hazardous Toxic Waste Disposal on Communities,* pp. 31–56. Springfield, Ill.: Charles Thomas.

Hamilton, Lawrence. 1985a. "Concern about Toxic Wastes: Three Demographic Predictors." Paper presented to the American Sociological Association, August.

———. 1985b. "Who Cares About Pollution: Opinions in a Small-Town Crisis." *Sociological Inquiry,* 55, 2: 170–181.

Hardin, Garrett. 1968. "The Tragedy of the Commons." *Science* 162: 1243–1248.

Harmon, Willis. 1976. *An Incomplete Guide to the Future.* San Francisco: San Francisco Book Company.

Harr, Jonathan. 1995. *A Civil Action: A Real-Life Legal Thriller.* New York: Random House.

Harris, David. "Health Department: Enemy or Champion of the People?" *American*

Journal of Public Health 74 (1984): 428–430.

Hartsough, Don M. 1989. "Legal Issues and Public Policy in the Psychology of Disasters." In Richard Gist and Bernard Lubin, eds., *Psychological Aspects of Disaster*, pp. 283–307. New York: Wiley.

———. 1985. "Measurement of Psychological Effects of Disaster." In J. Laube and S. Murphy, eds., *Perspectives on Disaster Recovery*, pp. 22–61. Norwalk, Conn.: Appleton-Century-Crofts.

Hartsough, Don M., and Jeffery C. Savitsky. 1984. "Three Mile Island: Psychology and Environmental Policy at a Crossroads." *American Psychologist* 39, 10: 1113–1122.

Hatcher, Sherry Lynn. 1982. "The Psychological Experience of Nursing Mothers upon Learning of a Toxic Substance in Their Breast Milk." *Psychiatry* 45: 172–181.

Hayes, Pat. 1984. Comments in A. Armour, ed., *The Not-In-My-Backyard Syndrome*, pp. 15–17. Downsview, Ontario: York University.

Hayward, D. Geoffrey. 1977. "An Overview of Psychological Concepts of 'Home.'" Paper presented at the Environmental Design Research Association Conference, Champaign-Urbana, Illinois, April.

Hayward, Geoffrey. 1976. "Home as an Environmental and Psychological Concept." *Landscape* 20: 2–9.

Heider, Fritz. 1958. *The Psychology of Interpersonal Relations*. New York: Wiley.

Heiman, Michael. 1996a. "Race, Waste, and Class: New Perspectives on Environmental Justice." *Antipode* 28, 2: 111–121.

———. 1996b. "Waste Management and Risk Assessment: Environmental Discrimination Through Regulation." *Urban Geography* 17, 5: 400–418.

Heller, Kenneth, et al. 1984. *Psychology and Community Change: Challenges of the Future*. Homewood, Ill.: Dorsey.

Hewitt, Richard. 1981. "Toxic Waste: A Long, Winding Freight Train to Nowhere." *Times Herald Record (Middletown, N.Y.)*, June 28.

Hilgartner, Stephen. 1985. "The Political Language of Risk: Defining Occupational Health." In Dorothy Nelkin, ed., *The Language of Risk: Conflicting Perspectives on Occupational Health*, pp. 25–65. Beverly Hills, Calif.: Sage.

Hill, Gladwin. 1984. "Stringfellow Toxins May Be Headed for Tap Water Supply: Big Test Ahead for E.P.A. Superfund." *New York Times*, August 26.

Hinchey, Maurice. 1986. "Organized Crime's Involvement in the Waste Hauling Industry." Report to the New York State Assembly Environmental Conservation Committee. Albany. July 25.

Hird, John. 1994. *Superfund: The Political Economy of Environmental Risk*. Baltimore: Johns Hopkins University Press.

Hoff, M., and J. G. McNutt, eds. 1994. *The Global Environmental Crisis: Implications for Social Welfare and Social Work*. Aldershot, U.K.: Avebury.

Hofrichter, Richard. 1993. *Toxic Struggles: The Theory and Practice of Environmental Justice*. Philadelphia: New Society.

Hohenemser, C., R. W. Kates, and P. Slovic. 1983. "The Nature of Technological Hazard." *Science*, April 22, pp. 376–383.

Hollander, E. P. 1958. "Conformity, Status, and Idiosyncrasy Credit." *Psychological Review* 65: 117–127.

Holman, Thomas. 1981. "The Influence of Community Involvement on Marital Quality." *Journal of Marriage and the Family*, February, pp. 143–149.

Horlick-Jones, Tom. 1995. "Modern Disasters as Outrage and Betrayal." *International Journal of Mass Emergencies and Disasters* 13, 4: 305–315.

Horowitz, Jordan, and Michael Stefanko. 1989. "Toxic Waste: Behavioral Effects of an Environmental Stressor." *Behavioral Medicine*, Spring, pp. 23–28.

Houts, Peter. 1989. *The Three Mile Island Crisis: Psychological, Social, and Economic Impacts on the Surrounding Population*. University Park: Pennsylvania State University Press.

Hunsperger, Wayne. 2001. "The Effects of the Rocky Flats Nuclear Weapons Plant on Neighboring Property Values." In James Flynn, Paul Slovic, and Howard Kunreuther, eds., *Risk, Media, and Stigma*. London: EarthScan.

———. 1993. "Heavy Metal Pollution and Residential Property Damages." *Environmental Watch* 6, 3: 1–7.

Hurley, Andrew. 1995. *Environmental Inequalities: Class, Race, and Industrial Pollution in Gary, Indiana, 1945–1980*. Chapel Hill, N.C.: University of North Carolina Press.

Ibsen, Henrik. 1979. *An Enemy of the People.* Adapted by Arthur Miller. New York: Penguin.

ICF, Inc. 1981. "Analysis of Community Involvement in Hazardous Waste Site Problems." A report to the Office of Emergency and Remedial Response, U.S. Environmental Protection Agency, July.

Ichheiser, Gustav. 1970. *Appearances and Realities.* New York: Jossey-Bass.

Illich, Ivan. 1977. "Disabling Professions." In Ivan Illich et al., *Disabling Professions.* London: Marion Boyars.

———. 1999. *Limits to Medicine: Medical Nemesis: The Expropriation of Health.* New York: Marion Boyars.

Irwin, Alan. 1995. *Citizen Science: A Study of People, Expertise, and Sustainable Development.* New York: Routledge.

Isaacs, Colin. 1984. Comments in A. Armour, ed., *The Not-In-My-Backyard Syndrome,* p. 7. Downsview, Ontario: York University.

Ittelson, William. 1970. "Perception of the Large-Scale Environment." *Transactions of the New York Academy of Sciences* 32: 807–815.

Jacob, Gerald. 1990. *Site Unseen: The Politics of Siting a Nuclear Waste Repository.* Pittsburgh: University of Pittsburgh Press.

Janis, Irving. 1971. *Stress and Frustration.* New York: Harcourt, Brace, Jovanovich.

Janis, Irving, and Leon Mann. 1977. *Decision Making.* New York: Free Press.

Janoff-Bulman, Ronnie. 1986. "The Aftermath of Victimization: Rebuilding Shattered Assumptions." In Charles Figley, ed., *Trauma and Its Wake,* 2:15–35. New York: Brunner/Mazel.

Janoff-Bulman, Ronnie, and Irene Hanson Frieze. 1983. "A Theoretical Perspective for Understanding Reactions to Victimization." *Journal of Social Issues* 39, 2: 1–17.

Jasinoff, Sheila. 1999. "The Songlines of Risk." *Environmental Values* 8: 135–152.

Johnson, Eric, and Amos Tversky. 1983. "Affect, Generalization, and the Perception of Risk." *Journal of Personality and Social Psychology* 45, 1: 20–31.

Johnston, Barbara Rose, ed. 1994. *Who Pays the Price? The Sociocultural Context of Environmental Crisis.* Washington, D.C.: Island.

Johnston, Barbara Rose, and Susan Dawson. 1994. "Resource Use and Abuse on Native American Land: Uranium Mining in the American Southwest." In Barbara Rose Johnston, ed., *Who Pays the Price? The Sociocultural Context of Environmental Crisis,* pp. 142–153. Washington, D.C.: Island.

Jones, Edward, et al. 1984. *Social Stigma: The Psychology of Marked Relationships.* New York: Freeman.

Jordan, W. S., Jr. 1984. "Psychological Harm Done After PANE: NEPA's Requirement to Consider Psychological Damage." *Harvard Law Review* 8: 1.

Jorgensen, Joseph. 1995. "Ethnicity, Not Culture? Obfuscating Social Science in the *Exxon Valdez* Oil Spill Case." *American Indian Culture and Research Journal* 19, 4: 1–124.

Jorling, Thomas. 1990. Decision in the Matter of the Application of CECOS International, Inc., with respect to the proposed Secure Chemical Residue Facility no. 6, March 13.

Kameron, Joel. 1975. "Man–Nature Value Orientations." Ph.D. diss., City University of New York.

Kahn, Mitchell and Susan Scher. 2000. "Infusing Content on the Physical Environment into the BSW Curriculum." Paper presented at the 2000 BPD Conference, Destin, Florida, October 20.

Kahn, Peter. 1999. *The Human Relationship with Nature: Development and Culture.* Cambridge: MIT Press.

Kahneman, Daniel, Paul Slovic, and Amos Tversky. 1982. *Judgment Under Uncertainty: Heuristics and Biases.* New York: Cambridge University Press.

Kaminstein, Dana. 1995. "A Resource Mobilization Analysis of a Failed Environmental Protest." *Journal of Community Practice* 2, 2: 5–32.

Kasperson, R. E., Dominic Golding, and Seth Tuler. 1992. "Social Distrust as a Factor in Siting Hazardous Facilities and Communicating Risks." *Journal of Social Issues* 48: 161–187.

Kasperson, R. O., et al. 1988. "The Social Amplification of Risk: A Conceptual Framework." *Risk Analysis* 8: 177–187.

Kasperson, R. E., and K. D. Pijawka. 1985. "Societal Response to Hazards and Major Hazard Events: Comparing Natural and Technological Hazards." *Public Administration Review* 45: 7–18.

Kasperson, Roger, ed. 1978. *Equity Issues in Radioactive Waste Management.*

Cambridge, Mass.: Oelgeschlager, Gunn & Hain.

Katz, Daniel, and Robert Kahn. 1978. *The Social Psychology of Organizations.* 2d ed. New York: Wiley.

Kaufman, Stephen. 1995. Conflict and Conflict Resolution in Citizen Participation Program: A Case Study of the Lipari Landfill Superfund Site." *Journal of Community Practice* 2, 2 : 33–55.

Kelley, Harold. 1972. "Attribution in Social Interaction." In E. Jones et al., *Attribution: Perceiving the Causes of Behavior,* p. 197. Morristown, N.J.: General Learning.

Kiefer, Chris, and Medea Benjamin. 1993. "Solidarity with the Third World: Building an International Environmental-Justice Movement." In Richard Hofrichter, *Toxic Struggles: The Theory and Practice of Environmental Justice,* pp. 226–236. Philadelphia: New Society.

Kiel, Katherine, and Katherine McClain. 1995. "Housing Prices During Siting Decision Stages: The Case of an Incinerator from Rumor Through Operation." *Journal of Environmental Economics and Management* 28: 241–255.

Kim, Nancy, and Daniel Stone. 1980. "Organic Chemicals and Drinking Water." Report to the New York State Department of Health.

Kleese, Deborah. 1982. "Mother as a Mediator of Environmental Hazards." *Childhood City Quarterly* 9, 3: 3–7.

Koffka, Kurt. 1935. *Principles of Gestalt Psychology.* New York: Harcourt Brace.

Kohlhase, J. 1991. "The Impact of Toxic Waste Sites on Housing Values." *Journal of Urban Economics* 30: 1–26.

Kraft, M. E., and B. B. Clary. 1991. "Citizen Participation and the NIMBY Syndrome: Public Response to Radioactive Waste Disposal." *Western Political Quarterly* 44: 299–329.

Kramer, Shira. 1997. "Orange County Landfill Health Survey." Report of Ridgecom, Inc., to Orange County, New York, July 10.

Krause, Celene. 1994. "Woman of Color on the Frontline." In Robert D. Bullard, ed., *Unequal Protection: Environmental Justice and Communities of Color,* pp. 256–271. San Francisco: Sierra Club.

———. 1993. "Blue-Collar Women and Toxic-Waste Protests: The Process of Politicization." In R. Hofrichter, ed., *Toxic Struggles: The Theory and Practice of*

Environmental Justice, pp. 107–117. Gabriola Island, B.C., Canada: New Society.

Krawetz, Natalia. 1979. "Hazardous Waste Management: A Review of Social Concerns and Aspects of Public Involvement." Staff Report 4, Alberta Environment, November.

Kriesel, W., J. C. Terrance, and A. G. Keeler. 1996. "Neighborhood Exposure to Toxic Releases: Are There Racial Inequities?" *Growth and Change* 27, 4: 479–499.

Krimsky, Sheldon, and Alonzo Plough. 1988. *Environmental Hazards: Communicating Risks as a Social Process.* New York: Auburn House.

Kristof, Nicholas. 1997. "Asian Pollution Is Widening Its Deadly Reach." *New York Times,* November 29, pp. A1, A7.

Kroll-Smith, J. Stephen. 1995. "Toxic Contamination and the Loss of Civility." *Sociological Spectrum* 15: 377–396.

Kroll-Smith, J. Stephen, and Stephen Couch. 1993a. "Technological Hazards: Social Responses as Traumatic Stressors." In J. P. Wilson and B. Raphael, eds., *International Handbook of Traumatic Stress,* pp. 79–91. New York: Plenum.

Kroll-Smith, J. Stephen, and Stephen Couch. 1993b. "Symbols, Ecology, and Contamination: Case Studies in the Ecological-Symbolic Approach to Disaster." *Research in Social Problems and Public Policy* 5: 47–73.

Kroll-Smith, J. Stephen, and Stephen Couch. 1990. *The Real Disaster Is Above Ground: A Mine Fire and Social Conflict.* Lexington: University of Kentucky Press, 1990.

Kroll-Smith, J. Stephen, and Stephen Couch. 1984. "Fear and Suspicion in Centralia: Doing Fieldwork in a Community in Crisis." Paper presented at the Society for the Study of Social Problems Conference, San Antonio, Texas, August.

Kroll-Smith, J., Stephen R. Couch and Adeline G. Levine. 2002. "Technological Hazards and Disasters." In Riley E. Dunlap and William Michelson, eds., *Handbook of Environmental Sociology.* Westport, Conn.: Greenwood.

Kroll-Smith, J. Stephen, and H. Hugh Floyd. 1997. *Bodies in Protest: Environmental Illness and the Struggle over Medical Knowledge.* New York: New York University Press.

Kroll-Smith, J. Stephen, and Samuel Garula Jr. 1985. "The Real Disaster Is Above Ground: Community Conflict and Grass Roots Organization in Centralia." *Small Town* 15: 4–11.

Kroll-Smith, J. Stephen, and Valerie Gunter. 1998. "Legislators, Interpreters, and Disasters: The Importance of How as Well as What Is Disaster?" In E. L. Quarantelli, ed., *Explorations in Disaster Theory*, pp. 160–175. London: Routledge.

Kroll-Smith, J. Stephen, Valerie Gunter, and Shirley Laska. 2000. "The Symbolic, the Physical, and Sociology Analytic Stances and Theorizing Environments." *American Sociologist*, Spring.

Kroll-Smith, J. Stephen, and Pamela Jenkins. 1996. "Old Stories, New Audiences: Sociological Knowledge in Courts." In Pamela Jenkins and J. Stephen Kroll-Smith, *Witnessing for Sociology: Sociologists in Court*, pp. 1–18. Westport, Conn.: Praeger.

Kroll-Smith, J. Stephen, and A. E. Ladd. 1993 "Environmental Illness and Biomedicine: Anomalies, Exemplars, and the Politics of the Body." *Sociological Spectrum* 13, 1: 7–33.

Kuhn, Thomas. 1962. *The Structure of Scientific Revolutions*. Chicago: University of Chicago Press.

Kulik, James, and Heike Mahler. 1987. "Health Status, Perceptions of Risk, and Prevention Interest for Health and Nonhealth Problems." *Health Psychology* 6, 1: 15–27.

Kunreuther, H., D. Easterling, W. Desvousges, and P. Slovic. 1990. "Public Attitudes Toward Siting a High-Level Nuclear Waste Repository in Nevada." *Risk Analysis* 10: 469–484.

Kunreuther, H., W. Desvousges, and P. Slovic. 1988. "Nevada's Predicament: Public Perceptions of Risk from the Proposed Nuclear Waste Repository." *Environment* 30: 17–33.

Kurzman, Dan. 1987. *A Killing Wind: Inside Union Carbide and the Bhopal Catastrophe*. New York: McGraw-Hill.

Kushnir, Talma. 1982. "Skylab Effects: Psychological Reactions to a Human-Made Environmental Hazard." *Environment and Behavior* 14, 1: 84–93.

Landy, Mark. 1986. "Cleaning Up Superfund." *Public Interest* 85: 58–71.

Lang, Kurt, and G. E. Lang. 1964. "Collective Responses to the Threats of Disaster." In G. H. Grosser, H. Wechsler, and M. Greenblatt, eds., *The Threat of Impending Disaster*, pp. 58–75. Cambridge: MIT Press.

Lasch, Jonathan, et al. 1984. *A Season of Spoils: The Story of the Reagan Administration's Attack on the Environment*. New York: Pantheon.

Lash, Scott, Bronislaw Szerszynski, and Briane Wynne. 1996. *Risk, Environment, and Modernity*. Thousand Oaks, Calif.: Sage.

Lazarus, Richard. 1966a. *Psychological Stress*. New York: McGraw-Hill.

———. 1966b. "The Study of Psychological Stress: A Summary of Theory and Experimental Findings." In Charles Speilberger, ed., *Anxiety and Behavior*, pp. 225–231. New York: Academic.

———. 1964. "A Laboratory Approach to Psychological Stress." In G. H. Grosser, H. Wechsler, and M. Greenblatt, eds., *The Threat of Impending Disaster*, pp. 34–57. Cambridge: MIT Press.

Lazarus, Richard, and R. Launier. 1978. "Stress-Related Transactions Between Person and Environment." In L. A. Pervin and M. Lewis, eds., *Perspectives in Interactional Psychology*, pp. 287–327. New York: Plenum.

Lee, Brenda. 1984. "The Social Impact Assessment of Hazardous Waste Management Facilities: Covering the Bases." Publication of the University of Toronto, March.

Lee, Terrence. 1983. "The Perception of Risks." In The Royal Society, *Risk Assessment: A Study Group Report*. Luton, Belfordshire, U.K.: Luton.

Lerner, Melvin J. 1980. *The Belief in a Just World: A Fundamental Delusion*. New York: Plenum.

Levine, Adeline. 1982. *Love Canal: Science, Politics, and People*. Boston: Lexington.

Levine, Adeline, G., and R. A. Stone. 1986. "Threats to People and What They Value." In A. H. Lebovits, A. Baum, and J. E. Singer, eds., *Advances in Environmental Psychology*, pp. 109–130. Hillsdale, N.J.: Erlbaum.

Lewin, Kurt. 1936. *Principles of Topological and Vector Psychology*. New York: McGraw-Hill.

Lewis, Sanford. 1993. *The Good Neighbor Handbook*. Acton, Mass.: CSPP.

Lewis, Sanford, Brian Keeting, and Dick Russell. 1992. *Inconclusive by Design: Waste, Fraud, and Abuse in Federal Environmental Health Research*. Boston: National Toxics Campaign Fund; Harvey, La.: Environmental Health Network.

Lifton, Robert Jay, and Eric Olson. 1976. "The Human Meaning of Total Disaster: The Buffalo Creek Experience." *Psychiatry* 39: 1–18.

Lindell, Michael, Timothy Earle, and S. M. Nealey. 1981. "Comparative Analysis of Risk Characteristics of Nuclear Waste Repositories and Other Disposal Facilities." Battelle Human Affairs Research Center Report, June.

Lipscomb, Jane, et al. 1991. "A Follow-up Study of the Community Near the McColl Waste Disposal Site." *Environmental Health Perspectives* 94: 15–24.

Llewellyn, Lynn G., and William R. Freudenburg. 1989. "Legal Requirements for Social Impact Assessments: Assessing the Social Science Fallout from Three Mile Island." *Society and Natural Resources* 2, 3: 193–208.

Louisiana Advisory Committee to the U.S. Commission on Civil Rights [LACUSC-CR]. 1993. *The Battle for Environmental Justice in Louisiana: Government, Industry, and the People*. Washington, D.C.: LACUSCCR.

Lovins, Amory. 1977. *Soft Energy Paths: Toward a Durable Peace*. New York: Friends of the Earth.

Lumsden, D. Paul. 1975. "Towards a Systems Model of Stress: Anthropological Study of the Impact of Ghana's Volta River Project." In I. Sarason and C. Spielberger, eds., *Stress and Anxiety*, 2:191–228. New York: Wiley.

Lynch, Kevin. 1990. *Wasting Away*. Edited by Michael Southworth. San Francisco: Sierra Club Books.

MacClennan, Paul. 1993. "Environment." *Buffalo Evening News*, January 17, p. 1.

MacDonald, H. Ian. 1984. "Welcome address" in A. Armour, ed., *The Not-In-My-Backyard Syndrome*. Downsview, Ontario: York University Press.

MacGregor, Donald, et al. 1994. "Perceived Risks of Radioactive Waste Transport Through Oregon: Results of a Statewide Survey." *Risk Analysis* 14, 1: 5–14.

Madisso, Urmas. 1985. "A Synthesis of Social and Psychological Effects of Exposure to Hazardous Substances." Report to the Inland Waters Directorate, Ontario Region, January.

———. 1984. "An Annotated Bibliography of the Literature on the Social and Psychological Effects of Exposure to Hazardous Substances." Report to the Inland Waters Directorate, Ontario Region, September.

Maguire, John. 1996. "The Tears Inside the Stone: Reflections on the Ecology of Fear." In Scott Lash, Bronislaw Szerszynski, and Briane Wynne, eds., *Risk, Environment, and Modernity*, pp. 169–188. Thousand Oaks, Calif.: Sage.

Maltoni, Cesare, and Irving J. Selikoff. 1998. Preface to *Living in a Chemical World: Occupational and Environmental Significance of Industrial Carcinogens*, pp. xv-xvi. New York: New York Academy of Scientists.

Markham, Adam. 1994. *A Brief History of Pollution*. New York: St. Martin's.

Markowitz, Jeffrey, and Elaine Gutterman. 1986. "Predictors of Psychological Distress in the Community Following Two Toxic Chemical Incidents." In A. H. Lebovits, A. Baum, and J. E. Singer, eds., *Advances in Environmental Psychology*, pp. 89–107. Hillsdale, N.J.: Erlbaum.

Marples, David R. 1988. *The Social Impact of the Chernobyl Disaster*. New York: St. Martin's.

Marshall, Elliot. 1982. "NRC Must Weigh Psychic Costs: Environmental Law Protects Mental Health, an Appeals Court Finds; Federal Attorneys See Broad Implications." *Science* 216 (June): 1203–1204.

Marshall, Elliot. 1982. "EPA's High Risk Carcinogen Policy." *Science* 218 (December): 975–978.

Marx, Leo. 1964. *The Machine in the Garden: Technology and the Pastoral Ideal in America*. New York: Oxford University Press.

Maser, Chris. 1996. "Resolving Environmental Conflict: Towards Sustainable Community Development." Delray Beach, Fla.: St. Lucie.

Maser, J. D., and S. D. Solomon. 1990. "Psychosocial and Psychological Consequences of Exposure to Extreme Stressors." *Journal of Applied Social Psychology* 20, 21: 1725–1732.

Masters, Kay. 1986. "Life Stage Response to Environmental Crisis: The Case of the

Love Canal, Niagara Falls, New York." Ph.D. diss., SUNY-Buffalo.

Masterson-Allen, Susan Brown, and Phil Brown. 1990. "Public Reaction to Toxic Waste Contamination: Analysis of a Social Movement." *International Journal of Health Services* 20: 485–500.

Mazmanian, Daniel, and David Morell. 1992. *Beyond Superfailure: America's Toxics Policy for the 1990s.* Boulder: Westview.

Mazur, Alan. 1998. *A Hazardous Inquiry: The Rashomon Effect at Love Canal.* Cambridge: Harvard University Press, 1998.

———. 1991. "Putting Radon and Love Canal on the Public Agenda." In Stephen Couch and J. Stephen Kroll-Smith, eds., *Communities at Risk: Collective Responses to Technological Hazards,* pp. 183–204. New York: Peter Lang.

———. 1989. "Communicating Risks in the Mass Media." In Dennis Peck, ed., *Psychosocial Effects of Hazardous Toxic Waste Disposal on Communities,* pp. 119–138. Springfield, Ill.: Charles Thomas.

———. 1981. *The Dynamics of Technical Controversy.* Washington, D.C.: Communications Press.

McClelland, Gary H., William Schulze, and Brian Hurd. 1990. "The Effect of Risk Beliefs on Property Values: A Case Study of a Hazardous Waste Site." *Risk Analysis* 10, 4: 485–497.

McCullough, David. 1968. *The Johnstown Flood.* New York: Simon & Schuster.

McGee, Tara. 1996. "Shades of Grey: Community Responses to Chronic Environmental Lead Contamination in Broken Hill New South Wales." Ph.D. diss, Australian National University.

McKibben, Bill. 1989. *The End of Nature.* New York: Doubleday.

McQuaid-Cook, Jennifer, and Kenneth Simpson. 1986. "Siting a Fully Integrated Waste Management Facility in Alberta." *Hazardous Waste Management* 36: 1031–1036.

Melief, Willem. 1986. "The Social Impacts of Alternative Policy Approaches to Incidents of Toxic Waste Exposure." In Henk Becker and Alan Porter, eds., *Impact Assessment Today,* 2:825–834. Utrecht, The Netherlands: Jan van Arkel.

Metropolitan Edison Company, et al., and United States Nuclear Regulatory Commission, et

al., v. People Against Nuclear Energy, et al., 103 Sup. Ct. 1556 (1983).

Metz, William. 1996. "Historical Application of a Social Amplification of Risk Model: Economic Impacts of Risk Events at Nuclear Weapons Facilities." *Risk Analysis* 16, 2: 185–193.

Michaels, Robert. 1988. "Health Risk Assessment: WTE vs. Peanut Butter." Solid Waste and Power, October: 22–27.

Milbrath, Lester. 1989. *Envisioning a Sustainable Society: Learning Our Way Out.* Albany: SUNY Press.

———. 1984. *Environmentalists: Vanguard for a New Society.* Albany: State University of New York Press.

Miller, David T., Sr. 1981. "One View from Jackson." *Jackson News (Jackson Township, New Jersey),* April 28.

Miller, J. G. 1964. "A Theoretical Review of Individual and Group Psychological Reactions to Stress." In G. H. Grosser, H. Wechsler, and M. Greenblatt, eds., *The Threat of Impending Disaster,* pp. 11–33. Cambridge: MIT Press.

Miller, Robert. 1984. "I'm from the Government and I'm Here to Help You: Fieldwork at Times Beach and Other Missouri Dioxin Sites." Paper delivered at the Society for the Study of Social Problems, San Antonio, Texas, August.

Miller, Vernice. 1993. "Building on Our Past, Planning for Our Future: Communities of Color and the Quest for Environmental Justice." In Richard Hofrichter, ed., *Toxic Struggles: The Theory and Practice of Environmental Justice,* pp. 128–135. Philadelphia: New Society.

Mitchell, Robert C. 1986. "Property Rights, Protest, and the Siting of Hazardous Waste Facilities." *American Economic Review* 76, 2: 285–290.

———. 1984. "Rationality and Irrationality in the Public's Perception of Nuclear Power." In William R. Freudenburg and Eugene Rosa, eds., *Public Reactions to Nuclear Power: Are There Critical Masses?* pp. 137–179. Boulder: Westview.

Mohai, P. 1990. "Black Environmentalism." *Social Science Quarterly* 71, 4: 744–765.

———. 1996. "Environmental Justice or Analytic Justice? Reexamining Historical Hazardous Waste Landfill Siting Patterns in Metropolitan Texas." *Social Science Quarterly* 77, 3: 500–507.

Mohai, P., and Bunyan Bryant. 1992. "Race, Poverty, and the Environment: The Disadvantaged Face Greater Risks." *EPA Journal* 18, 1: 6–10.

Mohai, Paul, and Bunyan Bryant, eds. 1992. *Race and the Incidence of Environmental Hazards.* Boulder: Westview.

Molotch, Harvey, and Marilyn Lester. 1975. "Accidental News: The Great Oil Spill as Local Occurrence and National Event." *American Journal of Sociology* 81: 235–260.

Monat, Alan, and Richard Lazarus, eds. 1977. *Stress and Coping: An Anthology.* New York: Columbia University Press.

Montague, Peter. 1984. "The Limitations of Landfilling." In Bruce Piasecki, ed., *Beyond Dumping: New Strategies for Controlling Toxic Contamination.* Westport, Conn.: Greenwood.

Moore, Richard, and Louis Head. 1993. "Acknowledging the Past; Confronting the Future: Environmental Justice in the 1990s." In Richard Hofrichter, *Toxic Struggles: The Theory and Practice of Environmental Justice,* pp. 118–127. Philadelphia: New Society.

Morehouse, W., and M. A. Subramaniam. 1986. "The Bhopal Tragedy: What Really Happened and What It Means for American Workers and Communities at Risk." Preliminary Report for the Citizens Commission on Bhopal. New York: Council on International and Public Affairs.

Morrison, Denton. 1983. "Doomseers, Boomseers, Techseers, Socseers: The Future as Seen in the Rearview Mirror." *World Future Society Bulletin,* November-December, pp. 7–13.

Morrison, Denton, and Riley Dunlap. 1985. "Is Environmentalism Elitist?" In Frederick Buttel and Craig Humphrey, eds., *Environment and Society.* University Park: Pennsylvania State University Press.

Mueller, Claus. 1973. *The Politics of Communication.* New York: Oxford University Press, 1973.

Mumford, Lewis. 1964a. *The Pentagon of Power: The Myth of the Machine.* Vol. 2. New York: Harcourt Brace Jovanovich.

———. 1964b. "Authoritarian and Democratic Technics." *Technology and Culture* 5, 1: 1–8.

Mushkatel, Alvin, Joanne Nigg, and David Pijawka. 1993. "Nevada Urban Residents' Views of Nuclear Waste Repository Siting in Nevada." In Riley Dunlap, Michael Kraft, and Eugene Rosa, eds., *Public Reactions to Nuclear Waste: Citizens' Views of Repository Siting,* pp. 239–262. Durham, N.C.: Duke University Press.

Napton, M. L., and F. A. Day. 1992. "Polluted Neighborhoods in Texas: Who Lives There?" *Environment and Behavior* 24, 4: 508–526.

Nelkin, Dorothy. 1992. *Controversy: Politics of Technical Decisions.* Newbury Park, Calif.: Sage.

———. 1987. *Selling Science: How the Press Covers Science and Technology.* New York: W. H. Freeman.

Nelkin, Dorothy, ed. 1985. *The Language of Risk: Conflicting Perspectives in Occupational Health.* Beverly Hills: Sage.

Nelson, Arthur C., John Genereux, and Michelle Genereux. 1992. "Price Effects of Landfills on House Values." *Land Economics* 68: 359–365.

Neutra, Raymond, Jane Lipscomb, Kenneth Satin, and Dennis Shusterman. 1991. "Hypotheses to Explain Higher Symptom Rates Observed Around Hazardous Waste Sites." *Environmental Health Perspectives* 94: 31–38.

New Jersey Department of Health, Division of Epidemiology and Disease Control. 1980. "Groundwater Contamination and Possible Health Effects in Jackson Township, New Jersey." July.

New Jersey Department of Health. 1993. "Public Health Assessment: Jackson Township Landfill, CERCLIS no. NJD980505283, December 13. <www.atsdr.cdc.gov/HAC/PHA/jackson/jtl_toc.html>.

New Jersey Supreme Court, A–83–84, decision in *Ayers v. Jackson Township,* May 7, 1987.

New York State Department of Health. 1988. "Love Canal Emergency Declaration Area: Decision on Habitability." Albany, N.Y.

Norris, Ruth, ed. 1982. *Pills, Pesticides, and Profits: International Trade and Toxic Substances.* Croton-on-Hudson, N.Y.: North River.

Novick, Sheldon. 1983. "What Is Wrong with Superfund?" *Environmental Forum* 2: 6–11.

Novotny, Patrick. 1998. "Popular Epidemiology and the Struggle for Environmental Health in the Community Environmental Justice Movement." In Daniel Faber, ed., *The*

Struggle for Ecological Democracy: Environmental Justice Movements in the United States, pp. 137–156. New York: Guilford.

Nuclear Regulatory Commission. 1975. "Reactor Safety Study: An Assessment of Accident Risks in U.S. Commercial Nuclear Power Plants (WASH–1400), October.

Ocean County Department of Planning. 1981. "General Statistical Information, Ocean County, New Jersey." Toms River, N.J.

Office of Technology Assessment. 1983. *Technologies and Management Strategies for Hazardous Waste Control*. Washington, D.C.: U.S. Congress, March.

Olsen, Marvin, Dora Lodwick, and Riley Dunlap. 1993. *Viewing the World Ecologically*. Boulder: Westview.

O'Riordan, Timothy, and James Cameron, eds. 1994. *Interpreting the Precautionary Principle*. London: EarthScan.

Orr, David. 1994. *With Earth in Mind: On Education, Environment, and the Human Prospect*. Washington: Island.

Ottum, Margaret, and Nancy Updegraff. 1984. "Local Residents' Perception of the Williamstown Pollution Problem." Unpublished research summary.

Packard, Vance. 1960. *The Waste Makers*. New York: McKay.

Page, G. William, and Harvey Rabinowitz. 1993. "Groundwater Contamination: Its Effects on Property Values and Cities." *Journal of the American Planning Association* 59: 473–481.

Paigen, Beverly. 1982. "The Ethical Dimensions of Scientific Conflict: Controversy at Love Canal." *Hastings Center Report*, June, pp. 29–37.

———. 1979. "Health Hazards at Love Canal." Testimony presented to the House Subcommittee on Oversight and Investigations, March 21.

Palinkas, Lawrence A., Michael Downs, John S. Petterson, and John Russell. 1993a. "Social, Cultural, and Psychological Impacts of the Exxon Valdez Oil Spill." *Human Organization* 52, 1: 1–13.

Palinkas, Lawrence A., John S. Petterson, John Russell, and Michael A. Downs. 1993b. "Community Patterns of Psychiatric Disorders after the Exxon Valdez Oil Spill." *American Journal of Psychiatry* 150, 10: 1517–1523.

Palinkas, Lawrence A., John Russell, Michael A. Downs, and John S. Petterson. 1992. "Ethnic Differences on Stress, Coping, and Depressive Symptoms After the Exxon Valdez Oil Spill." *Journal of Nervous and Mental Disease* 189, 5: 287–295.

Pannell, Kerr, Forster. 1985. "Tourism Impact Study: Proposed OWMC Hazardous Waste Treatment Facilities." February. Niagara Falls, Ontario.

Pearce, Frank, and Steve Tombs. 1998. *Toxic Capitalism: Corporate Crime and the Chemical Industry*. Brookfield, Vt.: Ashgate.

Pearlin, Leonard, Elizabeth Menaghan, Morton Lieberman, and Joseph Mullan. 1981. "The Stress Process." *Journal of Health and Social Behavior* 22: 337–356.

Pearson, Jessica. 1980. "Hazard Visibility and Occupational Health Problem Solving: The Case of the Uranium Industry." *Journal of Community Health* 6, 2: 136–147.

Peck, Dennis, ed. 1989. *Psychosocial Effects of Hazardous Toxic Waste Disposal on Communities*. Springfield, Ill.: Charles Thomas.

Perin, Constance. 1977. *Everything in Its Place: Social Order and Land Use in America*. Princeton: Princeton University Press.

Perrow, Charles. 1984. *Normal Accidents: Living with High Risk Technologies*. New York: Basic.

Perry, Ronald, Michael Lindell, and Marjorie Greene. 1982. "Threat Perception and Public Response to Volcano Hazard." *Journal of Social Psychology* 116: 199–204.

Perry, Ronald, H. Parker, and D. Gillespie. 1976. *Social Movements and the Local Community*. Beverly Hills: Sage.

Peterson, Christopher, and Martin Seligman. 1983. "Learned Helplessness and Victimization." *Journal of Social Issues* 39, 2: 103–116.

Peterson, D. J. 1993. *Troubled Lands: The Legacy of Soviet Environmental Destruction*. Boulder: Westview.

Petterson, John. 1988. "Perception vs. Reality of Radiological Impact: The Goiania Model." *Nuclear News*, November, pp. 84–90.

Pettit, C. L., and Charles Johnson. 1987. "The Impact on Property Values of Solid Waste Facilities." *Waste Age*, April, pp. 97–204.

Picou, J. Steven. 2000. "The 'Talking Circle' as Sociological Practice: Cultural transformation of Chronic Disaster Impacts." *Sociological Practice: A Journal of Clinical and Applied Sociology* 2, 2: 77–97.

———. 1996a. "Sociology and Compelled Disclosure: Protecting Respondent Confidentiality." *Sociological Spectrum* 16, 3: 1–23.

———. 1996b. "Toxins in the Environment, Damage to the Community: Sociology and the Toxic Tort." In Pamela Jenkins and J. Stephen Kroll-Smith, *Witnessing for Sociology: Sociologists in Court*, pp. 211–224. Westport, Conn.: Praeger.

Picou, J. Steven, and Duane Gill. 1997a. "Commercial Fishers and Stress: Psychological Impacts of the Exxon Valdez Oil Spill." In J. Steven Picou, Duane Gill, and Maurie Cohen, eds., *The Exxon Valdez Disaster: Readings in a Modern Social Problem*, pp. 211–236. Dubuque: Kendall-Hunt.

———. 1997b. "The Day the Water Died: Cultural Impacts of the Exxon Valdez Oil Spill." In J. Steven Picou, Duane Gill, and Maurie Cohen, eds., *The Exxon Valdez Disaster: Readings in a Modern Social Problem*, pp. 167–192. Dubuque: Kendall-Hunt.

———. 1996. "The Exxon Valdez Oil Spill and Chronic Psychological Stress." In F. Rice, R. Spies, D. Wolfe, and B. Wright, eds., *Proceedings of the EVOS Symposium*, pp. 879–893. American Fisheries Symposium 18. Bethesda, Md.: American Fisheries Society.

Picou, J. Steven, Duane Gill, and Maurie Cohen, eds. 1997. *The Exxon Valdez Disaster: Readings in a Modern Social Problem*. Dubuque: Kendall-Hunt.

Picou, J. Steven, Duane A. Gill, Christopher L. Dyer, and Evans W. Curry. 1992. "Stress and Disruption in an Alaskan Fishing Community: Initial and Continuing Impacts of the Exxon Valdez Oil Spill." *Industrial Crisis Quarterly* 6, 3: 235–257.

Picou, J. Steven, and Donald Rosebrook. 1993. "Technological Accident, Community Class-Action Litigation, and Scientific Damage Assessment: A Case Study of Court-Ordered Research." *Sociological Spectrum* 13, 1: 117–138.

Pijawka, Dennis, and A. H. Mushkatel. 1992. "Public Opposition to the Siting of the High-Level Nuclear Waste Repository: The Importance of Trust." *Policy Studies Review* 10: 180–194.

Piller, Charles. 1991. *The Fail-Safe Society: Community Defiance and the End of American Technological Optimism*. Berkeley: University of California Press.

Pirages, Dennis, ed. 1996. *Building Sustainable Societies: A Blueprint for a Post-Industrial World*. Armonk, N.Y.: Sharpe.

Pirages, Dennis. 1978. *The New Context for International Relations: Global Ecopolitics*. North Scituate, Mass.: Duxbury.

Polanyi, Karl. 1944. *The Great Transformation*. Boston: Beacon.

Pollock, P. H., and M. E. Vittas. 1995. "Who Bears the Burdens of Environmental Pollution? Race, Ethnicity, and Environmental Equity in Florida." *Social Science Quarterly* 76, 2: 294–310.

Portnoy, Kent. 1991. *Siting Hazardous Waste Treatment Facilities: The NIMBY Syndrome*. New York: Auburn House.

Powell, John Duncan. 1988. "A Hazardous Waste Site: The Case of Nyanza." In Sheldon Krimsky and Alonzo Plough, eds., *Environmental Hazards: Communicating Risks as a Social Process*, pp. 239–297. New York: Auburn House.

Preston, Valerie, S. Martin Taylor, and David Hodge. 1983. "Adjustment to Natural and Technological Hazards: A Study of an Urban Community." *Environment and Behavior* 15: 143–164.

Public Health Service. Agency for Toxic Substances and Disease Registry. 1997. "Public Health Assessment for Nease Chemical, Salem, Columbiana County, Ohio." CERCLIS no. OHD980610018, February 6. Prepared by the ODH for U.S. Department of Health and Human Services.

Purcell, Arthur. 1981. "Setting Priorities in Managing Toxic and Hazardous Substances." *The Environmental Professional* 3: 9–13.

Purcell, Kristen, Lee Clarke, and Linda Renzulli. 2000. "Menus of Choice: The Social Embeddedness of Decisions." In Maurie Cohen, ed., *Risk in the Modern Age: Social Theory, Science, and Environmental Decision-Making*, pp. 62–82. New York: St. Martin's.

Quarantelli, E. L. 1988. "Citizen Groups and Hazardous Waste: Their Careers and Conditions for Emergence." Article 203,

Disaster Research Center, University of Delaware.

Quarantelli, E. L., and Russell Dynes. 1977. "Response to Social Crisis and Disaster." *Annual Review of Sociology* 3: 23–49.

Rapoport, Amos. 1969. *House Form and Culture*. Englewood Cliffs, N.J.: Prentice-Hall.

Radelfinger, Sam. 1965. "Some Effects of Fear-Arousing Communications on Preventive Health Behavior." *Health Education Monographs* 19: 2–15.

Raffensperger, Carolyn, and Joel Titchner, eds. *Protecting Public Health and the Environment: Implementing the Precautionary Principle*. Washington, D.C.: Island, 1999.

Rathje, William, and Cullen Murphy. 1992. *Rubbish! The Archeology of Garbage*. New York: Harper Perennial.

Rehner, Timothy, et al. 2000. "Depression Among Victims of South Mississippi's Methyl Parathion Disaster." *Health and Social Work* 25, 1: 33–40.

Reich, Michael. 1991. *Toxic Politics: Responding to Chemical Disasters*. Ithaca, N.Y.: Cornell University Press.

———. 1983. "Environmental Politics and Science: The Case of PBB Contamination in Michigan." *American Journal of Public Health* 73, 3: 302–313.

Reim, B., D. Glass, and J. Singer. 1971. "Behavioral Consequences of Exposure to Uncontrollable and Unpredictable Noise." *Journal of Applied Social Psychology* 1: 44.

Reko, H. Karl. 1984. "Not an Act of God: The Story of Times Beach." Unpublished report.

Rich, Richard, David Conn, and William Owens. 1993. "'Indirect Regulation' of Environmental Hazards Through the Provision of Information to the Public: The Case of SARA, Title III." *Policy Studies Journal* 21, 1: 16–34.

Rich, Richard, Michael Edelstein, William Hallman, and Abraham Wandersman. 1995. "Citizen Participation and Empowerment: The Case of Local Environmental Hazards." *American Journal of Community Psychology* 23, 5: 657–676.

Rich, Vera. 1991. "USSR: Chernobyl's Psychological Legacy." *Lancet*, May 4, p. 1086.

Ridington, Robin. 1982. "When Poison Gas Came Down Like a Fog: A Native Community's Response to Cultural Disaster." *Human Organization* 41, 1: 36–42.

Ridley, Scott. 1987. *The State of the States*. Washington, D.C.: Fund for Renewable Energy and Environment.

Roberts, Leslie. 1987. "Radiation Accident Grips Goi'ania." *Science* 238: 1028–1031.

Robertson, John. 1983. "Geohydrologic Aspects of Hazardous Waste Disposal." In Denise Wiltshire and Dan Hahl, eds., *Information Needs for Tomorrow's Priority Water Issues*. Albany: U.S. Geological Survey.

Robinson, Ronald. 1994. "West Dallas Versus the Lead Smelter." In Robert D. Bullard, ed., *Unequal Protection: Environmental Justice and Communities of Color*, pp. 92–109. San Francisco: Sierra Club.

Rodin, Mari, Michael Downs, John Petterson, and John Russell. 1992. "Community Impacts Resulting from the Exxon Valdez Oil Spill." *Industrial Crisis Quarterly* 6: 219–234.

Rogers, Ronald. 1975. "A Protection Motivation Theory of Fear Appeals and Attitude Change." *Journal of Psychology* 91: 93–114.

Rogge, Mary. 1998. "Toxic Risk, Community Resilience, and Social Justice in Chattanooga." In Marie Hoff, ed., *Sustainable Community Development: Studies in Economic, Environmental, and Cultural Revitalization*, pp. 105–122. New York: Lewis.

———. 1996. "Social Vulnerability to Toxic Risk." *Journal of Social Service Research* 22, 1–2: 109–129.

———. 1995. "Coordinating Theory, Evidence, and Practice: Toxic Waste Exposure in Communities." *Journal of Community Practice* 2, 2: 55–76.

Roseland, Mark. 1995. *Toward Sustainable Communities*. British Columbia: New Society.

Rouse, Mary A., Tracy L. Shelley, and B. Kim Mortensen. 1990. "Assessment of Exposure to Mirex Associated with the Nease Chemical Company Superfund Site in Salem, Columbiana County, Ohio." Ohio Department of Health, October 4. Attached as Appendix C to Public Health Service 1997.

Ruesch, Jurgen, and Weldon Kees. 1956. *Nonverbal Communication*. Berkeley: University of California Press.

Russell, John C., Larry A. Palinkas, and Michael Downs. 1993. *Social, Psychological, and*

Municipal Impacts Related to the Exxon Valdez Oil Spill. Or: Briker, Nodland, Studenmund, Inc.

Ryan, W. 1971. *Blaming the Victim.* New York: Pantheon.

Sandman, Peter. 1990. "Getting to Maybe: Some Communications Aspects of Siting Hazardous Waste Facilities." In Theodore Glickman and Michael Gough, eds., *Readings in Risk,* pp. 233–245. Washington, D.C.; Resources for the Future.

Sandweiss, Stephen. 1998. "The Social Construction of Environmental Justice." In David Camacho, ed., *Environmental Injustices, Political Struggles: Race, Class, and the Environment,* pp. 30–57. Durham, N.C.: Duke University Press.

Sarason, Seymour. 1974. *The Psychological Sense of Community.* Washington, D.C.: Jossey-Bass.

Savitsky, Jeffrey, and Donald Hartsough. 1986. "Use of the Environment and the Legal Impacts of Resulting Emotional Harm." In Charles Figley, ed., *Trauma and Its Wake,* 2:378–397. New York: Brunner/Mazel.

Schacter, Sidney. 1959. *The Psychology of Affiliation.* Stanford, Calif.: Stanford University Press.

Schaeffer, Marc, and Andrew Baum. 1984. "Adrenal Cortical Response to Stress at Three Mile Island." *Psychosomatic Medicine* 46, 3: 227–237.

Schneekloth, Lynda and Robert Shibley. 1995. *Placemaking: The Art and Practice of Building Communities.* New York: Wiley.

Schooler, Tonya, and Andrew Baum. 1996. "Memories of a Petrochemical Explosion: A Cognitive-Phenomenological Study of Intrusive Thoughts." In Linda Williams and Victoria Banyard, eds., *Trauma and Memory,* pp. 189–201. Thousand Oaks, Calif.: Sage.

Schroeder, Christopher. 1993. "Cool Analysis Versus Moral Outrage in the Development of Federal Environmental Criminal Law." *William and Mary Law Review* 35: 251.

Schroeder, K., ed. 1990. "Chernobyl: The Intangible Catastrophe Continues." Report of the World Council of Churches/Commission on Inter-Church Aid, Refugee, and World Service Team Visit to Moscow and Byelorussia from June 23 to July 4 1990. New York: World Council of Churches.

Schroyer, Trent. 1998. *A World That Works: Building Blocks for a Just and Sustainable Society.* New York: Bootstrap.

Schwab, J. 1994. *Deeper Shades of Green: The Rise of Blue-Color and Minority Environmentalism in America.* San Francisco: Sierra Club Books.

Sclove, Richard. 1995. *Democracy and Technology.* New York: Guilford.

Scott, W., and M. Wertheimer. 1962. *Introduction to Psychological Research.* New York: Wiley.

Seelye, Katharine. 2002. "Bush Proposing to Shift Burden of Toxic Cleanups to Taxpayers." *New York Times,* February 24, pp. 1, 24.

Seley, John, and Julian Wolpert. 1983. "Equity and Location." In Roger E. Kasperson, ed., *Equity Issues in Radioactive Waste Management,* pp. 69–93. Cambridge, Mass.: Oelgeschlager, Gunn & Hain.

Selye, Hans. 1976. *The Stress of Life.* New York: McGraw-Hill.

Shaw, L. G., and Lester W. Milbrath. 1983. "Citizen Participation in Governmental Decision Making: The Toxic Waste Threat at Love Canal, Niagara Falls, New York." Rockefeller Institute Working Papers, no. 8.

Sheehan, Helen, and Richard Wedeen. 1993. *Toxic Circles: Environmental Hazards from the Workplace into the Community.* New Brunswick, N.J.: Rutgers University Press.

Shkilnyk, Anastasia. 1985. *A Poison Stronger Than Love: The Destruction of an Ojibwa Community.* New Haven: Yale University.

Short, James, Jr., and Lee Clarke, eds. 1992. *Organizations, Uncertainties, and Risk.* Boulder: Westview.

Shrader-Frechette, K. S. 1993. *Burying Uncertainty: Risk and the Case Against Geological Disposal of Nuclear Waste.* Berkeley: University of California Press.

———. 1985. *Risk Analysis and Scientific Method: Methodological and Ethical Problems with Evaluating Societal Hazards.* Boston: Reidel.

Shrivastava, Paul. 1987. *Bhopal: Anatomy of a Crisis.* Cambridge, Mass.: Ballinger.

Shusterman, Dennis, Jane Lipscomb, Raymond Neutra, and Kenneth Satin. 1991. "Symptom Prevalence and Odor-Worry Interaction Near Hazardous Waste Sites." *Environmental Health Perspectives* 94: 25–30.

Silbergeld, Ellen, Michael Gordon, and Lynn Kelly. 1993. "Dioxin at Diamond: A Study in Occupational/Environmental Exposure." In Helen Sheehan and Richard Wedeen, eds., *Toxic Circles: Environmental Hazards from the Workplace into the Community,* pp. 55–80. New Brunswick, N.J.: Rutgers University Press.

Singer, Eleanor, and Phyllis Endreny. 1993. *Reporting on Risk.* New York: Russell Sage Foundation.

Sitarz, Daniel, ed. 1994. *Agenda 21: The Earth Summit Strategy to Save Our Planet.* Boulder: Earthpress.

Skaburskis, A. 1989. "Impact Attenuation in Nonconflict Situations: The Price Effects of a Nuisance Land Use." *Environment and Planning* 21: 375–383.

Slater, Philip. 1974. *Earthwalk.* Garden City, N.Y.: Doubleday.

Slovic, Paul. 1993. "Perceived Risk, Trust, and Democracy." *Risk Analysis* 13: 675–682.

———. 1992. "Perceptions of Risk: Reflections on the Psychometric Paradigm." In D. Golding and S. Krimsky, *Theories of Risk.* New York: Praeger.

———. 1991. "Perceived Risk, Trust, and the Politics of Nuclear Waste." *Science* 254: 1603–1607.

———. 1990. "A Risk Communication Perspective on an Integrated Waste Management Strategy." In Howard Kunreuther and M. V. Rajeev Gowda, eds., *Integrating Insurance and Risk Management for Hazardous Wastes,* pp. 195–216. Boston: Kluwer Academic.

Slovic, Paul, Baruch Fischhoff, and Sarah Lichtenstein. 1982. "Psychological Aspects of Risk Perception." In David Sills, C. P. Wolf, and Vivian Shelanski, eds., *Accident at Three Mile Island,* pp. 11–42. Boulder: Westview.

——— 1980. "Facts and Fears: Understanding Perceived Risk." In R. Schwing and W. A. Albers Jr., eds., *Societal Risk Assessment: How Safe Is Safe Enough?* pp. 181–214. New York: Plenum.

Slovic, Paul, James Flynn, and Mark Layman. 1991. "Perceived Risk, Trust, and the Politics of Nuclear Waste." *Science* 254: 1603–1607.

Slovic, Paul, Mark Layman, and James Flynn. 1990a. "What Comes to Mind When You Hear the Words 'Nuclear Waste Repository'? A Study of 10, 000 Images." Unpublished paper prepared for the Nevada Agency for Nuclear Projects, Yucca Mountain Socioeconomic Project, Phase IV-B, Tasks 8.5 and 8.6, November.

———. 1990b. "Images of Place and Vacation Preferences: Implications of the 1989 Surveys for Assessing the Economic Impacts of a Nuclear Waste Repository in Nevada." Unpublished paper prepared for the Nevada Agency for Nuclear Projects, Yucca Mountain Socioeconomic Project, Phase IV-B, Tasks 8.5 and 8.6, November.

Slovic, Paul, Mark Layman, Nancy Kraus, James Flynn, James Chalmers, and Gail Gesell. 1990. "Perceived Risk, Stigma, and Potential Economic Impacts of a High-Level Nuclear Waste Repository in Nevada." Unpublished paper, Decision Research, 1201 Oak St., Eugene, Oregon, August.

Smith, E. M., et al. 1986. "Psychosocial Consequences of a Disaster." In J. H. Shore, ed., *Disaster Stress Studies: New Methods and Findings,* pp. 50–76. Washington, D.C.: American Psychiatric Press.

Smith, Elizabeth, Carol North, and Paul Price. 1988. "Response to Technological Accidents." In Mary Lystad, ed., *Mental Health Response to Mass Emergencies,* pp. 52–95. New York: Brunner/Mazel.

Soliman, Hussein. 1996. "Community Responses to Chronic Technological Disaster: The Case of the Pigeon River." *Journal of Social Service Research* 22, 1–2: 89–107.

Solomon, Susan D. 1989. "Research Issues in Assessing Disaster's Effects." In R. Gist and B. Lubin, eds., *Psychosocial Aspects of Disasters,* pp. 308–340. New York: Wiley.

———. 1986. "Mobilizing Social Support Networks in Times of Disaster." In Charles Figley, ed., *Trauma and Its Wake,* 2:232–262. New York: Brunner/Mazel, 1986.

Sonnenfeld, J. 1966. "Values in Space and Landscape." *Journal of Social Issues,* October, p. 71.

Sorenson, John, et al. 1987. *Impacts of Hazardous Technology: The Psycho-Social Effects of Restarting TMI–1.* Albany: State University of New York Press.

Sowder, Barbara, ed. 1985. *Disasters and Mental Health: Selected Contemporary Perspectives.* Rockville, Md.: National Institute of Mental Health.

Stallen, Pieter Jan, and Arend Tomas. 1985. "Public Concern about Industrial

Hazards." Paper presented at the annual meeting of the Society for Risk Analysis, Washington, D.C., October.

Staples, Susan. 1996. "Human Response to Environmental Noise: Psychological Research and Public Policy." *American Psychologist* 31, 2: 1–8.

Stephens, Sharon. 1987. "Lapp Life After Chernobyl." *Natural History*, December, pp. 33–40.

Stefanko, Michael, and Jordan Horowitz. 1989. "Attitudinal Effects Associated with an Environmental Hazard." *Population and the Environment* 11, 1: 43–53.

Stoffle, Richard, et al. 1991. "Risk Perception Mapping: Using Ethnography to Define the Locally Affected Population for a Low-Level Radioactive Waste Storage Facility in Michigan." *American Anthropologist* 93, 3: 611–635.

Stone, Russell, and Adeline Levine. 1985. "Reactions to Collective Stress: Correlates of Active Citizen Participation at Love Canal." In Abraham Wandersman and Robert Hess, eds., *Beyond the Individual: Environmental Approaches and Prevention*, pp. 153–178. New York: Haworth.

———. 1984. "Residents' Perceptions of the Hazard of Love Canal: Problems and Changes to Self and Family." Paper presented at the American Psychological Association, Toronto, Canada, August 1984.

Struglia, Rachel. 1998. "The Social Ecology of Environmental Inequity: Ethnic Communities and the Decision-Making Process in Orange County, California." Dissertation, University of California at Irvine.

———. 1993. "The Politics of Groundwater Contamination: A Case Study of the Two Superfund Sites in Phoenix, Arizona." Masters Thesis, Arizona State University.

Sunday Star Ledger (Newark, New Jersey). March 11, 1984.

Susskind, Lawrence, Sarah McKearnan, and Jennifer Thomas-Larmer. 1999. *The Consensus Building Handbook: A Comprehensive Guide to Reaching Agreement*. Thousand Oaks, Calif.: Sage.

Szasz, Andrew. 1994. *Ecopopulism: Toxic Waste and the Movement for Environmental Justice*. Minneapolis: University of Minnesota Press.

Szerszynski, Bronislaw. 1999. "Risk and Trust: The Performative Dimension." *Environmental Values* 8: 239–252.

Tarr, Joel, and Charles Jacobson. 1987. "Environmental Risk in Historical Perspective." In Brandon Johnson and Vincent Covello, eds., *The Social Construction of Risk: Essays on Risk Selection and Perception*, pp. 317–343. Boston: Reidel.

Taylor, Bron R., ed. 1995. *Ecological Resistance Movements: The Global Emergence of Radical and Popular Environmentalism*. Albany: SUNY Press.

Taylor, Dorceta E. 1992. "Blacks and the Environment: Toward an Explanation of the Concern Action Gap Between Blacks and Whites." *Environment and Behavior* 21, 2: 175–205.

Taylor, S. M., et al. 1991. "Psychosocial Effects in Populations Exposed to Solid Waste Facilities," 382–394. Proceedings of the Technology Transfer Conference, Toronto, Canada, November 25–26.

Tester, David. 1982. Panel presentation at the session on impacts of regulatory proceedings, International Association for Impact Assessment, Vancouver, B.C., October.

Thornton, Scott, and Michael R. Edelstein. 1999. "Citizen Enforcers or Bothersome Meddlers? A Plaintiff's Perspective on the Orange County Landfill Case." *Environmental Law in New York*, 10, 6: 81, 88–96.

Times Herald Record (Middletown, N.Y.), February 25, 1985.

Times Herald Record (Middletown, New York), February 6, 1984.

Timmerman, Peter. 1984a. "Ethics and Hazardous Waste Facility Siting." Publication of the University of Toronto, March.

———. 1984b. "Ethics and the Problem of Hazardous Waste Management: An Inquiry into Methods and Approaches." Publication of the University of Toronto, March.

Titchner, James L., and Frederic T. Kapp. 1976. "Family and Character Change at Buffalo Creek." *American Journal of Psychiatry* 133, 3: 295–299.

Tosteson, Heather. 1995a. "Communication and Negotiation at Hazardous Waste Sites: Some Psychological and Sociological

Influences on Scientific Debate." Paper
presented at the International Congress on
Hazardous Waste: Impact on Human and
Ecological Health, Atlanta, Georgia, June
5–8.

———. 1995b."Improving Communication in a
Climate of Uncertainty." Paper presented
at the Communication and the
Environment Conference, Chattanooga,
Tennessee, March 30–April 1, 1995, and
the meeting of the Society for Applied
Anthropology, Albuquerque, March
29–April 2.

Toth, Robert. 1981. "Life Without Chemicals:
Does Bad Outweigh Good?" in *Training
Manual on Toxic Substances, Book One.*
San Francisco: Sierra Club.

Tucker, Pamela. 2000. "Report of the Expert
Panel Workshop on the Psychological
Responses to Hazardous Substances."
ATSDR, U.S. Department of Health and
Human Services, Atlanta.

———. 2000. "Scientific Research Continues on
the Psychological Responses to Toxic
Contamination." *Hazardous Substances
and Public Health* 10, 1: 1–11.

Unger, David, and Abraham Wandersman. 1985.
"The Importance of Neighboring: The
Social, Cognitive, and Affective
Components of Neighboring." *American
Journal of Community Psychology* 13:
139–169.

Unger, David, Abraham Wandersman, and
William Hallman. 1992. "Living Near a
Hazardous Waste Facility: Coping with
Individual and Family Distress." *American
Journal of Orthopsychiatry* 62, 1: 55–70.

U.S. Army Corps of Engineers.
<www.hq.usace.army.mil/cecw/fusrap>.

U.S. District Court, Northern District of New
York, 99-CV–1449, *Leland v. Moran et al.,*
Justice David Hurd, April 13, 2000.

Van Eijndhoven, J. C. M., and G. H. E.
Nieuwdorp. 1986. "Institutional Action in
Soil Pollution Situations with Uncertain
Risks." In Henk Becker and Alan Porter,
eds., *Impact Assessment Today,* 11:
267–278. Utrecht, The Netherlands: Jan
van Arkel.

Van Eijndhoven, J. C. M., et al. 1985. "Hazardous
Waste in the Netherlands: Dutch Policies
from a Local Perspective." Report to the
International Institute for Applied Systems
Analysis, March.

Vaughan, Diane. 1989. "Regulating Risk:
Implications of the Challenger Accident."
Law and Policy 11, 3: 330–349.

Vaughan, Elaine. 1993. "Chronic Exposure to an
Environmental Hazard: Risk Perceptions
and Self-Protective Behavior." *Health
Psychology* 12, 1: 74–85.

Vaughan, Elaine, and Brenda Nordenstam. 1989.
"Farmworkers and Pesticide Exposure:
Perceived Risk, Psychological Distress, and
Health." Paper presented to the American
Psychological Association, New Orleans,
August 12.

Vissing, Yvonne. 1984. "The Difficulties in
Determining Elite Deviance: Dow
Chemical Company and the Dioxin
Controversy." Paper presented at the
Society for the Study of Social Problems,
San Antonio, Texas, August.

Von Uexküll, Thure. 1984. "Ambient and
Environment: Or Which Is the Correct
Perspective on Nature?" Paper presented at
the International Association for the Study
of People and Their Physical
Surroundings, West Berlin, West Germany,
July 25–29.

Vyner, Henry. 1984. "The Psychological Effects of
Invisible Environmental Contaminants."
Social Impact Assessment, July-September,
pp. 93–95.

———. 1988. *Invisible Trauma: The Psychosocial
Effects of the Invisible Environmental
Contaminants.* Boston: Lexington.

Wallace, Anthony. 1957. "Mazeway
Disintegration." *Human Organization* 14:
23–27.

Walsh, Edward J. 1988. *Democracy in the
Shadows: Citizen Mobilization in the Wake
of the Accident at Three Mile Island.* New
York: Greenwood.

Walsh, Edward J., and R. H. Warland. 1983.
"Social Movement Involvement in the
Wake of a Nuclear Accident." *American
Sociological Review* 48: 764–780.

Wandersman, Abraham. 1981. "A Framework of
Participation in Community
Organizations." *Journal of Applied
Behavioral Science* 17: 27–58.

Wandersman, Abraham, Steven Berman, and
William Hallman. 1989. "Hazardous
Wastes, Perceived Risk, Fears About
Cancer, Psychological Distress, and
Health." Paper presented at the American

Psychological Association Conference, New Orleans.

Wandersman, Abraham, William Hallman, and Steven Berman. 1989. "How Residents Cope with Living Near a Hazardous Waste Landfill: An Example of Substantive Theorizing." *American Journal of Community Health* 17, 5: 575–583.

Weart, Spencer. 1988. *Nuclear Fear: A History of Images.* Cambridge: Harvard University Press.

Webb, D. B. 1989. "PBB: An Environmental Contamination in Michigan." *Journal of Community Psychology* 17: 30–46.

Weinberger, Morris, James Greene, Joseph Mamlin, and Michael Jerin. 1981. "Health Beliefs and Smoking Behavior." *American Journal of Public Health* 71, 11: 1253–1255.

Weinstein, Neil. 1989. "Optimistic Biases About Personal Risks." *Science* 246: 1232–1234.

———. 1984. "Why It Won't Happen to Me: Perceptions of Risk Factors and Susceptibility." *Health Psychology* 3, 5 (1984): 431–457.

———. 1982a. "Unrealistic Optimism About Susceptibility to Health Problems." *Journal of Behavioral Medicine* 5, 4: 441–460.

———. 1982b. "Community Noise Problems: Evidence Against Adaptation." *Journal of Environmental Psychology* 2: 87–97.

Weller, Phil. 1984. Comments in A. Armour, ed., *The Not-In-My-Backyard Syndrome,* 76–78. Downsview, Ontario: York University.

Wendroff, Arnold. 1990. "Domestic Mercury Pollution." *Nature* 347: 623.

Westra, Laura, and Peter Wenz, eds. 1995. *Faces of Environmental Racism: Confronting Issue of Global Justice.* Lanham, Md.: Rowman & Littlefield.

Weterings, R. A. P. M., and Josee C. M. Van Eijndhoven. 1989. "Informing the Public about Uncertain Risks." *Risk Analysis* 9, 4: 473–482.

White, Lynn, Jr. 1967. "The Historical Roots of Our Ecologic Crisis." *Science* 155: 1203–1207.

Wicker, Allan. 1979. *An Introduction to Ecological Psychology.* Monterey, Calif.: Brooks/Cole.

Wigley, Daniel, and Kristin Shrader-Frechette. 1996. "Environmental Justice: A Louisiana Case Study." *Journal of Agricultural and Environmental Ethics* 9, 1: 61–82.

Wilkins, Lee. 1987. *Shared Vulnerability: The Media and American Perceptions of the Bhopal Disaster.* Westport, Conn.: Greenwood.

———. 1986. "Media Coverage of the Bhopal Disaster: A Cultural Myth in the Making." *International Journal of Mass Emergencies and Disasters* 4, 1: 7–33.

Wilkins, Lee, and Philip Patterson. 1990. "The Political Amplification of Risk: Media Coverage of Disasters and Hazards." In J. Handmer and E. Penning-Roswell, eds., *Hazards and the Communication of Risk,* pp. 101–106. Aldershot, U.K.: Gower Technical.

———. 1987. "Risk Analysis and the Construction of News." *Journal of Communication* 37, 3: 80–92.

Wilkinson, Charles. 1983. "Aftermath of a Disaster: The Collapse of the Hyatt Regency Hotel Skywalks." *American Journal of Psychiatry* 140: 1134–1139.

Wohlwill, Joachim. 1966. "The Physical Environment: A Problem for a Psychology of Stimulation." *Journal of Social Issues* 22, 4: 29.

Wohlwill, Joachim, and Imre Kohn. 1973. "The Environment as Experienced by the Migrant: An Adaptation-Level View." *Representative Research in Social Psychology* 4: 135–164.

Wolfe, Amy. 1986. "Risk and Confidence in Industrial Communities: A Comparative History of Perceptions of Industrial Pollution in Oak Ridge and Rockwood, Tennessee." Ph.D. diss., University of Pennsylvania.

Wolfenstein, Martha. 1957. *Disaster: A Psychological Essay.* Glencoe, Ill.: Free Press.

World Commission on Environment and Development. 1987. *Our Common Future.* New York: Oxford University Press.

Wynne, Brian. 1996. "May the Sheep Safely Graze? A Reflexive View of the Expert-Lay Knowledge Divide." In Scott Lash, Bronislaw Szerszynski, and Brian Wynne, *Risk, Environment, and Modernity,* pp. 44–83. Thousand Oaks, Calif.: Sage.

———. 1992a. "Misunderstanding Misunderstandings: Social Identities and Public Uptake of Science." *Public Understanding of Science* 1: 281–304.

———. 1992b. "Risk and Social Learning: Reification to Engagement." In S. Krimsky and D. Golding, eds., *Social Theories of Risk,* pp. 21–29. Westport, Conn.: Praeger.

———. 1980. "Technology, Risk, and Participation: On the Social Treatment of Uncertainty." In J. Conrad, ed., *Society, Technology, and Risk Assessment,* pp. 173–207. New York: Academic.

Yandle, T., and D. Burton. 1996. "Reexamining Environmental Justice: A Statistical Analysis of Historical Hazardous Waste Landfill Siting Patterns in Metropolitan Texas." *Social Science Quarterly* 77, 3: 477–492.

Zimmerman, Rae. 1993. "Social Equity and Environmental Risk." *Risk Analysis* 13, 6: 649–666.

———. 1989. "Public Acceptability of Alternative Hazardous Waste Management Services." In Dennis Peck, ed., *Psychosocial Effects of Hazardous Toxic Waste Disposal on Communities,* pp. 197–238. Springfield, Ill.: Charles Thomas.

INDEX

Abortion, *see* pregnancy
Abram, David, 83–84
Abstract vs. personal threats, 13, 67, 81–82, 83, 180, 215, 229–230, 280–282
Acceptance, *see* denial vs. acceptance
Acetone, 67
Action level, *see* safe, defining
Activism, *see* enabling response and grassroots organizations
Activists, 195–196
Acute toxic disaster, 10, 12, 20, 131–132
Adjudicatory hearing, 223, 225–227, 256–259
Administrative law judge (ALJ), 223, 225, 257
Affirmative Action, 272
Affluenza, 247
Aflatoxin, 187
African Americans, 8, 69, 86–87, 128, 134, 233–234, 237–238, 271–273
Agenda 21, 243, 286
Agent Orange, 5, 8
AIDS, 2
Air Pollution, 3–4, 230
    Indoor, 4
Airshed, 83
Alabama, 86
Alar, 187
Alaska, 87–89
Alpha radiation, 15
Al Turi Landfill, Inc., 46, 74, 143, 167–168, 171, 200, 225, 245, 258, 263
Ambient environment, 81–84, 88, 180–281
American Cyanamid, Linden, N.J., 127
American dream, 93, 96, 252, 255
American Cancer Society, 71
American Green Party, 218
American Psychological Association, 224
American Sociological Association, 224

Ames, Bruce, 187
Anderson v. W.R. Grace and Co.
Anger and hostility, 15, 17, 52–53, 67, 108, 125, 136, 195, 199
Aniline dye, 2
Announcement of contamination, 20, 29, 50–51, 66, 87, 169, 189
Anticipatory fear and dread, 24, 32, 71, 73, 79–80, 91, 120, 131, 142–144, 254, 257, 258–259, 262–264
Anxiety, 88, 91, 128, 130, 133
Appalachia, 94, 166
    Appalachian Trail, 261
Armour, Audrey, 266
Arsenic, 8, 85, 166, 230
Asarco smelter, 8, 85, 117, 166, 230, 287
Asbestos, 61, 157, 295
Asbury Park Press, 67, 100
Assimilative capacity, 247
Asthma, 4, 76, 145
Atomic Safety and Licensing Board, 241
ATSDR (Agency for Toxic Substances and Disease Registry), 62, 74, 134, 167, 171, 191, 218, 236
Australia, 80
Authoritarian vs. democratic technics, 249
Ayers v. Jackson Township, 220–221

Background dose, 261
Ballydine, Ireland, 252
Barton, Alan, 20, 155
Bass, Leo, 200
Bateson, Gregory, 163, 248
Baucus, Senator Max, 239
Baum, Andrew, 127–128
Beatrice Foods, 221–222

Beaver Indians, 242
Beck, Ulrich, 23, 279–281
Becker, Steven, 135
Bedford, Susan, 129
Beliefs about contamination, 10
  see also risk personality
Believers and nonbelievers, 55, 66, 69–70, 101, 106, 121, 154–155, 157, 164, 198, 202, 211, 230–231, 279–280
  see also denial
  see also values
  see also vulnerability, factors affecting
Bennis, Warren, 203
Benzene, 55, 67
Berger Peter, 294
Berman, Stephen, 71
Bhopal, India, 7,10, 242, 228, 273
Biomagnification and bioaccumulation, 14, 83, 87
  and storage in body fat, 18
Binghampton, New York, 7
Blame and blamelessness, 15, 17–18, 92, 105, 107–108, 113, 136, 169, 300
  Blaming the victim, 32, 92, 100, 106–109, 145, 156–157, 184, 202, 255
  Blaming the polluter, 116–117, 152, 300 *see also* PRPs
Bliss, Russell, 6
Bloody Run, 295
Blueberry Reserve, Canada, 242
Boston Massachusetts, 75
Bottled water, 5
Boundaries and bounding of contamination, spatially and temporally, 9, 11, 13–15, 20, 50, 67, 111, 165–167, 190, 194, 202, 211
Bowler, Rosemary, 128–129
Breast feeding, 77, 111, 120
Brennan, Justice Thomas, 225
Brio Superfund site, 8, 101
Broken Hill, Australia, 80
Brown, Michael, 121
Brown, Phil, 221, 237
Bruner, Jerome, 89, 184
Bruntland Report, 243
Buffalo Creek disaster, 17, 128, 130, 133, 220
Bullard, Robert, 233, 241, 271–272
Burden of proof, *see* exposure, proof of
Burford, Ann, 189, 219
Bush, Presidents George, 22, 173, 187
Byrne, Governor Brendan, 109

Cadmium, 257
California, 8, 45–46
  Waste management Board, 237
Cancer and carcinigeneity, 3, 14–15, 18, 73, 75, 79, 89, 175, 184–5, 241
  cancerophobia, *see* irrationality
  cause of, 74, 167, 241
  fear of cancer, 55, 62, 68, 71, 75–77, 79, 147, 306
  see also lifescape/ health pessimism
  impacts of cancer, 72
  natural carcinogens, 187, 241
Cancer Alley, 40, 295
Canon City, Colorado, 8
Cant (Citizens Against Nuclear Trash), 241
Carey, Governor Hugh, 65
Carson, Rachel, 3
Carter, President Jimmy, 66
Cartwright, Bob, 230
Catecholamines, 130
Cause and causality as a perceptual factor, 10, 13–17, 89–90, 113, 223–225
CECOS waste complex, Niagara Falls, New York, 135, 225–227
Center for Community Action and Environmental Justice, 218
Center for Health, Environment and Justice, 124, 215, 304, 235, 277
Centers for Disease Control (CDC), 74, 87, 167, 169, 189, 222, 263
Centralia, Pennsylvania, 6–7, 102, 157, 202, 210–212
CERCLA (Comprehensive Environmental Response, Compensation and Liability Act), *see* Superfund
Cerrell Associates, 237, 271
Certificate of occupancy (CO), 51–53, 99, 108, 208
Cesium, 5, 267–268
Challenger space shuttle disaster, 16
Chavis, Benjamin, 234
Chemical Control fire, 7, 127, 179–180
Chemicals, amount of, 3
Chemical hypersensitivity disorder, 74
Chemical Manufacturers Association, 285
Chemophobia, *see* irrationality
Chernobyl, 5,10, 133, 156, 182, 228, 267–268
Childhood Leukemia, 6, 75, 78, 221–222
Children, 141–151
  loss of, 72, 76–77, 125, 142, 146

special precautions, 47, 52, 57–58, 80, 85, 87, 101, 120, 136, 142, 153–154, 187, 189–190, 258, 263
 see health, pregnancy
China Syndrome, 228
Chlorine, chlorination, 3, 60, 77
 choracne, 77, 175
Chronic toxic disaster, 10–12, 21–22, 31, 73, 112, 131–132
Church World Service, 134
Churchill, Ward, 241
Citizen Attorneys General, 222
Citizen science, 288
Citizens, 183–184 *see* enabling response and experts
 Citizen's Bind, 165–168
 research, 12 *see* popular epidemiology
Citizens' Action, 217
Citizens' Action Committee (CAC), 278, 285–286
Citizens Clearinghouse for Hazardous Wastes, Inc., 215, 235 *see* Center for Health, Environment and Justice
Civil Action, A, 6, 203, 221–222
Civil rights
 Act, 240
 movement, 215, 272
Civility, 104
Class, as a variable, 69, 196, 229, 233–235, 237, 272
Clean Water Project, 217
Cleanup, 22, 88, 162, 166, 263 *see also* mitigation
Clinton, President Bill, 22, 223, 239, 272
Club of Rome, 248
Clues of contamination, 48–50, 66–67, 69
Coal tar and creosote, 8
Coalition formation, 231–233
Cognitive impairment, 120, 127–129
Cohansey aquifer, 50
Cohesiveness, 20, 70, 102, 156–159, 193, 207–209, 211–212, 214, 286
Collaborative process, 213, 287–289
Collateral damage, 23
Columbia space shuttle disaster, 16
Commission for Racial Justice, United Church of Christ, 234, 239
Commodification of nature, 311
Commoner, Barry, 218

Communication, 163, 169, 172–173, 189, 232
 see also information and distorted information
 distortion of, 74, 116–117, 163, 166, 172–178, 185–186
 and meta-communication, 163, 179–180, 185–186
 and mixed messages, 163–164, 177
 validity, 172–173
Communism, 311
Community
 group formation, 20, 42–43, 53, 193–209
 impacts to, 102–103, 157
 sense of, 39, 194–195, 202–203
 therapeutic, 197, 209–212
Compensation, lack of under Superfund, 22
Compost, 277
Concerned Citizens Committee of Legler, 53–54, 76, 100, 123, 138, 158, 197–200, 206–209
Confidentiality, 225
Conflict and contamination, 20, 117, 156–158, 201–213, 230, 286
Conformity pressure, 74, 251–252
Conoco, 309
Consensus vs. dissensus, 20, 53–54, 70, 74, 147, 193, 201–213, 215, 230, 286–287
Consequences of exposure as perceptual factor, 11, 13, 18
 likelihood, 13–15, 18
 severity, 13–15, 18
Constance, Lake of, 83
Consumption, 146
Contact or believed contact with contaminants, 10
Contaminated Community, definition, 9, 193
Contextualism, 24–26, 35–36, 135, 163, 183
Control and controllability as perceptual factors, 11, 13, 18, 95, 121–122, 127, 169
 see lifescape
Cooptation costs, 213, 286
Coping, 29–30, 51–52, 80, 105, 119–160, 300
 collective, 195
Cordova, Alaska, 87, 287
Corrosive community, 156, 286 *see also* conflict
Cost-benefit analysis, 173–174, 187
Couch, Steve, 12, 66, 102, 157, 210–211, 286–287
Couples, *see* relationships, spouses
Cradle to grave, 20, 275

Cree Indians, 242
Cross-generational impact, 11, 21–2
Culture of contamination, 252–255, 273–278
Cumbria, 267–268
Cumulative impacts, 258, 272, 288–289
Cuthbertson, Beverly, 157, 295
Cultural depravation, 87–88
Cultural Immunity, 279–282 *see also* denial
Cultural Survival, 309

Daily hassles, 31, 130–131
Daly, Herman, 246
Daubert ruling, 306
Davidson Laura, 130
DDT, 8, 86–87
DEC, *see* New York State Department of
    Environmental Conservation
Dechlorane, 13
Defacto environmental education, 84, 123,
    229, 252
Defoe, Daniel, 1–2
Democracy vs. technocracy, *see* risk
    paradigms
Dengue fever, 3
Denial vs. acceptance, 49, 54, 65–71, 79–81,
    106, 116, 120, 121, 149–151, 154–155,
    164, 230–231, 267, 279
    four pillars of denial, 245
    see also believers and non-believers
DEP, *see* New Jersey Department of
    Environmental Protection
Depression, 73, 88, 119, 125–128, 130,
    133–134, 152
Diamond Shamrock, 8
Dickens, Charles, 2
Dilemma, true, 23, 164–165, 245, 274
Dioxin, 5–7, 77, 105, 110–112, 116, 130, 145,
    175, 177
    Dying from Dioxin, 216
Direct action, 209–210, 257, 262
Direct impacts, 44–48, 143, 258, 271
Disabling response, 67, 73, 79–80, 89, 127,
    161–192, 239, 255, 257, 263, 264
Disaster response, 134–135
Discovery of contamination, 10, 20, 26, 50,
    110
Discrimination *see* environmental justice
Dissensus, *see* consensus
Distributive justice, 271–272
Distrust, 15, 17, 105

of government 60–61, 67, 76, 104,
    108–113, 117–118, 124, 161, 172, 181,
    190, 195, 198, 265, 268, 270
of environment, 61, 143–144, 146
see also lifescape
Divorce, *see* relationships, spouses
DOE (Department of Energy), 5, 178–179,
    181, 249–250, 260, 266, 307
Dominant Social Paradigm of Western
    Thought, 27, 89, 178, 196, 227, 229, 294,
    231, 253, 274, 276, 281
Dominion, 89
Donora, Pennsylvania, 3
Double binds, 162–164
    dialectic of double binds, 163–164,
    170–173, 185–186, 263
Dow Chemical, 116–117
Dreams, 125
Dredge spoils, 278
Drinking, 88
Driving, 187
Drug use, 88
Dunlap, Riley, 249–250
Dupont, Robert, 182
Duration of impact, *see* recovery
Dust, 47

Earth Summit, 243, 286
Ebola, 3
Ecohistorical context, 24–26, 29, 35, 94, 101,
    260
Ecological-symbolic disasters, 12
Economic impacts, 59, 61, 90, 94, 97, 99–101,
    103, 139, 153, 165, 230, 268, 276
    boom and bust, 88, 260
Ecosocial change, 274, 283
Ecosystem impacts of contamination, 12–14,
    18, 87–89, 162, 267–268
Ecuadoran Amazon Campaign, 309
EDB (Ethylene Di-Bromide), 8
Educational level, 69–70
Eisenhower, President Ike, 249
Elderly, 41, 61, 68, 138, 154–155, 259
Elite deviance, 116
Elizabeth, New Jersey, 7, 127, 179–180
    and Relocated Bayway, 7, 179–180
Employment, 271 *see also* working for
    polluting industry
Empowerment, *see* enabling response
Enabling response, 90, 115, 121–123, 128–129,
    135, 193–244, 263, 265, 284

Endocrine disrupter, *see* hormone disrupter.
Enemy of the People, 251
Engineering fallacy, 247–248, 250, 252, 254, 269
Entropic principle of contamination, 166
Environmental Action Foundation, 218
Environmental Defense Fund, 218–219
Environmental Health Network, 196, 217–218
Environmental illness, 4, 74
Environmental Impact Assessment (EIA), 248, 289
Environmental Justice, 174–175, 233–244, 278
  Environmental Justice (EJ) Movement, 233–242, 272–273
Environmental Pendulum, The 293
Environmental racism, 234, 237, 278
Environmental Research Foundation, 217
Environmental Turbulence, Theory of, 24, 193–194, 280–282
EPA (U.S. Environmental Protection Agency), 4, 85, 110–111, 169, 173, 175, 177–178, 180, 189, 213, 222, 230, 236–237, 239–241, 272
Epidemiology, 15, 74, 241
  and disease clusters, 74–76, 166–167, 184–185, 221–222, 241
  see also popular epidemiology
Equity, 270–273, 283
Erikson, Kai, 22, 156, 299
Erin Brockovich, 222
Error, Type I vs, Type II, 184–186, 188
Essex County, New Jersey, 7, 260, 263
Ethanol, 278
European Union, 243
Evacuation, 75, 189, 260, 261
Evidence, 74
Executive Order 12898, 223, 239–241, 272
Expanding vs. limiting models of expert testimony, 226
Experts and expertise, 12, 24, 54, 73–74 , 111, 114, 117, 161–162, 174, 178–184, 232, 256–257, 265–270, 306–307
  Expert/public dichotomy, 181, 183–184, 190–191, 199–201, 250, 257, 266–270, 307
  Expert elitism vs. expert error, 182–183, 267–268
  local expertise vs. technical expertise, *see* expert/public dichotomy
Exposure, 218
Exposure to contaminants, 18, 111

archetypes, 295
context, 12
half life and persistence, 14, 19, 87, 283 fill
  see also biomagnification
pathway, 18–19, 74, 79–80, 165, 167
proof of, 74, 78–79, 109, 111, 113–114, 163–165, 167–168, 175–176, 184, 188
Exxon, 241
  Valdez, 7, 87–88, 287
Eyak village, Alaska, 287

FACE (For a Cleaner Environment), 221–222
Facts of contamination, 12–15, 18
Familiarity as a perceptual factor, 10
Family *see* relationships
Farms, farming and farmers, 9, 18, 95, 115, 152, 165, 187, 252, 256–258, 262, 267–268
Fauntroy, Congressman Walter, 234
Fear, Factors influencing, 10, 55, 111
Federal Creosote, 8, 191
Fetal exposure, 71
Finality, lack of, 21–22
First National People of Color Leadership Summit, 236
Fish and fishing, 86–89
Florence, New Jersey, 46
Florio, Congressman James, 234
Floyd, Hugh, 74
Fowlkes, Martha, 112, 157
Frank, Arthur, 72
Freedman, Tracy, 146
Freeze, Alan, 183, 293
Freudenberg, Nicholas, 200
Freudenburg, William, 23, 182, 225, 307
Frye standards, 306
Fundamental attribution error, 135, 300
FUSRAP (Formerly Utilized Sites Remedial Action Program), 5
Future expectations, 73, 89–92, 146–147 *see also* Lifescape, loss of control

Gardening, 8, 18, 62, 85–87, 263
Gatchel, Robert, 120
Geiser, Ken, 229
General Accounting Office (GAO), 234, 238, 271, 275
General Electric, 8
Gerrard, Michael, 183
Gestalt Psychology, 81–83

Gibbs, Lois Marie, 124, 142, 145–146, 200, 215–216, 219, 229, 231, 232, 235
Gibbs, Margaret, 75, 119, 126–127, 129, 131, 134, 210
Gill, Duane, 73, 87, 102, 131
Glaser, Barney, 293
Glidden Corporation and mine, 42, 59–60
Globe, Arizona, 157, 295
Goiana, Brazil, 5
Good Neighbor Project, 285
Gore, Senator Al, 239
Gorsuch, Ann, see Ann Burford
Goshen, New York, 74, 225, 258–259
Government role, 17–20, 28, 110, 112. 115, 118, 123, 168, 176, 180, 185
    agency context (bureaucracy, interagency relations, etc.) 28, 62–63, 107–115, 117, 161, 166, 168–70, 176, 178, 186, 189–191
    blame of, 17–18, 52–53, 67, 92, 113, 259–260
    fiduciary responsibility, 67, 113, 115–117, 170, 191
    officials, 28, 169, 170–171, 179–180, 189–190 see also regulator's bind
Grass Roots groups, 193–209
    environmental movement, 196, 229, 235
        see also toxic victims' movement
    legitimacy, 209
    membership in, 195
    organization, 206, 209
Grassy Narrow Ojibwa, 88–89, 102, 242
Great Britain, 267–268
Greenberg, Michael, 272
Greenpeace, 240
Greens, 299
Grounded theory, 293
Gulf Coast, 259
    Tenants Association, 234
Guilt, 126, 142, 148, 153

Habermas, Ju..rgen, 172
Habitability study, 6
Hanford Nuclear Reservation, Washington, 252, 263
Hardeman County, Tennessee, 306
Harr, Jonathon, 221–222
Harris, David, 174, 187
Harrisburg, Pennsylvania, 6
Harvard University, 222, 296
Hastrup, Janice, 184
Hazardous wastes, 3–4, 7–8, 75, 94, 254

Health effects' characteristics as perceptual factor, 1–3, 11, 68–69, 73, 75–76, 196
    see cancer and carcinogeniety,
    childrens' health, 68, 80, 121, 140, 213
    environmental causes for, 73–74, 76, 241
    long latency and delayed onset, 11, 14–15, 18, 73, 76–77
    mutagenetic/genetic, 11, 21, 71, 73, 77–79, 140, 146
    neurotoxicity, 71, 129
    perception of, 75
    physical vs. psychological symptoms, 129
    preventability, 11, 15
    survey, 76, 167, 268
    severity, 11
    somatogenic, 71, 76
    symptoms, 11, 55, 67–68, 73–74, 76–77, 88, 120, 129, 131, 168
    teratogenic, 71, 77, 140, 179
    testing and screening, 78–80, 87, 176–177
    well-being affected by illness, 72, 81
    visibility, 11, 15
    see also lifescape
Hearsay, 225
Heiman, Michael, 174, 237
Helplessness, see disabling response
Heuristics, 182, 267
    availability, 228, 267
High Level Nuclear Waste Repository, 249, 259, 269 see also nuclear waste repository
Hilgartner, Stephen, 182
Hinkley, California, 222
Hispanics, 234, 237–238
Hodgkin's disease, 184–185
Hoffman, Madelyn, 218
Holman, Thomas, 300
Home, psychology of, 17, 39–41, 57–58, 61, 93–104, 143, 202, 274
Hooker Chemical, 6, 13, 116, 176
    Hooker bumps, 77
Hormonal disruption, 3, 71
Houk, Vernon, 174
Houston, Texas, 8, 101, 271
HTMA (Hazardous Materials Transportation Act), 183
Hudson River, 8, 278
Human-caused disaster, 10, 14, 16–18, 90, 105, 130
Hydrochloric acid, 252
Hydroflouric acid, 8, 273

Hysterectomy, 72, 76

Iatragenic impacts, 162
Ibsen, Henrik, 251–252
Illegal dumping, 8, 67, 257
Illich, Ivan, 161
Impact Assessment, Inc., 88
Incubation of a toxic event, 19, 38–39
Indigenous Environmental Health Network, 236
Induced growth, 260
Industrial ecology, 277
Industry and contamination, 19, 202
Information, 58, 70, 161, 172, 177, 181, 198–199, 216–217, 227 *also* communication
Innovative learning, 248, 252, 283
Insomnia and nightmares, 125, 142–143, 146
Instrumental vs. coherent rationality, 268–269
International Atomic Energy Agency, 133
Invisibility of contaminants, 9–12, 14, 18–20, 45, 70, 74, 88–89, 112, 180
Iraq, 5
Irrationality vs. rationality, 74, 135, 165, 173, 178–179, 182, 226–227, 265, 269, 276
Irwin, Alan, 268, 288
Islip Long Island garbage barge, 245–247
Isolation of victims, 20–21, 152–158, 193–194, 197–198, 212, 276, 287
Issues infrastructure, 219
Ittelson, William, 82

Jackson County, Mississippi, 128, 133, 300
Jackson Township, New Jersey, 35, 37–63, 100, 107, 108, 156, 263
municipal landfill, 42–63, 99
Jacob, Gerald, 250
Japan, 5
Johnstown (Pennsylvania) flood, 16–17
Jones, Edward, 32
Jones, Timothy, 225
Jorgenson, Joseph, 88
Jorling, Thomas, 226
Just world, belief in, 92, 281
Justice (*see also* environmental justice), 17, 270–271

Kameron, Joel, 84
Kapp, Frederick, 299
Kaufman, Stephen, 182
Kearny, New Jersey, 261

Kepone, 13
Kerr-McGee, 241
Kiev, 7
Kleese, Deborah, 140
Knowledge and what is known about contamination, 10, 12–15
Koffka, Kurt, 83
Korea, 5
Kraft, Michael, 250
Krause, Celene, 196
Kroll-Smith, Steve, 12, 66, 74, 102, 104, 157, 210–211, 286–287
Kuhn, Thomas, 294

Labor, 230
Last Chance Colorado, 276
Law of process momentum, 213
Laying Waste, 121
Lead, 8, 80, 85
Leadership, 123, 195, 198, 206
leader burnout, 206, 208
leader isolation, 206–207
League of Women Voters, 231
Legislation, 219
Legler, 35, 37–63, 65–66, 75–78, 86, 90, 94–96, 104, 106, 109, 119–121, 123, 126–127, 134, 136, 138, 141–143, 146, 153, 156–159, 176, 197–200, 202, 205–209, 211, 220–221, 254
LEPCS (Local emergency preparedness committees), 285
Levine, Adeline, 10, 38, 74, 111, 147, 159, 161, 171, 175–176, 179, 186, 189, 196–197, 201, 300
Lewin, Kurt, 294
Lewis, Congressman John, 239
Lifecycle impacts, 22, 205, 304
Life expectancy, 79–80
Life, value of, 186–187
Lifescape, 27–28, 65–118, 294, 280, 284
and health pessimism, 66, 71–81, 90–91, 93, 133, 140, 166–167
and loss of control, 61, 66, 89–94, 121–122, 127, 161–192, 169, 201, 297
and distrust of environment, 66, 81–89, 133, 144, 146
and inversion of home and place, 61, 66, 87, 90–91, 93–104, 153–154, 241–242, 264, 274
and social distrust, 66, 74, 90, 104–118, 124–125, 161–192, 299

Lifestyle, 19, 27, 39–47, 51–63, 65, 71, 85, 87, 95–96, 136, 143, 264, 280, 284
Lifton, Robert Jay, 133
Linden, New Jersey, 127–128
Lipari Landfill, 182, 212
Litigation and lawyers, 6, 21, 36–37, 87, 89, 91, 100, 108, 113–114, 131, 183, 199, 203–205, 207, 210, 212, 220–227
   toxic torts, 220–222
   environmental citizens suits, 222–223
   civil rights, 223
   NEPA review and adjudicatory law, 223–227
Litter, 47, 143
Livingston, Louisiana train derailment, 75, 102, 131
Llewellyn, Lyn, 307
Local environmental resistence, *see* NIMBY
London, 1–3
Louisiana Energy Services, 241
Love Canal, 5-,6, 9–11, 13, 16–17, 49, 53, 65–66, 68–69, 71–78, 86, 93, 101, 109–110, 112–113, 116, 119, 122, 129, 134, 145–147, 157, 159, 161, 165–167, 171, 175, 177, 179, 185–186, 189–191, 196–197, 199–202, 206, 209–211, 228, 233, 254, 259, 275, 300
   Area Revitalization Authority, 6
   Homeowners Association, 124, 200, 210, 215
Low point, lack of, 21
Luckmann Thomas, 294
LULU (Locally undesirable land use), 253

Mad Cow Disease, 3
Makofske, William, 228
Malathian, 127
Manville, New Jersey, 8, 191
Marathon Oil refinery, 273
Margins and marginalization, 9, 11, 165–166, 242, 261, 272
Marples, David, 156
Mazur, Alan, 176, 228
McColl hazardous waste site, California, 131
McGee, Tara, 80, 158
Media, 12, 54–55, 58, 123, 135, 145, 154, 156–157, 181, 198, 208, 210, 212, 214–215, 226–229, 259–260, 264, 280
Medical invisibility, 18, 73–75, 78–79
Men, 196, 206

Mental health as guise for regulatory action, 166, 190
Mercury contamination, 5, 102, 242
Merk, Sharp and Dohme, 252
Merion Blue Grass Sod Farm, 171, 255–258, 263, 278
Methane, 210
Methyl parathion, 128, 133–134
Metropolitan Edison, 224
Mexico, 263
Michaels, Robert, 187
Michigan PBB contamination, 77, 115, 165–166
Middle Fork of Little Beaver Creek (Ohio), 8, 13–14, 17, 19, 78–80, 87, 120
Middletown, New York, 285
Midland, Michigan, 116
Midway Landfill, 46
Milbrath, Lester, 231
Military-Industrial Complex, 249
Mill tailings, 5,7
Miller, Patricia, 112, 157
Miller, Robert, 110–112
Middletown, New York, 278
Mikkelsen, Ed, 221
Minimata, Japan 5
Minorities, 69, 128, 233–242, 308
Mirex, 8, 13–14, 16–19, 78, 120
Mississippi, 260
Missouri
   dioxin, *see* Times Beach
   State Division of Health, 110–112, 177
MIT (Massachusetts Institute of Technology), 183
Mitchell, Robert Cameron, 182
Mitigation and mitigability, 13, 15, 19, 21–22, 59, 162, 166, 177–178, 186, 190, 200, 203, 213, 263, 289, 311
Mitigatory gap, 18, 80, 162
MMPI, 75
Mobility, 94
Modern era, 23, 244, 282
Molybdenum, 8
Montclair, New Jersey, 261
Monitored Retrievable Storage, 309
Montague, Peter, 217
Mueller, Claus, 173
Multiple Chemical Sensitivity, 4
Mumford, Lewis, 249

Nader, Ralph, 218

National Academy of Science, 4
National Campaign Against Toxic Hazards (National Toxics Campaign), 214, 217–218
National Cancer Institute, 295
National Institute for Environmental Health Sciences, 236
Native Americans, 235, 241–242
Native peoples, 87–89, 242, 287, 309
Natural disaster and hazard, 10, 15–19, 104, 130, 298
Natural Resource Community, 87–89
Natural Resources Defense Council, 309
Nature, 9, 86
Navajo People, 241
Nease Chemical, 13–14
NGOs, 243, 286
Neighborhood identity, 50, 158–159
NEPA (National Environmental Policy Act), 223, 240–241, 248, 272, 288–289 *see also* litigation
Netherlands, 199–200, 209
Networks, social, 12, 158, 194, 214
    institutional, 194
    relational, 158 *see also* relationships
    spatial, 158–160, 197–198
Newark, New Jersey, 7, 271
    Ironbound section of, 7, 271
Newberry, Benjamin, 120
Newburgh, New York, 278, 285, 288–289
Newman, Penny, 218
New Environmental Paradigm, 281
New Jersey Department of Environmental Protection (DEP), 50, 54, 76, 176, 261–263, 310
New Jersey Grass Roots Environmental Organization, 218
New Jersey Radium/radon Advisory Board, 263
New York City, 3, 23–2
New York State Department of Environmental Conservation (DEC), 81, 256–259, 262
New York State Department of Health, 74, 161, 167, 171, 175, 184, 186, 189, 191, 213
New York State Environmental Quality Review Act, 289
New York Times, 229
New York Toxics in Your Community Coalition, 218

Niagara Falls, New York, 5, 13, 86, 225–227
Niagara River, 86
NIMBY (Not-in-my-backyard-syndrome), 181, 215, 253–270, 273–278
Nixon, Richard, 288
No Safe Place, 221
Noise, 46, 143
Normal accidents, 16
Notification of contamination, 50–51, 54, 66–67, 263
Not in anybody's backyard, 215, 311
NPL (National Priority List), 9, 21–22, 203, 308
NRC (Nuclear Regulatory Commission), 183, 224, 241
Nuclear Phobia, *see* irrationality
Nuclear Waste Policy Act, 249
Nuclear waste repository, 12, 26, 178–179, 181, 249, 307
NUMBY, 279, 282
Nutrient Uptake, 256–257

Oak Ridge, Tennessee, 263
Object perception, vs. environment, 82
Ocean County, New Jersey, 100
O'Connor, John, 214
Odors, 44–46, 67, 129, 131, 143, 167, 256
Office of Technology Assessment, 4
Olson, Eric, 133
Orange County Landfill, 114, 168, 258
Orange Environment, Inc., 114, 168, 200, 218, 259, 278, 284–285
Orange Recycling and Ethanol Production Facility, 278, 285
Organized Crime, 81, 171, 258
Outsiders vs. insiders, 106, 153–160, 197–198, 212, 280–282

Pacific Gas and Electric, 222
Packard, Vance, 246
Paigen, Beverly, 71, 116, 175, 199
PALLCA, 213
PANE (People Against Nuclear Energy), 224–225
PANE v. NRC, 223–227, 307
PANE v. Metropolitan Edison, 241
Panic, 110–111, 163–164, 169–170, 232 *see also* vigilance and hypervigilance
Parenthood and contamination, 1, 18, 52, 57, 68, 80, 85, 97, 101, 120–1, 125–126, 136, 138–155

Participation costs, 137, 141–142, 145,
     148–151, 212–213, 265, 286, 300
Pascagoula River, 260
Pastor, S.K., 182
PCBs and PBBs, 5,7–8, 77, 111, 115, 120, 165,
     187, 192, 234, 278
PCE (tetrachloroethylene), 163, 165, 186, 188
Peanut butter, 187
Pennsylvania DER, 46
Perkin, W.H., 2
Perpetual jeopardy, 26, 260
Persistence of chemicals, 14, 62
Personal threats, *see* Abstract vs. Personal
     threats
Personalistic bias, 135
Perrow, Charles, 16
Personal growth experiences, 123–124, 201
Pesticides, 3–4, 6, 8, 13–14, 23–4, 127–128,
     268, 297
Phillips, Stephen, 220–221
Physicians, 73–75, 77–79, 101, 177, 295
Picou, Steven, 73, 87, 102, 131, 287
Place, 87–88, 94, 97, 102, 196, 202
     identity of, 93, 97
Plague, 1, 3, 153
Poison Stronger than Love, 88
Politics and contamination, 109, 123, 166,
     169, 176, 190, 233, 260–262, 274
Polluter, *see* PRPs, *see also* blame of
Popular epidemiology, 75–76, 166–167, 178,
     210, 217–218, 221–222, 268, 296
Post-disaster equilibrium, 21
Post Traumatic Stress Disorder (PTSD), 88,
     128–130, 132
Poverty, *see* class
Power, 199–201, 271
Precautionary principle, 167, 185, 188–189,
     277
Pregnancy and miscarriage, 77, 79, 89,
     146–147, 175, 179
     fear of deformity, 77–79, 140, 146
Prevention, 19–20, 80, 105
     as perceptual factor, 13
Price-King, Linda, 196, 217
Prince William Sound, 7, 87
Prions, 3
Privacy, 39–41, 57, 93, 95–96, 101, 155, 204,
     258
Private property, 270, 274 *see also* home and
     lifescape/home

Proactive empowerment vs. reactive, 265,
     284–286, 289
Proximity, 44, 75, 180, 237–238, 258, 272
PRP (Potentially Responsible Parties), 22,
     114–116, 300
Prypyat, U.S.S.R. (Ukraine), 156
Psychology, 134
Psychopathology and individual psychological
     impacts, 90, 119–135, 145
Psychosocial disaster and impacts, 3,10, 162,
     224–225, 227, 272
Public health, 3, 74–75, 111
Public meetings, 123, 125, 163–164, 170–171
Publicity, *see* media

Qualitative vs. quantitative research, 226
Quality of life, 3, 27, 100

Rabe, Ann, 218
Race and racial justice, 196, 233–241
     institutionalized racism, 233, 238–239, 271
Rachel's Hazardous Waste News, 217
Radical Environmental Populism, 244
Radioactivity, 3,5,7, 14–15, 73, 133, 156,
     259–260, 267–268
     Gamma radiation, 7, 261
     radium-contaminated soil, 11, 260–263
Radiophobia, *see* irrationality
Radon gas, 4,7, 14, 16–19, 228, 241, 295, 261
Rasmussen, Norman, 183
RCRA (Resource Conservation and Recovery
     Act), 4, 183, 275
Reactor Safety Study, 182
Reagan, President Ronald, 173–174, 187, 214,
     219
Real Danger Is Above Ground, The, 157
Real estate impacts, 53, 101
Recovery, 21–22, 59, 62, 93, 97, 99, 112, 120,
     127, 130–131, 133, 147, 149–151, 162,
     166, 202–203, 287
Recreancy, 117
Reflexive Modernity, 279
Rehnquist, Justice Thomas, 224
Regulation as guidance for decisions, 173,
     178, 183
Regulator's bind, 168–173, 227
Regulatory capture *see* government agency
     context
Reich, Michael, 112, 115, 169, 192
Relationships, affected by contamination, 59,
     103, 105–106, 136–160, 196–198

family, 141–155
friendships, 58–59, 152–155, 158–159
government, 104
spouses, 56, 59, 136–141, 151
Religion, 102, 134–135, 149–152
Relocation, 21, 69, 74, 87, 92–93, 98, 100–102,
    126, 131, 133, 147, 153, 157, 166,
    177–178, 211, 261
Reko, Karl, 169
Remedy, remediation and remediable, *see*
    mitigation.
Renewable resources, 247
Renters, 69
Residential expectations, 39–41
Respiratory problems, *see also* asthma, 8
Responsibility, 273–274, *see also* PRPs,
    blaming, and cause and causality
    attributions of, 17, 113, 115
Reverse Commons Effect, 270, 276
Richton, Mississippi and the Richton Dome,
    25, 259, 263
Right to a clean and healthy environment,
    235–236, 269, 272
Right-to-know, 20, 219
    Emergency Planning and Community
    Right-to-know Act, 4
RI/FS (Remedial Investigation and Feasibility
    Study), 9, 22, 114, 213, 298
Rio Conference on the Environment, 197, 243
Risk, as a naive construct, 12–13, 23, 281
    acceptable risk, 174, 180, 184–188, 227,
    279, 307
    amplification, 13, 111, 227
    assessment, 74, 162, 174
    comparative risk, *see* relative vs. absolute
    risk
    crossover, 23
    mobilizing vs. qualifying characteristics,
    15, 164
    perceived risk, 223–225, 307
    paradigms, technocratic vs. democratic,
    178–191, 250, 268, 307 *see also*
    instrumental vs. coherent rationality
    perception shadow, 9
    personality, 12–15, 18–19, 29, 163–164,
    227, 303
    relative vs. absolute risk, 18, 173, 183,
    186–188, 269, 281
    Society, 23, 279, 281, 301
    threshhold, vs. linear, 188, 267
ROD (Record of Decision), 9, 22, 213, 237

Rosa, Eugene, 250
RSR, 285
Rule 702 standards, 306
Rural, 39–61, 69, 148
Rushton, Washington, 8, 85, 117, 166, 230,
    287

Safe, defining, 69, 87, 111, 118, 161–165, 170,
    173, 183–190, 210, 230, 260, 267, 279
Salem, Ohio, 13–14
Sampling error, 36, 131
Sanitary Movement, 2
Santaria, 5
SARA (Superfund Authorization and
    Reauthorization Act), *see* Superfund
SCA (Service Corporation of America), 271
Schizophrenia, 163
Science and scientists, role, 24, 171–172,
    181–182, 185–186, 189–191, 250
Schlictmann, Jan, 222
SeaTac airport, 46
Seattle, 46
Security, sense of, 21, 83–85, 89, 91–94, 97,
    100, 104, 201
Seley, John, 270
Self, sense of, 89–90, 93, 129, 201
Sellafield Nuclear Reprocessing Plant, 268
SEPA (State Environmental Policy Act), 289
Seppi, Pat, 191–192
Seveso, Italy, 5, 243
Shintech, 240
Shkilnyk, Anastasia, 26, 88–89, 102, 242
Shock learning, 83
Shrader-Frechette, 249
Sick Building Syndrome, 4
Signal Events, 6
Significance, interpretation of, 185–186
Siting, 250, 265–266, 271, 273–278
Skagit River Valley, 8
Slater, Philip, 203
Slovic, Paul, 181, 250, 267, 269
Smith, Elizabeth, 130
Smog, 3
Smoking, 15, 124, 187, 241
Social learning, 248, 275, 283, 288
Social and Psychological Impacts, *see* Psycho-
    social impacts
Social Process Model, 24–26, 274
Social support vs. undermining, 158, 194,
    197–198, 242 *see also* relationships and
    environmental stigma

Social work, 134
Soil contamination, 85
Sontag, Susan, 71
South Carolina, 75
Southern Organizing Committee for
    Economic and Racial Justice, 236
Southwest Organizing Project, Southwest
    Network for Economic and
    Environmental Justice, 237
SPIA (Sustainability Planning and Impact
    Assessment), 289
Stages of toxic disaster, 19
    pre-disaster, 19–20
    disaster, 20
    post-disaster, 21–22
Standard, *see* safety, defining
Staten Island, 67
State College, Pennsylvania, 13
State-of-the-art, 275–277 *see also* engineers'
    fallacy
State University of New York at Buffalo, 184
Status, 94
Stern, Adam, 219
Sterling v. Velsicol, 306
Stigma
    courtesy, 264
    environmental, 31–32, 70, 94, 100,
        103–105, 107, 117, 145, 155–158,
        164–165, 181, 187, 246, 251, 255, 256,
        260, 264–265, 268–271, 273, 282, 286
    social, 11, 14–15, 20, 24, 31–32, 66, 71, 106,
        204, 260, 263, 273, 277
Stockman, Thomas, 251–252, 277
Stone, Russell, 111, 159, 201, 300
Strauss, Anselm, 293
Stress, psychological, 10, 24, 27–31, 85, 90,
    103, 120–160, 224, 226
    chronic vs. acute, 127
    inherent stressors, 10
    stressors, 19, 29, 44–48, 87, 90, 133
Stringfellow Acid Pits, 8, 219
Systems perspective, 28
Subjective vs. objective, 224–225, 257, 266,
    268, 274, 307
Subpublics, 295
Suburbia, 39–61, 69, 85–86
Suicide, 73, 147
Superfund, 4, 8–9, 13–14, 21–23, 74, 87,
    114–116, 166–167, 174, 177–178, 183,
    203, 219–220, 230–232, 237–238, 257,
    285, 300

Support, social (*see also* relationships),
    119, 159–160
Supreme Court hypothesis, 225
Sustainability, 197, 242–243, 246, 283–290
    environmental sustainability, 277
Symptom Checklist SCL–90R, 120
Szasz, Andrew, 214, 219, 228–229, 244

Tacoma, 85, 166, 230
    landfill, 48
    the Tacoma Process, 230
Talking circle, 287
Tatum dome, 259
Technology and technocracy, 16, 162, 176,
    178–179, 181–186, 226–227, 247, 250,
    266, 307, 267, 274, 276
Technocracy vs. democracy, *see* risk
    paradigms
Technological disaster, 16, 84, 112, 130
Technological fix, 19, 247
Teenagers, 78
Tennessee River, 86
Tester, David, 171
Territoriality, 264
Texas City, Texas, 8, 273
The 3 C's of risk, 13–14
Thin and Thick risk, 269
Third Path Analysis, 245, 287, 289
Thomas Commission, 175–176, 190–191
Threat Belief System, 66
Three Mile Island (TMI), 6, 10, 90, 127, 129,
    130, 132, 224, 228
Time and temporal effects, 9, 11, 20–21,
    202–203
Times Beach, Missouri, 6, 73, 101–102, 105,
    109–112, 128, 130, 169, 177, 189, 202,
    233
Timmerman, Peter, 268–269, 271
Titchener, James, 299
Tosteson, Heather, 169, 171–172
Toxic Release Inventory, 238
Toxic victims' movement, 213–219, 229–233
    decentralized nature of, 214
    networking approach of, 214
Transformative methods, 287–288
Trauma, 299
Tradition, loss of, 88
Traffic impacts, 46–47, 143, 260
Tragedy of the Commons, 270
Treatment, mental health, 130,
    133–135

Triana, Alabama, 8, 86, 233
Trust, *see* lifescape
Tucker, Pamela, 134, 191–192
Tulane University Environmental Law Clinic, 240
Tulleytown landfill, 46–48

Ubiquity of contaminants, 9
Uncertainty and unknowns, 10–12, 18, 52, 58, 73–75, 78–80, 88, 90–92, 110–112, 120, 128, 165, 168–169, 171–172, 198, 202, 267, 279
Undermanning, 212
Unger, David, 197
Union Carbide, 7
United Nations, 243
    U.N. Commission on Environment and Development, 243
United Nuclear, 241
University of Michigan, 236
Uranium
    mill tailings, 260
    miners, 15, 241
Urban, 69, 84–85
U.S. Army Corps of Engineers, 5
U.S. Appeals Court for the District of Columbia, 224
U.S. Supreme Court, 224–225

Valdez, Alaska, 87
Validity, logical vs. statistical, 36, 131, 167, 174, 268–269, 271
Values, 70, 162, 172, 178–179, 207, 227, 229, 231, 274
Vectors, 47
Vermont, 165
Vernon, New Jersey, 260–263, 310
Victims and victimization, 11, 17, 70, 83, 88–90, 105–106, 113, 124, 157, 161, 165–166, 179–180, 255, 265, 277, 287
Vigilance and hypervigilance, 29–30, 32, 68, 105, 264–265
Violence, 88
Visual impacts, 47–48, 82–83
Vivendi, 259
Voluntariness, 10, 17. 89
Von Uexküll, Jakob, 81–83
Voodoo, 5, 174
Vulnerability, factors influencing, 37, 66–68, 69, 91–93, 102, 105, 238

age and presence of children, 37, 67–70, 88, 95, 97, 101, 121, 125, 131, 138, 196, 206
dependence on local resources, 87
length of residence, 68–70, 206
location/proximity, 67–70, 237–238
working for polluting industry, 70, 116–117, 196, 233, 241–242, 311
Vyner, Henry, 73

Wallkill, New York, 285–286
Wallkill River, 257
Wandersman, Abraham, 71, 197
Warren County, North Carolina, 234
Warwick, New York, 8
WASH–1400 study, *see* Reactor Safety Study
Washington Heights, Wallkill, New York, 163, 188
Waste and waste disposal, 245–246, 252, 273, 276, 285
Water, contamination of, 50–63, 67–68, 76, 103, 127, 144, 163–164, 222, 246, 251, 258
    supply, 55–60, 90, 98, 103, 139, 207
Watersheds, 83
West Nile Virus, 23–4
Whistleblowers, 252
Wilderness, 84
Wilkens, Lee, 228
Wilkey, Judge, 224, 226
Woburn, Massachusetts, 6, 10, 75, 221, 295–296
Wolfenstein, Martha, 92
Wolpert, Julian, 270
Women, 68, 88, 128, 131, 196, 206, 235, 264
    womens' movement, 196–197
Work and livelihood, disruption of, 7, 28, 59, 87, 103, 124, 155
World Bank, 243
Worry, 18, 93
Worst case scenario, 18, 80, 185, 264, 276
W. R. Grace, 221
Wynne, Brian, 16, 23, 267–268

Y2K, 16
YIYBY (Yes, in your backyard), 273–274
Yucca Mountain, Nevada, 12, 249, 310

11629758R0021

Made in the USA
Lexington, KY
19 October 2011